THE BUSINESS GUIDE TO SELLING THROUGH INTERNET AUCTIONS

Other Titles of Interest From Maximum Press

Internet Marketing for Less Than $500/Year, Second Edition: Yudkin, 1-885068-69-7

Marketing With E-Mail, Second Edition: Kinnard, 1-885068-51-4

Business-to-Business Internet Marketing, Third Edition: Silverstein, 1-885068-50-6

Marketing on the Internet, Fifth Edition: Zimmerman, 1-885068-49-2

101 Internet Businesses You Can Start From Home: Sweeney, 1-885068-59-X

The e-Business Formula for Success: Sweeney, 1-885068-60-3

101 Ways to Promote Your Web Site, Third Edition: Sweeney, 1-885068-57-3

Internet Marketing for Information Technology Companies, Second Edition: Silverstein, 1-885068-67-0

Internet Marketing for Your Tourism Business: Sweeney, 1-885068-47-6

Exploring IBM Technology, Products & Services, Fourth Edition: Hoskins, 1-885068-62-X

Exploring IBM RS/6000 Computers, Tenth Edition: Davies, 1-885068-42-5

Exploring IBM @server iSeries and AS/400 Computers, Tenth Edition: Hoskins, Dimmick, 1-885068-43-3

Exploring IBM @server xSeries and PCs, Eleventh Edition: Hoskins, Wilson, 1-885068-39-5

Exploring IBM @server zSeries and S/390 Computers, Seventh Edition: Hoskins, Frank, 1-885068-70-0

Exploring IBM e-Business Software: Young, 1-885068-58-1

Building Intranets With Lotus Notes and Domino 5.0: Krantz, 1-885068-41-7

Exploring IBM Network Stations: Ho, Lloyd, & Heracleous, 1-885068-32-8

For more information, visit our Web site at *www.maxpress.com* or e-mail us at *moreinfo@maxpress.com*

THE BUSINESS GUIDE TO SELLING THROUGH INTERNET AUCTIONS

A Proven Seven-Step Plan for Selling to Consumers and Other Businesses

Nancy L. Hix

MAXIMUM PRESS
605 Silverthorn Road
Gulf Breeze, FL 32561
(850) 934-0819
www.maxpress.com

Publisher: Jim Hosk

Manager of Finance/Administration: Joyce Reedy

Production Manager: ReNae Grant

Cover Designer: Lauren Smith Designs

Compositor: PageCrafters Inc.

Copyeditor: Andrew Potter

Proofreader: Jacquie Wallace

Indexer: Susan Olason

Printer: P.A. Hutchison

This publication is designed to provide accurate and authoritative information in regard to the subject matter covered. It is sold with the understanding that the publisher is not engaged in rendering professional services. If legal, accounting, medical, psychological, or any other expert assistance is required, the services of a competent professional person should be sought. ADAPTED FROM A DECLARATION OF PRINCIPLES OF A JOINT COMMITTEE OF THE AMERICAN BAR ASSOCIATION AND PUBLISHERS.

Recognizing the importance of preserving what has been written, it is a policy of Maximum Press to have books of enduring value published in the United States printed on acid-free paper, and we exert our best efforts to that end.

Library of Congress Cataloging-in-Publication Data

Hix, Nancy L.
  The business guide to selling through internet auctions : a proven seven-step plan for selling to consumers and other businesses / Nancy Hix.
     p. cm.
Includes index.
  ISBN 1-885068-73-5
  1. Internet auctions. I. Title.
  HF5478 .H588 2001
  381'.17'028854678—dc21
                                    2001003602

For my beloved Jeff

Acknowledgements

This book would not have been possible without the help of many people. I'd first like to thank Bill Meyer and Andy Roe from AuctionWatch.com. Special thanks to Jim Hoskins of Maximum Press and ReNae Grant of PageCrafters, along with Jan Zimmerman, Shannon Kinnard, and Susan Sweeney; whose works provided a wealth of information. My gratitude to Scott Samuel from Ándale, Ina and David Steiner of AuctionBytes.com, Michelle Weiss from the Top 100 Network, and Lisa Stroup from Collector Books.

I appreciate the input I received from Josh Piestrup from SmoothSale, Bill Marger from Merchants Square, Inc., Patrick Byrne, J. P. Werlin, and Jacob Hawkins from Overstock.com, Andrew Kantor of TradeOut, and Gail Hotchkiss and Leon Herr from SoupGirl.com. More thanks to Jen Hessler and Karen Siddiqi from the Online Auction User's Association, and independent online auction sellers Deanne Summer & Elizabeth Hohns. Thanks also to the AlphA NetizeN, Dennis Kemery. Way cool, man.

I'm proud to belong to the eBay Community at the Online Trader's Web Alliance, where many folks responded to my research questions. I gratefully acknowledge Serenity Long, Suzette Assink, Mike Rudi, Jim & Crystal Wells-Miller, Hope Larsen, Melinda Boeh, Rob Broder & Wayne Hume, Susan J. Templeton, Michelle Pear, Linda Covino, Vikki Boese, Darryl Taylor, Jeff Real, Jill Morgan, Karyl Blakeman, Debbie Lucero, Paula & Jim Adwell, Kathleen Becker, StormThinker, Marjie S., Alexis Forrester, ToyRanch, Lynn Berry, Kathy Danis, Stephanie Lee, Cathe Bianchi, Metziya, Linda Solomon, Michelle Stevens, Maridele Neikirk, Teri Rosvall, AD, and so many others.

Special thanks to eBay user John Hannon (parrothead88) for sharing his "shooting star" selling experiences with me, and also to eBay user Puzzlegoddess for reminding me to warn sellers about where not to slap adhesive tape. Thanks also to B&M business owner Janet Cole for sharing her marketing philosophies.

Huge hugs to Anne Hawkins of Bod Squad, who made sure I dragged myself to the gym at least two hours each week, and also to Nancy J. Davies, who will forever be my writing coach whether she knows it or not.

Thanks to John C. King for legal information, Carol Angelo for her advertising ideas, and Classmates.com for putting me back in touch with both of them. Thanks to Jeff Savage of Drexel Grapevine Antiques for creating an Internet auction seller's doorway page to help demonstrate its use, and to Jeanne Cseri-Martin for providing information on Reverse Auctions used by Lucent Technologies.

Supportive friends and family: My parents James and Rita Brodsky, my mother-in-law Barbara Hix, Michael Trenteseau, James C. Armstrong, Jr., Tricia Hyrowski, Charlynn Muehle, Jim and Linda Brodsky, Jane Sralla, Mark E. Sunderlin, Jane Brodsky, Sylvia Richards, Alice Blount, Larry Riccio, Christine J. Williams, Michael H. Conroy, Kathryn J. Barker, Ron and Lauren Atlas, David L. Hix, Chuck and Laurie Capan, Patti Warren CNM, and the two best sons in the world, Chris J. Colucci and Jeffrey J. Hix.

Disclaimer

The purchase of computer software or hardware is an important and costly business decision. While the author and publisher of this book have made reasonable efforts to ensure the accuracy and timeliness of the information contained herein, the author and publisher assume no liability with respect to loss or damage caused or alleged to be caused by reliance on any information contained herein and disclaim any and all warranties, expressed or implied, as to the accuracy or reliability of said information.

This book is not intended to replace the manufacturer's product documentation or personnel in determining the specifications and capabilities of the products mentioned in this book. The manufacturer's product documentation should always be consulted, as the specifications and capabilities of computer hardware and software products are subject to frequent modification. The reader is solely responsible for the choice of computer hardware and software. All configurations and applications of computer hardware and software should be reviewed with the manufacturer's representatives prior to choosing or using any computer hardware and software.

Trademarks

The words contained in this text which are believed to be trademarked, service marked, or otherwise to hold proprietary rights have been designated as such by use of initial capitalization. No attempt has been made to designate as trademarked or service marked any personal computer words or terms in which proprietary rights might exist. Inclusion, exclusion, or definition of a word or term is not intended to affect, or to express judgment upon, the validity of legal status of any proprietary right which may be claimed for a specific word or term.

Foreword

I sit in a New York hotel room eyeing the ruins of the first great Internet building boom. On my table lie the business plans and financial statements of several collapsed dot-coms. The plans read like artist renditions of a futuristic city, replete with fantastic skyscrapers of improbable design. The financial statements of these failed firms, however, read as though those renditions were handed to architects who ignored their training in materials, structural design, and engineering and built strictly to their own visions. They later saw the firms collapse of their own twisted weight. I make my living picking through this rubble for the pieces worth preserving, so I appreciate from a unique vantage point the need for a book such as the one Nancy L. Hix produced. I admire the skill with which she has tackled the task.

To understand the need for and significance of this book, let's start with some theory. Why did the first Internet building boom self-destruct? Forget the Internet entrepreneurs' widely shared belief (entirely wrong) that a business is worth its brand, traffic, sales, "stickiness," or any of the other metrics in vogue over the last few years. In the long term, a business is worth some multiple of its cash flow and the capital it needs to generate it. Also, set aside the pernicious role of the venture capitalists and their bankers, feeding dreams of the entrepreneurs as they slyly profited from them. At its core, the great fallacy of the first Internet boom was that it was inspired by a George Jetson-like image of reality: the day would come when we pressed a button and a product showed up at our door. When in fact, there's nothing about the Internet that sucks distribution costs out of the system of retail. It's no cheaper to FedEx dog food to customers than it is to truck it to their neighborhood store and have them drive in to pick it up themselves. That fact leads to one basic insight: the only thing that works well on the Internet is whatever doesn't work well *off* the Internet. And with rare exception, retailing works well in the physical world. Retail is a mature, efficient industry from which most of the fat has been wrung. Therefore, essentially all of the companies built from this George Jetson-like vision of the world are doomed.

So if the Internet is only good for doing what doesn't do well off-line, what then? A few oddball examples exist such as luggage, which is a non-dollar-dense product that is expensive to retail because of the storage requirements per dollar of sales. We're still waiting for a dominant player to emerge in online luggage. The travel business is another bad meatspace business to be in, for the ticket agent sells the consumers knowledge and service, and these can be increasingly automated. The closeout, bankruptcy, and liquidation business is another tough meatspace business to be in. The odd lots and assortments of products that become available in the market cause the normal efficiencies of mass retail to elude them (hence the emergence of my firm, Overstock.com, geared to bridge those difficulties). Leaving aside the example of luggage, then, the basic truth of the Internet emerges: it is lousy at sucking *distribution* costs out of the system, but it is wonderful at sucking *information* costs out of it.

Isn't information what liquidation is all about? To see this, take the problem to the extreme. Pretend I am one of the few hundred collectors of rare carved fish decoys in this country, and I want to sell mine at the best possible price. There is some "market-clearing price" such that, if all fish decoy collectors knew that I was selling my collection, we could find the exact price where the market demand would match my supply. I could run to hundreds of flea markets around the country, show my fish decoys to millions of people, take their bids, and haggle until I had found just the right price that would sell them all, but not a penny less.

Alternately, I can post them on eBay, show them to millions of people, and learn same thing for the cost of a few listing fees. Looked at from the economist's perspective, eBay has sucked all the costs of information (running to many flea markets, exposing them to people, haggling) out of the system. The same force that brought into being the market towns of ancient China and the bazaars of the Near East is thereby unleashed on a global scale.

Therefore, liquidation is all about information. Another way to say this is that liquidation is all about *traffic*. In meatspace, it's expensive to gather information about the market-clearing price of a product because it's expensive (in money and time) to expose a product to millions of potential purchasers. On the Internet, however, it is cheap to generate that much traffic to a product. The day will come, if it hasn't already arrived, when the investment community is going to smack its collective forehead and say, "How could we ever have thought the Internet was about retail? The Internet is a horrible place to do retail. The Internet is purely for liquidation."

Thus the chain of reasoning runs like this: the Internet is good at doing whatever is not done well in meatspace. Something not done easily in meatspace is delivering millions of eyeballs to a product. Above all normal retailing, liquidation is about delivering millions of eyeballs to a product; therefore liquidation is the one form of commerce in physical products that makes sense to do on the Internet. (Well, that and luggage.)

Within that theoretical framework, the value of Ms. Hix's book should be apparent. eBay emerged as a bazaar for collectors' items, tchotchkes, and various attic leftovers. Over time, however, and with no obvious planning, it emerged as the owner of the most valuable asset on the Internet—millions of value-conscious shoppers creating a perfect market in which unprecedented volume of transactions could be accomplished.

The problem is, many of the institutions and practices (English auctions, reputation-enforcements, etc.) of eBay and other online auctions originally geared to trade between collectors. For example, they can be ill suited to the needs of someone selling large volumes of mass merchandise. eBay in particular, however, recognizes that the value of their asset will be enhanced by expanding their bazaar to accommodate mass-market sellers of consumer products. They have therefore taken steps to enlarge their institutions and practices in their favor. Navigating these systems is no easy matter. Determining what sells, and for how much, and whether it's worthwhile to be in the business, are concepts that have occupied many of us at Overstock.com in recent months. We have learned through trial and error many of the lessons Ms. Hix proposes in this book. Pleasantly surprising for me was that the system she developed for testing a variety of products at auction, tracking their success, and deciding which direction to take one's business is very close to what we developed at Overstock.com in the first several months of 2001. I wish, in fact, that we had had access to her manuscript a few months earlier, as it would have saved us many hundreds of hours of experience. With that in mind, along with my earlier comments about what works on the Internet and why, I recommend this book for its clarity and organization, and for the need that it fills. It will become a bible for the increasing numbers of people who wish to use the Internet auction industry as an arena to liquidate large volumes of consumer products. And it will surely repay any reader who takes the time to learn and apply its method, which might be summarized thus:

"Time spent in reconnaissance is seldom wasted."
—Napoleon

Best of luck in your own liquidations.

Patrick M. Byrne, Ph.D.
CEO
Overstock.com

Table of Contents

Chapter 1:
Internet Auctions—The Emerging Marketing Channel 1

Chapter 2:
Your Seven-Step Internet Auction Strategy   61

Chapter 3:
Will Your Products Sell? 82

Chapter 4:
Selecting the Right Auction Site and
Type of Auctions for Your Business   108

Chapter 7:
Promoting Your Online Auction Listings   267

Chapter 8:
The Internet Auction Transaction—
A Seller's Responsibilities   305

Chapter 9:
Assessing Your Internet Auction Success   **348**

Chapter 10:
Becoming an Internet Auction Entrepreneur   371

Chapter 11:
Winning with Your Customers   411

Chapter 12:
Problems, Resolutions, and Online Support   **440**

Introduction

Do You Need This Book?

Are you the right audience for this book about selling through Internet auctions? Find out by taking this short, easy quiz:

- Do you have products you need to market quickly?

- Do you plan to sell to consumers and/or businesses?

- Do you want to make money from selling products on the Internet?

- Are you intrigued by the marketing possibilities that Internet auctions offer?

- Do you need to develop an Internet auction strategy that will help you get the most out of your venture?

If you answered yes to any of these, then this book is for you. It will aid you in using Internet auction sites to bring success and profit to your business.

What It Is

This book will help you develop your Seven-Step Internet Auction Strategy in order to get the most profit out of selling through Internet auctions. It demonstrates how a large company, midsize business, or small business operator can use a structured approach with a relatively new and very exciting online selling medium. Each step is covered in enough detail to get the main points across while leaving you plenty of options. I'll also explain what tools you need and what you can expect the results to be if you use each step to your best advantage.

My goal is to encourage you to be as confident as possible when you take your products online. The Internet Auction Strategy steps I've included may seem overwhelming at first, but you'll probably find that you already know much of the information from your original business planning. Think of the steps in this book as guidelines that will help you expand your business to include another selling platform.

Further on, we'll explore what you need to know in order to carry out the online auction process from start to finish. You'll read about what to do when the auction ends and comes off the Internet into real life, and the best way to analyze and organize your business. I've also included a chapter for independent auction sellers who want to apply the Seven-Step Internet Auction Strategy to their entrepreneurial venture. All auction sellers can read about how to win with customers, and how to handle any "problem" situations that may arise while marketing products at the cyber-auction sites.

By the time you finish Chapter 12, you'll be proficient at winning with your customers and you'll know how to attract repeat business and referrals. You'll become an online customer service expert. Additionally, you'll be able to volley any problems that may arise and handle them like a pro when they do.

What It Isn't

This book isn't about writing a formal business plan. Many other books now on the market can give you all the details you need to write the very best business plan possible if you're seeking a business loan or a buy-in.

This book is also *not* about snagging a bargain on Amazon Auctions, matching your china pattern on Yahoo Auctions, or sniping in a last-minute bid on eBay, Inc. If the main objective of your online auction experience involves bidding and/or buying, then put this book back on the shelf and pick up the next one. It's probably packed with everything you need to bid with confidence.

This book is specifically for people who want to make money using Internet auctions to sell large quantities of items—overstock, discontinued items, or promotional products—to businesses or individuals.

What You Already Know

To make the most of this book, it's assumed that you're familiar with the Internet, the hardware and other essentials you need in order to access the Internet, and a working knowledge of the main communication medium used for Internet commerce, which is electronic mail, or e-mail.

It's also assumed that you currently have an e-mail address and an account with an Internet Service Provider (ISP), that you know how to use it to access the Internet, and that you can send and receive e-mail.

How to Use This Book

The chapters in this book introduce, describe, and dissect the 7 Steps in the Internet Auction Strategy, and provide a systematic guide in planning your Internet auction selling.

- **Chapter 1, Internet Auctions—The Emerging Marketing Channel**, introduces you to and chronicles the emergence of the Internet and its impact on business. You'll read about what Internet auctions are and how they work. You'll also read about how and why Internet auction sites became such hot marketplaces, and look at a few of the more popular ones.

- **Chapter 2, Your Seven-Step Internet Auction Strategy**, outlines your Seven-Step Internet Auction Strategy and covers some essential elements of your business. The seven chapters that follow cover each of the steps in detail.

- **Chapter 3, Will Your Products Sell?**, guides you in product and market analyses to determine your target market, your probability of reaching your market, and your product pricing. You'll learn to identify the essential elements of your business and how they map into your Internet auction strategy.

- **Chapter 4, Selecting the Right Auction Site and Type of Auctions for Your Business,** details the different types of auction sites and various auction types, and helps you decide which format is best for your business. You'll read about auction types like Dutch, English, reverse, and fixed price and determine which is best for your selling campaigns.

- **Chapter 5, Payment, Billing, and Escrow,** covers how your high bidders will pay you, such as via personal check, credit card, online payments, and billing services; and also covers escrow and verification services that are available online.

- **Chapter 6, Listing Your Auctions,** prepares you for selling at online auction sites and instructs you in creating your individual auction listings. The chapter then covers tips for writing good ad copy, how to include photographic images with your auctions, and how to keep your customers interested.

- **Chapter 7, Promoting Your Online Auction Listings,** gives you some tips for getting the word out about your products up for auction. You'll read about how best to promote your auctions on your business Web site, compiling e-mail lists, and setting up link exchanges. You'll also see a few tips for promoting your auctions at no cost.

- **Chapter 8, The Internet Auction Transaction—A Seller's Responsibilities,** outlines your rights as an Internet auction seller, and also covers what your customers have the right to expect from you. You'll read about the importance of providing truthful and honest information about the items that you sell. We'll discuss the importance of having a policy for returned goods, and how to conduct productive communication with your customers.

- **Chapter 9, Assessing Your Internet Auction Success,** covers the final step in your Internet auction strategy before you start the process over with another online auction sales campaign. You'll calculate your profit, determine if you met your sales goals, and decide if selling at Internet auctions is right for your business.

- **Chapter 10, Becoming an Internet Auction Entrepreneur,** targets independent sellers who plan to make Internet auction selling a full-time venture. You'll see tips for organizing your time and your business, and information that needs to be included in your business Web site. Testimonies of full-time sellers will give you an idea about what you can expect when you sell at online auctions.

- **Chapter 11, Winning with Your Customers,** explains ways to provide online auction customer service in order to win with your customers, earn their confidence, and guarantee repeat business. We'll discuss the best ways to word the e-mail messages that you send your customers, when to enter feedback after successful transactions, and what the other books tell prospective buyers to look for when they surf the auction sites. You'll also read about packing and shipping items to ensure their safe transport, and the different shipping carriers and their policies.

- **Chapter 12, Problems, Resolutions, and Online Support,** is a crucial chapter for Internet auction sellers. Here you'll learn the best way to deal with the inevitable problems that arise in the course of every Internet auction seller's routine. You'll read about how to handle problems caused by the auction site, making final value fee requests, and fielding other problems that crop up during the Internet auction selling process. In the Online Support section, you'll read about online auction portal sites, available news and articles about the Online Auction Industry, and Web addresses for online chat with other Internet auction users in discussion forums.

- **Appendix A** contains a site directory of various types of Internet auction sites, auction tools, online advertising businesses, and image hosts.

- **Appendix B** is your HTML reference guide. You'll learn some quick and easy formatting tips so you can create visually pleasing auction descriptions. At the end of this appendix, you'll see a formatted auction description that you can copy and adapt for your own sales.

- **Appendix C** provides worksheets to help you plan your Seven-Step Internet Auction Strategy. The worksheets will help you study your competition, calculate your pricing, select auction sites, and examine other essential elements of your strategy before taking it online.

Members-Only Web Site

Purchasing this book entitles you to have access to the Members-Only Web site. Since the Internet is a living, growing medium, it's subject to constant change. Web sites and auction support products available at no charge today may command fees tomorrow. Sites change their name and their location on the Web, or close entirely. New sites spring up with information you don't want to miss. The Members-Only Web site for this book contains updated information and live links to many of the sites included in this text.

To access the companion Web site, go to the Maximum Press Web site located at www.maxpress.com. Follow the links to *The Business Guide to Selling Through Internet Auctions* and locate the companion Web site area. You will be prompted to enter a user ID and password. Type in the following:

- User ID: *auction*

- Password: *pump*

You will then be granted full access to the Members-Only area. Once you arrive, bookmark the page in your browser and you'll never have to enter your ID and password again. Visit the site often for the latest information about the effervescent Online Auction Industry, and enjoy your success. We ask that you not share the user ID and password for this site with anyone else.

If you would like to suggest topics or Web sites for the next edition or if you have questions about this edition, you can e-mail the author from the companion Web site.

1

Internet Auctions—The Emerging Marketing Channel

Have you spent a little time on the Internet? That question is facetious, of course. Nobody spends a little time on the Internet. When asked if a person has heard about the Internet, the answer would be either "Yes" or "No, I've been living on Neptune for the past several years."

If you've done some surfing, or if you follow the stock market or watch the news, you've heard about eBay, Inc., the pioneer Internet auction Web site that started the "bidding online" craze and spearheaded a whole new way to buy and sell goods. You may not be familiar yet with how eBay works, but you're probably interested in learning more. You're also about to find out that many different auction sites exist with varied auction formats that target different users.

This chapter will familiarize you with exactly what an Internet auction site is. We'll discuss how the concept emerged, how the auction sites work, and how running Internet auctions can be a boon to your business. Perhaps you'd like to launch a product promotion by offering introductory items to the largest audience possible and need an economical sales plan to carry it through. Or, you're looking for a way to sell large quantities of items, such as surplus inventory or discontinued items. Either way, Internet auctions will generate profits for you.

The Internet—A New Way of Life

There's money to be made online. Given the growing number of computer-literate people who are connected to the Internet, that should come as no surprise. Netscape Communications reports that 105 million copies of its groundbreaking Navigator and Communicator Internet browsers were downloaded from Netcenter between January 1998 and December 1999, and that was just last century. We're years ahead of that now, but before discussing where we are and what we can do with this medium, let's rewind to the start.

The Internet's Beginning

It started out as a late 1960s effort to set up a nationwide communications network that could withstand a nuclear war. According to the plan, the destruction of any one computer would not disrupt the network. Called ARPAnet (Advanced Research Projects Agency network of the U.S. Department of Defense), it was mainly used by DOD defense contractors and academic institutions. At first, it had some definite size and capability limitations. But not for long.

As technology advanced, ARPAnet's potential to reach a limitless audience drew the attention of both corporations and small businesses that saw its potential as a way to reach customers in limitless directions. In the mid-1990s, we started seeing company URLs in television and print advertising.

The Browser
The **Web browser** communicates over the Internet with **Web servers** using **HTTP** (HyperText Transfer Protocol). The browser is your tool for accessing the Web. It's the software that allows you to look at Web pages, send messages via e-mail, safely transmit encrypted confidential data through cyberspace via Secure Sockets Layer (SSL) sites, hold real-time "chat" sessions with others connected to the Internet, and sell stuff. With specialized software called plug-ins, you can access various kinds of text, images, and sound.

In its early stages, when computers connected to the Internet could send and receive only text messages, the first browser was a WYSIWYG (What You See Is What You Get) viewer/editor (that word is actually pronounced "wizzy-wig"). It was called the World Wide Web because it was the only way to view the Web. Later, it was renamed Nexus to avoid confusing the product for the actual World Wide Web. The first browser with the point-and-click graphical user interface was NCSA Mosaic, developed at the University of Illinois. Other browsers based on graphical user interfaces (GUIs) evolved from Mosaic. Today, the two most popular browsers are Microsoft's Internet Explorer and Netscape Navigator.

If you're new to the Internet and want an experience in viewing today's Web with early browsers and tools, visit Deja Vu at *www.dejavu.org* (Figure 1.1). You'll be amazed at how far Web viewing has come in a relatively short time.

The Web Page

A **Web page** is a text document created with hypertext markup language (HTML) tags. These markup tags assign images, formatting, colors, and hypertext links to the page.

Your browser reads documents written in the HTML language and displays them on your computer screen. To access a Web page, your browser sends a network request for the HTML file to the Web server where the file resides. The Web server responds to your browser's request and sends the document to your browser, which interprets the HTML file and displays the page on your screen.

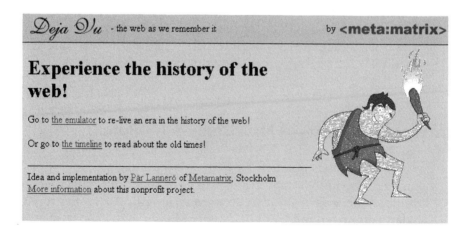

Figure 1.1. Deja Vu lets you surf the Web with yesterday's tools (*www.dejavu.org*).

The Internet's Growth

The Internet started slowly and for the first 15 years stayed at a moderate walk. It picked up speed in the late 1970s, and sometime in the mid-1990s it hopped on a springboard and vaulted its way into communications technology history. Never before had a communications medium grown so fast.

According to Netstats.com, as of March 2001, the total number of domain names registered worldwide was 32,302,665. Of these, 22,092,172 are commercial domains, or "dot coms" (which is a trendy term coined from the domain extension .*com*). While not all of these domains have an active site, over 300,000 new domains are registered each week. There's a tremendous amount of Internet growth happening every day, and with this growth come new business opportunities.

Today's World Wide Web

Most of us are familiar with the part of the Internet called the World Wide Web, or "the Web," which is the most popular and fastest-growing segment of the Internet. The Web contains sites, called Web sites (recently, and probably through misuse, our language accepted the word "website," but it's still considered an abomination in many circles).

You'll frequently see the term **online**, which means that you're connected to the Internet by way of an **Internet service provider** (ISP). Similarly, when one claims to have gotten some information "online," it means it was acquired via the Internet. "Online auctions" and "Internet auctions" are used synonymously throughout this book.

Internet Auctions—A New Selling Medium

Auctioning goods online is an extremely popular way to sell products. Just ask the million and a half folks registered at eBay, and the five million who visit *www.ebay.com* every month. According to Rodrigo Sales, cofounder and CEO of AuctionWatch, many companies are discovering Internet auctions as a marketing channel and are still determining how to leverage it. The Internet auction sites sprang up fast, caught on quick, and maintain a stronghold as an e-commerce medium.

The **Online Auction Industry**, or OAI, has its own following of self-confessed addicts.

What's an Auction?

Historical evidence exists of auction activity around 500 BC, when the Greek historian Herodotus documented a Babylonian auction. The Romans held public auctions to sell items seized from their opponents in battle.

The word *auction* originates from the Latin root *auctus*, meaning "to increase." As the term implies, an auction involves potential buyers offering to pay an amount higher than the previous person's offer. This process is called *bidding*. When you list goods at auction, your starting bid represents the item's current value unless someone bids it up higher. Your bidder is essentially making a "best offer." The person offering the highest amount buys the goods when the auction ends or the bidding stops.

Live auction experience helps, but it's not necessary in order to become a successful Internet auction seller.

What's an Internet Auction?

An Internet (or online) auction is an auction that's conducted on the Web. A seller lists an item, and bidders place bids via text entry fields in their Web browsers. The original auction concept is still there, but the process has changed. The popularity of auctions has increased dramatically since bidding went cyber.

Both buyers and sellers can initiate Internet auctions. Sellers run **standard auctions**, where prospective sellers bid against each other, ultimately raising the price until the auction ends. Buyers run **reverse auctions**, where sellers attempt to undercut each other with their offers. In both cases, the host specifies the starting price and the time limit for the auction, and all necessary auction rules and terms. The product, shipping, and related information appear in the text part of the auction, called the **auction description**.

Note: You'll read more about the auction terms such as "standard" and "reverse" in Chapter 4.

The OAI has also stretched the term "auction" to new limits with another type of listing called a **fixed-price** auction. A seller lists an item with an opening price, and the first person to bid the opening price buys the item and the auction ends. Many business-to-consumer and business-to-business Internet transactions are conducted via fixed price listings.

An online auction can be open to any registered user at the particular auction site, or it can be by invitation only. Bidding can be either open (all parties are aware of the others involved) or closed (bidder's identities kept private). One of the common strengths of online auctions is that bidding and pricing are conducted from wherever the user chooses to access the auction site via the Internet. Bids can be posted instantly from anywhere in the world. Given the speed and reach of the Internet, this leads to real-time prices that reflect the latest supply-and-demand balance in the global marketplace.

The Internet as a Seller's Haven

People shop on the Internet, making it an excellent place to market products. Folks who were once too timid to use their credit cards for Internet purchases now have much more confidence conducting transactions that way.

Once you take your business online, you'll have a plethora of potential customers waiting for you. Gross revenues from Internet sales increase every year. Forrester Research, an online consulting firm, predicts that U.S. business-to-business e-commerce will hit $2.7 trillion in 2004. The whole e-marketplace is projected to capture 53 percent of all online business trade by 2004.

With these numbers, you'd be hard pressed to find a better place to sell your products than on the Internet. Its growth will speed up as various e-marketplaces evolve, including Internet auctions. Now's the time to jump right in.

The World Is Your Marketplace

Everyone is online these days. Millions of folks connect to the Web every hour of every day and very quickly learn to conduct day-to-day routines via their desktop PCs. These newly automated tasks include banking, literary research, chatting with friends, posting messages on public bulletin boards, and making a living. Most of these routines traditionally required leaving home—or at least getting off one's chair.

It's increasingly obvious that "being online" has turned the business world head over tail. With so many people connected to the Web, the whole world can be your target market. With Internet auctions, you can sell goods to private consumers or other businesses. It all depends on who wants to buy what you're selling. The online version of auctions allows people to participate at their own pace, driven only by the price and duration of your auction. Furthermore, Internet auctions allow customers to set the price (**dynamic pricing**) while sellers can study the market to best determine their sales strategies.

Dynamic Pricing

A traditional deal takes place at a specific location, such as at the hotel desk, the ticket counter at an airport, or at a department store cashier stand. Since the Internet came along, these transactions can now transpire in cyberspace, and not necessarily at a fixed amount. A hotel room that used to cost a flat $52 a night may run anywhere from $23 to $78, for the same room at the same hotel, depending on what kind of deal you can get online.

Internet auction business is based on dynamic pricing. You'll either pay $450 for the new sofa, or you'll pay $530 if someone tries to outbid you and raises your high bid in the process. There's also the chance that an item listed at way below retail will sell at a loss if the listing doesn't have enough exposure. This is why sellers want to target Internet auction sites with plenty of active bidding. Dynamic pricing is a favorite of both customers and sellers with benefits for both. Customers like to have some say-so over what they're paying, and sellers know they'll move their inventory at prices consumers are willing to pay.

Conducting Market Studies Through Internet Auctions

Internet auctions offer a rich crop of market statistics. With considerable ease and a closed auction search feature, you can find out what's selling and what's not. You can launch low-cost promotions to entice sales and future interest in your products. Property that's promoted and exposed to a multitude of interested buyers usually commands top dollar.

You can use online auctions to determine part of your pricing plan:

- Set prices for goods based on previous auction performance.

- Time your auctions for optimum sales and product exposure.

- Determine the demands of both businesses and consumers for your products.

The information you can derive from Internet auctions is invaluable in setting up your Internet Auction Strategy. You'll read more about studying your market through closed auctions in Chapter 3.

The Internet Auction Language

It's a sure sign that a new idea is evolving into a major trend when it generates its own lexicon. Remember when the word *mouse* used to conjure up an image of a small furry mammal with cute pink ears? And a *monitor* was the kid who had the privilege of clapping erasers on the school playground? You'd find a *keyboard* on a piano, a *bus* picked you up from school, and a Frisbee was your favorite *disk*.

In this computer age, these words have different uses. The OAI is full of its own newfangled terminology.

Who's Who at the Site?

The people who create the Web pages and write the programs that drive the auction site are the **site developers**. People who register to buy or sell are called **users**. Those who make and enforce the site's rules are the **site administrators**. Aside from users to whom you sell items, you'll probably deal with the site administrators the most. You'll e-mail them whenever you need to contact someone at the auction site. The customer-service contact and the person to whom you report site violations are both examples of site administrators.

An Auction Site vs. a Listing

eBay, Yahoo, Gegy, and the several hundred others are not themselves auctions. They are **Internet auction sites**. At these Internet auction sites, sellers put items up for sale in what are called **auction listings**. An auction listing is sometimes called an **auction**, and it's sometimes called a **listing**. They are actually the same thing—a page at an auction site where someone offers an item for sale.

Buzz Words

To **snipe** means to bid at the very last possible second, right before the auction clock runs out, in order to end up the high bidder. To **shill** is a term for the unsavory practice of bidding on your own auction, or having a friend bid on your auction, with the sole intent of falsely inflating the price. When the bidding meets the **reserve** price, the seller must sell the item to the high bidder. When you **neg** someone, it means you enter negative user-rating **feedback** to warn others of his or her unsavory practice. This might result from his or her being an **NPB** (non-paying bidder.) A **retaliatory neg** is what you might get in return.

Speaking of letters, we now have B&Ms (Brick & Mortar stores). These are also called RL (real life), RW (real world), or 3-D (three dimensional, not Web-based) stores.

In Other Words: Different Terms for the Same Feature

You'll notice that many auction sites have different terms for the same thing. Perhaps they don't want to use another site's phrases, or maybe they worry about copyright infringement. It's similar to the fast-food industry, where to "Super Size" at McDonald's and "Go Large" at Burger King mean essentially the same thing—more pop and a larger order of fries.

Feedback, user rating, comments, and **rating votes** are all terms used by different sites to define the little number appearing after consumer-to-consumer site user IDs (business-to-business accounts typically aren't rated). When you click on that number, you'll see a list of comments that other users have left about that person, usually noted as positive, negative, or neutral.

When you enter a bid amount that's higher than what shows up as your high bid, the site bids for you up to your maximum bid if someone tries to outbid you. This has also been known as **proxy bidding** or **automatic bidding**, depending on which Internet auction site you've used.

For fixed-price auctions, where the seller sets the price and the first person to agree to pay it buys the item, every Internet auction site calls it something else. Depending on the site, it's the **Take-it Price, Buy it Now,** or **Quick Win** feature. Your customers can find out more about you by calling up your **My AuctionPlace** and **AboutMe** page, which are different names for a personal page you can create for yourself at an Internet auction site.

If you decide to use a variety of different sites, it's important to not be too hung up on terms, but rather, learn the concepts. They will be covered in detail in the chapters that follow.

Internet Auctions as a New Marketing Channel for Business

Limitless possibilities exist for you to market your products through Internet auctions. Dealers and suppliers have a demand for an automated, online alternative to traditionally costly and time-consuming liquidation channels. Over the past few years, Internet auctions have changed from offering novelties or collectibles to presenting legitimate e-commerce opportunities. Today's Internet auctions should be a part of any e-business plan.

There are over 300 Internet auction sites currently operating. The table below shows statistics on how many users are signed up at some of the most popular auction sites as of March 2001. The sites are listed in their ranking order of popularity:

Auction Site	Web Address	Type of Site	No. of Users
eBay	*www.ebay.com*	C2C, B2B	22,500,000
Yahoo! Auctions	*auctions.yahoo.com*	C2C, B2C	10,150,000
Amazon Auctions	*auctions.amazon.com*	C2C, B2C	10,000,000
Priceline	*www.priceline.com*	B2C	9,000,000

These rankings, of course, can change overnight. It's frustrating for authors to provide Web addresses, names, and statistics because the nature of the Internet continues to be growth and with that comes change. A site that isn't mentioned here today could stand out by omission tomorrow. That's the way it is.

Advantages

With a limitless audience comes numerous sales opportunities. Besides the obvious advantage of reaching the whole world with one Internet auction listing, the most notable advantage, especially for a business, is cost. You can generate profits and set your own hours while the auction site does much of the work for you.

Low-Cost Advertising

"Not only does selling at online auctions feed my techno junkie habit," says Jill Morgan, a horse enthusiast from Ontario, Canada, "but it has enabled me to operate and turn a profit sooner than had I just opened a shop. I have a worldwide audience without shelling out for expensive advertising. That would have required 10 times the bank loan I secured to get started and it would have been 4 or 5 years before I began showing a profit."

Jill appreciates economical online auctions. "Advertising and marketing would have eaten every piece of my financial pie just to get my name out there," she says. "Suppose I took out an ad in a September issue of a horse magazine to get some Christmas business. I'd have to take the ad then because I can only afford a one-time expenditure. Then the September issue comes out and there's an error in my ad, like the wrong telephone number, incorrect site URL, or the wrong products listed. I'd have totally lost my Christmas market with no way of fixing it. They aren't going to reprint the issue and reship them because of me. And they won't compensate me for the loss of business."

In the online world, you can fix these types of errors instantly, depending on how quickly you spot and fix your error. You can have total control without being at anyone's mercy.

Depending on the print medium and circulation, a business-card sized ad could cost $500 or more. When liquidating products or selling overstock, you can avoid the high cost of print advertising in favor of a $2 Dutch auction.

Doing the 24/7

Since Internet auction sites are always open, you can have around—the-clock hours too. Janet Cole, a small-business owner in San Dimas, California, appreciates selling at online auctions because it allows her some recreational time. Her interests are split between sailing and serving her customers, so running Internet auctions and having a business Web site allows her to do both—sail *and* sell. "My shop is always open, even when I'm on the high seas and the lights are out in the store," she says. "The Internet keeps me from becoming a total workaholic but allows my business to generate the type of profits it would if I was one."

Janet is one of many online auction sellers who lets the auction site work for her while she's seeing to other things.

Enjoying the One-on-One Contact

With traditional over-the-counter sales, it's sometimes difficult to locate the product specialist if you have questions. Moreover, the seller may know very little about the piece other than the manufacturer and the price.

Person-to-person Internet auctions usually facilitate a way for the buyers and sellers to communicate with each other while the auction is running. A potential bidder can contact the seller to find out more about the item, and the seller can answer any questions promptly and thoroughly. This rapport builds confidence between seller and potential buyer. Since the communication happens via e-mail, you have a record of the conversation.

While there's no substitute for your customer physically seeing an item and interacting with you in person, the Internet is a close second. Plus, there are some advantages:

- You can answer your customer's e-mail after locating the information.

- Your customer can print out your e-mail as a record, and not have to take notes while you speak.

- You can think your response through before you send it, to ensure that you project the right business image.

That last item may be the most important. When you deal with customers in person, you don't always have time to answer every question in a way you'd feel proud of later. When you communicate in e-mail, you can take the time to let each customer know that his or her question is important to you.

Photos—Building your Customer's Confidence

By including digital photographs with listings, sellers can exhibit their wares to literally millions of potential customers with minimal expense. It's nice to see an item in person, but with today's digital cameras and high-resolution monitors, a seller can replicate its likeness from all angles and zoom in on the nooks and crannies.

If you invest in a good digital camera, you can post a clear, sharp picture of an item with your auction description. You can zoom in on tags, monograms, or flaws. You can also present it from several angles, and even show the packaging if you think it's important.

The seller should always include close-up photos of any imperfections. Not only is it an honorable approach to selling, but potential buyers will sense this honesty. Unless they disqualify the item because of the imperfections, they'll bid with confidence. Plus, disclosing any flaws protects the seller if a dispute arises later. You'll learn more about creating photographic images for Internet auctions in Chapter 6.

Small Business Benefits

In addition to allowing businesses an economical online presence, Internet auctions offer some other benefits:

- The ability to liquidate obsolete items, overstock, or outdated inventory

- The ability to personally interact with your customers without leaving your office

- The opportunity to work from home

- Expanded customer base

Inventory Liquidation

If a merchant discontinues a product line, they can quickly liquidate their stock by listing the items for auction. If a market idea doesn't catch on in their area, they can use the Internet to reach places where sales might thrive. Instead of discounting and thus taking a huge loss, they can sell the goods at or above the retail price on the Internet. Items that might sit on store shelves unclaimed for many years could sell at a premium at auction online.

In-Home Operations

Sandy, a full-time online auction seller, prefers working at home to selling over the counter as she used to.

"I had my own shop," she says. "I paid for the rent, advertising, utilities, and insurance. I operated the store seven days a week. I greeted each customer and kept 'want to buy' lists." Sandy claims that she misses having folks bring in their treasures for her to sell and the one-on-one interaction, but she does not miss certain things about running a Brick & Mortar store.

"I'm happy without the bills, the time spent away from my family, and the shoplifting. I also don't miss being cornered near my car by the husband and wife team of panhandlers after I closed shop one night. I had a narrow escape." Sandy lists from 50 to 75 auctions every week. You'll read more about independent Internet auction sellers like Sandy in Chapter 10.

Expanding Your Customer Base

The Internet auction venue docs more than just generate sales. Businesses can and do gain exposure from their auction listings. By viewing the auctions, potential buyers find out about the main Brick & Mortar business. The Internet, in turn, gives these sellers access to an unlimited number of customers.

Sandy speaks of the e-commerce arena in terms of an increase in customers. "The world is now my marketplace. I've 'met' some very interesting people. No way would I have had a buyer from Japan walk into my store to buy my Herman Miller chair. I could not have sold a set of five postcards to a man in England for $110. I wouldn't have even dreamed of tagging them for that much! I've sent cameras to Germany, pottery to California, and a vanity set to Canada."

Sandy attributes her contentment with being a full-time auction seller to money and a worldwide marketplace.

Sites like the Big Three—Amazon, Yahoo, and eBay—all have hundreds of thousands of auctions running constantly. Millions of users have active accounts on these sites. With numbers like those to throw around, there's no better way to attract customers than by listing an item for auction.

Midsize Business Benefits

Regional or midsize businesses that normally target retail consumers should take advantage of the potential Web presence at every consumer or business-to-consumer Internet auction site with more than ten thousand registered users. Listing low-cost popular items with competitive pricing can have extremely profitable consequences.

Increase Your Marketing Area

If your business is a regional chain, dropping a few consumer auctions on eBay, Amazon, and Yahoo expands your marketing area to the whole world—or at least to the countries you specify in your auctions. A business based in the Midwest can establish regular customers in all parts of North America, and beyond the continent if your business chooses that much expansion, in a matter of weeks. Maybe faster.

Study the Market Area Prior to Expansion

If you're planning to open a branch of your business in a particular geographic area, you can see how many items sell to folks in that area when you list them for sale on a consumer Internet auction site. There is no better way to test a region for your product's appeal than by letting customers in those areas "sample" them at the auction sites.

Large Business Benefits

While smaller businesses can test market products at the consumer sites, large companies eagerly (and economically) expose their products to all of these willful shoppers with minimal work force and practically zero overhead costs. Consumers can turn into new corporate clients. When concentrating on selling your products through Internet auctions, the idea is to draw customers to your Web site, on which they'll see a link to your Internet auctions. Many corporate businesses do just the opposite. They list auctions as a way to promote their business Web sites. Listing products for auction on several different Internet auction venues can have benefits at the varied corporate operating tiers.

Consumer Site Benefits for Corporations

Many corporations have a presence on consumer sites like eBay. The driving idea was to test market their products. Corporate marketing specialists are also well aware of the glaring fact that eBay has over 20 million registered users. For twenty-five cents, a well-drafted and nicely presented Internet auction listing can reach a staggering number of them. High bidders turn into pre-qualified buyers for the company's products. They can be targeted for other sales. Even if buyers don't bid on the auction, the listing can raise interest in the product. Some auction sites allow external links within your auction descriptions. A prominent link to the business Web site can draw the interested potential customer there to read even more about the intriguing product, and possibly place an order. These consumers become leads for high-end corporate sales at the business-to-business auction sites. Many corporations have caught on.

Sun Microsystems

They're a hardware and software manufacturing giant, and they've used auction sites to entice new customers and develop new markets. Sun Microsystems realized the rapid growth of the Internet auction market and sells products through a number of auction sites. Sun has a business arrangement with eBay to sell products directly to end-users. The dynamic pricing involved in competitive bidding reveals what retail consumers will pay for products such as Sun Workstations and Workgroup Servers. They've also run auctions on DoveBid, a business-to-business auction site that you'll read about in Chapter 4. Marketing products at the business auction sites allows Sun to target companies that they weren't reaching in other ways.

J. C. Penney's

Cashing in on its century-old credo of good products at affordable prices, J. C. Penney's launched JCPenney Auctions *(auction.jcpenney.com)*, their own Internet auction site (see Figure 1.2) that offers an alternate auction format where the price gets increasingly affordable as the auction clock ticks away. To establish itself in the online auction game, the company hooked up with the FairMarket Network. JCPenney Auctions is a business-to-consumer site where you can bid via traditional high bid wins auctions or falling price auction listings.

JCPenney Auctions offers regular English and Dutch auctions. In another type of auction, which FairMarket calls "AutoMarkdown" listings, bidders know in advance how far the price will decline. The falling-price method lures buyers to bargains. Every few hours, the going price falls lower until the specific quantity of items offered sells out. A buyer can also bid early and pay a higher price to ensure getting the item. J.C. Penney's brought "first come, first served" clearance rack sales online. Penney's is just one retail giant with its own online auction site.

Terms and Conditions

When you auction products online, you're responsible for following the site's rules. All Internet auction sites list their terms and conditions. Most of them have the same general guidelines. Here's a sampling:

- You must be an adult (18 or older) who can form a legally binding contract.

Figure 1.2.   JCPenney Auctions' home page (*auction.jcpenney.com*).

- You can't sell illegal or certain restricted items.

- You can't bid on your own auctions.

- You must sell the item to the high bidder, provided he or she met any reserve price you set.

- You must contact the buyer after the auction closes to complete the transaction.

- You must adhere to the terms and conditions of the site.

You'll usually find a link to that information right from the home page. Be aware that the sites keep you in line. If you break the rules, you'll eventually hear from them. If you keep it up, you'll be booted.

The Appeal for Buyers

Whatever product you're selling, regardless of its previous sales history, will be dynamically priced once you sell it on the Internet. Online shoppers like that. They're reading the other online auction handbooks right now, eagerly learning how to grab a bargain in this new online shopping medium.

Once seen as the last resort for liquidating property, auctions had negative connotations. Auctions were commonly used during property foreclosures, which meant that an individual or family was involuntarily losing their property. But in the past several decades, we've seen a staggering array of items sold at auctions by retail merchants, such as:

- Consumer electronics

- Antiques

- Automobiles

- Clothing

- Garden supplies

- Furniture

- Jewelry

- Fine art

Aside from the desire to buy something for the best price, people are naturally drawn to the competition of bidding. This is a perfect match for the online auction seller.

It's Private

Privacy is one appealing aspect of the Internet. When you turn on your computer, nobody cares what you're wearing, or even if you're dressed. At checkout time, there's no fumbling around for your checkbook and driver's license. You won't run into an elderly neighbor or the local chaplain while you're waiting in line to pay for black lace underwear and spike heels.

Bidding online does wonders for limiting inhibitions. Many folks find competing with others too aggressive in person, but easy behind a computer monitor. Online, a person doesn't have to operate outside of his or her comfort level.

Buyers Go Wild

Oh, sellers do love bidding wars! The most common "happy face" threads at the Online Trader's Web Alliance eBay Community Forum are started by sellers who report a phenomenal auction sale. They'll post a link to their auction featuring some gadget that they picked up for a bargain—maybe for a quarter at a garage sale—hovering at a bid of ten or even a thousand times that.

My personal eBay objective last year was to get my coveted purple star, which appears by the site IDs of sellers with 500 or more feedbacks from unique users. I was approaching 400 and wanted to "turn purple" by the end of 2000. Engaged in some late-summer treasure hunting in Union Pier, Michigan, I picked up items to sell on eBay. One particular yard sale yielded all kinds of things I knew would do well, such as:

- Crochet yarn, the older the better

- Puzzles

- Character mugs

- Out-of-print books

- Cast-iron trivets

With an armload of treasures, I was about to cash out when my mother tossed what looked like a tiny claw foot bathtub onto my booty pile. It was jet black.

"Take this," she said knowingly. I paid fifty cents for it. The thing was about the size of my fist, and it was filthy. At home, she handed me the silver polish and a cloth. After an hour of blister-inducing labor, a beautiful sterling silver salt cellar appeared from under ages of tarnish. Each tiny leg had a touch of ornate filigree. It was lovely.

Now shiny and distinguishable from gunmetal, I listed it on eBay with a starting price of three dollars. Within the first hour, the bidding had jumped to twelve dollars. Whenever I reloaded my browser, the price went up. Two bidders were engaged in a bidding war. They both wanted it.

When the price leveled off at $41, I emailed the high bidder and asked what made this little silver tub so appealing. She explained that she ran a silver matching service and needed this exact item for one of her clients. Apparently, her contender had the same idea. And I, the seller, love telling this story. The item closed at $52.

This is just one example. Almost every Internet auction reseller has had a similar windfall. You never know when or why something you list will bid high. All hundred million or so people currently using the Internet have an equal opportunity to spend money on your stuff. Once you decide on your product line, find the right site, and learn how to draw customers, you'll be saying "Wow, check out the bidding on my auction!"

Familiarizing Yourself with Internet Auctions

Access your favorite auction portal and you'll read about new Internet auction sites starting up all the time. Some of the specialized business-to-consumer sites attract buyers and sellers of a specific commodity. You'll find Internet auction sites for hardware, automotive parts, box lot clothing sales, office furniture, and anything else that can be bought and sold. Other sites, like eBay, are enormous garage sales, offering anything from candles to weaving looms to tee shirts to English teapots. Ambitious new sites promise a new and different type of auction process to set them apart from the rest.

Most online auction addicts by now have a favorite online auction site. Internet auction sites have become the status quo for buying anything on the Internet. But where did these sites come from, how did they get where they are, and what good are they for your business? This section will answer these questions.

eBay—The Internet Auction Pioneer

The first online auction site was eBay (see Figure 1.3), and it remains the most popular. Pierre Omidyar, a former software programmer for Apple Computer, Inc., who in 1991 cofounded an online mall called eShop, says his goal for creating eBay was to help independent sellers market products online. He later started eBay when his wife wanted a place on the Web to swap Pez dispensers with other enthusiasts. Omidyar launched eBay on Labor Day, 1995. The software that recorded the bidding and regulated the auction duration was sophisticated for its time, but rudimentary considering eBay's present capabilities. According to reports from Nasdaq, eBay estimates that 2.5 million users access its site every day.

We can guess that the "e" stands for "electronic" and "Bay" refers to the San Francisco Bay area, since that's where eBay is based. That first Internet auction site rapidly became the leading online "auction bay," making headlines with its initial public offering of stock in September 1998.

Note: It's trendy to use a lowercase letter as the first letter of a proper noun and capitalize the second letter, but this poses a problem for writers. It's awkward to start a sentence with a word like that. Do you capitalize the trendy letter, or leave it small? This wreaks havoc with the auto-correct functions on most word-processing systems. I left the trendy initial lowercase letters small in this book no matter where they occur in the sentence. Why spoil the mood?

You'll find that at most sites, bidding is a process that can be self-taught, with a little help from the ever-present site tutorials. Selling, however, takes a lot more practice and a developed strategy. The Seven-Step Internet Auction Strategy introduced in Chapter 2 will help you plan your new venture.

Auction Portal Sites

A successful Internet auction business seller should regularly visit at least one of the Internet auction portal sites. Any of several can become your auction home on the Web.

Portal sites are designed to be your first stop on the Web. A portal is actually a grand entranceway with many doors and windows, and por-

Figure 1.3.   eBay, The world's online auction marketplace (*www.ebay.com*).

tal Web sites are just that—your doorway to the Web. The idea is for you to set a multipurpose portal page as your browser's "home" page so that it comes up whenever you invoke your browser. On the portal page, you'll find links to wherever you want to go in your ride through cyberspace. Some portals, such as *www.yahoo.com* or *www.msn.com*, open the door to the whole Internet.

An auction portal is specialized. It puts you right at the threshold of the online auction world. You'll find any of the following information resources:

- Breaking news in the Internet auction world

- Auction site profiles

- Message boards

- Links to auction sites

- Internet auction business information

Auction portal sites like *www.AuctionWatch.com* and *www.Honesty.com* offer auction tools and maintain lists of online auction sites. There's no shortage of online auction support on the Internet, and you'll read more about sites that provide it in Chapter 11.

Learn to Sell by Being a Buyer

While reasonably simple, the online auction process does require a short learning time before you'll develop a comfortable routine. The very best way to feel out an auction site is by bidding on something. Be a buyer before selling, and review plenty of listings in various categories. Notice which auctions draw your attention, and why. This is the first exercise in your "Becoming an Internet Auction Seller" training. Pause here and go bid on something. Win the auction and carry through the transaction. Take copious notes.

Back in 1997, when I placed my first bid on an eBay auction, I found the experience rather intimidating. Someone immediately outbid me. I hadn't read the site tutorial nor had I ever bought anything online before, so I thought someone eager to place a bid higher than mine just happened to be at his or her computer waiting for a contender. Of course, this wasn't true. The high bidder used proxy bidding to raise his bid above mine.

The first auction I ever listed closed with no bids. I'm not surprised. I didn't include a picture, relied on the plain-text default formatting, and I set the opening bid at what should have been the reserve price. I'd use that auction as an example of one to avoid if I were coaching online auction buyers.

Choosing a Favorite

Picking a favorite auction site will require spending some time poking around the Internet. Don't hesitate to drop a bookmark when you find a site with plenty of links to online auctions. You can return to the list later to examine the sites one at a time. You can check the endless supply of auction site lists available online—further proof that there's a huge world thrown open to anyone who wants to list items for sale.

In Chapter 4, you'll learn how to explore the Internet to find the type of Internet auction site that best suits your business needs.

How Internet Auction Sites Operate

Most online auction sites claim that they're "only a venue." This means that they provide a medium for sellers to list items and buyers to bid on them, but that's where their involvement ends. The transaction takes place between the seller and the buyer, with the auction site typically out of the picture when the auction ends.

When you list an online auction, your customers compete with each other to purchase your goods. You set the opening price and they raise it by bidding against one another. As an online seller, though, you don't have to pay an auctioneer and your customers don't have to wait patiently for other auctions to complete before they can bid on your item. They can bid in real-time, right from their own computers.

Normally, the sellers prepare their own auctions, determine how long they should run, and then launch them. Depending on the site, auctions can run from ten days to thirty minutes (these are called **flash** auctions, and are usually used for retail Internet auctions).

At business-to-consumer sites, the opportunity to buy goods at ridiculously low prices is supposed to tempt bidders. Some of these sites debit the customer's credit card for the high bid immediately after the auction closes and the goods ship right away. At other sites, the seller collects the payment and ships the item, and the site charges a percentage to the seller's account.

When you first access an Internet auction site, you'll usually locate auctions in one of two ways—by text and criteria searches, or by browsing through listing categories. As a seller, you want your auctions to target both types of searches. You'll learn more about that in Chapter 3, as you begin planning your Seven-Step Internet Auction Strategy. Here we'll discuss how your prospective customers will find your auctions.

Searching for Auctions

Internet auction sites typically have powerful search tools that let you draw out specific auction listings. Your customers can search for items in two ways with a few options:

Text Searches:

- Key words in the title

- Certain words in the description

- Auction number

Criteria Searches:

- Price range

- Seller's user ID

- Buyer's user ID

- Active auctions

- Closed auctions

Most sites also let you call up closed listings with their "search completed auctions" option. It may also be "search finished auctions" or something similar. It does the same thing—it performs your search on auctions that have closed. As an Internet auction seller, studying closed auctions can help you conduct a variety of valuable market studies.

The Search Page

eBay has a comprehensive search function in which you can select several different search pages to carry out the different search criteria. While they may have changed their screen by the time this book goes to press (which is typical), Figure 1.4 shows how the main eBay "Smart Search" page appears at this writing. This search page allows you to search by category, but it's not always the most effective way to narrow down your search.

If your customers follow your auctions, some sites let them enter your seller site ID to view your current listings. If you know the number of the auction you want to view, you can go there directly by entering the number in the space provided in the Item Number search screen.

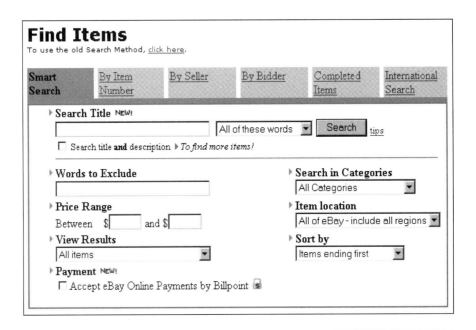

Figure 1.4.   eBay's Smart Search (*pages.ebay.com/search/items/search.html*).

Paring Down Searches

These auction site search tools function just like those on search engines such as Lycos and AltaVista. If you want to limit your search results, enter the main search text in quotes and use a minus sign (-) in front of any terms that you don't want included. Here's an example:

> "men's slacks" -jeans
>
> This will return listings for men's slacks but ignore listings for jeans.

Search Results

Suppose you're seeking auctions for novelty items. Figure 1.5 shows part of the Yahoo site's screen containing a list of active auctions that came up when I did a search for the word "novelty."

A typical page of listings returned by a search, like Yahoo's in Figure 1.5, includes the following information:

- Auction number

- Title of the auction

- Type of auction

- Whether the auction contains a picture

- Whether it's a reserve price auction

- Current bid price

- Starting and ending dates of the auction

- Time remaining in the auction

- What types of online payments the seller accepts

- Whether the seller has a merchant account

From this page of listings, you can click on the auctions one by one and decide which ones interest you. Amazon shows you thumbnail images of the auction photo by each line that comes up in the search.

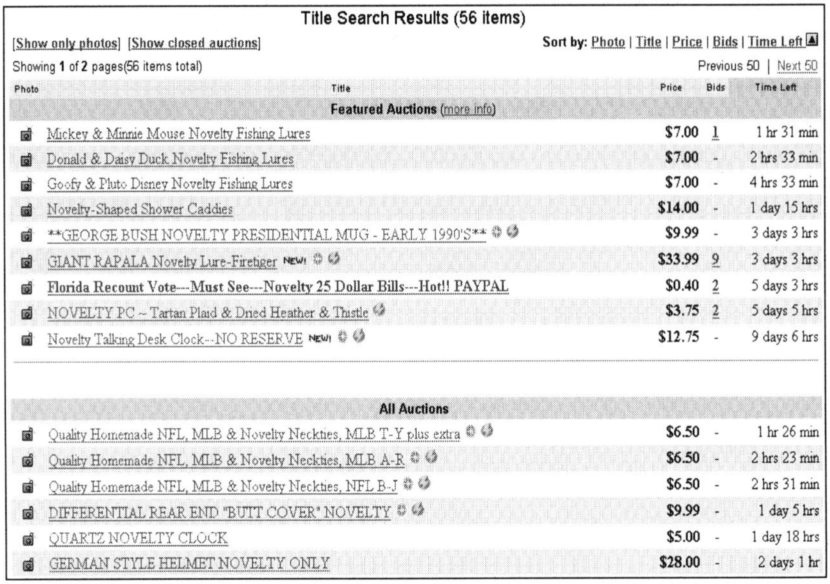

Title Search Results (56 items)

[Show only photos] [Show closed auctions] Sort by: Photo | Title | Price | Bids | Time Left

Showing 1 of 2 pages(56 items total) Previous 50 | Next 50

Photo	Title	Price	Bids	Time Left
	Featured Auctions (more info)			
	Mickey & Minnie Mouse Novelty Fishing Lures	$7.00	1	1 hr 31 min
	Donald & Daisy Duck Novelty Fishing Lures	$7.00	-	2 hrs 33 min
	Goofy & Pluto Disney Novelty Fishing Lures	$7.00	-	4 hrs 33 min
	Novelty-Shaped Shower Caddies	$14.00	-	1 day 15 hrs
	GEORGE BUSH NOVELTY PRESIDENTIAL MUG - EARLY 1990'S	$9.99	-	3 days 3 hrs
	GIANT RAPALA Novelty Lure-Firetiger NEW!	$33.99	9	3 days 3 hrs
	Florida Recount Vote---Must See---Novelty 25 Dollar Bills---Hot!! PAYPAL	$0.40	2	5 days 3 hrs
	NOVELTY PC ~ Tartan Plaid & Dried Heather & Thistle	$3.75	2	5 days 5 hrs
	Novelty Talking Desk Clock--NO RESERVE NEW!	$12.75	-	9 days 6 hrs
	All Auctions			
	Quality Homemade NFL, MLB & Novelty Neckties, MLB T-Y plus extra	$6.50	-	1 hr 26 min
	Quality Homemade NFL, MLB & Novelty Neckties, MLB A-R	$6.50	-	2 hrs 23 min
	Quality Homemade NFL, MLB & Novelty Neckties, NFL B-J	$6.50	-	2 hrs 31 min
	DIFFERENTIAL REAR END "BUTT COVER" NOVELTY	$9.99	-	1 day 5 hrs
	QUARTZ NOVELTY CLOCK	$5.00	-	1 day 18 hrs
	GERMAN STYLE HELMET NOVELTY ONLY	$28.00	-	2 days 1 hr

Figure 1.5. Listings returned by Yahoo! Advanced Search (*list.auctions.yahoo.com/show/searchoptions*).

Note: To keep this book from being classified "for mature audiences only," I excluded adult items with the "-adult" notation included in my search string.

Searching by User ID

Some online auction sites allow you to track only your own auction activity. At other sites, however, you can also monitor other users, such as your competition. This is a very important marketing tool. Checking your competitor's auctions allows you to conduct auction site "detective" work in situations like these:

- Before you list your items, you can see how items sold for another seller.

- You can time your auctions so they don't compete with anyone else's listings for similar products.

- You can see if your regular customers are bidding on another seller's auctions, and determine what it is about that seller's listings that cost you a customer.

The user ID search can definitely be handy for shrewd sellers.

And the Drawbacks...

Sellers occasionally encounter buyers who think that their sole purpose for existing is to make your Internet auction selling a nightmare. Perhaps you had to leave negative feedback for a non-paying bidder and he or she is determined to get even somehow. Or maybe the user just can't get over a deal that didn't meet outlandish expectations. This misanthrope could search for your auctions, find out who your sellers are, and e-mail them with all kinds of nasty, ugly lies about your business practice. This gets old.

Luckily, the major sites are "on" to this type of misuse and have implemented features that only allow e-mail to transpire via a user interface at the site. Most business-to-consumer sites don't reveal the high bidder's identity, or at least not his or her e-mail address. Others won't give you any contact information about either party unless you're connected to the same successfully closed auction. Nonetheless, it's an unpleasant experience when someone interferes with your auction selling.

➥ **Note:** You'll read more about auction interference in Chapter 12.

Global Auction Search Sites

Some of the Internet auction service providers, such as AuctionWatch, Ándale, and Bidder's Edge, provide a function that allows you to search through hundreds of auction sites for a single text string. For instance, if you enter "baseball cap" in the search box, the site returns listings for baseball caps at any of 300 Internet auction sites.

Figure 1.6 shows what Bidder's Edge, or BidXS as it's also called, returns when you search for baseball caps.

You can search all auction sites, or one at a time. A feature like this enables your customers to search for the best value on hundreds of Internet auction sites without surfing from site to site.

BidXS New Search GO! All Categories | All Sites / Amazon Auctions

Site	Description (Click on column header to sort results)	Pic	Price	Bids	Expires
Yahoo	New babies Tweety Taz Bugs red **baseball cap** - KiSta		$3.00	0	7 days 17 hrs 59 mins
Yahoo	Grateful Dead Skull **Baseball Cap** #59		$9.99	0	7 days 22 hrs 59 mins
Yahoo	Grateful Dead Guitar BLACK **Baseball Cap** #58		$9.99	0	7 days 22 hrs 59 mins
Yahoo	STAR TREK Omnipedia The History of the Future black **baseball CAP**		$3.00	1	8 days 8 hrs 59 mins
Yahoo	BATMAN FOREVER black logo **baseball CAP**		$3.00	0	8 days 8 hrs 59 mins
Yahoo	SAILOR MOON denim **Baseball CAP** 7-14 New PAYPAL		$5.00	0	8 days 23 hrs 59 mins
Yahoo	Dr. Who 1986 U.S.A. Tour **Baseball Cap** MINT Sealed		$6.98	0	9 days 10 hrs 59 mins
Yahoo	Tool **Baseball Cap** #65		$9.99	0	9 days 22 hrs 59 mins
eBay	1940s Figural Cuban **Baseball Cap** Pins (2)		$9.99	1	2 days 17 hrs 12 mins
eBay	**Baseball cap** Black with Marthas Vineyard		$3.99	0	1 day 23 hrs 2 mins
eBay	SPIDERMAN: **Baseball** Style **Cap** with Blue Brim		$8.75	0	16 hrs 32 mins

Figure 1.6. Search results from Bidder's Edge (*www.bidxs.com*).

Browsing Categories

When you browse a particular Internet auction category, you'll see all of the items listed in that group. Use a category search if you plan to spend hours browsing the auctions. Actually, you should browse the categories when you're checking out a site for the first time. It will give you an idea of what sells well there. If there are plenty of listings with bids, this means there are more chances to lure customers when you eventually launch your auctions.

Figure 1.7 shows a sample of a category page at DealDeal.com, a business-to-consumer site for computers and electronics. The site returned this page when I clicked on the "Computer Products" tab from the home page. Clicking on any of the links on this page would bring up a page of active auction listings. The page looks similar to what a search would return, except that all of the auctions are in the same sub-category.

Note: Some sub-categories have sub-categories of their own. You may have to click a few times to actually see a list of auctions.

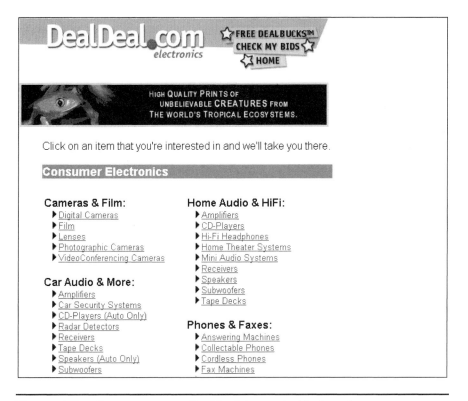

Figure 1.7. Category page at DealDeal (*www.dealdeal.com*).

Standard Auction Site Features

The sites want to make it easy for you. After all, if you like using the site, you might become a regular seller there. Moreover, the better your listings are, the more users you'll attract. If the site charges listing fees and commission, they'll earn more as you draw customers. If advertisements fund the site, higher traffic means more visits (or **click-throughs**) to the sponsors' Web pages.

The more popular the site, the better it is for everyone involved. To encourage your customers to participate, they've included certain features to help both the buyers and the sellers:

- Site tutorials

- Choice of auction duration

- Transaction-specific feedback

- HTML-enabled auction descriptions

- Bidding history

- E-mail notification

- Rules

Here we'll discuss these important auction site features in detail.

Tutorials

Some Internet auction site users have never read an HTML handbook, yet their auction descriptions are sharp and professional. This may be due in part to a well-written site tutorial.

The auction site benefits from providing instructions for users. Sellers can learn to list auctions that include everything the buyer needs to know about the item. Since these listings attract bidders, the site earns more commissions. In addition, sellers who feel comfortable using the site will keep listing auctions, which means more fees paid to the site. Buyers bid confidently if the site seems well trafficked. Everyone wins.

Where Do I Find It?
You'll usually find a link to the site tutorial right on the home page. You might see it called "How to use" or "How to sell and bid," or a curtly descriptive "Help."

I toured hundreds of Internet auction sites, and those that provided a site tutorial had the link to it clearly marked. Unfortunately, not all sites contain a tutorial. Some of the fledgling sites apparently haven't realized the need for one yet, but they will if the site plans to stay in business.

What Does the Site Tutorial Cover?

Some auction sites have a series of links that take you to special pages where you can learn the basic site functions. Regardless of what the site calls it, all of these pages make up the tutorial. Here's what most Internet auction site tutorials contain:

For all users:

- Locating a person's e-mail address

- Checking user feedback

- Leaving feedback after a transaction completes

- Browsing the site

- Frequently Asked Questions (the FAQ)

- Using escrow services

- Preparing and adding photos to your auctions

- How to use the site's special features

- How to report misuse of the site

For the buyer:

- Entering a bid

- Explanation of proxy bidding

- Last-minute bidding hints

- Canceling a bid

- How and when to contact the seller

- What to do if the seller refuses to sell you the item

For the seller:

- Listing an auction

- Formatting the description with simple HTML code

- Modifying an active auction

- Canceling an auction

- The best time to list an item

- Setting a reserve price

- How and when to contact your high bidder

- What to do if your high bidder doesn't pay

Some Internet auction site tutorials put others to shame. The sites lacking in that area probably assume that you already know everything. You can decide for yourself whether you want to be flattered, but your main concern should be with your prospective customers. Will they be able to easily bid on your auction if they can't figure out how to use the site? A good choice for you would be an auction site with good instructions—especially for bidders.

Choice of Auction Duration

When listing an auction, the seller decides how long it will run. Common auction lengths are seven, five, or three days. Some auction sites run auctions for fourteen days or longer. Flash auctions last several hours or less.

Note: Some auction sites keep auctions open as long as there's active bidding.

In Chapter 6, you'll read more about auction durations and the importance of timing your auction so it attracts the most bids.

Transaction-Specific Feedback

Most of the Internet auction sites won't allow you to enter feedback for another user unless you can link the comment to a successful auction. This prevents certain types of feedback misuse.

Note: Open feedback means you can leave any type of feedback for any user. Not many sites allow that anymore, with good reason. We'll discuss feedback misuse in Chapter 12.

Some sites let you enter open feedback only for positive comments, but unless the comment corresponds to a successful transaction, it doesn't count toward the person's final rating. Amazon Auctions uses that system.

Other sites allow open feedback only for positive and neutral comments. At most auction sites, you can only enter negative feedback that pertains to a particular auction. This prevents someone from tarnishing another user's report with multiple negative comments. This can irreparably damage his or her online auction reputation.

HTML-Enabled Descriptions

Earlier in this chapter, you read about how your Web browser interprets HTML files and displays them in your browser. Web pages appear on the screen as they do because of the directives included in the HTML markup code. Hypertext Markup Language, or HTML, is the coding language used to create pages on the World Wide Web.

When you list an auction, you'll enter certain information, such as the title, item category, reserve price, and starting bid. These entries are all just plain text. The most involved part of your auction listing is the **auction description**. This is where you describe the features of the item to make it attractive to bidders. Your HTML-coded auction description becomes part of the auction-listing page.

What's So Great About HTML?
HTML rules! It's your design tool for dressing up your auctions. With HTML formatting, your auctions will hold your customers' attention and not bore them silly.

All Web pages are the result of HTML codes. Some are sophisticated and include dynamic formatting, CGI programs, and other tools that make the site interactive. If you want to see the HTML code that creates your favorite Web page, it's easy to look at. If you're using Internet Explorer, from the main menu bar click on "View," and then on "Source." The HTML code for that page will open in a Notepad application. If you're using Netscape, click on "View," and then on "Page Source." You'll see the HTML page code on a separate screen. It will probably look very complex. Don't be put off by that. The HTML code that you'll use to dress up your auction descriptions, or even the code created automatically with some auction tool programs, is *much* simpler and easier to adjust than the code that represents a professionally created full-function business Web page where you can conduct searches and order products.

It's very handy to know at least the basics of HTML if you plan to do a lot of selling at Internet auction sites. In Appendix B, you'll find an HTML tutorial that will give you all the HTML codes you need to know to format auction descriptions that impress buyers and attract bids. In the meantime, Figure 1.8 shows an example of some simple HTML code, created in Microsoft's Notepad program.

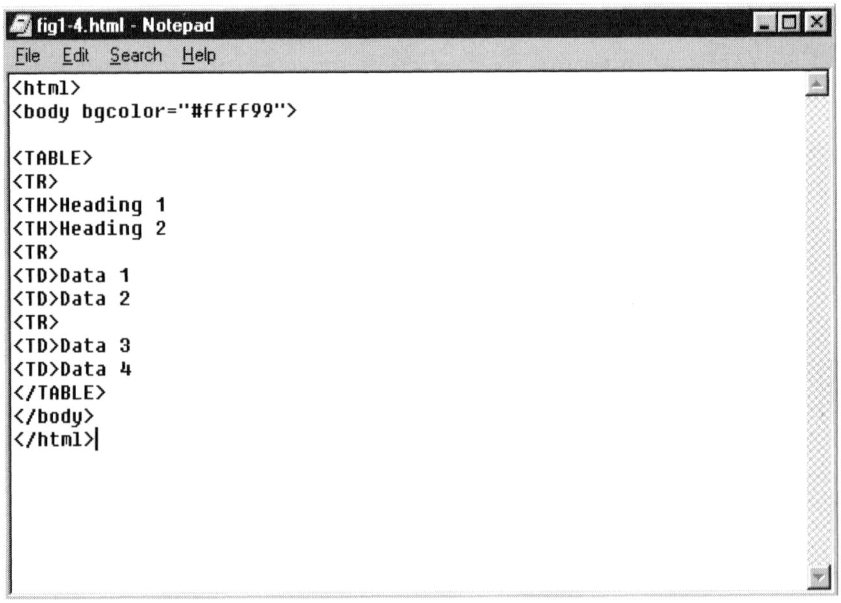

```
fig1-4.html - Notepad
File  Edit  Search  Help
<html>
<body bgcolor="#ffff99">

<TABLE>
<TR>
<TH>Heading 1
<TH>Heading 2
<TR>
<TD>Data 1
<TD>Data 2
<TR>
<TD>Data 3
<TD>Data 4
</TABLE>
</body>
</html>
```

Figure 1.8. Sample HTML code.

The HTML code file in Figure 1.8 produces the page shown in Figure 1.9 when you view it in a Web browser. This particular example is bland by comparison. The smartly formatted auction descriptions you see some experienced sellers use result from HTML code that was prepared before the listing went up.

Images and Hyperlinks

Auction sites provide a space in the auction entry form to enter the URL to an image you're including with your listing. The photo usually appears in its own area under your description. Using HTML tags, you can include pictures of the item and hyperlinks to other Web sites right in the description area of your auction. This is where you want the buyer focused. You'll find the HTML code you'll need for adding images and creating hyperlinks in Appendix B.

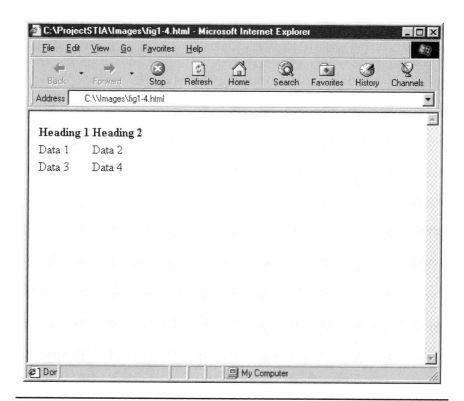

Figure 1.9. Sample HTML code output.

Here's a word of advice about hyperlinks. If you use eBay, you may not be allowed to include a hyperlink to your Web page. In late 2000, eBay began cracking down on links to business Web pages within your auction description and later banned hyperlinks to sites that offer products for sale. This resulted from certain sellers circumventing eBay's fees by offering the same product for less from their Web sites. Many other Internet auction sites still allow external links. Be sure you know the site's rules before you add hyperlinks in your auction descriptions.

Bidding History

At most consumer-to-consumer sites, you can view the bidding history while the auction is active. Others allow you to view the names of the bidders (their user IDs), but not their bids. You can see the bid amounts once the auction closes.

Amazon Auctions lets you view the bidding history, with the amounts and user names, as soon as a bid meets or exceeds the reserve price. If the auction has no set reserve, you can view the history as soon as the second bid enters. eBay keeps the bid amounts on standard auctions private until the auction closes, as shown in Figure 1.10.

To access the bidding history page, you'll typically find the link right on the auction listing. For an active auction, the bid amount usually doesn't appear—only the bidder's user ID.

If the auction is closed, the bid amounts appear. Figure 1.11 shows bidding history for the same auction in Figure 1.10, after it closed.

Notice that the bid amounts now show up along with the user ID and the time of his or her bid. Notice that my bid (I'm user ID "marble") came in after the winner's bid. This is because his maximum bid, placed before my attempt, outbid me by proxy.

Why Worry About Bid History?

By following bidding history, you can track how often the same users bid. This gives you an idea of how eager someone is to buy your products and how likely they are to become a customer of yours. You can also estimate how much they're willing to pay for what you're selling.

Here are a few more reasons:

- **Item interest**—Lots of bidding indicates enthusiasm. Your customers love it, so keep selling it.

---

eBay Bid History for
LITTLE SHOP OF HORRORS 1986 DVD Steve Martin (Item #1411179223)

Currently	$16.50		First bid	$9.99
Quantity	1		# of bids	7
Time left	2 hours, 17 mins +			
Started	Feb-18-01 17:19:02 PST			
Ends	Feb-25-01 17:19:02 PST			
Seller (Rating)	robbroder (947) ★ me			

View page with email addresses (Accessible by Seller only) Learn more.

Bidding History (Highest bids first)

User ID	Bid Amount	Date of Bid
██████ (35) ☆	-	Feb-24-01 15:40:57 PST
marble (518) ★ me	-	Feb-24-01 22:49:19 PST
marble (518) ★ me	-	Feb-24-01 22:48:51 PST
████████ (0)	-	Feb-22-01 11:30:45 PST
█████ (61) ☆	-	Feb-23-01 00:58:12 PST
█████ (61) ☆	-	Feb-23-01 00:57:48 PST
█████ (61) ☆	-	Feb-23-01 00:57:31 PST

Bid amount protected until close of auction. Remember that earlier bids of the same amount take precedence.

Figure 1.10. Bidding history for an active eBay auction (detail used with the seller's permission).

- **Item value**—Many bids usually means the reserve and current price are within the market value for the item.

- **Timing**—You can determine at what time during the auction's run most of the bidding took place. This can help you time your future auctions.

Check the bidding history to familiarize yourself with how and when your customers placed their bids, and use this knowledge to your best advantage.

E-Mail Notification

All auction sites I've used communicate with you via e-mail. That makes sense, since e-mail is the main communication tool of the Internet. Here's when you'll typically hear from the auction site:

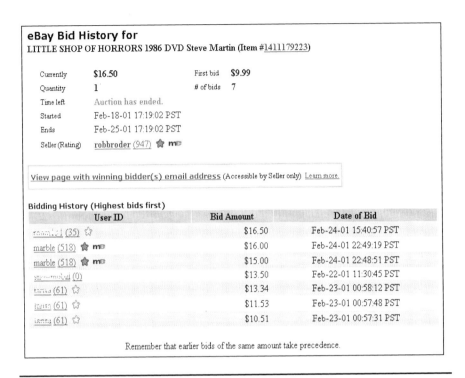

Figure 1.11.   Bidding history for a closed eBay auction.

- When you register

- When you change any personal information on your account, like your e-mail address

- When you place a bid

- When you're outbid

- When an auction ends and you're the high bidder

- When the auction ends and the reserve wasn't met

- When you list an auction

- When someone bids on your auction

- When the high bidding meets your reserve price

- When the auction closes

- When you've violated the rules (inadvertently, of course!)

- When you receive your daily activity summary

Not all sites contact you in all of these cases. However, each message from the site helps you manage and keep track of your auction activity.

You'll usually receive a daily e-mail message summarizing your current site activity—bids you placed and items you've listed. You'll also hear from the site at billing time. They inform you if they billed your credit card, or if your charge wasn't approved and you need to arrange another payment method with them.

Rules

No, you can't do whatever you want, especially when you use Internet auctions to sell stuff. There are rules, many of which protect users. Who wants to participate at a poorly regulated site?

If you encounter a user with unethical practices that affect your transactions, the rules provide a basis for seeking assistance from the site administrators. There are certain restrictions at online auction sites. Most sites maintain strict policies to prevent users from conducting business that's unfair or annoying for other users. For instance:

- At most sites, you cannot bid on your own auctions.

- You cannot simultaneously list the item at another auction site.

- There may not be any interaction between user IDs owned by the same person or organization.

- You cannot list bogus auctions.

- You cannot charge the high bidder excessive fees.

- You cannot sell anything that's illegal.

- You cannot state in the auction description that the item is illegal.

- You cannot require the winning bidder to purchase additional items.

- You cannot interfere with another seller's auction by contacting the current bidders for any reason.

- You must honor sales or bids as long as the high bid met or exceeded any reserve price.

- You cannot set absurdly high reserve prices with the sole intent of seeing how high the auction will bid up to.

- You cannot build lists of user IDs for the purpose of sending spam.

- You cannot enter shill bids.

Unless the auction site is the type that takes possession of the merchandise and handles shipping, the site takes no responsibility for the sale or delivery of auctioned items. eBay doesn't, and neither do the other major sites. Remember—it's just a venue. Though most have an e-mail address to which you can send site-violation reports, they usually won't intervene if the buyer and seller don't see eye-to-eye. Some online auction sites provide links to Internet third-party mediation services if anyone needs such resources to resolve an issue.

No Illegal Activity
This one is universal to all Internet auction sites—don't break the law. Sellers must not list anything that is illegal to sell or possess. The list below breaks down the restricted items. Furthermore, it's illegal to sell stolen merchandise or controlled substances anywhere. Here's an example of illegal or restricted items:

- **Firearms**—Antique, sport, hunting, silencers, air guns

- **Unlawful weapons**—Brass knuckles, some types of mace dispensers

- **Alcohol or tobacco products**—Liquor, cigars, cigarettes

- **Controlled substances**—Narcotics, barbiturates, hallucinogens

- **Pirated copies**—Music, software, videos

- **Law-enforcement items**—Badges, uniforms, documents

- **Counterfeit items**—Collectibles, money, diplomas, IDs

- **Live animals**—Any type of living animals, including your neighbor's children

- **Endangered species and all human remains**—Skins, bones, tusks, and teeth

- **Illegal drugs or drug paraphernalia**—Controlled substances, hash pipes

- **Racist items or Nazi memorabilia**—You may find your auctions canceled by the site if you list this stuff.

We all expect the seller to sell and the bidder to pay, but those are rules established by the site. Whether refusal to honor a high bid at an Internet auction site is illegal depends on individual state laws.

No Shills

When someone bids for the sole purpose of altering the high bid with no intent to purchase the item, this is **shill bidding**. It's illegal in all 50 states and many countries outside the United States.

Features Unique to Some Sites

All Internet auction sites strive to offer features that set them apart from the rest. Other sites choose not to include certain features if the site powers-that-be don't find them effective or necessary, or perhaps the software to power the programs is too costly. To each his or her own. What you like about one site may not exist at another one. Have in mind the features that would be right for your Internet auction selling venture when you explore an auction site.

The following paragraphs include unique online auction features a few sites offer. You might find some of them useful.

First Bid Privileges

To entice people, some sites let you specify certain privileges for the first bidder on your auction. Amazon.com lets you offer that person 10% off the final bid amount if he or she eventually wins the auction. At eBay, you can list a "Buy It Now" price. If someone accepts that price and places a bid for that amount, the auction ends and he or she pays that price for the item. These "first bid" options are very helpful to sellers, as they entice quicker bids and shorter turnaround. You can list an auction at 3 P.M., receive a "Buy It Now" bid at 5 P.M., and ship the item out the next day. (You'll read more about instant payment methods in Chapter 5.)

Merchant Account User IDs

Most of the general consumer-to-consumer sites are also business-to-business sites. They encourage businesses to sell at their site. You can charge reasonable prices for items, which draws bids, which increases revenue for the Internet auction site.

Some of the sites will charge reduced listing fees if you register a merchant account with them, and offer special services as well. Yahoo Auctions has several small business services that are designed to lure entrepreneurs to use its site. Figure 1.12 shows Yahoo's small business services page.

Notice in the Yahoo Web page that they also offer something called the Yahoo Store. Many auction sites allow sellers a similar feature. The next section explains more about that.

Storefronts

To encourage business accounts, some of the Internet auction sites will allow business sellers to set up their own page of listings. This creates an environment much like an online store for the seller. Amazon Auctions offers a feature called zShops Storefront. Every zShops merchant with active listings gets a free storefront. The zShops Storefront allows merchants to pitch their merchandise to several million Amazon customers. Buyers discover your store while browsing through other listings.

When you register and list items in zShops, the site creates a default storefront that you can later access and customize with features you select. The features make it easy for your customers to check out your listings. You can add a few tools to your zShops Storefront, such as:

- Brand bar

- Search box

Figure 1.12. Yahoo Auctions small business services page.

- Your featured items

- Link to your feedback

- Store description and photo

If you have active listings on the Amazon Auctions site, your zShops Storefront automatically includes a link to your open auctions on your storefront page. Other Internet auction sites have a similar feature.

Photo Galleries

eBay has a unique feature called the Gallery. This feature presents miniature pictures, called **thumbnails**, for all of the items for which their sellers have supplied JPG pictures. The Gallery displays the same information as the regular auction listing pages, but your customers will see each item's picture without clicking on the title.

To have an auction image included in the Gallery, you must supply a JPG image when listing your item for sale, and click the checkbox indicating you want to be included in the Gallery. You can use the same JPG image that you used for your main listing, or you can supply a different image in the Gallery URL field. Figure 1.13 shows an example of what you'll see when browsing eBay's Gallery. Sellers who wish to use this feature have an additional 25¢ added to the listing fee for that item.

Personal Paging

Here's the ultimate way to tether yourself to your business and carry your online auctions with you wherever you go. Auction notifications can arrive on your personal pager, cellular phone, or a special paging unit. The site will page you at certain times:

Figure 1.13. eBay's Gallery page.

- When you're outbid (if you're buying)

- When you've won an item

- When a bid enters on one of your listings

- When you've sold an item

The eBay personal paging feature is called "eBay a-go-go," which is a service provided by SkyTel *(www.skytel.com)*. You can purchase a paging unit right from SkyTel or enable the feature to interface with your own paging device.

Frequent Seller Benefits

Some auction sites like to reward their frequent users with special privileges. These privileges include special customer support, high-visibility listings, or special rates. Several Internet auction sites offer benefits to high-volume sellers.

LiveAuctionOnline Anchor Tenants
At the consumer-to-consumer Internet auction site called LiveAuction Online, you can become an anchor tenant. As an anchor tenant, your auctions show up in a special featured category and a banner you create appears with listings in a category you choose. This increases the chance that customers will see your listings.

Here are a few more specifications:

- You must provide a banner that fits into a 455 x 60-pixel space.

- You must provide a business profile.

- You must maintain a minimum of 100 auctions (may vary) at all times.

- There should be a minimum of 500 visitors a day to your business Web site.

- You should only be running a maximum of 500 auctions in your category at one time.

- Your listings are free—you only pay if your item sells.

You can find out more about LAO's Anchor Tenant program at *www.liveauctiononline.com.*

eBay PowerSellers

eBay implemented this program for members who run a full-time online trading business on eBay. PowerSellers enjoy certain benefits and privileges depending on which level they have achieved: Bronze, Silver, or Gold. You reach these levels by maintaining a certain volume of sales within a given period. The various benefits include:

- You can display a special logo on your Web site and in your eBay listings.

- Special customer-support persons handle your questions.

- You can have your own success story included on eBay's site.

- You're invited to attend special events that eBay hosts throughout the year.

- There's an account manager assigned to your account to handle any issues you may have during normal business hours.

- Receive telephone support via a 24-hour hotline.

You can find more about eBay's PowerSeller's program at the link from their Site Map.

All-in-One Auction Status Pages

Some auction support services, such as AuctionWatch, offer all-in-one auction status pages as part of their tool package. The auction sites have pared-down (but functionally adequate) versions of them. Amazon.com offers a "Member Profile" page. They both serve the same purpose. You can track all of your auction activity—auctions you listed and any on which you placed active bids—from one Web page.

Figure 1.14 shows an early example of my Amazon Auctions Member Profile page. The layout changes periodically.

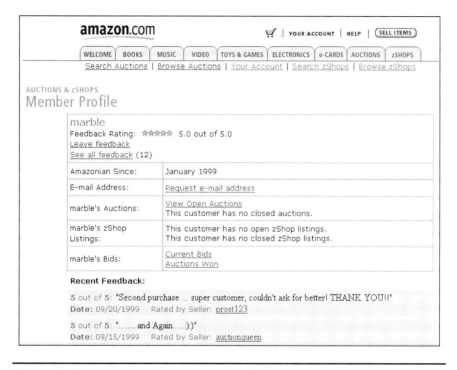

Figure 1.14. Amazon.com customer details page.

This is a convenient way to see all my auction activity at a glance. I can click on any link to keep track of what I'm doing at the site.

Understanding the Auction Listing

The auction listing is your customer's doorway to your goods. It tells them the most important things they need to know about the item and the auction:

- The product offered

- How many are up for auction

- The lowest price you'll accept (which is the opening bid, unless you establish a reserve price)

- How long they have to decide to bid

- Any users who have bid before them and at what price

- The seller's site ID

The customer will also find your prepared item description and, of course, a photograph of it. Not all of these are found at business-to-consumer auction listings, but consumer-to-consumer listings usually show enough information to make the customer feel comfortable with placing a bid on the auction.

In the chapters that follow, we'll cover the auction listing in painstaking detail in order for you to present your items to your customers in the best and most effective ways possible. For the meantime, the following paragraphs contain an overview of what the typical Internet auction listing contains.

Auction Title

The title is a one-line summary of the item being listed. When you learn how to enter an auction listing in Chapter 6, you'll understand why being as specific as possible with a limited amount of space is extremely important to the success of your auction.

The title is what comes up in lists created by searches, and many potential bidders will use those few words to determine whether they'll view the auction, and whether they'll bid. Your title is an important part of your listing, so it had better be good.

Quantity of Items Listed

This lets you know how many of the item are up for auction. If it's more than one, the auction is probably a Dutch auction, meaning that more than one bidder will take home the goods. You'll read more about Dutch auctions later.

It's important to note that even if the auction is for one carton of individually packaged golf balls, the quantity will still be "one" since you are in effect auctioning one lot of golf balls. The bidder will purchase all of them with one high bid. If you're auctioning more than one lot, then you're running a Dutch auction.

Starting Bid

The starting bid is usually the lowest price the seller will accept for the item. For single-item auctions, the seller must assume up front that the auction will have only one bid, since one bid is all it takes to have the auction close with a sale. More than one bid means selling at a higher price and a happier seller.

The exception is if the seller sets a **reserve price**, which is the level the bidding must reach before the seller will part with the item. Then the starting bid is usually meaningless unless the site specifies that it must be at least a certain percentage of the reserve.

Current High Bid

This number indicates where the bidding is currently. If your customer chooses to place a bid, it must be over this price, and possibly by an increment set by the site. For instance, if the current bid is $25 and the required bidding increment is $5, the site won't accept a bid of $27. The customer must bid at least $30.

If no bids have entered, then the price will indicate the opening bid set by the seller.

Start and End Time

It's important for your customer to know when the auction will end, in case he or she wishes to snipe in a last minute bid to avoid competitive bidding.

If your favorite Internet auction site uses **open-ended bidding**, then the end time will extend by a certain amount of time for each bid placed. In other words, the auction will stay open as long as there have been bids placed within the last five minutes, as a more realistic "going, going, gone" approach typical to real life auctions. This supposedly allows sellers to receive the maximum amount for their items. The jury is still out on how users really feel about open-ended bidding. Many sites have discontinued it. Bidders like to snipe (place last-second bids).

Seller and Current High Bidder ID

These fields let you know who has the item for sale, and who's the current high bidder. In the case of a Dutch auction, you'll usually just see an indication of how many bids have been placed on the auction. At business-to-consumer and business-to-business sites, you may not see these fields. Instead, you'll simply see how many bids have been placed on the item.

Auction Description

Your customers will probably scroll right to the description. This is the seller's "ad" for the item. Here you must educate and interest the customer by presenting details about the item, and then entice them with selling points. It's how you succeed in the Internet auction business. In order to be effective, the description must hold the customer's attention. Here are some examples:

Specifics:

- Name and type of item

- Color of the item

- Catalog information (style number, manufacturer, model number, etc.)

- Appearance and condition of the item

Selling points:

- What's unique about it?

- Why is it a great value?

- Is it hard to come by at the price you're asking?

- Why can't your customer live without it?

This is the bare minimum for an effective auction description. There's a lot you can do in a very small space. The chapters that follow contain helpful hints for effective product marketing by way of what you include in your description.

Photographic Images

Never list an auction without including an image. If you don't have a digital photograph to upload and use with your auction, don't list the auction until you have one.

Is that blunt enough? Well it's true. Auctions with photos attract more bids than auctions without them. And you can bet you'll read more about creating effective photographs for your auctions further on in this book. I'll drive this point home so often that the reviewers will hound me for it—but so what? Including photographs with your Internet auctions is essential if you want to be a successful seller.

The Bidding Field

The bidding field is where your customer will enter the amount that he or she wishes to bid. Some sites require the person to log in with a user ID and password first. The bidder can then proceed to the auction page to bid.

Figure 1.15 shows the bidding area of an auction at Amazon. The bidding field at other auction sites is typically similar to this. Notice that Amazon remembered my site ID via a "cookie" placed on my computer during a previous session when I logged onto the site. If I wanted to bid on this item, I'd enter a bid amount and click "Bid Now." A password and bid confirmation then appears on the next screen.

Note: A cookie is a very small text file sent by an Internet site to your computer's hard drive. Its purpose is to track your visits to the site. Most browsers accept cookies by default. You can set your preferences to deny them if you wish to remain anonymous at Web sites that use them.

Figure 1.15. Bidding field at an Amazon auction (found on any active listing page).

This particular auction also specified a Take-It price. Had I bid $4.50 on the item, the auction would have closed and I'd be the winner. Notice there is also a hyperlink below the bidding field that would take me to more instructions.

Bid-entry forms may differ, depending on the auction site. If you encounter a site that does things in a unique way, refer to the online instructions. The Internet auction sites like their users to know exactly what they're doing when they bid. So do the sellers.

Maximum Bid

Suppose you're the bidder. You'll enter a maximum bid, which is your self-imposed spending limit. You can usually raise this amount while the auction is active.

If you're the first bidder, the amount shown as your current bid will probably be lower than your maximum bid. The amount will match the minimum price set by the seller. The only exception is if your maximum bid meets the reserve price—then your current bid matches that, even if your maximum bid exceeds it.

Once you enter your bid, you can usually review it before it's official. This safeguards you in case you've made a grave error with the decimal point. Your bid takes effect as soon as you confirm it. If you're the high bidder, the program returns a screen to notify you of this. Your user ID then appears on the auction page as the current high bidder. If someone attempts to outbid you, the site proxy bids for you.

The Proxy Bid

This feature lets you set a bidding limit that will automatically increase your bid if someone attempts to outbid you. If you're the first bidder, the amount shown as your current bid will probably be lower than your maximum bid. The amount will match the minimum price set by the seller. The only exception is if your maximum bid meets the reserve price. Your current bid then matches the reserve price, even if your maximum bid exceeds it.

Here's an example. If the starting bid on an item is $20 and you enter a maximum bid of $100, you'll only see $20 as your current bid. If another user then enters a bid of $25, your bid will automatically (by proxy) raise to $30 (or the next increment). This will keep going until someone bids more than $100. Then you've been outbid and you have to enter a higher price. Let's hope your customers set high maximum bids and have plenty of bidding competition. That drives the price up.

Site Registration—Setting Up a User Name

Most sites let you browse listings as much as you want without a user ID, but in order to bid on an auction or sell anything, you must be a registered user.

Before you register, be sure to review the site's Terms and Conditions. If the site has a user agreement or something similar, read that also. To register, you're required to enter certain personal information that's retained by the Internet auction site in case someone needs to contact you. This information also puts the seller and buyer in contact when the auction closes.

As with many other registration processes on the Web, you might have to complete optional online questionnaires. These usually include multiple-choice items you select with a mouse click. This information determines which banner ads you'll see if the auction site runs them. You'll read more about those in Chapter 7.

Business Site Registration

At a business auction site, you may be asked for your business name, Federal Tax ID number, and business contact information.

Figure 1.16 shows the business account registration screen at uBid *(www.uBid.com)*, a noted business-to-business and business-to-consumer Internet auction site you'll read more about in Chapter 4.

Consumer Site Registration

Although the registration process varies from one site to another, and also varies depending on the type of auction site you choose, you can expect to provide the same type of information at all consumer-to-consumer sites including:

- E-mail address

- Site ID you'd like to use

- Full name

- Company name (if applicable)

- Street address

- City

- State or province

- Zip or postal code

- Country

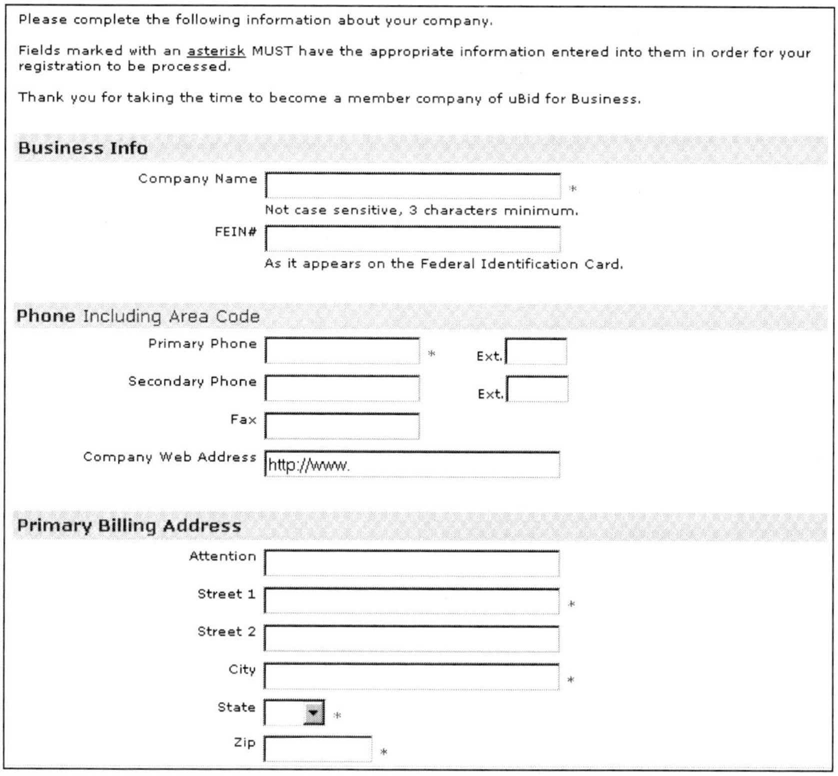

Please complete the following information about your company.

Fields marked with an asterisk MUST have the appropriate information entered into them in order for your registration to be processed.

Thank you for taking the time to become a member company of uBid for Business.

Business Info

Company Name *

Not case sensitive, 3 characters minimum.

FEIN#

As it appears on the Federal Identification Card.

Phone Including Area Code

Primary Phone * Ext.

Secondary Phone Ext.

Fax

Company Web Address http://www.

Primary Billing Address

Attention

Street 1 *

Street 2

City *

State *

Zip *

Figure 1.16. Business account registration screen at uBid.com.

- Daytime and evening phone numbers
- Fax number
- A credit card number

The consumer sites require your personal information, such as your address, telephone number, and occupation. Figure 1.17 shows you what you'll see when you register a buying or selling ID at Yahoo Auctions.

Almost every business Internet auction site asks for your credit card number when you register, and runs an authorization right away. It's very safe as long as the site uses SSL (Secure Sockets Layer) software when taking your personal information.

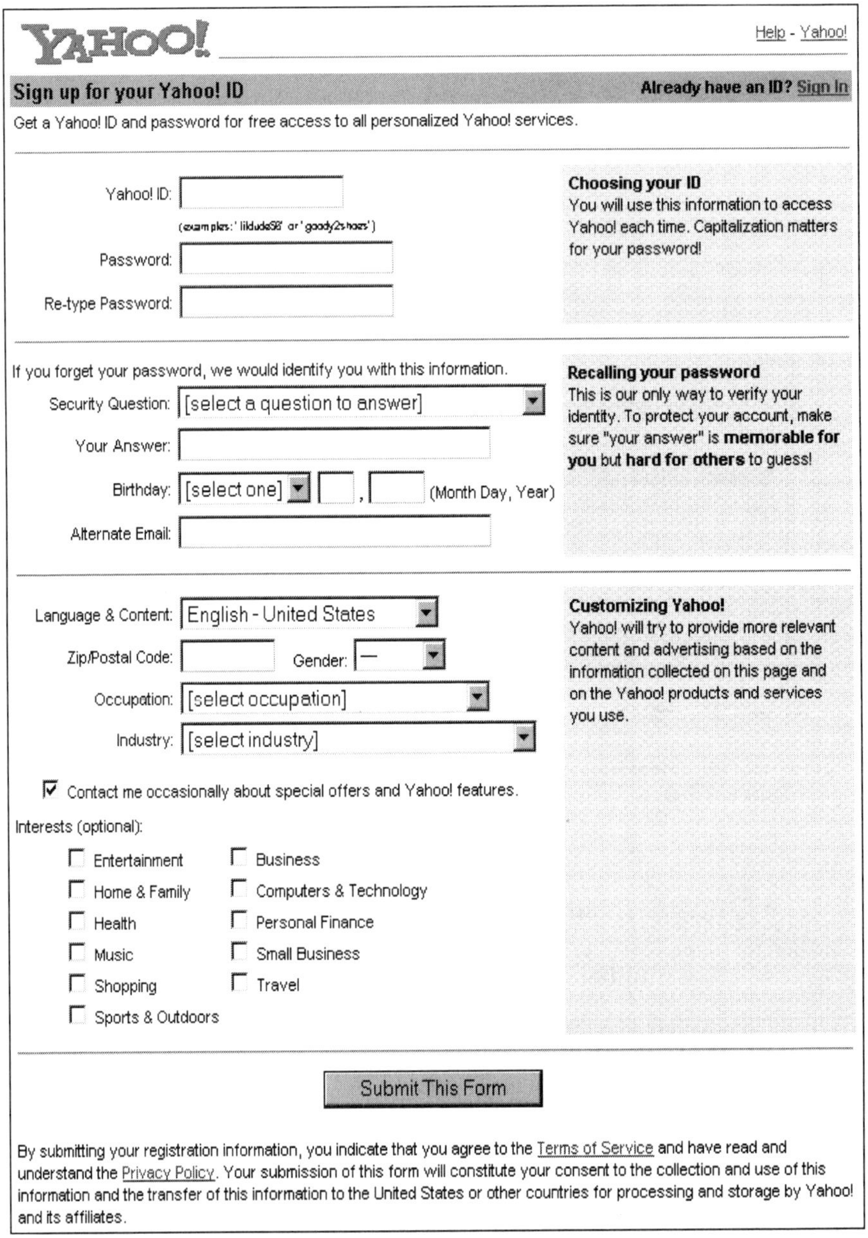

YAHOO!   Help - Yahoo!

Sign up for your Yahoo! ID   **Already have an ID?** Sign In

Get a Yahoo! ID and password for free access to all personalized Yahoo! services.

Yahoo! ID: [_____]

(examples: 'lildude98' or 'goody2shoes')

Password: [_____]

Re-type Password: [_____]

Choosing your ID
You will use this information to access Yahoo! each time. Capitalization matters for your password!

If you forget your password, we would identify you with this information.

Security Question: [[select a question to answer] ▼]

Your Answer: [_____]

Birthday: [[select one] ▼] [___] , [___] (Month Day, Year)

Alternate Email: [_____]

Recalling your password
This is our only way to verify your identity. To protect your account, make sure "your answer" is **memorable for you** but **hard for others** to guess!

Language & Content: [English - United States ▼]

Zip/Postal Code: [_____] Gender: [— ▼]

Occupation: [[select occupation] ▼]

Industry: [[select industry] ▼]

☑ Contact me occasionally about special offers and Yahoo! features.

Customizing Yahoo!
Yahoo! will try to provide more relevant content and advertising based on the information collected on this page and on the Yahoo! products and services you use.

Interests (optional):

☐ Entertainment   ☐ Business

☐ Home & Family   ☐ Computers & Technology

☐ Health   ☐ Personal Finance

☐ Music   ☐ Small Business

☐ Shopping   ☐ Travel

☐ Sports & Outdoors

[Submit This Form]

By submitting your registration information, you indicate that you agree to the Terms of Service and have read and understand the Privacy Policy. Your submission of this form will constitute your consent to the collection and use of this information and the transfer of this information to the United States or other countries for processing and storage by Yahoo! and its affiliates.

Figure 1.17. Registration screen at Yahoo.

Secured Sites

SSL protocol ensures that your browser sends the information you enter in a secure, encrypted form that nobody can intercept. If the site lets you choose whether you want to use SSL, definitely do, even if you aren't submitting a credit card number. It never hurts to protect your privacy.

Your browser may prompt you with a window when you enter or leave an SSL site. To double check, look for the little lock image in the very bottom frame of your browser. It's normally unlocked, but if you're on a page with SSL, the lock will be closed—or locked.

Here's what the lock icon looks like up close:

Unlocked   Locked

Check for the locked lock at any site that requires you to submit personal information, such as a credit card number. You definitely don't want this information in the wrong hands, and a secure site prevents that from happening.

Your User ID

At some Internet auction sites, your e-mail address is your **user ID**, also called a site ID. Other sites let you pick your own unique site nickname after you register. A few sites specifically won't allow you to use an e-mail address as your site ID. You must choose a "nickname" by which your customers will come to identify your auctions.

Note: Avoid using an underscore in your user ID. Since your user ID usually appears in hyperlink text, it's underlined. The underscore isn't visible in underlined text, and other users might think it's a space.

Password

You need a password to participate. Some sites let you enter your own password, but others send you a temporary one in e-mail to use when confirming your registration. You can then change it to something else.

Auctions and Your Business

If you've decided to take your business to Internet auctions, you couldn't have picked a better time. The next phase of your new venture is planning your Seven-Step Internet Auction Strategy. It will help you determine your Internet auction marketing plan. As you delve headfirst into setting up auction listings and waiting for bids to come rolling in, these steps will become your game plan. The Seven-Step Internet Auction Strategy will help you launch your online auction business.

2

Your Seven-Step Internet Auction Strategy

There has *never* been a better time to sell at Internet auctions. All you need are the right products, the right auction site, and the right selling strategy. An idea might be brilliant and loaded with potential, but it won't work if you try to carry it out without some kind of plan. That's why, in addition to creating your Seven-Step Internet Auction Strategy, you must examine the essential elements of your business before you use another selling platform. These elements include your strengths, weaknesses, goals, and assets.

All of these are adjuncts to your Seven-Step Internet Auction Strategy. By the end of this chapter, you'll be ready to take your business online. This chapter will help you examine your business and formulate a Seven-Step Internet Auction Strategy for selling through Internet auctions.

Your Seven Steps To Success

You definitely need a structured approach in order to succeed in a business based on something as new as selling at Internet auctions. The most common reason that businesses fail is lack of an adequate plan. When you examine your business in depth, it's a great opportunity to carry out the most beneficial kind of market research. The Seven-Step Internet Auction Strategy encourages you to keep the crucial elements of your business in mind.

First, determine whether you're a good candidate for online auction product marketing. Then it's time to map your strategy. You will create a plan you can tailor-make in the best interest of both your own needs, and the needs of your business.

Is This a Formal Business Plan?

No. Most likely, you compiled a formal business plan when you first launched your business. It contained information about the business concept, the business objective, product manufacturing, marketing, overall financial information, and ownership. You may want to have that handy as you develop your Seven-Step Internet Auction Strategy for selling at Internet auctions, because you'll review some of these here.

Since it's advisable to keep your formal business plan up to date, this will be an excellent opportunity to add information about your new marketing venue to it. Internet auction selling, if carried out in the organized manner outlined in this book, will become an important and profitable part of your overall business plan.

Key Elements of Your Seven-Step Internet Auction Strategy

Perhaps you're a small business entrepreneur or a large company assigned you to set up their Internet auction marketing division. Either way, you'll use your auction strategy to get your products to your customers. Here we'll explore the essential aspects of your business, and address these questions about the key business elements:

- What products will you sell?

- Who is your target market?

- Which auction sites will you use?

- What type of auctions will you run?

- How will your customers pay you?

- How do you get the auctions running?

- How do you get the word out about your auctions?

- When is the transaction complete?

- How do you assess your success?

You'll organize all of this information and convert it to a systematic marketing strategy. The worksheets in Appendix C will help you organize each element of the Seven-Step Internet Auction Strategy.

How to Use the Steps

You should examine the steps shown in Figure 2.1 before you start listing items for auction. By reading the steps through, you will be better able to anticipate your next move as you complete the step before it.

If you're as excited about selling at Internet auctions as current market trends indicate you should be, you might be tempted to skim through the chapters and go right to the sites. I urge you to read the Seven-Step Internet Auction Strategy very carefully, beginning with Step 1.

Your Seven-Step Internet Auction Strategy

Step 1: Select Your Products and Identify Your Market

Step 2: Identify the Best Payment Method for Your Customers

Step 3: Identify the Appropriate Auction Site and Type of Auction for the Products

Step 4: List the Products for Auction

Step 5: Promote Your Auctions

Step 6: Complete the Transaction

Step 7: Assess Your Success and Return to Step 1

Figure 2.1. Your seven-step Internet auction strategy.

Step 1: Select Your Products and Identify Your Market

What are you going to sell? Most users of the traditional consumer-to-consumer sellers are, right now, out combing the yard sales and thrift shops to pick up a bargain that they can sell on eBay for a huge profit. That's great, and you can make a lot of money that way as one of the home-based independent sellers addressed in Chapter 10. However, if you already run a business or plan to list auctions on behalf of a corporate enterprise, you already have the goods on hand to sell.

Some independent sellers operate on a "25-hour working day." They track down every bargain that's laying out for sale, clean it up, research what kind of item it is, write and design an auction ad, and then launch and track the listing. As a business seller, you should concentrate on the surplus or overstock items that you have that would amount to a huge loss if unsold. Take these to the online auction block.

Your Current Stock

Seasoned Internet auction users advise against listing retail-priced goods at the online auction sites. "If you have a brand new pair of Levi jeans, you're not going to get the full retail price for them no matter what site you list them on," says one veteran eBay seller. "You have too much competition from the retail giants like J.C. Penney's, who run falling price auctions for their own jeans. You also have the yard sale hunters who will list a slightly used pair of the same Levi's at a fraction of retail. If people are going to pay full retail for brand new Levi's, they'll buy them at the store where they can try them on and have the exact selection they want." Be sure the goods you list can sell below retail.

The best items to sell online are the ones you can't move for a steady profit over the counter. Here are some examples:

- **Overstock**—Items you over-ordered

- **Surplus items**—Leftovers from a promotion

- **Discontinued items**—Items that are not big sellers on the market, or models replaced by newer versions. This could include discontinued items you bought at a discount, or items you no longer plan to carry.

You'll make your best profits by listing items that you would have otherwise taken a huge loss on. If you list them online, you stand the chance of breaking even—at least. Also, decide if you want to become a clearinghouse for surplus and overstock, or if you just want to sell items from your own business supply.

What Must You Sell Quickly?

Some products may be too costly to maintain in stock. This depends on how much you have invested in them, of course. If the value of the goods combined with the cost of stocking space is eating up your profits, designate these goods for the Internet auction block. They'll turn into revenue, and make room for stock with a faster over-the-counter turnover.

Numerous reasons could make it necessary for you to need to sell a large amount of stock quickly:

- You need to make room for updated items or newer models.

- You have too many of them and need to turn them into revenue.

- Your local Brick & Mortar customers aren't ordering as much as they used to.

This also holds true for items that are nearing the end of their "15 minutes of fame." If you see that a fad has run out, it's time to move anything related to it. If you move the items by selling them at an Internet auction site, you're more likely to reach folks getting in on the fad just as it's dying out. They'll happily purchase your soon-to-be passé stock.

Pricing Your Products

Pricing your product is one of the most important decisions you'll make when selling at Internet auctions. You must list your products at a starting bid that's in line with what your target market is willing to pay. At the same time, you either must produce a profit or break even, depending on your expectations for moving the stock. There are several approaches to setting your minimum bids.

Consider the least you can charge for your products without incurring a loss. You also need to think about the amount of profit that you want to earn from the sales. How high can you price your goods and still be ahead of your competition?

Can you discount your prices below the Manufacturer's Suggested Retail Price and still fall under any guidelines they may have? You may also want to consider offering quantity discounts to steady customers. You'll read more about pricing your products in Chapter 3.

New Product Promotions

Are you interested in testing the market for a new item? Perhaps it's a line of items your business manufactures, or maybe it's just an idea you had for the next "pet rock" that you're certain will vault you into the Fad Hall of Fifteen-Minute Fame.

There's no better place for test-marketing your item than at a site like eBay, where you have customers from every possible demographic type imaginable. In addition, they all have user IDs, which means that they can all bid on your products.

If you have a patent on an item and need a manufacturer's buy-in, you'll have a much better chance of holding their interest if your business proposal has a ready-made sales record backing it. A closed eBay Dutch auction that sold 1,500 of your brainchild would definitely be convincing.

In Chapter 3, "Will Your Products Sell?", you'll read more about selecting products that will do well at auction. For now, think about who your customers will be.

Your Target Market

To whom are you selling? To put it in angler's terms, where will you find the most richly stocked trout pond? That's where you want to drop your bait. When you're marketing products, your trout pond is the place you'll find the most possible customers with the least amount of effort.

Well, we already know where that is—on the Internet, of course. However, even with the millions of people who are on the Internet auction sites, your auction ad still has to target those most likely to buy your products. You need to identify who they are, and then make your auctions both attractive and accessible to them.

Most Internet auction sites have you list your items in categories. Part of the reason they're set up that way is so sellers can reach their **target market**. When potential buyers surf along looking for what they want to buy, they check the auction categories.

You can best define your target market as "that group of customers with a set of common characteristics that sets them apart from other customers." Knowing who your customers are helps you define your Internet auction marketing strategy. In order to do that, you need to consider the characteristics of your potential customers:

- What are their buying trends?

- Where do they live, work, and shop?

- What's their average income?

- What are their hobbies, pastimes, or interests?

- Are they online?

- Are they impulsive enough to confidently bid online?

Once you have the answers, you can determine your customers' needs, and then determine how your products can serve your target market. In your auction descriptions, you need to get the point across that your products are right for them.

Market Trends

Smart marketers follow popular trends and learn to anticipate products that will sell. Fads bring new products to the marketplace; so does new technology. Keep an eye on the market.

You'll want to view closed auctions—and not just your own—to see what is selling and what isn't. You may want to follow technical or trade journals to keep abreast of developments in the Internet auction world. It's important to know what products are selling well on the Internet. Read newspaper ads. Watch commercials on TV. Follow the stock market. In other words, know what is selling and what isn't.

Of course, your own sales will help you determine this over time also.

Identifying and Analyzing the Competition

If you analyze your competition, you can determine your position in the industry. You don't have to be the leader or potential leader to be profitable, but it helps to know where you stand. This will help you promote your company and products.

Some businesses may offer the same products as you do, and others may target the same customers. Both are your competition. It's important to know your competition because they, in addition to your customers, help you define your business. Once you identify your competition, you need to decide if you want to tap their market, or alter yours. You have a few decisions to make at this point:

- Do you plan to carve your own niche?

- Are you comfortable sharing the niche?

- Are you aggressive enough to do both?

You also need to anticipate what the competition will do once your business is successful. Will they copy you? Will they attempt to denigrate your products by listing better ones on the same Internet auction site you're using? Knowing your competition inside and out will help you stay a step ahead of them.

Step 2: Identify the Appropriate Auction Site and Type of Auction for the Products

eBay isn't the only Internet auction site. It was the first, and may well be the best in its class. However, the OAI, or Online Auction Industry, has come so far since Omidyar sold Pez dispensers that a dedicated seller—especially one selling items in large quantities or lots—needs to explore many different options.

Know the Types of Sites

Within the OAI, different types of sites support certain types of sales. Sellers have separate classifications. Either they sell as consumers, or they sell as a business. Folks who do not run a business and sell on their own are considered consumers, and those who sell at online auctions usually sell to other consumers. If you're selling goods that will exchange through a licensed business, then you are a business seller.

All Internet auction sites classify according to the types of sales they support. Here is the key to the auction site terms you'll read more about in Chapter 4:

- **C2C (Consumer-to-Consumer)**—Individuals list items, which are purchased by other individuals.

- **B2C (Business-to-Consumer)**—Businesses list items, which are purchased by individuals.

- **B2B (Business-to-Business)**—Businesses list items, which are purchased by other businesses.

- **B2E (Business-to-Exchange)**—Businesses list items, which are viewed at Auction Exchange sites.

A good example of a B2C site is Egghead.com. For C2C and B2C selling, eBay leads the industry. DealDeal, which you'll read more about, is a well-known B2B site. AuctionWatch is, among other things, an established B2E site.

Quantity of Items

Are you selling ten office chairs, or are you selling ten thousand of them? If you have ten, you should see how well they sell on a site like eBay. If you have ten thousand, you'll want to list them through a B2B site that can sell the whole lot for you.

In certain cases, your business customer may want to bid on the entire lot, which will typically cut down on shipping and transportation costs. If you sell the items individually, your customers will pay more per item but you'll have more cost and labor involved in packing and shipping.

Who Is Your Customer?

Regardless of the quantity of items you're selling, it's important to know to whom you'll end up selling them. You should try to anticipate this before you list the items. Not whether you're selling them to Bob or Mary, but whether you're selling them to Bob, to Mary, or to Lisa Peters & Co.

If your target customer is another business, select a B2B site that offers the best service and takes the least amount of commission from your sales. You may have to hunt around a little to find information for sellers, and you may have to make telephone contact with site representatives who will set up your selling account.

Listing Tools

Every quantity seller uses some kind of listing tool to manage auctions. To enter each one manually is a time-consuming task. John Hannon, an eBay shooting-star seller, uses Auction Works, and it takes him only a few seconds to list a week's worth of auctions. He can schedule them for the next week and go away on vacation if he wants to.

Note: An eBay shooting star user is one who has accrued more than 10,000 positive feedback comments from unique users.

We'll talk more about auction listing tools in Chapter 6.

Step 3: Identify the Best Payment Method for Your Customers

Collecting money from your customers is a fundamental business issue, of course. Unlike your shop, where goods exchange for payment over the counter, your Internet auction customers are typically scattered all over the place. Hand over hand payments are not likely. Additionally, if you decide to sell to international customers, you need to determine how your customers can send funds to you conveniently. Always make it as easy as possible for your customers to pay you.

Mail-In Payments

Mailing payments to the seller was the standard procedure when Internet auction sites first came about. The seller's end of auction (EOA) e-mail included his or her address and the total amount due for the item (plus shipping and optional insurance). The buyer would send a personal check (if the seller accepted them), cashier's check, or money order to cover the cost. Then the seller shipped the item. According to an estimate by eBay, 80% of the transactions at the site still take place through the mail.

If you aren't set up with a merchant account or an online payment system, mail-in payments still work. However, they're not always the easiest payment method for your customers.

Credit Cards

Do you need a merchant account? Chances are if you're already an established retailer or wholesaler, you have one. This is good, as some customers will be much more likely to bid if they know they can put the purchase on plastic. If you plan on doing a lot of online business, opening a merchant account so you can accept credit cards is advisable. If you can't open one for some reason, you do have another option open that will allow your customers to pay for their purchase from you with a credit card.

Online Payment Services

Most people have heard of PayPal and BidPay, two of the best-known online payment services. There may be more by now. Some of the Internet auction sites have their own system in place to allow buyers to pay for purchases through the site with a credit card. You'll have to check at each site to find out if they have such a program in place. Since they're a solid source of income for the Internet auction sites, rest assured that most of them do.

Sellers should register with at least one online payment service. If you're using a C2C or B2C site, check auctions in the appropriate listing category for your products to see which service the sellers most commonly use. Since most sellers include payment services they accept within their auction descriptions, you can also do a global site search for the words "PayPal" and see how many listings come up. This is a good indication of the current popularity of the service. Do the same with other online payment services and make your own decision about which one you want to use. Alternatively, register at as many as you feel you can reasonably manage.

You'll read more about online payment services in Chapter 5.

Step 4: List the Products for Auction

Listing your products is a lot like unlocking the front door, turning the "Closed" sign around, and opening your business for the day. The goods are out, and you're ready to sell them. For the most part, you can kick back and let the auction site and the search engines take over until the auctions close.

There are ways to promote your auctions, but you'll read about that in the next step.

Learn How the Site Works

You have to know your way around any auction site that you use. Chapter 1 provided an overview to start you off. I recommend two preliminary steps to anyone who seriously considers selling goods at any Internet auction site:

- Browse the site thoroughly and read the Terms and Conditions, Restrictions, Site Tutorial, and any other information included at the site.

- Register as a user, and buy something. Don't just place a bid, but actually win. If another user outbids you at the last minute, find another auction and try again. Track the auction until it ends and be sure you're the high bidder when it does. Then carry through the transaction with the buyer, making note of what you like and dislike about both the site and the transaction.

From these studies, you can make the best assessment of the site and decide if it's right for your business needs. You'll also learn a lot about what your customers will expect from you.

Run a Test Auction

Your test auction has to be a real auction. In other words, if you have a high bidder, you have to sell the item. However, with your test auction, you'll learn to feel comfortable listing auctions. You can practice editing a live auction, appending information to the description, or using any other feature that the site allows on live auctions. This will also help you see how your auction looks when it's live. You can use HTML to make your auction look professional, or use an auction description tool to make it look sensational.

Describe the Item Accurately

As an Internet auction seller, you must tell the bidder the specifics of the item up for auction. In addition to the finer qualities of the item, or its selling points, you need to mention anything that's wrong with it. This can include:

- Missing parts or packaging

- Damage to the item

- Unclear product markings

- Wear and tear on the item

If you're honest when you list the item, you can fall back on your auction description if problems arise later. The books on buying at auction warn sellers to read the auction description before bidding. It's up to you, the seller, to drive that point home.

State Your Terms

You will want your customers to know your terms of sale up front. These can include:

- When and how you expect payment

- How long you will wait to hear from the buyer before you relist the item

- Your policy on leaving feedback

- Whether you accept returns, and under what conditions

Here also, if you state your terms clearly in the auction description, you've covered yourself in case the buyer brings up any issues later. In Chapter 8, you'll read more about clearly stating your terms.

Select Your Listing Tools

Start your first auction from scratch. Code it yourself with simple HTML (have Appendix B handy) and keep it simple. List one auction at a time until you get the hang of it. After that, you will want to explore some bulk listing and auction-formatting tools that allow you the following benefits:

- Schedule your auctions so they'll start automatically.

- List many auctions at the same time.

- Format your auction descriptions with different fonts, colors, and images.

- Reuse your auction description formats with just minor tweaking.

Web sites that provide tools for auction sellers are often called Internet auction service providers. Some of the leaders in the business are Ándale, AuctionWatch, and AuctionWorks. These sites provide automated tools that make listing numerous auctions a breeze. Here's a sampling:

- Bulk uploading of auctions

- Auction scheduler (starts your auctions at a time you specify)

- Image hosting

- Hit counters for your auctions (so you can check your traffic)

- Automatic invoicing

- Bulk feedback posting

- Generated sales reports

These sites charge a nominal fee for their services. Most sellers who use them find that the tools are well worth the fees.

Step 5: Promote Your Auctions

To get the most hits to your listings, you have a few options for promoting them. Promotion of your business involves using all means available to get the message out that your product or service is good or desirable. Listing products for auction at eBay is not always sufficient to get the message across to your customers. You need to let them know that your products are available at such-and-so auction site and they need to visit there *pronto* to place a bid.

Links Within Your Auctions

As we discussed in Chapter 1, most Internet auction sites allow you to use HTML code within your auction descriptions. With HTML, you can include a link to your seller list, which contains links to all other auctions you have running at that site. This is an essential element of a volume seller's auction description. If you include an incentive for multiple purchases, such as free or reduced shipping, your customers will be more likely to visit your other listings. More visits to your listings mean a chance for more bids.

Your Business Web Site

Any successful business has, or should have, a great Web site. An essential link on your business Web site should be the one that takes your customers right to your Internet auction listings. You need to let your customers know that your Internet presence also includes your online auction business. Your link will take them there, and your listings will keep them interested.

You could even offer purchase incentives to encourage steady Internet auction business. For instance, offer your customers 10% off their next Web site purchase for every one of your auctions they've won.

Link Exchanges

Got a friend with a Web page? Trade links! That's how we upped our hit counters back when we were making our personal home pages. The concept works for consumer and business Internet auction sellers as well.

Gail Hotchkiss and Leon Herr had a great idea for a link exchange. Together with their friends at the Online Traders' Web Alliance (OTWA), they created a site called SoupGirl.com, at which they include links to sellers' auctions. They also have a message board where users can discuss topics of interest to Internet auction users, and they host a featured seller each week.

Paid Advertising

If you really want to invest some cash to promote your auctions, you could pay for a banner ad at one of the Internet auction service provider's sites. Expect to shell out upwards of $1,000 for a limited-run banner ad on a high-profile site. Web advertising isn't cheap, as it funds most of the freebies that the site offers to its users.

Step 6: Complete the Transaction

The Internet auction transaction moves in phases, from start to finish. Each step is as important as the next, and it's especially important to complete the transaction properly. To be successful as an Internet auction seller, you need to keep your customers happy. Just as you expect certain things from your customers, they will expect certain things from you in return.

Your Responsibility as a Seller

Selling at an Internet auction site carries certain responsibilities. If your auction receives bids at or above your stated minimum or reserve price, you're obligated to complete the transaction with the highest bidder. You also have a few other responsibilities once the auction ends successfully:

- Contact the buyer when the auction closes.

- Inform the buyer of how much he or she owes for the item, plus shipping and insurance.

- Be sure the item is in the condition you stated in the auction description.

- Charge accurate amounts for shipping and insurance.

- Send the buyer the correct item.

- Insure the item, if the buyer requests and pays for it.

- Pack the item securely.

- Address the package clearly and accurately.

If you use care when completing the transaction, your customers will be more likely to remain your customers. In Chapter 8, you'll read more about your responsibilities as a seller.

End-of-Auction E-mail

Most of the C2C and B2C sites have provisions in place that put you in contact with your high bidder when the auction ends. It's up to the seller to contact the high bidder to work out the specifics of the transaction. Therefore, you must contact your high bidder as soon as the auction ends. Your **End-of-Auction** (EOA) **e-mail** should contain the following:

- A thank you for bidding on your auction

- The auction number and name of the lot or item purchased

- The buyer's high bid

- The charge for shipping

- The charge for insurance, at the customer's option

- The address to which the customer will send payment

- Your account name at an online payment service site

- Reiteration of your return policy

The B2B sites also ensure that the high bidder receives notification at the end of the auction.

Packaging Your Items

You need to decide whether to sell your products packaged in multiples, individually packaged, or loose (no packaging but securely packed). Your item packaging depends on who your customer is. If you're selling multiples of items, a lot will depend on what your customers plan to do with the item. There are three possible types of customers:

- End-user, or consumer

- Resale business

- Wholesale business

Each type of customer will have different expectations where item packaging is concerned.

Packing and Shipping

No matter how meticulously you handled the transaction up to here, none of it will make any difference if the customer receives a broken item. You, the seller, are responsible for adequately packing the item so it withstands the trip once it's out of your hands. Choosing a carrier that's economical for you and convenient for the customer is also an issue. Here is what you need to consider:

- **Packing products**—Packing puffies (peanuts), shredded paper, braces

- **Adequate carton**—Priority-mail boxes, mailing cartons

- **Your transmittal note**—Always include a note with the products you ship.

- **Carrier**—United States Postal Service, or another shipping company

You will read more about adequate packing, reliable shipping methods, and what your transmittal note should include in Chapter 8.

Follow-Up E-mail

When you ship the item, you need to let the customer know so he or she can be on the lookout for it. Be sure to send e-mail notifications to your customers to keep them apprised of the status of their shipment. You should also request that your customers notify you via e-mail when their package arrives, so you can assess their satisfaction.

Feedback

As you read in Chapter 1, feedback, or user rating, is how Internet auction participants rate each other. Different sellers have varied ideas about one aspect of the transaction—when to enter feedback for the buyer.

Some sellers post feedback for customers as soon as they receive payment. These sellers feel that at that point, the customer has fulfilled his or her end of the deal and is under no further obligation to the seller. Other sellers don't enter feedback until after the customer has received the item and is satisfied with it. There are pros and cons to each method, which you'll read about in Chapter 8. Under no circumstances should the seller expect the buyer to enter feedback first.

Step 7: Assess Your Success and Return to Step 1

Once the transaction has completed to your and your customer's satisfaction, there are a few essential steps to take before returning to Step 1 to start the process over. You need to record the transaction and assess your profit. Was it worthwhile?

Recordkeeping

Later in this chapter, you'll read about the importance of keeping adequate financial records. You'll also want to keep a record of each Internet auction transaction you carry out. The success of your auctions will tell you some important information for future sales campaigns:

- Which products sell

- Which auction site yielded the best sales results

- Your market—individual or business?

- Net profit earned

These records will come in handy when you consider selling the same or similar items later. The FTC recommends that when the auction closes, the sellers should print all the information about the transaction, making a note of the buyer's identification, the description of the item and the time, date, and price of the bid. Print and save a copy of every e-mail message that you send or receive from the auction site, or from your successful bidders.

Did You Make a Profit?

Keep a record of your profits so you know what you can expect if you list this type of item again. This will help you determine where to set the starting bid, and how many you can expect to sell—assuming the market hasn't drastically changed.

Include these costs in your profit calculations:

- Listing fees

- Auction management and image hosting service fees

- Site commission

- Cost of shipping and materials not covered by the buyer

- Any associated expenses not covered by the buyer

These figures will be important in helping you decide whether to list that item again at auction.

Auction Site Fees

Internet auction sites typically don't operate free. There is a charge for selling. When the concept first came about, a few sites offered free listings, but they became too expensive to operate. One example is the now-defunct auction site called Up4Sale. Their credo was "free auctions forever," but once eBay bought them out, they ceased operation. It soon became apparent that Internet auction sites are a rich source of income for those who operate them.

In Chapter 9, you'll read more about what to expect in Internet auction site fees and how to account for them.

3

Will Your Products Sell?

Step 1 of your Seven-Step Internet Auction Strategy is to select your products and identify your market. Can you sell your products online?

Some products are surefire sellers on the Internet: electronics, clothes, collectibles, and toys. Other products have tiptoed onto the Internet, making a surprise appearance and leaving consumers amazed. Whoever thought there would be an online market for eye shadow? Or that anyone would order garden shrubs from a Web site? Yet both businesses are booming in the browsers.

This chapter will help you decide what you're going to sell, who will buy it, and how you'll market it.

What Will Sell

The optimistic answer to this question is "anything you present right." The word *right* in this context means:

- You've presented the item to the correct target market.

- The prospective customers are receptive to the item.

- The item is priced correctly.

• You're presenting your item better than your competition.

All four of these issues are essential if you want to succeed in your new e-commerce venture. This section will help you decide if you've selected the right products to sell through Internet auctions.

Internet Sales Statistics

Not every business sells on the Internet. Small businesses number over 23 million in the United States, but only 9% have their own Web site and less than 5% conduct sales online. Large corporations, however, are involved in the Internet at a much greater level because they have larger resources for funding their Internet involvement. For all types of businesses, Internet sales climb every year.

➠ **Note:** Small businesses are those with less than 100 employees and under $5 million in sales.

The following 5-year statistics from Forrester Research published in late 2000 show the projected online shopping revenue by category:

Online Shopping Revenue by Category, 1996-2000 (millions)

Category	1996	1997	1998	1999	2000
Computer Products	$140	$323	$701	$1,228	$2,105
Travel	126	276	572	961	1579
Entertainment	85	194	420	733	1250
Apparel	46	89	163	234	322
Gifts/Flowers	45	78	149	227	336
Food/Drink	39	78	149	227	336
Other	37	75	144	221	329
TOTAL	$518	$1,138	$2,371	$3,990	$6,579

This table shows a steady increase in items sold via the Internet between 1996 and 2000. Current trends indicate that the numbers will continue to climb.

What the Customer Wants

With your marketing worksheets in Appendix C, you can determine the basics of your marketing and operations. Now you need to figure out whether your products will sell online, and who will buy them. You need to consider a few things:

- Is there a demand for the product?

- Is it practical to purchase the product online?

- Is it easy to locate the product on the Internet with the intent to purchase it?

- How quickly can the product be delivered?

This section will help you determine whether you can meet your customers' needs in these areas.

Demand for Product

Is your product line already selling well on the Internet? If it's selling marginally well from a business Web site, then you know that your customers are seeking the product online. Getting your customers online is an important first step in getting them to your auctions.

There is one way you can find out if a product is selling online. Check closed auctions at C2C and B2C sites. Closed auctions with bids indicate successful sales. Auctions that closed after bidding wars indicate products you should get on the market right away—they're hot! You'll read more about the importance of studying closed auctions as you progress through your Seven-Step Internet Auction Strategy.

Is an Online Purchase Practical?

Are you marketing products that don't have to be purchased in person? For the typical consumer, the more difficult or time-consuming it is to buy something, the more he or she will prefer to use the Internet instead of traditional over the counter shopping. But does this apply to all products?

Traditional business trends might indicate that customers prefer to purchase some products in stores. The look, touch, and try principal would logically apply to items a customer wants to see in person. Here are a few examples:

- Cosmetics

- Shoes and Clothing

- Jewelry

- Giftware

Although logically, customers would rather purchase these items in person, all of these commodities sell very well from manufacturer and retailer Web sites. When you check the auction listings at eBay, Amazon, or Yahoo, you'll find they're selling well at Internet auctions, too. Some megastores claim that online sales have replaced the traditional catalog phone-in orders.

Therefore, the answer to the question "Is an online purchase practical?" is yes. There is an online market for virtually any commodity.

Locating the Product on the Internet

If consumers are seeking something online, one of the first places they'll look is at the Internet auction sites. When a customer goes online in search of a product with the intent to make a purchase, one of two things is likely to happen:

- They'll check eBay first, and then go to the manufacturer's Web site.

- They'll call up a search engine like Google or Yahoo and do a text search for the item.

Why would a person shop online as opposed to going to the store? The first answer, of course, is convenience. If a person can economically buy something using his or her computer, time spent running to the store can be used in other ways.

Speed of Delivery

Customers want their products as soon as they're paid for. Since you'll have the products in inventory, you have some control over the speed at which your customers will receive their orders. With a credit card or online payment, you can ship the items the next business day. Otherwise, you need to wait for the cashier's check or money order to arrive, or a personal check to clear the bank. Then you can ship.

You can offer your customers premium shipping options, provided they know in advance what the cost will be and are willing to pay for it.

The Ideal Online Customer

That's easy. The ideal online customer is someone with lots of money and plenty of room on his or her credit card. Right? Well, to a certain point. The best Internet auction customers are those who are comfortable buying things over the Internet. There's nothing worse for a seller than dealing with someone experiencing Internet paranoia, which translates to extreme reluctance to send money to someone they don't know. They'll e-mail you endlessly asking you to prove your reliability and doubt every response you give. They'll take forever to pay you, or they won't pay you at all. This is all very annoying but, unfortunately, Internet marketers must be prepared to deal with it.

Understandable Concerns

Buyers may also have issues that are *not* born of paranoia, and you must react to them with polite patience. Experienced or not, any Internet customer is likely to have these concerns:

- Will the item I want be too expensive to ship?

- Where can I direct questions about the product?

- What if the seller cheats me?

These questions are not the mark of a squeamish buyer—they are quite practical. Of course, your auction description will solve the first two dilemmas, since you'll include the estimated shipping cost and your contact information. Your solid online reputation and confident attitude in your correspondence hopefully will appease the third concern. But you can expect online customers to be at least a little bit worried at first, since the Internet is still new to so many.

It would be nice if you could always choose your customers, but that's not typically possible. Here you'll learn to identify and target the ideal Internet customers.

Experience with Auctions

The ideal customers have purchased things through Internet auctions before and know how they work. You can identify Internet auction veterans in several ways:

- **Feedback score**—A high number consisting of mostly positive and few neutral comments means the user knows the Internet auction circuit.

- **User profile**—Many of them include the date the person registered his or her online auction account.

- **The tone of their correspondence**—A person's confidence with the Internet auction process will reflect in their understanding of your terms of sale.

Remember that you'll get your share of newbies, too. You need to be sure you can deal with customers at all levels of online auction experience. In Chapter 9 you'll read about ways to make newcomers feel confident that your transaction will turn out exactly as they want it to.

Ample Cash and Credit Line

Your ultimate high bidder might be the nicest person in the world, but that won't do you much good if he or she can't pay you. Hopefully, you'll target customers who can make good on their bids, whether they're small businesses or individuals. Unfortunately, as your Internet auction sales increase, so will your encounters with non-paying bidders (NPBs). Handling that is one downside of the Internet auction business. The ideal customer, of course, is the one who puts his high bid right where it belongs—in your pocket.

Your terms of payment should offer options, such as personal checks, cashier's checks, money orders, credit cards, or online payment service transactions. Some customers prefer to pay by check, and others will phone you with a credit card number. If your customers are Internet auction regulars, they'll probably have an account with an online payment service like PayPal. All the better.

➠ **Note:** You'll read more about online payment services in Chapter 5.

Pricing Your Goods

Pricing is crucial, and requires research. You don't want to price your items so high that nobody bids on your auctions, but you also don't want to incur losses or you won't be in business very long. It's very important to use care in determining your opening bid amount.

Cost vs. Price

Successful marketing is all about making more for an item than you paid for it. Two terms to consider here are **cost** and **price**.

- **Cost** is the total amount of your fixed and variable expenses to manufacture or offer your product.

- **Price** is the selling price per unit that your customers will pay for your product or service.

If customers ask, "How much does this cost," your answer is "the price is $7.00." The idea here it to set your price above your cost.

Price Floor and Price Ceiling

Two terms define the most you can charge while staying competitive, and the least you can charge without taking a loss:

- **Price floor** is the lowest amount at which you can offer your product and still cover your cost and expenses associated with marketing the product. If you set the price at or below cost, you should have a temporary, specific purpose, such as to run an introductory promotion.

- **Price ceiling** is the highest cost a consumer will pay for a product or service. Think of the price ceiling as the customer's perceived value of the item. Several factors create this perception, such as the product's popularity, quality of advertising (yours and the manufacturer's), and packaging. Also involved is the comparison your customers make between you and your competitors.

Remember that the revenues from your online auction sales must generate a profit if you intend to be successful at it. If you're moving stock to avoid a loss and can bear a break-even result, then your price floor is easy to determine. The merchandise pricing worksheet in Appendix C will help you determine your pricing range.

Operating Overhead

Your overhead is any expenses associated with the following:

- Rent and storage expenses

- Staff wages

- Computer hardware

- Telephone and fax

- Internet Service Provider

We will assume that your overhead costs are in place whether you're listing Internet auctions or not. These won't be included in your cost and price analysis—only auction site fees since those are dynamic depending on your ratio of closed sales. Fees can vary at every Internet auction site.

Expect to Sell Below Retail
Remember the two main reasons why consumers go to the Internet auction sites:

- To seek out a rare item

- In search of a bargain

Presumably, you're not selling antique tomes or rare single pieces of chinaware. You're liquidating stock, selling surplus items, or marketing a new product. Chances are nothing on your sales list qualifies as "rare." So, you need to market items that you can sell below the suggested retail price. If you sell items at retail, you're going to compete with regular straight-sale business Web sites that may charge less for shipping and don't have auction site fees as additional overhead. You want to make money or at least break even—not take a huge loss. On a positive note, remember that these are *auctions*. People can bid and outbid each other. If you get more than one bid, you may end up selling the item at or above retail. Just keep in mind the least amount you can take for the item when you decide at what amount the bidding will start.

Setting Your Minimum Bid
The minimum bid is the price at which you start your auction. Where you start the bidding, or at what price you set your reserve, is crucial to whether your items will sell.

Always assume that your minimum bid—the amount at which your auction starts—will end up as the winning bid when the auction closes. In other words, always count on only one bid. This mirrors the phrase "expect the least and you won't be disappointed" because the bidding may go higher than that one bid. You can't assume that a bidding war will drive the price wildly high. Depending on your expected outcome of the sale, set your minimum bid far enough above your price floor to generate some profit and make worthwhile the effort involved in preparing the listing. Your customers will be drawn to the best value and the greatest bargain.

Be Competitive

Be sure to price your items competitively without incurring too great a loss for yourself, and always anticipate being undercut by someone who wants to divert your sales. At most sites, you can't change your starting price once the auction is running, regardless of whether it has bids or not. If someone undercuts you, all you can do at that point is pray, end your auction, and restart at a lower price and thus incur listing fees, or hope that your auction ads convince your market that they're wise to pay a little more for your stuff. Good luck.

What Won't Sell

The best answer is "anything you present poorly." The word *poorly* in this context means the opposite of what *right* meant under "What Will Sell." For instance, here's an example of items that won't do well at Internet auctions:

- An item listed on a site that doesn't target that market (for instance, a washing machine listed at an Internet auction site that specializes in toys)

- An item that your prospective customers have no use for (for instance, if it's unusable or completely obsolete)

- An item priced at ten times its actual value

- An item that your competition is selling cheaper

Notice that I don't list specific products that won't sell. There is no such classification when it comes to selling at Internet auctions. You can sell just about anything that can be legally sold, and is within the guidelines of your chosen venue.

Knowing Your Product Marketing Business

Can you sell your products through Internet auction sites? Sure you can. It might seem like a long stretch right now, especially if you're new to the Internet, but it's possible if you're prepared to do the extra work. Remember that in addition to the work involved in managing both the online and offline duties of Internet auction sales, you're going to deal with a whole new set of customers.

One important step in marketing your products through Internet auctions is to take a close look at your business. You need to examine several essential elements of your present operation before you find the online market for your products. Know thyself first.

Internet Auction Manager's Job Description

As any independent marketer could tell you, selling at Internet auctions is no organizational cakewalk. The more auctions you list, the more you have to keep track of, and this multiplies as the size of the company in question increases.

On an AuctionWatch message board, someone asked if it was wise to put your Internet auction sales experience on a professional résumé. Of course it is. Selling at Internet auctions is going to tax your personal business sense and expose you to a plethora of valuable business experience. If you were to present your résumé to someone who's stuck dealing in Real Life and sees the Internet only as a means for entertainment, you have to word your Internet auction experience carefully.

Here's a sample:

> **Internet Sales Manager:**
> Ran small business operation through online sales medium that relied on dynamic pricing as a success incentive. Formatted virtual sales showroom and wrote ad copy to appeal to target market. Grossed $44,500.00 in first 12 months in business.

Sound contrived? Not at all. Once you get your Internet auction business underway, you'll realize that it's true.

Business Elements Involved in Online Auction Product Marketing

Initially, you'll need to pinpoint your objective for heading over to the Internet auctions. As you progress through Step 1 of your Internet Auction Strategy, you'll need to examine a few other areas of your business:

- Can your business handle the additional work involved in listing online auctions?

- What are your Internet auction business goals?

- Who will manage the Internet auction part of your product marketing?

- How do you handle your Internet auction finances?

- What are your Internet auction sales and operating expenses?

- How much will you pay for the goods you list for auction?

- What will the Internet auction sites charge you to sell at their site?

All of these are essential elements in figuring out how you're going to operate when you start listing online auctions. You'll also identify your long-term Internet auction mission, your strengths and weaknesses, and your Internet auction sales goals.

Internet Auction Product Marketing Mission Statement

Your original business plan probably included a statement of your operation's mission. You need to find that plan and have it nearby as you set up your Internet auction venture because you'll want to include this new operation in your overall business plan. When you update that business plan, you should be specific about what you intend to accomplish by marketing products at Internet auctions. You'll need a separate mission statement for your Internet auction division.

Who Writes It?

Entrepreneurs should determine, write, and make known their Internet auction mission statement. It should include the company's vision, process, and purpose for selling products at Internet auction venues.

A Mission Stated

Just like when writing your Internet auction titles and descriptions, choosing the right words is essential. Words play an important role in marketing. Here's an example of an Internet auction seller's mission statement:

> "To offer quality goods at prices buyers will pay through Internet auctions, a medium on which they are comfortable buying, in order to generate profits and/or reduce losses."

This might be a good item to print out and tape to the front of your computer monitor when you list your first few auctions.

Your Marketing Strengths and Weaknesses

While it's hard to be objective about your own business or company, you have to make an honest assessment in order to know on which capabilities you should rely, and which ones need work. You need this in order to have any success with your auctions. Here's an example of strengths and weaknesses you can identify:

Strengths include:

- Assets

- Resources

- Manpower

- Tools

- Motivation

Weaknesses include:

- Lack of assets

- Lack of knowledge, inexperience

- Too much competition

- Being afraid to change, grow, or succeed

Once you identify them, you can work on improving the weaknesses and then build your Internet auction strategy on your company's strengths.

Defining Your Internet Auction Selling Goals

Internet auctions should be one element in an overall e-business strategy. Here's an example of a three-year goal for a small to midsize business that's taking its products to Internet auctions with the goal of eventually operating that way full time:

- To earn net profits from Internet auction sales of $100,000 by the second year

- To earn 30% of those profits in the first year, and 60% the second year

- To operate exclusively on the Internet within three years

In order to achieve this type of goal, you need to rely on your Seven-Step Internet Auction Strategy during the three main phases of your growth. These phases include when you start out, while you're working toward your goals, and once you achieve them.

Can Your Business Handle the Workload?

It's not just bright lights and the roar of the crowd. There are also numerous backstage (offline) issues to consider. Managing Internet auctions takes time, dedication, and specific skills at all levels of the venture. Since most auction sites are strictly selling venues, all tasks involved in the transaction are typically between your company and the buyer. Therefore, the responsibility of listing the auction, fielding questions or comments received via e-mail, managing Internet auction stock inventory, and all of the steps involved in closing the sale is in your company's hands. You will need to either acquire these skills, or hire someone who already has them.

Your Internet Auction Manager

If you're not the one who will manage your company's auctions, then you need to select someone with a few essential qualifications:

- Experience using the Internet

- Comfort communicating via e-mail

- Good customer-service skills

- Knowledge of page design and HTML

- Ability to test and use different types of auction-management software

- Good reputation for follow-through

- Inventory management skills

If you plan to list at only one site, managing your auctions should be no problem. Many of the C2C and B2C sites have built in auction-management programs for use at their site.

Large Company Internet Auction Marketing Staff

If you're a large corporation intending to sell inventory at Internet auctions, your Internet auction manager may require a staff skilled in writing software programs to upload auctions and manage inventory. You may also need an administrator to manage your server.

Knowing Your Market

When you start selling at Internet auctions, it's imperative that you select a specific type of product to focus on, particularly something that you know very well. You'll want to start right off as a credible seller, and you have a better chance of that if your auction descriptions reflect a thorough knowledge of your goods.

If your Brick & Mortar business specializes in office supplies, select items of that genre as your test items. Within that category, select items that you know won't sell for very high prices. As a new seller, your customers will have more confidence buying low-cost items from you.

Sell One Test Item

For your first auction at a C2C or B2C site, select a low-cost item that you can list with a low minimum bid. Check closed auctions at the auction site you plan to use to see which types of items in your product line are steady sellers. Choose something that's currently selling well so you're guaranteed a winning bid; then carry out the transaction exactly as described in Chapter 7. When you complete the transaction and you're satisfied with the result, enter positive feedback for your new customer and encourage him or her to do the same for you. Once you have one positive feedback rating, list a few more of the same type of item. You can improve on your original auction description as you see fit.

Your new customers might want to order multiple items from you, or similar merchandise, and will be tempted by the opportunity to consolidate shipments and save shipping costs. We can count on regular postal rate increases, which means that the cost of shipping sometimes runs higher than the item purchased. This is one reason why you should include a link to your other auctions within your auction description. It's good incentive for your customers, who might push their bids higher in order to buy from you.

Establish a Market Reliability Record

As you slowly build a customer base, you're also building an Internet auction reputation if the site has user rating, or feedback. Most of the C2C and B2C sites show your feedback score and incremental awards (like eBay and Amazon's colored-star system). These symbols are very important to your bidders, since they attest to your reliability and record of good Internet auction practices.

Your Internet auction rating puts your business up for public inspection by a huge audience, too.

Test Market a New Product

Once you have a good feedback record—perhaps 40 or more positive marks—you can then experiment with other types of products. You may want to use eBay to test market a new product. It might be something your company patented, or products you acquired in a lucrative box-lot deal. Listing a moderate lot of them at an Internet auction site can help you determine whether the product will sell, who the market is, and what price you should charge for the product in future auction listings.

When test marketing products, be mindful of seasonal items. Only list the best of your stock when you know the market is ripe for it.

Knowing the Customers Who Buy Your Products

You won't know each of your customers personally, of course, but you will be communicating with them after your auctions close if you sell at a B2C or C2C site. The advice in this section pertains to your prospective customers, who are also your target market. Depending on what you sell, your target customers may be a large group, or a relatively small group. Either way, you'll want to know certain things about them.

Who Are Your Customers?

If you list items at a B2C or C2C Internet auction site, you'll deal one-on-one in e-mail with each winning bidder. Having participated in over 600 online auction transactions as of this writing, I don't always know the demographics of those I buy from and sell to. Occasionally the e-mail correspondence becomes informal and friendly and I get to know the person whom I'm dealing with a little better, but that doesn't happen often. I usually don't know that much about my customers because I rarely have a reason to ask.

Selling through online auctions would be the perfect opportunity to survey your customers. Folks may be reluctant to offer too much personal information, but if you're clear about why you're asking, they may at least tell you their age and general interests. You can guess their gender by their names, and you'll have a good idea what region they're from by their shipping address. This is one entry for your Customer Satisfaction Worksheet. When the transaction is closed, send your customers a short survey including these non-intrusive questions:

- How old are you?

- Did you purchase this item for yourself, or as a gift?

- Are you satisfied with the product?

Tell them why you're asking, and let them know that while their participation is appreciated, they're under no obligation to answer. This might ease any pressure or suspicion. Invite them to add any comments they wish to include. Let them vent. Whatever they send you is valuable information in getting to know the customers who are buying your products. You'll want to tailor your auction to appeal to that market if you list the product again.

Is the Customer in Control Now?

As you target customers, you're building a customer base to generate repeat business. The rise in popularity of online business brings with it a shift in power from vendors of goods and services to the customers who buy them. If you know that your customers will occasionally be the "boss" of the transaction and you willfully secede the authority (without jeopardy to your business, of course), you'll build a base of loyal customers. Sellers who figure this out quickly will be the first to gain from the advantage. As long as the venture results in profits for you, it's a smart move to let the customer feel that he or she is in control.

Retaining Your Customers

While most Internet auction feedback ratings only increment for comments entered by unique users, to only target unique users would be foolish. The most successful Internet auction users rely on repeat customers, or "regulars." How you conduct your business will determine if you keep your customers or lose them. Chapter 9 covers all you need to know to build good customer relations as you list items online.

There's an important lesson here for anyone interested in doing business on the Internet. Successful Internet auction selling is not about routine transactions and form letters. It's about the one-on-one communication you have with your customers. You can use online auction tools and bulk auction loaders to sell your items, but when the online part of the auction ends, you have to communicate with your customers one by one, in e-mail. Building good relationships with your customers will keep your online business afloat.

Your Selling Style

Internet auction selling requires charisma and style. My first impression of parrothead88, an eBay shooting-star seller I interviewed, was that his telephone voice sounded as friendly as his auction descriptions read. I asked him how it is that he always sounds so friendly.

"I love the people," John Hannon answered, "and I love what I do." It shows. His selling style has been the cornerstone of his success. John's been able to close all of his Brick & Mortar stores and makes a comfortable living selling his products exclusively at online auctions. He accepts returns on damaged goods and reimburses the customer for the return shipping charge. He answers all of his e-mail personally, and remembers names. His products are always exactly as he describes them in his auction descriptions.

Anticipate Changes from Growth

Businesses that enter the online market often find themselves pleasantly surprised as their business increases in unprecedented and unanticipated ways. If you make the best of this growth opportunity, you're bound to profit from it. As your business grows, you need to project this to your customers. Let them know that you're there, you've made it, and you're a seller who will deliver the goods for the best price.

Consumer Concerns

When we discussed the ideal Internet auction customer, there were several issues mentioned that represent valid customer concerns. According to the Federal Trade Commission, Internet auction fraud has become a significant problem. Most consumer complaints center on sellers who:

- Don't deliver the advertised goods

- Deliver something far less valuable than they advertised

- Don't deliver in a timely way

- Fail to disclose all the relevant information about the product or terms of the sale

Customers will be concerned that any of these problems might come up. You can instill confidence in them with a clearly written auction description, easy to understand terms and conditions, and pleasant e-mail communication. Reassure your customers that you are a fair and honest seller, while being clear about your expectations of the buyer.

Your Auction's Presentation

Nobody knows right off the bat whether an idea will sell or not. One thing's for certain, though—how you present your product or idea will make a huge difference. With Internet auctions, you have one place in which to present your perfected sales pitch, and that's in the auction listing itself. The better you get at presenting items, the more money you'll make. That's why this book devotes so much space to creating great auction descriptions that will sell products.

In Chapter 6, you'll read more about writing auction descriptions that attract bids and instill confidence in your bidders.

How's Your Sales Charisma?

Are you an upstanding sales associate, or would you make a killing on the snake oil market? You won't be dealing face to face with your customers, but your business ethics will reflect in how well you handle your Internet auction transactions. You'll also reveal them within the context of your auction description. Always keep in mind that how you write is how you represent yourself. You'll need to appeal to your target market while establishing an aura of credibility. The following sections demonstrate how you can accomplish that.

Honesty and Integrity

Don't promise your customers things that you know your product or business can't deliver. If you know that your claim is far-fetched, there's a good chance that your customers will know it too. The basic intelligence that got the person on the Internet and registered with an auction site is reason enough to target smart people with your ads. In other words, cut back on the hooey.

Here are a few examples of believable product claims from seasoned Internet auction sellers:

> **Example:**
> We guarantee our flowerpots to be 100% terra cotta and free of defects. Since we value your repeat business, we will replace any defective items.

> **Example:**
> Our fine scented candles are hand-poured into Austrian crystal decanters and have slow-burning, centered wicks. They will ship to you securely packaged.

> **Example:**
> These are brand new Motorola clip-on organizers for StarTAC phones, still in their original packaging and have all of the standard features. They're covered under the original manufacturer's guarantee and by our 3-day inspection policy.

All three of these present the important aspects of the product in a straightforward manner with no phony gushing. The guarantees mentioned are an important confidence-building part of your auction description, and you'll read more about writing them in Chapter 6.

Product Knowledge

You must know the details of what you're selling so that you can answer questions correctly and thoroughly. Don't list an item unless you can be a knowledgeable sales representative for it. Be sure this knowledge reflects in your auction ad. You may receive questions from potential bidders, and you want to have answers handy in order to give them enough time to bid before the auction closes.

Know Where You Can Operate

Deciding where you want to compete requires some knowledge of where you *can* compete. Choosing the right site is imperative to success in the Internet auction industry. Both Chapter 4 and Appendix A list Internet auction sites and their specialties. Know which ones have the biggest concentration of your target market as registered users by the amount of bids placed on certain types of items.

General C2C or B2C Sites
Test the market at a mega-site like eBay, where your customers are everybody and anybody. eBay offers specialty sites where you can list qualifying items. You can start out by listing your products in one of those areas, or launch a standard listing to the general eBay population. If you're a first-time Internet auction seller, I strongly advise you to list your test auctions at any one of the three mega-sites instead of listing at a B2B site right away. You can explore those when you have some Internet auction selling experience.

Specialized Sites
If you know that your target market will be looking for your automobile deodorizer products at an Internet auction site that specializes in automotive products, you'll eventually want to list them there once you've conducted your test auctions. You'll need to research the auction sites in advance to make the best choice.

Credibility Through Specialization
Just like some Internet auction sites specialize in buying and selling items in a particular niche, you should strive to be something of a specialist in the products you're marketing. You don't need to be the person who engineered and developed the product, but you should know some specific information about it so you can answer questions, such as

- How it works

- What colors it comes in

- How long it lasts

- What features it has

- Who makes it

- Is there a warranty?

You get the idea. If you're a product specialist as well as a marketer, you're likely to have an edge on your competition. This will also help you build trust and confidence with your customers.

Common E-Business Product Marketing Mistakes

Internet auctions have clearly shaped options for both small and large businesses. Small businesses can liquidate stock on auction sites where consumers or other small businesses shop. Large businesses that already have an established Web presence can start their own online auction sites, like J. C. Penney's *(auctions.jcpenney.com)*, or list items at a site where businesses sell to other businesses.

When you market products at the Internet auction sites, at least as an option or alternative to your Brick & Mortar business, you stand to profit from it. Those who play by the old rules may fall behind and devalue their business, or even obliterate it. Let's examine some of the most common e-business mistakes.

Hasty, Costly Decisions

Which auction sites will you use, and how many different ones? Which online payment services will you sign up with? What types of products will you list, and how many of each? Here are a few common pitfalls to avoid when making these decisions:

- Setting your price too high in an attempt to make a fast profit

- Listing at an auction site that's not appropriate for your products

- Not making your auctions appealing

- Using a poor quality photo, or neglecting to include photos at all

- Not knowing enough about the product you're selling

- Forgetting to proofread your auction titles and descriptions

- Using the wrong photo or product description

All of these can cost you bids and money, and all of them are avoidable if you take the necessary time to plan your auctions. When asked to offer advice to a business that plans to market products through Internet auctions for the first time, Patrick Byrne, CEO of the hugely successful Overstock.com says, "Don't get too greedy. Price your items competitively and start small."

Not Mentioning Your Business Web Site in Your Auctions

Your business Web site is the most powerful tool that you have for e-commerce marketing, of course. You want links to your site to appear in as many places as possible. You have your site URL on your business cards, your product brochures, your shopping bags, in your Yellow Pages ad, and anywhere else you can sneak it. Add your auction descriptions to that list, and always include a link to your business Web site when you create them (if the auction site allows it). You'll also include a link to your auctions from your business Web site. This way you can advertise your two main Internet selling venues in tandem. You'll read a lot more about other ways of promoting your auctions in Chapter 7, when you plan Step 5 of your Internet auction strategy.

Neglecting Customer Service

If you sell on the Web, you'll do business with people you'll never meet in person. This lack of personal contact often means impersonal and unsatisfactory customer service. If you don't think you'll ever sell to the same customer twice, perhaps you can get by this way. But if you'd like to enjoy repeat business from steady customers who can generate referrals, become an expert at delivering quality Internet auction customer service. It doesn't start when the auction closes. You'll also deal with customers, or potential customers, while your auction is live.

- Answer all product queries from potential bidders honestly and accurately. Don't consider any question too insignificant to answer.

- Send your end of auction notices promptly, and include all of the necessary information that you'll read about in Chapter 9.

- Let your customers know when you've received their payment, and when you've shipped their merchandise.

- Answer e-mail promptly.

- Always leave feedback for your customers after a successful transaction if the auction site you're using has that feature.

Do you want to be a successful Internet auction seller? Treat your customers with the same respect you use when you interact with them in person or on the telephone. Be nice.

Failing to Prepare for Success

Businesses are enjoying great success and huge profits at the online auctions. It's an e-business that grew at a phenomenal rate and will continue to grow. With your inevitable success, you run the risk of falling behind if you neglect to do some advance planning. Consider how you'll handle certain situations that may bring you more business than you're used to:

- **Auction site promotions:** If the site you're using launches a huge promotional campaign for new members, or offers a system of bonus points for users who meet certain buying criteria, you may end up with twice as many successfully closed auctions as you anticipated. Stay apprised of any plans the auction site has to bring more bidders to your auctions, and be sure that you have adequate resources to handle the additional business.

- **Instant demand:** You have several Dutch auctions listed for an item that suddenly becomes a hot seller because of a media or news event. Be sure that you can satisfy an influx of buyers with the same level of customer service that your regular customers expect from you.

- **Seasonal commerce:** Plan for the additional business around holiday seasons or during special media events.

Even if you didn't intend to make Internet auctions a permanent part of your business plan, you need to consider this possibility: you stand to be very successful at it. Map out in advance how you'll increase your staff to handle the additional business so you don't miss a profitable opportunity.

Outdated Products and Auction Description Content

If your stock is way out of date, decide whether selling it would degrade the image you want for your business. For what you do sell, be sure your ad copy doesn't allude to passé news. For example, the Florida votes were recounted and we know who won the 2000 Election, so don't use "as subtle as a dimpled chad" to describe your product features. Update your auction ad text periodically. Outdated content gives the impression that your products are stale and the seller isn't really paying attention. This can put consumers off. Be sure that you refresh your auction description content at least once for every six auction runs.

Computer Reluctance

Early on, certain businesses resisted the idea that the Internet would "catch on" and be used for commercial purposes. Don't let technology scare you off, and don't give in to the notion that "the Internet has passed you by" because you didn't join the cause right away. You can jump in any time and quickly gain the expertise you need to be successful.

Technological Inundation

Don't be seduced by the fancy technological operations you see other businesses muck their Web pages with. You risk overdoing your auctions if you overload them with techno-dazzle. Internet auction success is not about using the best or most powerful technology. Instead, research and select the online resources you need to start building an impressive and professional Internet auction presence.

Paradigms

Throw out blueprints, organization charts, and five-year plans. Internet auction selling requires a new mindset and a fresh management approach.

Successful product marketing with Internet auctions may require a conscious effort to discard "pre-Internet" attitudes that could only hamper your chance for success. The chart below offers some attitude adjustments when planning your Internet Auction Strategy.

Paradigm	Attitude for Internet Auction Success
We've always relied on our Brick & Mortar business and it's never failed us.	Internet auctions can supplement our business and increase our customer base.
We may not be able to reach our market on the Internet.	Our customers shop on the Internet.
What if we try this, and fail?	We stand to succeed in this popular new market.
What if this Internet thing doesn't catch on?	E-commerce is projected to reach $8 trillion by 2004.

Total Reliance on the Internet

This is not a standalone business opportunity that someone can take or leave as they wish. Internet auction selling has irrevocably altered the way you can market and sell to customers, perhaps with your existing Brick & Mortar store as your core business—at least initially. This change demands a new way of thinking about your approach and marketing.

4

Selecting the Right Auction Site and Type of Auctions for Your Business

This chapter will help you carry out Step 2 of your Seven-Step Internet Auction Strategy, which is to select an Internet auction site and type of auction for your business. In order to select the right type of auction site, you need to be familiar with what's up for grabs in the Internet auction arena.

This is an important chapter to review once you have Internet access and you're comfortable navigating through Web sites. It will help if you have your computer on and connected to the Internet so that you can call up each auction site in your browser. This will be helpful for a few reasons:

- You can compare the site's pages to those shown here. Since the Internet is always changing, the site may look different on the day you access it. It may also refer you to another URL with **client pull**, which is an automatic redirection to another Web address. Unfortunately, the site also may not be active anymore either. If that happens read the text anyway. You may encounter another site that operates similarly.

- Since I can't demonstrate hyperlinks on this static hard copy, you can click on the site's navigation links to see where they take you.

- It would take an enormous volume to include every page of every site, so I included a sampling of the essential site pages. Since the number of Web pages you can visit online is only limited by the speed of your ISP, you can take a complete tour of the site while you're online.

- The sites are much more appealing in living color.

Selecting an Auction Site

The eBay site started out as primarily consumer-to-consumer (C2C), soon went to business-to-consumer (B2C), and now has eBay Business, Office, and Industrial, which is a dedicated area of its site for business-to-business (B2B) auctions. Since there's more revenue in top-dollar sales, most of the C2C sites also offer B2B auctions. Businesses now have the advantage of being able to sell at any site they choose. Sun Microsystems is selling at a B2B site called DoveBid, and they have listings on eBay. Here's a quote from Sun's AboutMe site at eBay:

> With online auctions rapidly emerging as an important venue in the Internet economy, these online B2B exchanges are revolutionizing many large companies and Sun is a leader in this space offering a new way to purchase a variety of Sun Solutions through auctions.
>
> From http://members.ebay.com/aboutme/auctions.sun.com

Selling at an auction giant like eBay will usually turn reasonable profits for you as long as you have a marketable product and your potential customers know about your auctions. An auction giant like eBay, with its twenty or so million users, will return at least your starting bid with the possibility of premiums. The premiums, in this case, are any bids over your starting bid.

Each type of auction site offers certain advantages, which allows you to select one based on your business goals.

Big Site vs. Small Site—Advantages

Big sites have many users. Millions of them. You can get bids from users who run across your listings by accident. If you list pigtail holders, for instance, your auction will come up in searches run by pig enthusiasts. If you sell at an auction site that only lets you list hair accessories, your audience is much smaller. While it's great if your listings attract many viewers, you don't need millions of people to see your item. All it takes is two enthusiastic bidders to raise the price and earn profits for you. Three bidders are better, and so on, and so on.

One disadvantage of a big site is that users have so many auctions to choose from that yours might slip away unnoticed, especially if you're not actively promoting your listings. There are several online auction sites giving eBay a run for its money, but that isn't a bad reflection on eBay. It just means they have competition.

As you determine the best site for your business needs, decide if you want to use a major site with guaranteed high traffic or a smaller, more specialized site that may target your audience for a direct hit.

Web Site Traffic

In Web language, **traffic** is the volume of visitors to a particular page. Not how many unique people access the page, but how often anyone visits the page. Each time the Web page loads in someone's browser, it's a **hit**. If the site has a page counter, it will usually increment by one with each hit. A high-traffic site is one with tens of thousands of daily page hits.

The Mega-Sites

Amazon Auctions, Yahoo! Auctions, and eBay each claim to have millions of users. They probably have the best results for users, but it's hard to compare the bottom-line figures. eBay claims a 50% sales turnover, which is great, but other sites don't have the figures listed so it's hard to determine a success ratio among users.

Note: **Sales turnover** means the percentage of listed items that actually sell.

Choosing your best auction site will be a combination of personal preference and knowing how well auctions that you list on a particular site will reach your market in order to help you attain your sales goals. When you study the major Internet auction sites, you'll notice that they offer certain advantages over smaller sites.

Plenty of Servers

A Web server is a high-powered computer that holds the data for a Web site. To keep up with the high amount of selling and bidding activity, high-traffic online auction sites always use more than one server. The search engine for the site might be on one server, and auctions in popular categories might be on another. As you browse from one part of the site to another, and through the various categories, your session moves from one server to another.

This enables the site to handle the traffic, and it's transparent to the user. So, why is a site with multiple servers advantageous? Because if one server has problems, your session can be rerouted through another server, similar to the way telephone calls are redirected when lines go down in a storm. And if you can access the site, so can your important customers.

Many More Category Choices

Jeans. Not just jeans, but blue jeans. Not just blue jeans, but Levi's blue jeans. And not just Levi's blue jeans, but Levi's blue jeans in zipper or button fly.

On a major auction site, these category trees can be endless and the big Internet auction sites keep adding more of them. A high-traffic auction site like eBay has thousands of item categories, and you can test list items in as many as you wish.

Lesser-known sites have certain advantages too.

Smaller Internet Auction Sites

Most of what I call "smaller" auction sites are either newly started online auction sites, or those associated with a particular business or commodity. Comparatively light traffic and having fewer registered users classifies them as "small."

The Internet is still, by some standards, a very young medium. It changes constantly. What's obscure today makes headlines tomorrow. Definitely don't rule out the smaller sites. After all, eBay was once a small site. You never know what option an up-and-coming Internet auction site has that's perfect for how you want to operate.

Most of the smaller Internet auction sites I reviewed offer the same features and options that the main sites do, just to a more selective audience. Some have unique features.

Auctions Not Lost in Oblivion

If you're listing something very common, like electronic game systems or the latest holiday rage, your auctions might get lost in a sea of other listings for the same items at a high-traffic site. You have a much better chance of selling your goods for a higher price at a site that's not riddled with competition, as long as the site has users that will bid on your auctions. That you'll find out through your test auctions.

Fewer Categories—Shorter Searches

If your customers don't have that many categories to choose from, it won't take very long to find items to bid on. Some of the smaller sites don't even have sub-categories because they're not necessary. If the site is just for furniture, the main categories are specialized enough.

Auction Interactive 2000 *(www.auction2000.net)* demonstrates this type of listing. When you access the main page and click on "Auctions," you'll see five categories:

- Antiques

- Brittales

- Collectibles

- Jewelry/Gems

- Glassware

Click on any category for a complete table of active listings. Your customers will travel a much shorter route to your auctions once they access the site.

FairMarket Auction Network

Listing items at "smaller" auction sites doesn't necessarily mean your item will only draw the attention of the registered users at that particular site. The FairMarket Auction Network is a consortium of approximately 100 Internet auction sites that share auction listings. Based in Woburn, Massachusetts, the network hosts a database containing listings from nearly 100 participating network sites. If you list an item at an Internet auction site within the FairMarket Auction Network, it would also be listed throughout the entire network of auction sites.

This large and centralized auction network has a potential audience of close to 50 million users, if not more. In addition to the auction network, FairMarket also develops and delivers e-business selling and marketing solutions for retailers, distributors, and manufacturers. At least one major corporation selected the FairMarket Auction (see Figure 4.1) as part of its "click and mortar" e-commerce strategy, using the auction site as a market-making tool while selling excess and discontinued inventory.

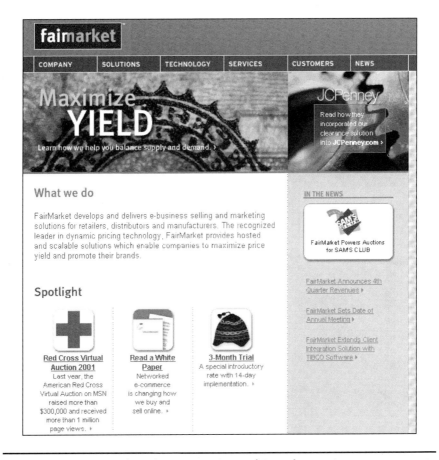

Figure 4.1. FairMarket's home page (*www.fairmarket.com*).

FairMarket provides powerful B2B online selling tools to help manufacturers and distributors earn more money selling surplus products than they would through traditional channels.

Top 100 Auction Sites

This independently run site is part of the Top 100 Network, part of which is shown in Figure 4.2. The Auction Site page lists Internet auction venues in order of popularity, according to how they rated in private user polls.

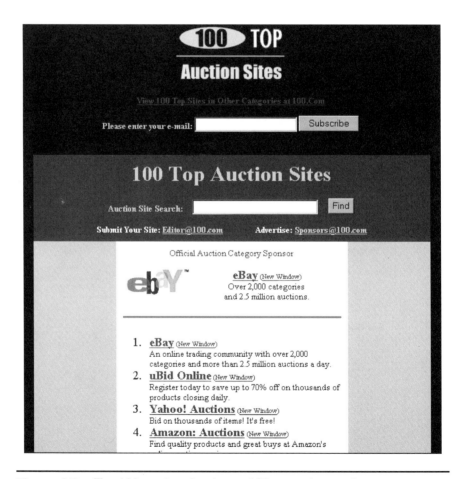

Figure 4.2. Top 100 auction sites (*www.100topauction.com*).

According to Michelle Weiss, an editor at the Top 100 Network, "We determine the top sites based on their overall content and appearance. The site should be operational and provide useful information and/or services to those who use the list. In addition, the site should not have any material that could be considered offensive."

Web Portal Auction Sites

Some folks enter the Web via a Web portal like Lycos or Yahoo. Both of these Web portals host online auctions. The auction-listing fees are similar to the most popular C2C sites, and they have a respectable amount of traffic. Things always change in the OAI, but as long as people sell and bid at Internet auctions, hosting an Internet auction venue will remain a good moneymaker for the portals.

Consumer-to-Consumer

Consumer-to-consumer, or C2C, Internet auction sites are those at which consumers, who represent themselves rather than an established business, sell items through Internet auctions to other consumers. They are also very aptly called person-to-person (P2P) auction sites. A seller who wishes to list items registers at the site, prepares auction listings, and launches them. A potential buyer places a bid, and may eventually be outbid by another user. By the time the auction closes, there might be one bid or 45 bids on the item. Then the transaction moves off the auction site and takes place in e-mail, via an on-screen messaging system, or on the telephone. The seller then contacts the high bidder by sending an end of auction e-mail, and the transaction completes according to the terms of sale specified by the seller. This methodology takes place at a consumer Internet auction site.

eBay

As you read about in Chapter 1, eBay, Inc. *(www.ebay.com)* was launched in September 1995. The eBay auction site was originally committed to helping individual buyers and sellers—not large companies—sell items to one another over the Internet. However, almost every type of individual or business seller now lists products for auction on eBay.

eBay leads the online auction business, with millions of registered users and close to a billion completed auctions. In the time it took you to read this paragraph, over one hundred new auctions started on eBay—it's *that* popular. The eBay Internet auction site receives more than 300 million hits each month. eBay users conduct over ten million searches each *day*. It's fair to say there's a tremendous amount of traffic on eBay. In addition to the U.S.-based eBay, there are several eBay Global Sites:

- eBay Australia

- eBay Austria

- eBay Canada

- eBay France

- eBay Germany

- eBay Italy

- eBay Japan

- eBay United Kingdom

You'll also find certain areas of eBay called "Specialty Sites" so sellers can list items that won't be obscured in the sea of eBay's regular listings. These special areas of eBay include dedicated places to list cars, fine art, and books. This helps target buyers specifically interested in shopping for these types of items:

- **eBay Motors**—Dealers and automobile enthusiasts can list auctions for automobiles, motorcycles, classic and antique vehicles, and motor vehicle-related products.

- **eBay Premier**—At this site, sellers can list auctions for fine art, high-end jewelry, prized manuscripts, and decorative arts.

- **Service for Business**—Service providers can bid on your projects through an eBay service called eLance, which is an Internet market for freelance business.

- Half.com—Booksellers can list fixed-price auctions for used books, music, movies, and video games at substantial discounts.

Sales at eBay are in U.S. dollars ($), or the currency specified by the Global Site. Also, some sellers may specify that payments should be in a specific currency. All eBay fees are in U.S. dollars.

eBay pioneered many of the features that have become the OAI standard at other online auction sites. eBay has also adapted some features that other sites offered first. The site adds more features every few months. When they do, you'll see announcements about them all over the site.

Edit Your Auctions

Once your auction is running, you can't go back and correct a mistake with your browser's "back" button. However, typos are embarrassing and can affect your credibility as a seller. To help you out, eBay allows you to revise your item title, description, image URL, payment options, or shipping terms before anyone bids on your auction. On the auction-listing page, you'll see this:

> **Seller:** *If this item has received no bids, you may <u>revise</u> it.*

Clicking on the word "revise" will take you to the Update User Information screen, where you can correct the information after entering your user ID and password. Once you revise your item, this line of text appears on the auction page:

> <u>*Seller revised*</u> *this item before the first bid.*

The "seller revised" hyperlink takes you to the Explanation of Seller Revisions page.

Buy It Now

eBay also offers fixed-price listings in the form of Buy It Now, or BIN. The listings run as normal auction listings do—the seller sets a minimum price and determines how long the auction will run. With a BIN auction, the seller also sets a price that a bidder can agree to pay to buy the item before the auction ends. Once someone bids the BIN price, the auction ends and the BIN bidder buys the item at that price. If the first bidder places a bid either at or above the starting bid but below the BIN price, the BIN feature is disabled and bidding progresses as it normally would.

Yahoo! Auctions

Yahoo! Auctions *(auctions.yahoo.com)* launched in September 1998. This popular Internet auction site—for both buyers and sellers—features 2,000 listing categories. They include arts and entertainment, toys, games, antiques, home and garden items, cameras, computers, and electronics.

This very successful Internet auction site is part of the very powerful Yahoo.com search engine and Web portal. The Santa Clara, California-based Yahoo! Web portal boasts more than 60 million worldwide users, has 18 worldwide portal sites, and offices in the United States, Europe, the Asia Pacific, and South America. Figure 4.3 shows the Yahoo! Auctions' home page.

Until January 2001, Yahoo! Auctions were free. Then they began charging listing fees. The fees range from $0.20 for items with starting

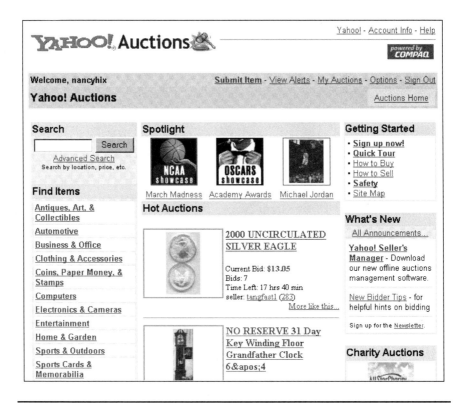

Figure 4.3. Yahoo! Auctions' home page *(auctions.yahoo.com)*.

prices under $10, to $1.50 for auctions beginning at $50 or more. You'll also pay fees for a few other auction features.

Image Hosting for Sellers

While most of the major sites offer image hosting now, Yahoo! Auctions was one of the first to allow sellers the option of hosting their auction images right on at the Yahoo! site. Sellers can upload as many as three images per auction. With image hosting sites now charging fees and occasionally experiencing site outages, this is a definite plus for sellers.

Auctions Booth

To give your auctions a personal touch, you can customize the page layout for your Auctions Booth and item pages by using the Yahoo! PageBuilder. Figure 4.4 shows a sample Yahoo! Auctions Booth.

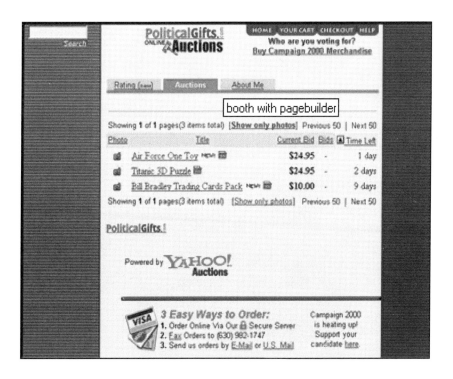

Figure 4.4. Sample Yahoo! Auctions Booth (*auctions.yahoo.com/phtml/auc/ us/promo/booth2.html*).

Your Auctions Booth helps you spotlight your listings. Using PageBuilder, you can customize your page layouts, insert images, change your background, and add text. You can add a list of your active auctions, and a link to your user feedback. The idea is to give you more control of how your auctions look.

Amazon Auctions

Amazon Auctions *(auctions.amazon.com)* launched its auction division in March 1999. All ten million existing users of the book-selling branch of Amazon became automatic registered users of Amazon Auctions, giving the site a ready-made crowd of regulars. Since high traffic helps sell items, it was a hit from the start. Amazon Auctions is an easy Internet auction site to navigate, making it a great site for a first-time seller. You can get anywhere on the site right from the main page, and you can get back to the main page from anywhere on the site. Figure 4.5 shows an example of what appears when you call up the home page.

Figure 4.5.   The Amazon Auctions' home page *(auctions.amazon.com)*.

Sellers will see a comprehensive Seller's Guide that will walk you through listing auctions. There's a list of Top Questions and links to the answers. Figure 4.6 shows how easy it is for Amazon Auction sellers to learn how to list auctions.

Open-Ended Bidding
All Amazon.com auctions run with open-ended bidding. This dynamic auction-ending feature ensures that an auction can't close until ten minutes pass without a new bid. Amazon.com calls it "Going, Going, Gone." Sellers get the most advantage out of dynamic-end auctions, but they're not popular with bidders.

Take-It Price
You may elect to set a Take-It Price, which makes your listing a fixed-price auction. The Take-It Price is the amount at which you're willing to end the auction and finish the transaction off line. If you offer a Take-It Price, you'll need to be available to get in touch with the winning bidder

Figure 4.6. Amazon Auctions Seller's Guide (*http://s1.amazon.com/exec/ varzea/ts/help/list-an-item/107-5543698-8604503*).

at any time. He or she may "Take-It" any time after the first minute of the auction.

You can alter the Take-It Price before anyone enters a bid. Once a bid is in place, the Take-It Price locks in.

Business-to-Consumer

A business-to-consumer, or B2C, site is one at which businesses list items and consumers bid on them. At some B2C venues, the site's involvement ends when the auction closes, and the seller ships the merchandise to the buyer. At some of the others, though, the site has physical control of the merchandise being offered and accepts payment for the goods. The merchandise, usually on consignment from the business, ships right to the buyer. The site handles the transaction from start to finish. The B2C Internet auction sites discussed in this section encourage business owners or operators to list their own auctions.

SmoothSale

Are you up to making live deals online with your customers? Several Internet veterans formed the B2C Internet auction site called SmoothSale in January 2000. Based in San Francisco, SmoothSale, Inc. *(www.smoothsale.com)*, is a privately held e-commerce software company that provides retailers, auctions, and B2B enterprises with tools to sell products at online auctions (see Figure 4.7). Their objective is to reduce what they call abandoned shopping carts, or uncompleted sales, with software that puts sellers in real-time touch with their customers.

According to Josh Piestrup, Director of Merchant Development at SmoothSale, "SmoothSale is focused primarily on enabling sellers to conduct business directly with consumers. The whole idea is for the seller and buyer to be online at the same time."

SmoothSale uses a combination of instant messaging and traditional e-commerce techniques to put sellers in touch with their customers. You can post items with a fixed price and then keep regular online hours in order to be available to answer shoppers' questions. This allows you to sell and offer special deals in a real-time shopping environment.

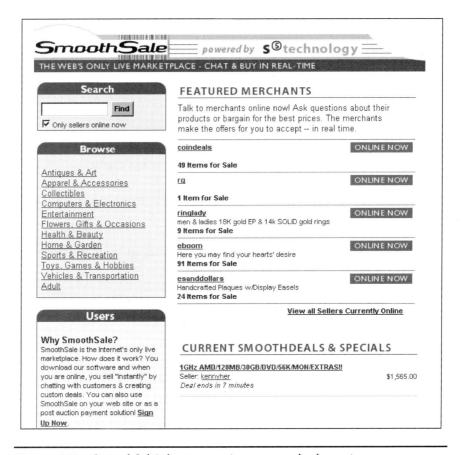

Figure 4.7. SmoothSale's home page (*www.smoothsale.com*).

After you download their software, you can "instantly" sell when you're online by chatting with customers and customizing deals.

Instant Selling

SmoothSale has more than 500 active merchants. With some unique features, they enable businesses of any size to communicate with customers and close sales online—not just through e-mail. SmoothSale offers its own Instant Selling software platform for retail auctions and for its other e-commerce offerings. The software includes an "online/offline" button that appears wherever you want to transact business. This is called the SellerOnline button.

Figure 4.8 shows an auction listing at SmoothSale with the SellerOnline button visible. This button invokes a live chat window in which the buyer can contact the seller in order to ask questions.

There are four steps involved with the SellerOnline registration process:

- Telling your customers who you are

- Downloading the SmoothDealer (the IM client)

- Uploading your product information for your auction titles and descriptions

- Placing the button on your Web site, in your auctions, and including it in your e-mail

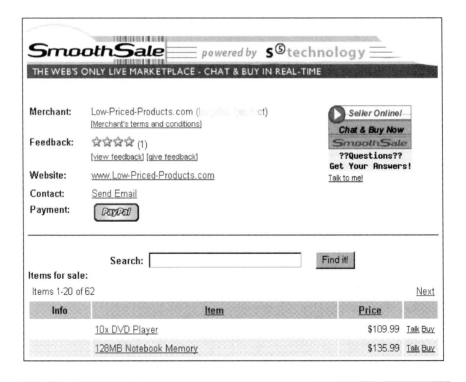

Figure 4.8. Auction listing at SmoothSale showing SellerOnline button.

The last step provides you with the HTML code that you can copy and include in your Web pages. The code creates the SellerOnline button, which lets your customers know when you're available.

SellerOnline Linked from Other Sites

Sellers can insert this button at other Web sites as a hyperlink, so customers can contact them and talk in real-time about the products. "I love using the SellerOnline button," says Jen Hassler of the Online Auction Users Association. "My customers seem to be more confident buying things from me once we've had the chance to chat online about the items I have listed for auction. I know it's increased my sales." The SellerOnline button can also be used at eBay auctions.

Note: If the SellerOnline button is used at eBay auctions, the seller must adhere to the eBay terms and conditions and may not use the SellerOnline feature to finalize deals until the eBay auction closes. In other words, you can't use "the button" to avoid paying eBay fees.

Egghead

You can't talk about B2C auction sites without mentioning Egghead, *(www.egghead.com)*, the leading B2C Internet auction site for computers and electronics (see Figure 4.9). Many heartbroken "computer geeks" watched with horror as the Egghead Brick & Mortar retail shops closed for business, but they were quickly appeased when the Egghead e-commerce site went into operation. Egghead now sells its products exclusively at its B2C Web site. You'll also find listings for typical Internet auction fare:

- Computers

- Cruises

- Electronics

- Golf items

- Jewelry and watches

- Sports and fitness items

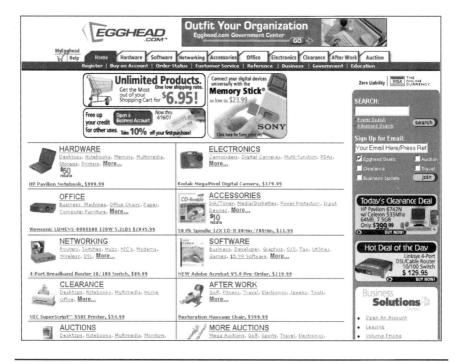

Figure 4.9. Egghead's home page (*www.egghead.com*).

- Tools and home items

- Travel packages

As a small or midsize business, you probably won't be selling at an Internet auction site like Egghead. However, it's a great site to study and peruse if you're thinking of online auctioning of similar products. Egghead does an excellent job with its B2C auctions and its site is very popular with consumers.

Egghead Auctions (Figure 4.10) has over 2,000 auctions opening daily in 24-hour, Express Auction, Free Freight Auction, and Mega Auction formats. Following is an explanation of each type of Egghead.com auction listing:

- **24-Hour Auctions**—As their name implies, these auctions run for 24 hours.

- **Express Auctions**—These listings run for 60 minutes and open at $1. They run nonstop from 5:00 A.M.–10:00 P.M. PDT every day, including weekends.

- **Free-Freight Auctions**—These auctions include free ground shipping via UPS to locations in the U.S.

- **Mega Auctions**—Look here for large quantities of items with competitive pricing.

From the Egghead home page, click on the Auctions tab and you'll see their active listings with the high bid prices.

Clearance and After Work Auctions

Their Clearance and After Work products supplement Egghead's auction format as its version of a fixed-price auction. Customers don't bid on

Figure 4.10. The Egghead.com auctions page (*www.egghead.com/aa/auctions.htm*).

these listings—they simply opt to purchase the products at the listed price. Clearance and After Work products are offered in limited quantities available up until the posted sale-closing time, or as long as supplies last.

Yankee Auctions

Most of the auctions at Egghead are what they call Yankee auctions, which is a modified type of Dutch auction that you'll read about later in this chapter. Egghead's Yankee auctions offer a large quantity of items and run for one or two days. The bidders offering the highest bids buy the item when the auction closes.

Reverse Auctions—eWanted

The idea to put customers in control of transactions led to the development of reverse auctions, in which buyers post requests for the items and the price they want to pay, and sellers attempt to bid the price down. Many large corporations use reverse auctions in their B2B transactions. Some of the B2C sites incorporate reverse auctions, and other business auction sites exclusively feature reverse auctions.

eWanted *(www.ewanted.com)* is an open marketplace, where anyone can post what they're looking for, and anyone can make an offer to sell it (see Figure 4.11). All requests on the eWanted site are for things that people want to buy. Sellers can browse through the listings and see if anyone is looking for their particular merchandise. Buyers on eWanted are not necessarily looking for the lowest price, but for specific or hard-to-find items. It's a lot like having customers lined up at your shop, holding signs up that tell you exactly what they want to buy.

How It Works

The process is very straightforward:

- Buyers request what they're looking for.

- Sellers browse these requests and make offers based on what buyers want. When making an offer, the seller can choose to extend the offer to other buyers in case the original requester doesn't accept. Or, if the seller has multiple quantities of this same item, he or she can include the extra quantity in the offer.

Figure 4.11. eWanted's home page (*www.ewanted.com*).

- The buyer only buys the desired quantity, or doesn't make a purchase at all if the offer does not meet his or her expectations.

- The sellers can then offer any items that are left for sale to the rest of the eWanted community.

- Anyone who wants the merchandise can click on the Buy Now button and purchase it immediately.

- Items sell on a first-come, first-served basis until they're all sold out.

- Buyers get what they want and sellers find customers ready to buy.

There are no fees for sellers until they sell something.

Advantage for Sellers

Sellers can browse buyer requests by category or enter a text search and see a list of all items that buyers want. (See Figure 4.12.) Here's the field where sellers look for buyers:

In the text entry area, I typed the word chair. When I clicked on the "Search" button, the screen in Figure 4.13 appeared, showing a list of buyers interested in purchasing chairs.

I am now able to contact buyers looking for the particular type of chair I'm offering to make a sale. If you don't find a current buyer request matching what you have, you can post your item for sale.

"People can put up general requests, like anything related to Marilyn Monroe, or they can put up a specific request for a Palm V," said Steven Nerayoff, Vice President of Business Development for eWanted. "We feel the site appeals to sellers because buyers do less browsing and more buying."

Business-to-Business

Business-to-business Internet commerce is the sale of goods and services for which the order-taking process completes via the Internet. Business-to-business, or B2B, Internet auction sites are selling platforms where one business sells to another business. Either the business itself owns

Seller overview:

- Browse buyer requests for FREE
- Find ready buyers for your items
- Save time and money
- You pay no transaction fees unless you sell something
- Free Buyer Leads service alerts you when someone posts a request that matches what you sell

Start selling now! What do you have to sell? [chair] [Search]

Figure 4.12. Seller search box at eWanted (*ewanted.com/introduction.cfm*).

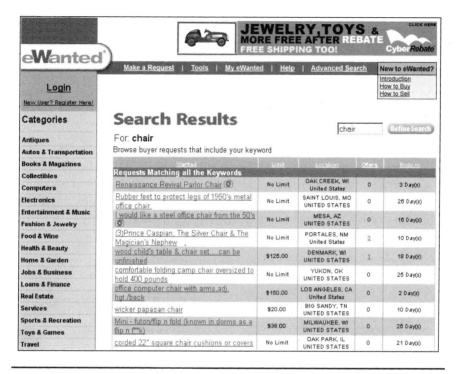

Figure 4.13. Search results at eWanted (*ewanted.com/search/searchLot.jsp*).

and operates the B2B site, or they've collaborated with another business to list their products there.

CommerceOne *(www.commerceone.com)* is a fully integrated e-commerce solutions provider and a B2B Internet auction supplier. CommerceOne will contribute to the $8.5 trillion dollar e-commerce explosion forecasted for the year 2005. These huge sales projections are the main reason corporations have turned to B2B Internet auctions. Many large corporations run Internet auctions from their main Web pages as a normal part of their e-commerce effort.

The following are a few examples of corporations and their B2B e-commerce Internet auctions, including partnerships:

- Microsoft, see Figure 4.14 *(auctions.bcentral.com)*

- Sun Microsystems *(www.sun.com/auctions)*

- Sears, Roebuck and Co. and Carrefour *(www.gnx.com/home.jsp)*

- DaimlerChrysler, Ford Motor Company, General Motors, Nissan, and Renault *(www.Covisint.com)*

- Lucent Technologies, AT&T, and Sun Microsystems *(ITParade.com)*

It's become commonplace for companies to collaborate with other companies to establish B2B e-commerce sites. This allows e-commerce specialization, competitive marketing, and a global reach when it comes to promoting their venture. It also helps the companies draw a critical mass of buyers and sellers to their Internet auction sites.

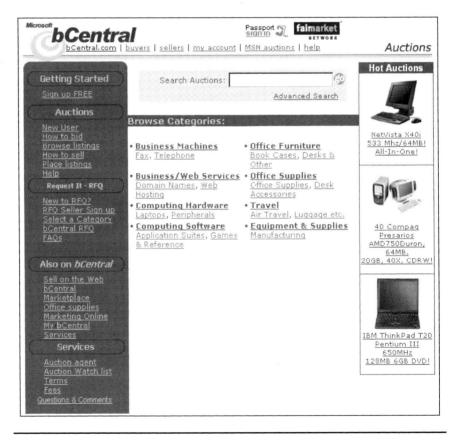

Figure 4.14. Microsoft's bCentral business-to-business auction venue *(auctions.bcentral.com)*.

XSLots.com

Formerly known as BoxLots.com, XSLots *(www.xslots.com)*, owned by Merchants Square, Inc., is a popular Internet marketplace to sell surplus inventory, using a specialized system of e-commerce for small businesses (see Figure 4.15).

"The XSLots.com site allows businesses to list and look for surplus inventory," says Bill Marger, President of Merchants Square, Inc. "Businesses set up an account online and then have the ability to list whatever they have for sale in surplus and can access the seller's contact information."

XSLots.com is a venue for members to conduct business with each other. Merchants Square, Inc., is not liable in any way for the transactions between members and any other user, nor do they handle the pack-

Figure 4.15. XSLots.com's home page *(www.xslots.com)*.

ing and shipping of merchandise. That takes place between the individual buyer and seller.

Members may enter online listings for themselves or on behalf of companies they represent through the XSLots Web Site, subject to the parameters of the preset format.

You and your customers will register an account on the New Member Sign Up Form shown in Figure 4.16. You can also register an ac-

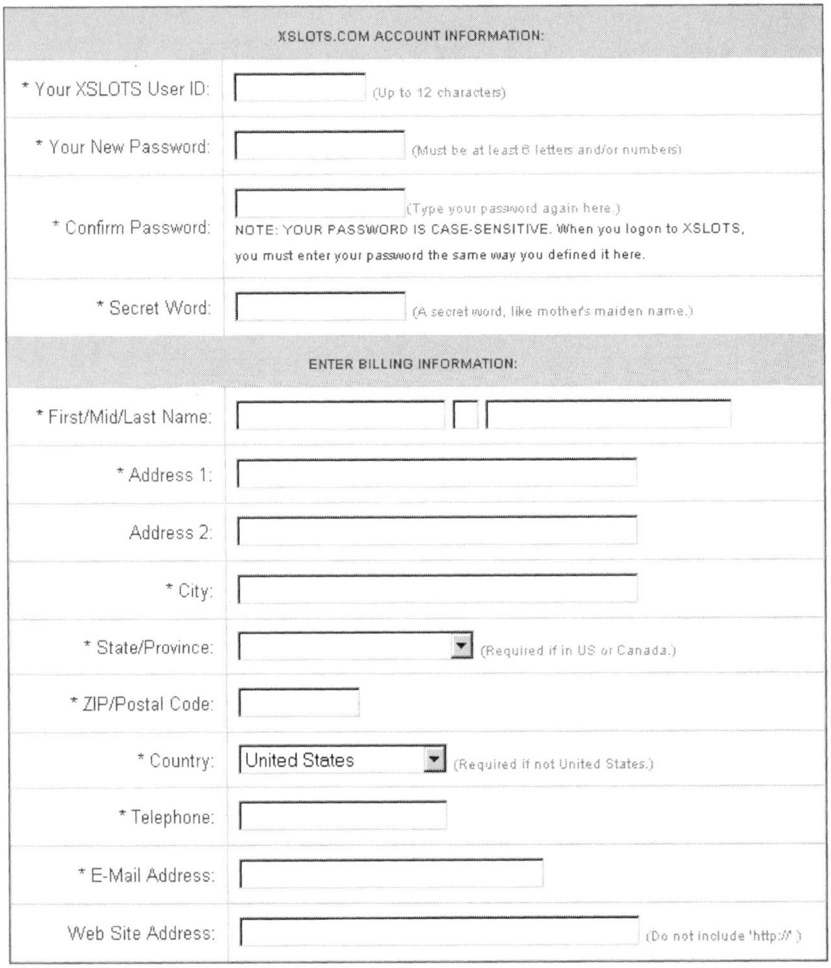

XSLOTS.COM ACCOUNT INFORMATION:

* Your XSLOTS User ID:	(Up to 12 characters)
* Your New Password:	(Must be at least 6 letters and/or numbers)
* Confirm Password:	(Type your password again here.) NOTE: YOUR PASSWORD IS CASE-SENSITIVE. When you logon to XSLOTS, you must enter your password the same way you defined it here.
* Secret Word:	(A secret word, like mother's maiden name.)

ENTER BILLING INFORMATION:

* First/Mid/Last Name:	
* Address 1:	
Address 2:	
* City:	
* State/Province:	(Required if in US or Canada.)
* ZIP/Postal Code:	
* Country:	United States (Required if not United States.)
* Telephone:	
* E-Mail Address:	
Web Site Address:	(Do not include 'http://')

Figure 4.16. XSLots' new member sign up form (*www.xslots.com/boxlots/blogin.asp*).

count for the XSLots merchant listings program, called Merchant's Square and Internet Mall.

Market Place

With your free membership, you can enter auction listings at the XSLots Market Place, where businesses can list surplus or wholesale inventory. The section of their site called the "Online Classifieds" hosts B2B e-commerce wholesale, surplus, and close-out merchandise. Listings must comply with the intent of the Web site to advertise wholesale, manufactured, or dealer lots (bulk merchandise) for sale.

To add or edit your listings, you'll log in with your Member ID and password, as shown in Figure 4.17.

Once you're logged in, you can view listings, add your own auctions, edit your active listings, and upload and remove images. Figure 4.18 shows the image-uploading screen where you'll upload photographs of your items that you have stored on your computer. You'll specify these images to appear with your auction listings. Figure 4.19 shows the online form where you'll launch your Internet auction listings as a registered seller.

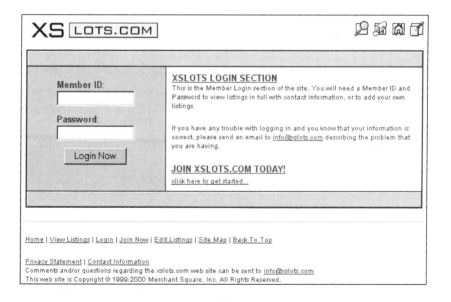

Figure 4.17. XSLots' member login screen (*www.xslots.com/boxlots/ blogin.asp*).

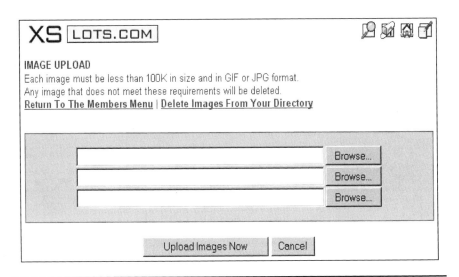

Figure 4.18. XSLots' image upload screen (*www.xslots.com/boxlots/getfile.htm*).

Merchants Square Internet Mall

One of the site's most attractive features for small businesses is its merchant listings program, called Merchants Square and Internet Mall (*www.merchant-square.com*). This site serves as the B2C venue for XSLots. A Merchants Square storefront is a Web page you create with the help of page-building tools at XSLots. You can list online auctions or sell items at a fixed price. You can also link to your Market Place auctions so your Internet auction customers have access to all of your sales.

From the Merchants Square main page, shown in Figure 4.20, you can edit or create your storefront, or browse other vendor storefronts to get some interesting design and content ideas.

Since storefront sites appear grouped by category, visitors who click on one link will see your link. This will help increase your traffic. When you list online auctions, either at XSLots or other Internet auction sites that allow external links, you can add a link to your Merchants Square storefront. You can also add a link to your business Web site. A nicely designed link ad and a few sample inventory items will make your Merchants Square storefront a great traffic generator for other Internet components of your business. The links will invite your customers to do some additional surfing.

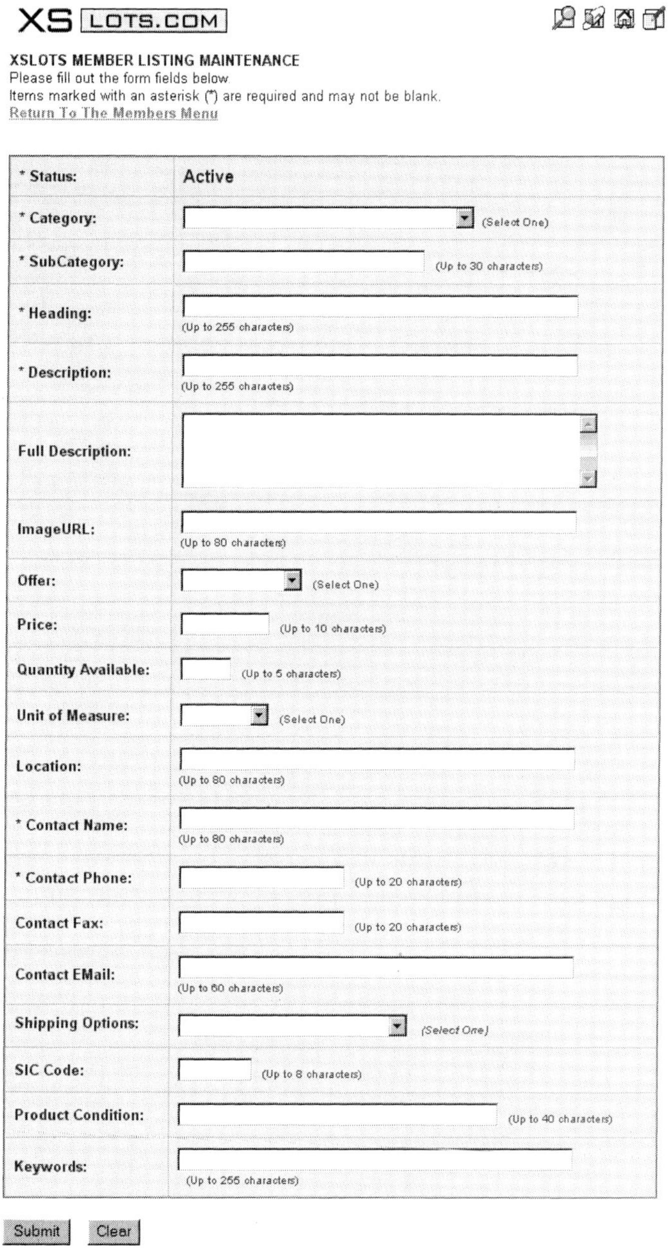

XS LOTS.COM

XSLOTS MEMBER LISTING MAINTENANCE
Please fill out the form fields below.
Items marked with an asterisk (*) are required and may not be blank.
Return To The Members Menu

* Status:	Active
* Category:	(Select One)
* SubCategory:	(Up to 30 characters)
* Heading:	(Up to 255 characters)
* Description:	(Up to 255 characters)
Full Description:	
ImageURL:	(Up to 80 characters)
Offer:	(Select One)
Price:	(Up to 10 characters)
Quantity Available:	(Up to 5 characters)
Unit of Measure:	(Select One)
Location:	(Up to 80 characters)
* Contact Name:	(Up to 80 characters)
* Contact Phone:	(Up to 20 characters)
Contact Fax:	(Up to 20 characters)
Contact EMail:	(Up to 60 characters)
Shipping Options:	(Select One)
SIC Code:	(Up to 8 characters)
Product Condition:	(Up to 40 characters)
Keywords:	(Up to 255 characters)

Submit Clear

Figure 4.19. XSLots' member listing maintenance screen (*www.xslots.com/boxlots/updtlisting.asp?fAction=New*).

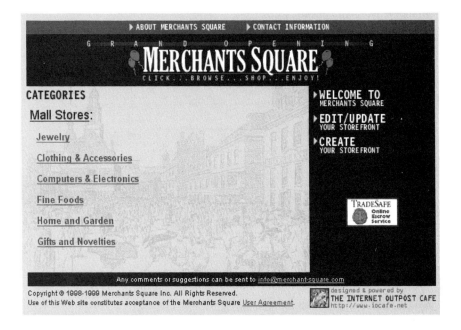

Figure 4.20.   Merchants Square mall store categories (*www.merchant-square.com/subnav_2.htm*).

You can set up your Merchants Square storefront within minutes at XSLots.com, which helps if your selling venture needs to be up on the Web quickly in order to take advantage of market timing. You can get your seller account instantly and start listing as soon as you've read and agreed to the site Terms and Conditions.

Standard membership is free. There are no set-up fees, activation fees, or monthly charges. You can upgrade to premium membership for a one-time fee. Premium members have their storefronts displayed in the Antique and Internet Mall directories and benefit from all of the traffic to Merchants Square.

DoveBid

DoveBid, Inc. *(www.dovebid.com)*, the successor to Dove Brothers, LLC, is one of the world's leading auctioneers and capital asset sale advisors (see Figure 4.21). Where XSLots.com is an ideal site for small and fledgling businesses, DoveBid is an auction Mecca for the corporate giants. For more than 60 years, DoveBid has helped corporations, government agencies, and financial institutions get maximum value for their capital assets by conducting thousands of industry-specific auctions to sell millions of individual lots. The goods transferred on DoveBid represent billions of dollars in assets.

With headquarters in Foster City, California, DoveBid, Inc., is a leader in Webcast industrial auctions, appraisals, and other capital asset disposition services for Global 2000 businesses. DoveBid has conducted thousands of industry-specific auctions on behalf of corporations, government agencies, and financial institutions worldwide. Its portfolio of asset disposition services includes live Webcast auctions, round-the-clock online auctions, featured online auctions, on-location auctions, sealed-bid Internet sales, and private-treaty sales. Buyers and sellers can

Figure 4.21. DoveBid's home page (*www.dovebid.com*).

also benefit from such transaction support services as appraisals, credit rating, financing, inspection, insurance, maintenance, photography, repair and operations procurement, and transportation and logistics.

Numerous Global 2000 businesses have participated in DoveBid programs, including AT&T, Boeing, DaimlerChrysler, Hewlett Packard, Lucent Technologies, Levi-Strauss, Lockheed-Martin, NEC, and Warner Brothers. Many have conducted multiple auctions with the B2B Internet auction site.

Prominent exposure on the Sun Microsystems and other participating companies' Web sites gives DoveBid something of an edge in the B2B Internet auction market. This popularity increases the opportunity for its customers to maximize returns on their capital assets. DoveBid helps customers with every aspect of asset disposition. They manage the entire Internet auction process, whether the transaction is for a single machine tool, a 100-location project, or somewhere in between.

The first thing you need to do is to register an account with DoveBid. Then you can register to bid via Webcast, and list, track, or bid on assets in the Global Marketplace. Registered users can make use of many other online auction services available through DoveBid. Figure 4.22 shows the contact information and user e-mail and identification portion of the user registration screen.

DoveBid Webcast Network

On DoveBid's Webcast auctions, Web-based users place bids online at the same time other bidders can place competing bids on the live auction floor. DoveBid conducted the first Webcast auctions in January 2000, and since then conducted scores of Webcast auctions for its corporate clients.

Valuation Services

DoveBid has a wholly owned and separately operated subsidiary called DoveBid Valuation Services that provides diversified asset appraisal services (see Figure 4.23). DoveTech, Norman Levy Associates, Inc., AccuVal, Philip Pollack, and Greenwich Industrial Services joined to form DoveBid Valuation Services, Inc. DVS can appraise a variety of assets, including:

- Personal property

- Inventory

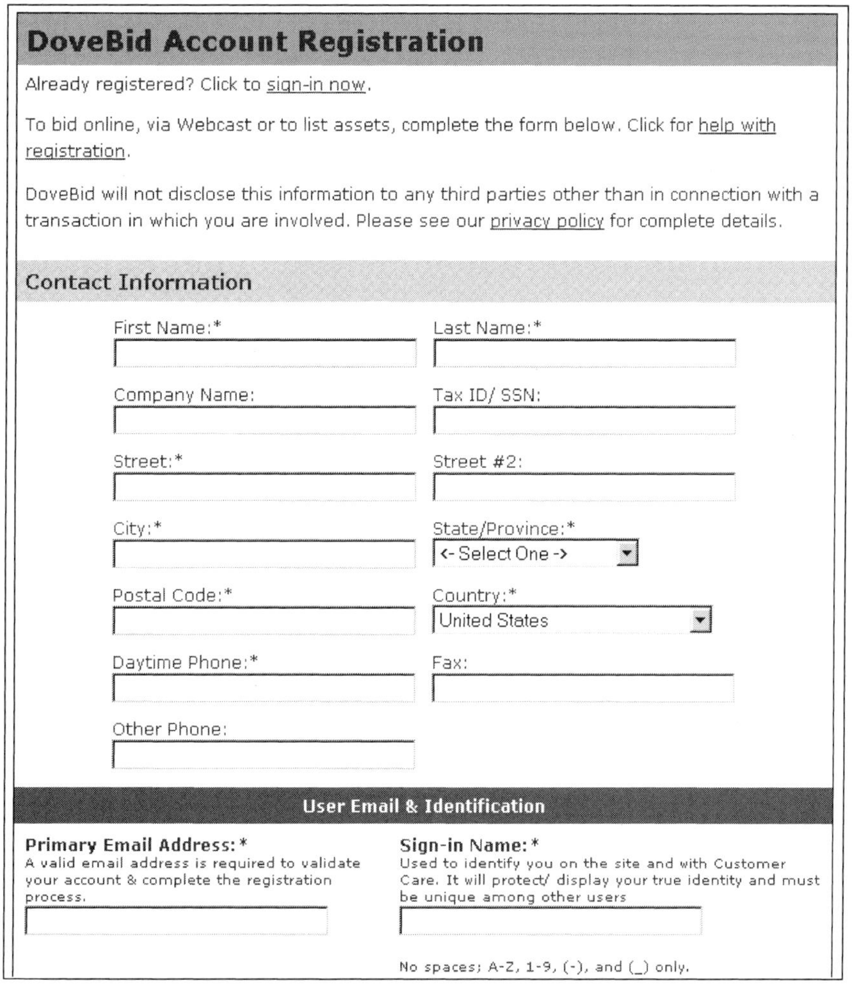

DoveBid Account Registration

Already registered? Click to <u>sign-in now</u>.

To bid online, via Webcast or to list assets, complete the form below. Click for <u>help with registration</u>.

DoveBid will not disclose this information to any third parties other than in connection with a transaction in which you are involved. Please see our <u>privacy policy</u> for complete details.

Contact Information

First Name:*

Last Name:*

Company Name:

Tax ID/ SSN:

Street:*

Street #2:

City:*

State/Province:*
[<- Select One -> ▼]

Postal Code:*

Country:*
[United States ▼]

Daytime Phone:*

Fax:

Other Phone:

User Email & Identification

Primary Email Address:*
A valid email address is required to validate your account & complete the registration process.

Sign-in Name:*
Used to identify you on the site and with Customer Care. It will protect/ display your true identity and must be unique among other users

No spaces; A-Z, 1-9, (-), and (_) only.

Figure 4.22. DoveBid's registration screen (*dovebid.com/accounts/register.asp*)

- Real property

- Intangible assets

- Business valuation

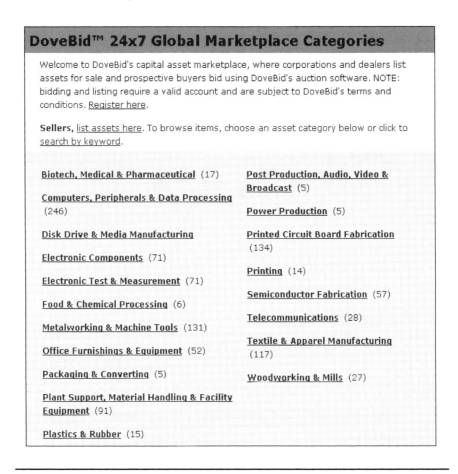

DoveBid™ 24x7 Global Marketplace Categories

Welcome to DoveBid's capital asset marketplace, where corporations and dealers list assets for sale and prospective buyers bid using DoveBid's auction software. NOTE: bidding and listing require a valid account and are subject to DoveBid's terms and conditions. Register here.

Sellers, list assets here. To browse items, choose an asset category below or click to search by keyword.

Biotech, Medical & Pharmaceutical (17)

Computers, Peripherals & Data Processing (246)

Disk Drive & Media Manufacturing

Electronic Components (71)

Electronic Test & Measurement (71)

Food & Chemical Processing (6)

Metalworking & Machine Tools (131)

Office Furnishings & Equipment (52)

Packaging & Converting (5)

Plant Support, Material Handling & Facility Equipment (91)

Plastics & Rubber (15)

Post Production, Audio, Video & Broadcast (5)

Power Production (5)

Printed Circuit Board Fabrication (134)

Printing (14)

Semiconductor Fabrication (57)

Telecommunications (28)

Textile & Apparel Manufacturing (117)

Woodworking & Mills (27)

Figure 4.23.   DoveBid's valuation services page (*dovebid.com/valuations*).

Whenever possible, they tailor each appraisal for any special circumstances the client may have. Valuations comply with the Uniform Standards of Professional Appraisal Practices (USPAP) and comply with local rules and regulations that apply in specific jurisdictions.

The accuracy of DoveBid's appraisals has also been recognized throughout the industrial sector as a whole, by leading organizations such as lending institutions, financial consultants, insurance companies, state and federal courts, crisis managers, and merger and acquisition firms.

From the "Company" navigation tab on the DoveBid home page, click on "Contact us" for more information about selling at DoveBid.

Auction Site B2B Marketplaces

Business-to-business Internet auction e-commerce has been so profitable that auction sites originally intended as C2C venues cannot pass up the generated revenue from B2B business. There's too much money in it to "just say consumer." eBay operates a few B2B ventures, and Yahoo! Auctions' B2B Marketplace has been a huge success.

eBay's B2B Business

The eBay Internet auction site's first B2B trading facility, called Business Exchange, targeted companies with fewer than 100 employees. The new auction facility enabled business sellers to list auctions in 34 business-related categories, including computer hardware, software, electronics, and industrial and office equipment.

You can access the Business Exchange from eBay's home page. Figure 4.24 shows the top part of the page. You'll find 34 business-related cat-

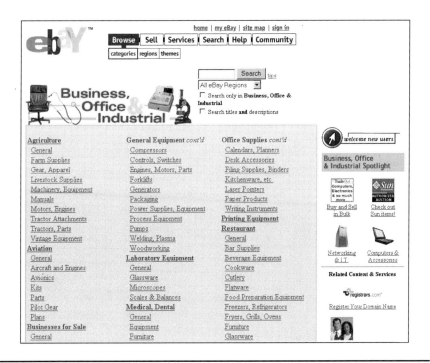

Figure 4.24. eBay's Business, Office, and Industrial Business Exchange (*pages.ebay.com/catindex/business.html*).

egories with as many as 60,000 listings. Some of the main categories include metalwork equipment, software, electronics, safety and security items, office equipment, and businesses for sale. eBay promotes Business Exchange listings with targeted banner advertising on business-related sites and through existing marketing relationships, including AOL.

Business Exchange auction listings are not distinguishable from regular eBay auction listings. The listing pages follow the same format as those entered by private sellers. For more information about selling at eBay's Business Exchange, send e-mail with your questions to business@eBay.com.

In another B2B venture, eBay has financial interest in TradeOut.com, a B2B site for selling overstock. You'll read more about TradeOut further in this chapter.

Yahoo's B2B Marketplace

They offer well over 48,000 items in more than 650 categories. Yahoo! B2B Marketplace (Figure 4.25) collaborated with DoveBid to launch an Internet auction site for business executives, small companies, and entrepreneurs. Businesses list goods for auction, and buyers can browse

Figure 4.25. Yahoo! Business to Business Marketplace (*b2b.yahoo.com*).

through many different Web sites, marketplaces, and business formats to quickly find and purchase products.

You'll find the Yahoo! B2B Marketplace linked from the Yahoo! B2B Industry Marketplace. This part of the Yahoo! Web portal serves as a one-stop destination for information and services aimed at helping industry professionals with product research, read the latest industry news, and make purchasing decisions. Among the Industry Marketplaces, you'll find links for business entities:

- Software

- Electronics

- Hardware

Each marketplace includes targeted categorized business information, feature articles, and informational resources such as white pages, industry-specific news, and a rich-media Webcast center. It's not an Internet auction site, but it's a great source of industry-specific e-commerce information.

Business-to-Exchange

A Business-to-exchange, or B2E, company really isn't an auction/hosting site. It's a services company that expedites the listing and uploading of your business merchandise to an exchange or auction site, and allows the seller to track and manage his or her sales while they're in progress. When the auctions close, the exchange helps the seller expedite the post-sale fulfillment part of the transaction.

Analysts at Keenan Vision estimate that by the year 2004, more than 60 percent of all e-commerce transactions will be performed using dynamic pricing. There will be 12.2 million memberships between businesses and Internet exchanges in 2004. This section profiles two of the best known B2E Web sites—AuctionWatch and GoTo.

AuctionWatch

You'll see AuctionWatch *(www.auctionwatch.com)* mentioned in many different parts of this book. Their B2E facility has an e-commerce platform that enables businesses of all sizes, both large and small, to benefit from dynamic pricing environments in addition to typical fixed price channels. AuctionWatch's comprehensive offering of services corners three main areas:

- Seller services

- Buyer services

- Fulfillment solutions

You'll read more about AuctionWatch and its seller online support in Chapter 12. Here, we'll discuss the two valuable business exchange tools that AuctionWatch provides:

- Customers can search auctions at hundreds of sites with one universal search.

- Sellers can register a user account at many different Internet auction and auction service provider (ASP) sites with a single effort.

- Sellers can upload auctions to multiple Internet auction sites with one effort.

Using the Internet to buy and sell merchandise is all about convenience and saving time. If you direct your customers to the AuctionWatch universal search and list items at Internet auction sites within their exchange, you can help increase your own Internet auction traffic. AuctionWatch's Universal Search feature helps your customers browse through listings at hundreds of Internet auction and fixed-price sites. A user conducts a multi-site search on one form. Figure 4.26 shows the Power Search page at AuctionWatch.

Universal Registration

AuctionWatch's Universal Registration allows you to sign up and store all of your auction account registration information in one location so you can launch, monitor, and manage all of your auctions at AuctionWatch. You'll register your accounts with auction sites like eBay, Yahoo!, and Amazon on one form. Then you can manage the information from one window instead of going to the auction sites one at a time. A timesaving feature such as Universal Registration leaves you

Figure 4.26. The Power Search page at AuctionWatch (*srch.auctionwatch.com/usearch*).

more time to plan your Internet Auction Strategy. Click on the Universal Registration navigation link from the main AuctionWatch pages to read more about this feature.

Upload Auctions

With Auction Manager Pro, you can launch multiple auctions at once to either Amazon, Yahoo!, or eBay. From the "Launch Auctions" link, you can create a new auction or use one of your stored auctions. When you store an auction and reuse it, the description, pricing, quantity, and other listing information is exactly as you last used it. You can make adjustments before you launch the auction.

AuctionWatch requires an auction venue ID and password on file in your Universal Registration preferences before you can create auction listings.

GoTo Auctions

Another well-known and heavily trafficked B2E Internet auction site, GoTo (*www.goto.com*) offers some powerful services that allow GoTo Auctions to enable any individual or business to participate in online auctions. GoTo Auctions is a fast and easy way to enter the Internet auction space and promote your products and services to targeted customers.

Search Auctions

GoTo Auctions provides a search capability so your customers can hunt for auctions at over 400 auction sites and B2B exchanges, including Amazon Auctions, eBay, and Yahoo! Auctions. Figure 4.27 shows GoTo Auctions' main search page.

As part of its B2E system, GoTo Auctions partners with other Web site owners, allowing them to add a search box to their site. Adding a GoTo Auction search capability to your business Web site can bring more Web surfers and potential customers your way.

GoTo Auctions offers its "Pay for Performance" option. An auction site selects the categories that are most relevant to its auction

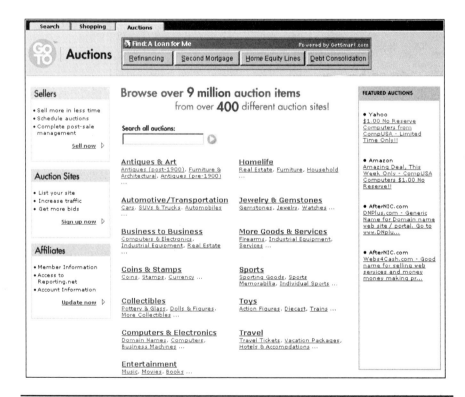

Figure 4.27. GoTo Auctions main search page (*search.auctions.goto.com*).

products and determines what to pay on a per-click basis. A higher bid means that their auctions will be more prominently listed on the search results page.

ChannelFusion Network

The GoTo Auctions community offers ChannelFusion, an auction management service. It includes provisions for listing auctions at numerous Internet auction sites with one listing effort. The divisions of the GoTo ChannelFusion Network offer three tiers of Internet auction service:

- Pro

- Merchant

- Concierge

Formerly known as AuctionManager, ChannelFusion Pro offers auction-management tools for individuals and small businesses. The program enables users to post at many different auction sites and exchanges, including eBay, Yahoo! Auctions, and Amazon Auctions. You'll also be able to use a comprehensive set of tools, such as image hosting, ad creation, sales tracking, and post-sale management.

For larger businesses, ChannelFusion Merchant provides advanced tools to efficiently post, sell, and manage high volumes of products through multiple e-marketplaces. It targets Internet auction sellers who want to move a large volume of product through the dynamic pricing channel.

ChannelFusion Concierge is the management package that includes full access to the ChannelFusion Network and the related Internet auction services. Concierge sellers can contact a ChannelAdvisor who can look at your product line and help you price your items to be in line with your market, and consequently achieve your selling goals. Concierge customers can post products to all sites in the ChannelFusion Network, increasing the possibilities of reaching their targeted demand.

Sites that Sell Overstock

Any B2C or B2B Internet auction site gives you a venue for selling overstock, but several Internet auction sites are dedicated to just that cause.

In some media channels, e-commerce liquidators are unceremoniously known as "vulture dot-coms" because they seek out belly-up Internet businesses to buy out their overstock at a bargain and sell it for a huge profit. If you're on the verge of shutting down your operation and need to immediately sell your stock, a liquidation site can mean avoiding an astronomical loss. For the e-commerce liquidators, it means big bucks business.

Not all overstock Internet auction sites hustle liquidations. Several run just like any other C2C or B2C site, where the sellers will list auctions and customers can bid on them. This section profiles several different types of surplus inventory Internet auction sites.

Overstock.com

Overstock.com, Inc. *(www.overstock.com)*, operates from a 100,000-square-foot warehouse in Salt Lake City, Utah, and has become one of the top 25 most-visited retailers on the Web, according to Media Metrix. Although they have been touted as a "vulture.com" by certain media, Patrick Byrne, CEO of Overstock, attributes only a small part of their business to liquidations. "Only 20 percent of our sales come from close-outs," he explained. "The other 80 percent are consignment, partner sales, and manufacturer excess inventory." According to Byrne, Overstock's mission is to provide manufacturers and businesses with a way to move small or large quantities of slow-moving inventory directly to the consumer, without polluting their sales channels. Channel pollution is what Byrne terms as discounting merchandise within the selling market where the same products are sold at retail. This greatly hinders retail sales. "They need some other channel to blow the products out to the market and get them into the customers' hands," he explained.

It started as a venture to support the flea-market business. They then sold goods to small "Mom and Pop" operations via faxes, and later started their consumer sales via Overstock's present fixed-price Web site, which remains a popular purchasing site for bargain seekers. Overstock offers quality name-brand merchandise to consumers at up to 70 percent off. Their categories include housewares, electronics, sporting goods, clothing, travel/leisure products, gifts, toys, and jewelry.

Home furnishing and fashions are Overstock's biggest sellers. Byrne's most memorable sale was for comforters. "We didn't expect to move as many as we did," he said, "but we sold them by the container load." He was also amazed by an immediate sale of vacuum cleaners—a lot of 55 sold out within days. Now they sell between 100 and 150 vacuums every day.

Figure 4.28 shows the Overstock.com home page that the consumers see when they call up the site in their browsers.

Their success has been overwhelming. According to the Wall Street Journal, Overstock is the 25th most visited shopping site on the Web among those who surf the Web from work. Most of its registered users are female—75 percent. Overstock has three channels by which it acquires merchandise to sell at its fixed-price site:

- Commissioned sales via Overstock's Partner Program

- Consignment sales

- Close-out buying

Figure 4.28. Overstock's home page (*www.overstock.com*).

At first, Overstock had possession of all of the merchandise it sold. Now the exception to that is merchandise sold by its partners. Overstock Partners will warehouse and ship their own merchandise.

Partner Program

Overstock helps other e-tailers clean discontinued or unwanted inventory out of their warehouses and ends up collecting an 18 percent commission. The partners enter their own listings at Overstock's site. "We anonymize the sales for them," says Byrne. "We handle the marketing, customer service, credit-card process, and any fraud or chargeback issues. We also create and host the listing photos."

According to J. P. Werlin of Overstock, 30 to 40 percent of its business is from the Partner Program. "We don't have to house the merchandise," says Werlin. "It's a great business and our partners love it."

Overstock Partners use the interface screens shown in Figures 4.29 and 4.30 to list products for sale. New partners receive the URL for an on-site tutorial, or Interface User Manual, and a unique user ID and password with which to reach the interface screens.

Partners can view pending orders, sales reports, and product returns on separate screens. They can also change an item's price and update their contact information via the Overstock site.

Consignment Sales

Overstock also takes goods on consignment, working with a manufacturer such as the Dr Martens shoe crafters, whose merchandise Over-

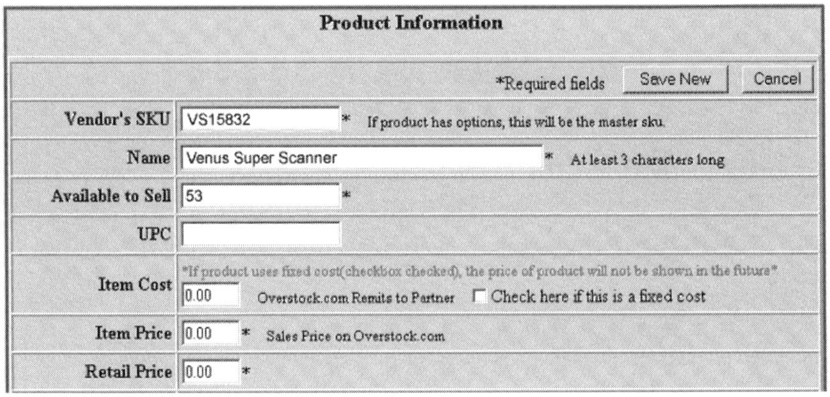

Figure 4.29. Overstock's partner interface product identification screen.

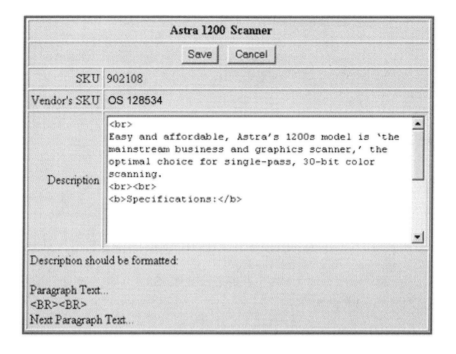

Figure 4.30. Overstock's partner interface product information screen.

stock buys at the manufacturer production price. Overstock warehouses it, so the manufacturer can make room for other stock. Then Overstock lists the goods on its site. Overstock doesn't charge the manufacturer to warehouse the goods when selling consignment—it stores the goods and handles the sales. If the manufacturer wants to move additional goods, Overstock takes possession of them, sells them, and gives the manufacturer the full price minus 18 percent commission.

"If the business or manufacturer prefers that Overstock buy the goods outright," says Byrne, "we'll give them bottom dollar for it. If we consign it, they earn more."

Close-out Buying
Overstock searches out inventory from unsuccessful e-commerce ventures and overstocked merchants, and resells the goods at a discount. For example, they bought out stock from both Gear.com and ToyTime.com when both businesses ceased operation. "Close-out buy-

ing has been around a long time," says Byrne. "Before the Internet, bargain basements and flea markets handled the goods."

To contact Overstock about liquidating surplus or leftover goods, or to inquire about becoming a partner, call 801-947-3100 or send e-mail to info@overstock.com.

B2Bstreet

A secure online B2B Internet auction site for business overstock and excess inventory, B2Bstreet *(www.b2bstreet.com)* is a venue for businesses to sell their stock without an intermediary in a secure online environment. Sellers pay a small transaction fee per listing only on items that sell. The site offers free escrow services and guarantees friendly customer support (see Figure 4.31).

According to Chairman Ronald K. Shelp, B2Bstreet was created specifically to address the unique overstock issues affecting small and

Figure 4.31. B2Bstreet's home page (*www.b2bstreet.com*).

midsize retail, manufacturing, and service businesses. The B2Bstreet marketplace brings buyers and sellers together to transact business. Security features include transaction technology that was developed in conjunction with a leading commercial bank and free escrow accounts that protect both buyer and seller.

Founded in 1999 with present headquarters in New York City, B2Bstreet also has offices in Connecticut, New Hampshire, Utah, and Washington, D.C. It is endorsed by the American Chamber of Commerce Executives (ACCE), having partnerships with more than 75 Chambers of Commerce. B2Bstreet has expertise in various overstock marketplaces, including excess retail inventory, discontinued product lines, manufacturing overruns, customer returns, office equipment replacements, and product liquidation.

Selling Merchandise

There are no fees to list goods with B2Bstreet. All you have to do is register and you can start listing right away. B2Bstreet gives you a unique user number that you'll enter at the bottom of the auction-listing screen. The input screen is very much like that at most Internet auction sites. You'll enter your item title, listing category (from a drop-down menu), unit of measure (lot, case, unit, pallet, etc.), and the item's location. You can schedule the auction start and end time; a handy feature that's not usually possible without using an auction scheduler that interfaces with the auction site.

You can designate the item as "hot" or "featured," and then enter the financial details of the sale in the fields provided on the input form (see Figure 4.32). Next, you'll enter the item description in an HTML-enabled form. For your auction image, you can either enter the image's URL if it's hosted on the Web somewhere, or you can upload an image from your computer's hard drive and the B2Bstreet auction site hosts it for you.

As you scroll to the end of the form, you'll enter your user verification information—the seller ID number that B2Bstreet issued to you, and your user password. Click on the Add Offer button and your auction goes live.

Services

B2Bstreet has plenty of seller services. Whether you are a buyer or a seller of business surplus, you can take advantage of B2Bstreet's transaction features, including:

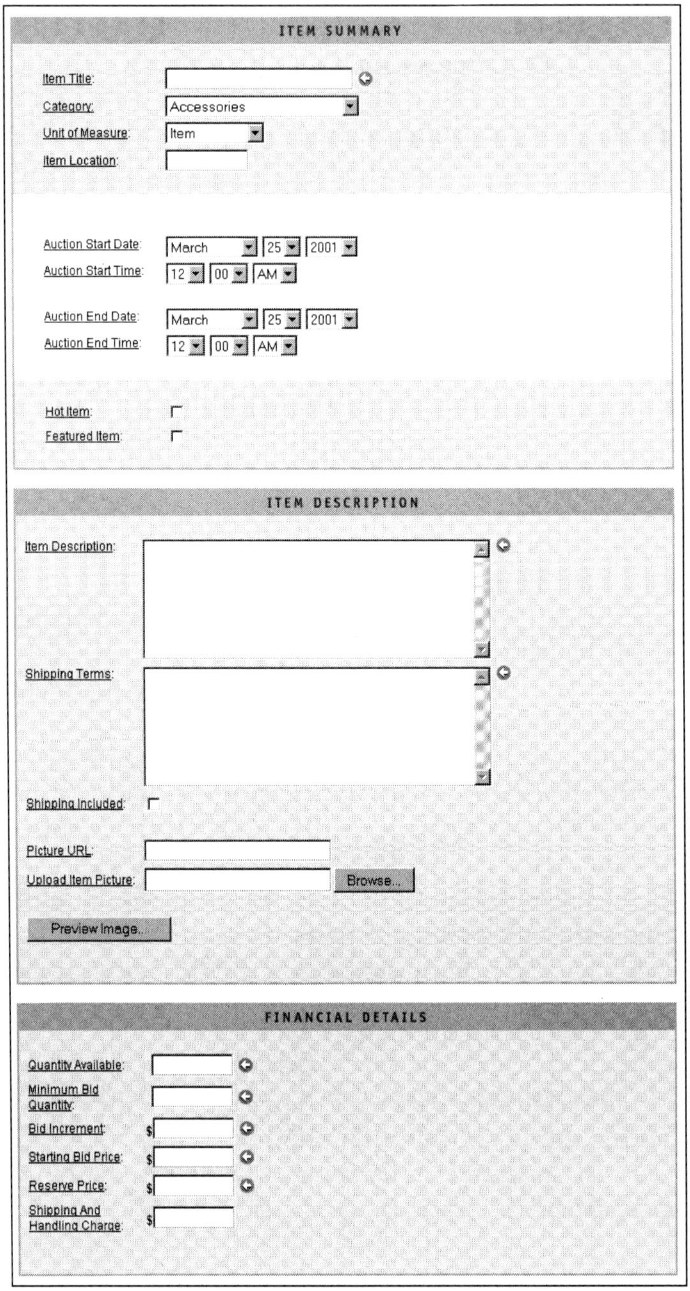

ITEM SUMMARY

Item Title:

Category: Accessories

Unit of Measure: Item

Item Location:

Auction Start Date: March 25 2001

Auction Start Time: 12 00 AM

Auction End Date: March 25 2001

Auction End Time: 12 00 AM

Hot Item:

Featured Item:

ITEM DESCRIPTION

Item Description:

Shipping Terms:

Shipping Included:

Picture URL:

Upload Item Picture: Browse...

Preview Image...

FINANCIAL DETAILS

Quantity Available:

Minimum Bid Quantity:

Bid Increment: $

Starting Bid Price: $

Reserve Price: $

Shipping And Handling Charge: $

Figure 4.32. The B2Bstreet's auction listing page.

- **Shipping**—A leading online freight service provider can take care of all of your shipping needs.

- **Escrow**—If you choose to, you can use third-party online escrow services provided by Internet Escrow Services.

- **Inspection**—You can request a physical inspection of the goods before shipment, ensuring the quality of the products and providing certification for transaction settlements.

- **Insurance**—All transactions receive complimentary shipping insurance from B2Bstreet.

- **Image management and uploading**—Send their services department a hard-copy photograph and they'll digitize it so you can add it to your listing.

TradeOut

Another popular online B2B surplus marketplace called TradeOut *(www.tradeout.com)* is another Internet auction venue available to retail executives concerned with improving their inventory return on assets. The company was formed in October 1998 and is headquartered in Valhalla, New York. TradeOut (Figure 4.33) is a haven for sellers who need tips and hints for successful online selling. In their Tips for Selling section, TradeOut offers suggestions for such selling interests as competitive pricing, listing appearance, managing your auction photos, and the importance of comprehensive product information.

The venue's mission statement is clear: "TradeOut will be the preferred transaction venue for businesses in the $350 billion surplus asset market. TradeOut will help improve business results for companies buying and selling surplus industrial equipment and consumer merchandise by making transactions more efficient and more profitable."

A number of interesting features exist at TradeOut. "You can use our Wanted Items section to tell sellers about your interest in items that aren't yet listed on TradeOut, or access our Partner services, including logistics, escrow and financing features," says Andrew Kantor, Vice President of Marketing at TradeOut. It's very easy to list items there.

Figure 4.33. TradeOut's home page *(www.tradeout.com)*.

Selling

TradeOut allows you to list fixed price, standard auction, and highest sealed bid auctions. Once you register, you can list items for sale. TradeOut calls this "product posting" and it's done in six steps:

1. Select a marketplace

2. Pick a category

3. Select an optional category if you want to list in more than one

4. Enter basic product information

5. Specify product and sale details

6. Review the item and then launch the auction listing

The next step takes you to the listing screen, which is shown in Figure 4.34.

When you scroll further down on the page, you'll enter important information about the product, the unit type (carton, case, pallet, dozen, etc.), and whether you'll entertain bids at less than your asking price. TradeOut notifies you of these offers in e-mail.

You'll also schedule the ending time of your auction (it starts as soon as you activate the listing), add warranty information and an image, and then select whether you want the auction automatically reposted if the item doesn't sell. Then you can review and submit the listing.

TradeWatch

TradeWatch is a resource to help companies buy and sell safely on TradeOut. You can review trading policies and services that enable your company and your high bidders to transact with confidence. You can read the TradeWatch frequently asked questions (FAQ) page by clicking on the TradeWatch icon on any main TradeOut page.

If you have questions, contact a TradeWatch representative at tradewatch@tradeout.com.

Assessing an Auction Site

Now that you know about the different types of Internet auction sites available for your business selling purposes, you probably have some idea which kind you'd like to use. Maybe you've decided on one, and maybe you'd like to carry out your Internet auction strategy at two or three different types of sites. Maybe more. This section will help you decide which site is best for helping you achieve your business goals and make the most out of your Internet auction venture.

In the next few sections, you'll learn the important points to consider when deciding which auction site will bring your business the best results:

- Ease of use

- Success of your trial auctions

- Success of other sellers at that site

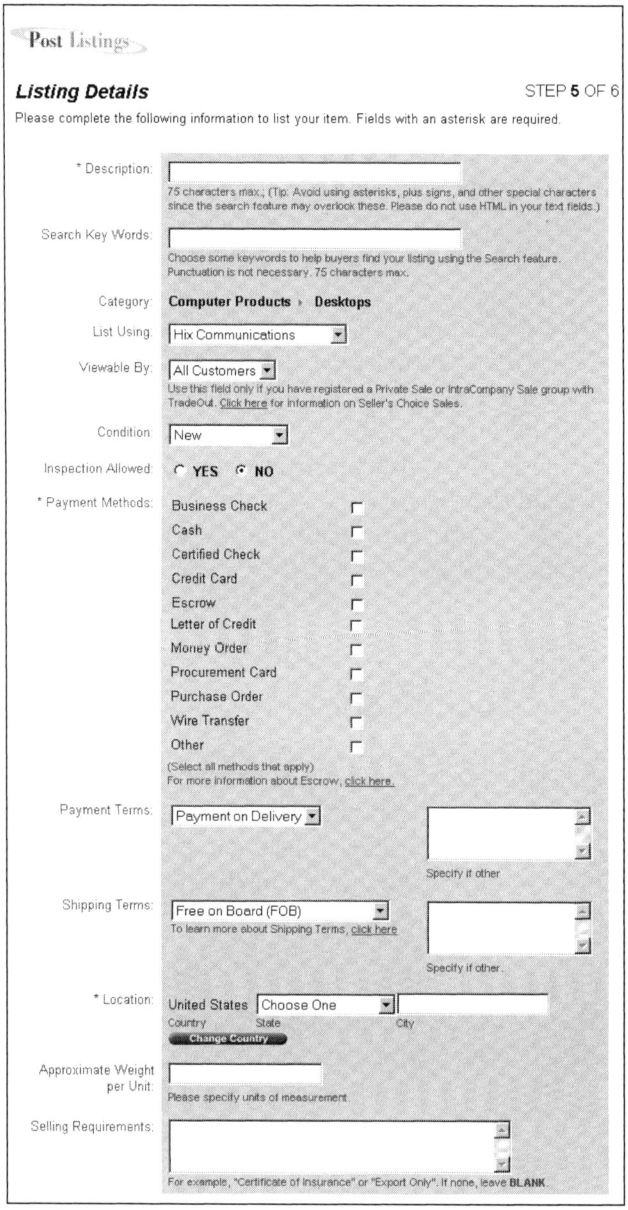

Figure 4.34. Auction entry page at TradeOut (*www.tradeout.com/shared/ post/postlistingdetails.jsp*).

- How other users feel about the site

- The site's overall rating

As you become more comfortable with browsing through Internet auction sites, you'll also develop your own criteria for assessing the site's potential for your business needs. Use an Auction Site Assessment Worksheet in Appendix C when you research any site you might end up using.

Is the Site Easy to Use?

Many of your customers may be using the Internet for the first time to bid on and buy your products. That's why it's important for you to be a buyer at a site before you're a seller. The notes you took when you purchased an item from an Internet auction site should include your assessment of how easy the bidding process is. Make sure that the site appeals to people with limited Internet expertise.

You should also be sure that listing an auction is a smooth process. Unless the site's customer base and your sales are phenomenal, don't waste your time at a site that doesn't have an easy auction listing procedure.

Check how the auction works. Don't assume that the rules used by one Internet auction site apply to another. Some sites offer systematic tutorials that take potential buyers through the bidding process. Check the tutorial that the site provides for bidders to make sure that it's an easy process for your customers. You may have to coach them if they want to place bids on your products but don't know how to bid. Taking a few minutes to go through the tutorial and become familiar with the site's process could earn you more business.

Features and Services
You should expect the site to offer certain services, such as seller support, e-mail notification, Secure Sockets Layer (SSL) site encryption to protect sensitive user information, free registration, HTML-enabled auction description areas, a search function, listing categories, and contact information for sellers who have questions or encounter problem users. Look for features like these, as well as those described in Chapter 1, at any site that you consider using. They should be standard functions.

Some auction sites exaggerate their features, or repeat them on another page as **services**. As a businessperson, you know that this is a normal part of promoting the goods, but you're also perceptive enough to know that a list of ten site features may translate into six that are unique from one another. For example, an "on-site information guide" and a "help page" are essentially the same thing, but they may appear as separate items on an impressively long list of site features. Don't judge a site by the length of its features list. In this case, size doesn't matter. Additionally, don't be taken in by a feature such as "buyers are never charged a fee for bidding." Of course they aren't.

Is There a Site Tutorial?

There must be, and it should cover everything both you and your customers need to know in order to successfully—and easily—use the Internet auction site. An effective auction site tutorial will step you through the auction listing process by showing the actual input forms you'll use, with notations and instructions for each field. It will also cover the bidding process so your customers will know how to bid on your products.

Notice in Figure 4.35 that eBay also has a photo tutorial. This is an excellent information resource, since photos are an integral part of your auction listings. If you find an auction site that lets you list a test item, this is the optimum in seller training. Give it a go!

Your Success with the Site

This section assumes that you've used the auction site and want to assess its overall usefulness for your business. Perhaps you used the site before as a private user and now wish to use it for your business sales. Keep in mind everything you remember about your experience with the site and how many auctions you participated in. Never judge an Internet auction site by a bad experience with one particular user, unless that user was operating on behalf of the auction site. Rather, judge the auction site by how well the administrators handled your situation when you reported it.

If you used a site for a few test auctions, you can make a solid assessment since you ran the auction as an agent for your business. If you used the site before your current Internet auction venture, you need to consider just how much you used the site as a buyer and as a seller.

- How many auctions did you list?

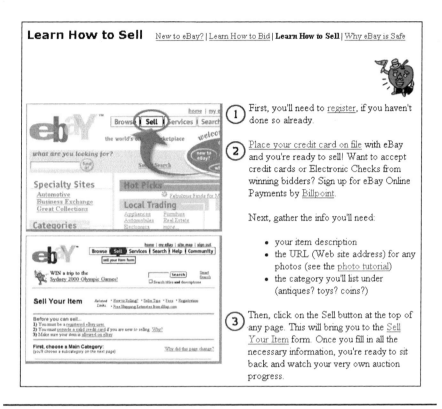

Figure 4.35. eBay's tried and true seller tutorial (*www.pages.ebay.com/help/basics/n-selling.html*).

- How many of the items that you listed sold successfully?

- How many of your listings closed with no bids?

- How many times have you bid on other sellers' items?

- How often have you been the high bidder?

Based on the above, consider whether your buying and selling volume at that site is adequate for you to make an assessment of it. If not, you need to spend more time there learning about how the auction site operates.

Adequate Administrative Support

It is imperative that you use a site that protects its users. If not, you're subjecting both yourself and your business to some potential migraines. Some sites provide free insurance or guarantees for items that are undelivered, inauthentic, or just not what the seller claimed. If the site has possession of the merchandise on consignment for you and handles the shipping, find out where your customers can direct questions or concerns. You don't want to leave them without recourse in a bad situation with the Internet auction site, as this may adversely reflect on you and your business.

Plenty of Site Traffic

The only way you'll be successful at Internet auction selling is if you have bidders, and the only way you'll have bidders is if they get to the auction site via some means (browser bookmark, hyperlink, or auction exchange search). You can check for adequate site traffic by looking at the number of active items that have had at least one bid placed on them. If you can check closed auctions, examine how many of them closed with bids.

Some of the sites let you know how many registered users they have. This isn't necessarily a measure of site traffic, but it's a good sign that, at least initially, the auction site promoted itself in a way that attracted users.

Other's Success with the Site

If your competition is making money at an Internet auction site, every reason exists that you will too. Even if sellers turning profits hand over fist aren't listing the same commodities you are, their high sales volume indicates plenty of site traffic and buyers looking to spend money. If you can see that the trout pond is stocked, drop your line.

To determine the overall success of an auction site, you can check some valuable information that's available right at the site.

Check Closed Auctions

Checking Internet auction closing prices is an exceptionally valuable tool for someone working to assess a site. Some auction sites have a full-function search feature for closed auctions, while others offer a selection of listings that resulted in high profits under the heading "recent sales." With this function, the site decides which closed auctions it will show you based on the amount of the winning bids. You'd rather see all of them, of course. Searching closed auctions with your own criteria is the most helpful, but something is better than nothing—as long as you can check closed auctions. Checking how well other sellers have done with a product is helpful for a number of reasons:

- You can get an idea for setting your starting price.

- If the item is a hot seller, you can set your opening price attractively low and know that you'll most likely sell high.

- You can get information from the other sellers' item descriptions to include in your own, as long as that information applies to your item too.

- If the item isn't selling well, you can concentrate on another commodity and wait for the market to pick up.

In Figure 4.36, you can see the results of an Amazon Auctions closed auction search for the word "marble." It shows the number of bids on each item and the closing price. Every auction visible in the screen figure sold, and most had multiple bids. For single-item auctions, multiple bids indicate that the items sold for more than the opening bid.

E-mail Questions to Users

E-mailing a seller at the site to find out what he or she thinks about the venue might be your only way to find out how other sellers like doing business at a particular Internet auction site. This is easy if the user's e-mail address is also his or her site ID. However, not every Internet auction site will reveal a user's e-mail address. eBay and a few other sites put you in touch with users through an on-screen e-mail interface at the site.

The Web page in Figure 4.37 is where "surreal" can send "marble" a message. Surreal reached this screen by clicking on the "Ask the seller a question" link from marble's main auction listing page. Surreal can enter a message, select whether to receive a copy of the message via e-mail, and then click on the Send button (not shown). Marble will receive e-mail to the address she registered with eBay, and it will be from surreal's registered e-mail address. They can conduct any further communication via their own e-mail addresses.

Figure 4.36. Results of a closed auction search at Amazon Auctions (*auctions.amazon.com*).

Comments from Users

Contacting another seller in e-mail isn't the only option you have for finding out how users feel about a particular auction site. There are dozens, maybe hundreds, of Web-based discussion forums just for online auction independent use and e-commerce.

Online Discussion Groups

In Chapter 12, you'll read about message boards and discussion forums dedicated to sharing information about online auction experiences. If you plan to be a regular Internet auction seller, or if your company has appointed you to head its Internet auction marketing division, you'll benefit from finding an online discussion forum where you can interact

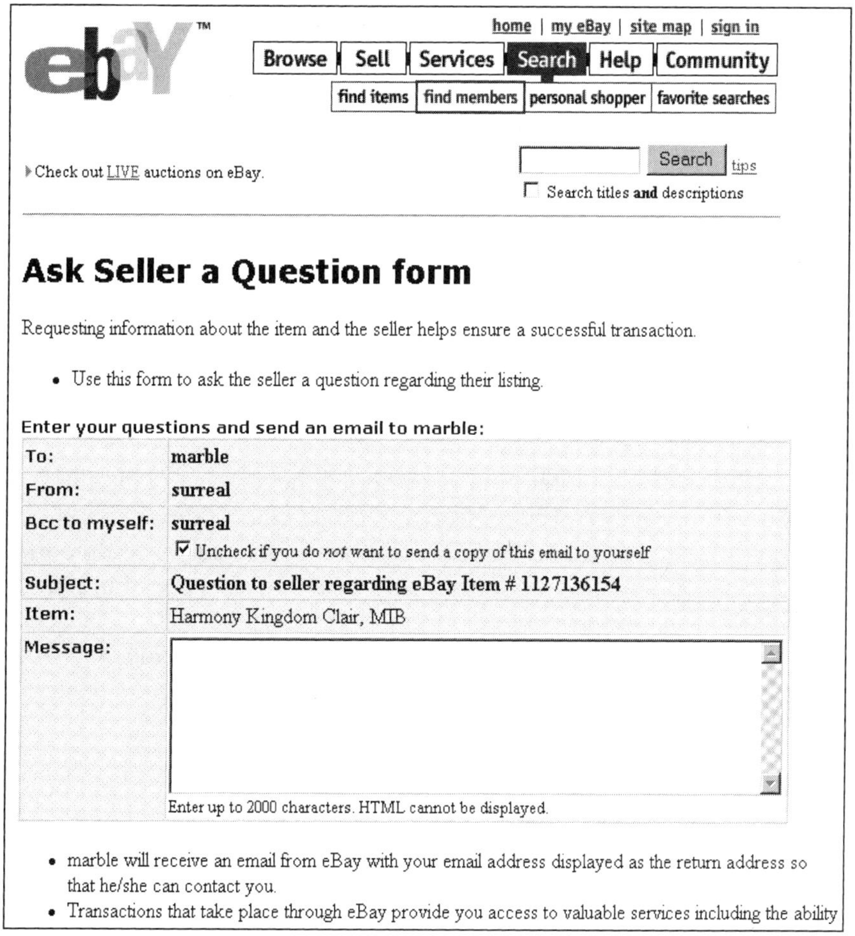

Figure 4.37. E-mail contact screen at eBay (*contact.eBay.com*).

with other auction sellers. A wealth of knowledge and experience exists in those groups.

Reading Auction Site Reviews

AuctionWatch presents monthly Internet auction site profiles written by commissioned authors. Hundreds of auction site profiles exist at the AuctionWatch site, with new ones appearing every month. You'll see profiles of auction sites that you may not have considered checking out. Access the site profiles by clicking on the "News & Information" navigation tab, and then on "Reviews." You'll find hours of interesting reading.

Further in this book, you'll read about Internet auction site e-newsletters that some auction portal and services sites offer if you subscribe at their Web site. Chapter 12 names several of them, including The Auction Guild and AuctionBytes. Both are valuable information resources that offer information about existing and fledgling online auction sites.

The Site's Overall Rating

Earlier in this chapter, you read about the Top 100 Network's auction site rating page. You can also visit Gomez *(www.gomez.com)* for Internet auction site rankings. Gomez provides a directory of online buying resources, and ranks auction sites by ease of use, types of users, customer confidence, and on-site resources.

As you can see in Figure 4.38, Gomez also provides reviews for the top-ranked Internet auction sites. The Gomez site offers plenty of information that is valuable for sellers.

How Long Has the Site Been Operating?

A site that's been operating for over a year has good Internet roots, especially if it has a good user base (plenty of registered users) and a good prove out of sales. New sites are worth a look as well, but you'll have to plant yourself in an online auction community in order to hear about them. Your favorite Internet auction portal or Auction Service Provider's site is the best place to learn about Internet auction upstarts.

Note: Be wary of any Internet auction site that has the identical look and feel of another existing site, and watch for the duplication of certain auction-management tools that you know another site developed. A site like this may be short lived due to copyright infringements.

Are the Other Sellers' Listings G-Rated?

Not too long ago, the eager new CEO of an Internet auction site upstart posted the link to his venue in a popular online auction discussion forum. I followed the link to the new site's home page and found the featured listings. I clicked on an auction title that read "Classic Photography."

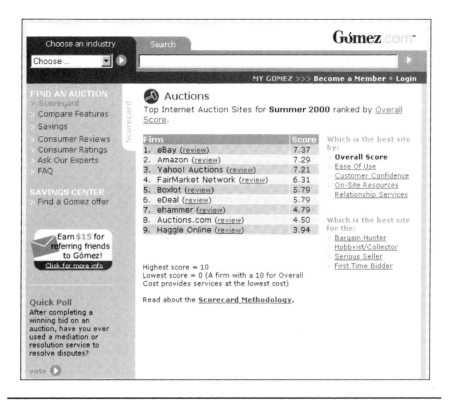

Figure 4.38. Auction site rankings at Gomez (*www.gomez.com*).

Classic indeed. The auction was for a large photograph of a naked woman in a suggestive pose. I'm glad that I wasn't viewing the site at the office, or at home with my kids nearby. I returned to the message forum right away, intent on posting a warning about the adult content. Other users had already seen it and weren't any more thrilled about it than I was. This new site, which also featured some copyrighted formats used without permission, became the subject of ridicule among veteran auction users very quickly.

While it's your business what you sell, you'd be safe to assume that your potential customers will prefer family-friendly listings unless soundly forewarned. Think about how they would react had you directed them to the site I mentioned above to purchase your products and seen your listing along with sex toys and adult videos. This is why selling at an established site—one with the kinks ironed out—is a safety net against these types of situations. It also pays to spend some time exploring a site before you list auctions there.

A Split Decision—Using More Than One Auction Site

Once you're an established Internet auction seller and operate comfortably with that selling method, you may want to pan out and list items at several different sites. Compare this to opening a new B&M store in another city. It certainly makes sense, since you'll be broadening your Internet market even wider. Membership at a B2E site will help you launch multi-site listings from one place. Before you do this, you need to feel comfortable with the Internet auction e-commerce process and have numerous successful auctions behind you. There are a few more things to consider, which you'll read about here.

Limitations

There is one standing rule that you'll see posted at most Internet auction sites. You may not list the same item at several different sites, hoping that one of them will net you a sale. This does not mean that if you have two items, you can't list one at eBay and one at Yahoo!. It means that you can't list the same item at both places if you only have one for sale.

For example, if you have a box lot of 100 pairs of shoes, you can list 50 pairs at eBay and 50 pairs at Yahoo!, or in some other combination to equal the amount of pairs you actually possess. You cannot list a Dutch auction for 100 pairs at each site. The reason for this should be obvious. You are responsible for selling any items you list for auction if the auctions close successfully. If you get successful bids for 45 pairs at one site and 75 pairs at the other, you'll have 20 unhappy customers who might make damaging complaints about your business. Unless you can produce goods for every single auction you list at every site, don't risk it. Be sure you don't overlist, so you don't oversell.

Managing Multiple Sites

It could be easy as cake and pie, or it could be a complex operation requiring dedicated personnel. It all depends on how large your business is and how "involved" your listings are. You can use auction management software to keep track, and keep your transaction records separate for each site. This would be a good case in which to rely on the auction manager tools provided by the site, since you're far less likely to confuse an auction at one site with an auction at another site.

If you're into mega-marketing on the magnitude of Sun Microsystems, hire a unique auction manager for each auction site you use. The styles and demands of listing at a site your company runs will differ from those at a C2C or B2C site. Your business will benefit from having personnel who specialize in each type of online auction listing.

Time Division

Be sure you list only the number of auctions that you or your staff can reasonably handle. Remember that for every closed auction, there's a customer (or a company) who will expect prompt service. Check out the planning tips for independent sellers included in Chapter 10. You'll find some time-management ideas that will benefit Internet auction sellers at all business levels.

Types of Auctions

All online auction sites run differently. Standard operating procedures at one site might be options at another one. Most of the major auction sites let you decide how you want your auction to run by offering you several choices of auction types. This section covers each of them in detail. First, we'll discuss one very important Internet auction goal—success.

What's a "Successful" Auction?

An auction that closed with at least one bid, or one in which at least one bid met the reserve price (if one was set), is a **successful auction**. When I use the term, it refers to an auction resulting in a transaction between the seller and a buyer.

On an Internet auction site, a transaction between the seller and high bidder takes place after the auction closes. There is one exception.

If the high bid is lower than any reserve price set by the seller, he or she is not obligated to sell the item.

There's no guarantee that every auction you list will meet your reserve price. However, if you know which types of auctions are right for the products you're selling, you have a greater chance of making a steady profit from your successful auctions.

Standard Auctions

Most online auction sites offer standard auctions. This is the bare-bones basic auction, where the seller lists an item and decides at what amount the bidding starts. The high bidder takes home the prize. There's one sale, no reserve, and no other special procedures except those typically performed by the auction site.

When the auction ends, the transaction completes off-line.

Reserve-Price Auctions

A reserve price represents the lowest price at which you're willing to sell an item that you list for auction. You can set the bidding to begin at a lower price (the minimum bid), and then set a higher reserve price. When you start the auction, only the minimum bid price is visible on the auction page. Bidders usually don't know the reserve price until the bidding reaches that amount. Some auction sites wait until the last hour of the auction to reveal if the bidding met the reserve price. Others don't reveal the high bidder's user ID until the auction meets or exceeds it.

You may be curious why sites allow reserve auctions. Since bidders don't know the reserve amount, they can place early bids in hopes of meeting it, and then others will bid too. However, since there's only one winning bidder, who cares if the auction draws many bids? The seller does. For some reason, bids attract more bids. When many people bid on the same auction, this tends to drive up the price. The seller is happy, the auction site gets a higher commission, and the high bidder has the thrill of winning.

Reserve auctions have certain drawbacks. In the fall of 1999, eBay revealed numerous complaints about reserve-price listings. Certain sellers set ridiculously high reserve prices to see what the item would bid up to, with no intention of actually selling it. To discourage this, eBay will charge an additional fee if you set a reserve price. If the high bid meets the reserve, they refund the fee. A few other Internet auction sites have since adopted this policy, although some sellers still use reserve price auctions to protect their profits.

Dutch Auctions

If you're selling large amounts of the exact same item, you'll be running Dutch auctions most frequently. It doesn't matter if you have three or 300 of them, as long as it's a multiple of the exact same item. This is thrifty; you can list multiple items and only pay one insertion fee. You'll typically pay site commission fees on every item that sells.

How Do They Work?

The seller specifies a starting bid that will apply to each unit of sale, and indicates how many items are available. Buyers have the option of bidding at or above the starting bid for as many as they care to acquire. When the auction ends, the highest bidders purchase the goods at the lowest successful bid.

It pays to bid early because the earliest successful bids win. Suppose that five of the same coffeepots are for sale at $22 each. Ten people bid $25 for one coffeepot. The first five bidders can each purchase an item since they all offered the winning amount.

If anyone bid over $25 for a coffeepot, that person would be among the winners for the item. The other four who bid $25 before any others did also would win. Each of the five coffeepots would sell for $25. If all ten bids exceeded $25, then the five items sell to the high bidders at the lowest offer.

Here's an Example

Let's say that a seller has five of the same pairs of aerobics shoes for sale and starts a Dutch auction with the minimum bid for each one at $50. At the end of the auction, the following bidding has taken place:

User	Amount of bid	Date of bid	Time of bid
TrishAloha	$51	Aug 2	12:54:06
AmandaK	$52	Aug 2	12:54:08
TuckerJH	$55	Aug 2	12:55:29
BigG	$52	Aug 3	08:03:51
BodSquad	$65	Aug 3	22:24:48

User	Amount of bid	Date of bid	Time of bid
Krafty	$90	Aug 3	23:26:06
JennyLynn20	$60	Aug 3	23:46:18
AmyMichele	$55	Aug 4	04:03:55
ArealLulu	$52	Aug 4	05:25:03
DoshJoey	$100	Aug 4	12:10:50

This auction would result in the following sales:

Winner	Amount paid
TuckerJH	$55
BodSquad	$55
JennyLynn20	$55
Krafty	$55
DoshJoey	$55

Since the low successful bid for the item was $55, each of the high bidders pays that amount for the item, even if their bids were higher.

TuckerJH and AmyMichele tied for the low bid, but since TuckerJH bid before AmyMichele, TuckerJH is one of the winners.

If the number of bids is less than the number of items offered in the Dutch auction, then only those items sell to the winning bidders. The same logic applies as shown in the example. If a bidder chooses to bid on more than one item, his or her offer must exceed the other bids in order to win the number of items included in the bid. When you list a Dutch auction, the site usually determines the winners and the winning amount for you. You'll receive this information in e-mail after the auction ends.

English Auctions

With an English auction, you don't specify the number of days that you want your auction to run. The clock starts running when your auction receives its first bid.

You'll list an English auction for a 3-day duration, just like any other item. If three days pass with no bids, the auction starts over for another three days. If after nine days no one places a bid, the listing falls out of the system. English auctions are open-ended, meaning that the auction only ends if no one has bid for twenty-four hours.

Open-Ended Auctions

Some auction sites use **open-ended auctions**, also called **dynamic-end auctions**. In these types of listings, the bidding remains open as long as bids enter. For each bid placed within a specific block of time before closing, such as in the final hour, a certain amount of time is tacked onto the end of the auction. If the auction receives another bid within that time, the listing remains active for another stretch. Dynamic auction extensions are usually five or ten minutes. Auction sites that offer this feature do so to allow sellers to get the maximum amount for their items.

Most bidders dislike dynamic-end auctions, because they can't snipe in a last minute bid. These types of auctions hamper the last-minute bargain price opportunities that some bidders hunt for. Dynamic-end auctions are not that popular with bidders; thus, they might discourage your potential customers for whom the last minute "going, going, gone" thrill is the whole appeal of online auctions.

It's optional at some sites, but at others you can't disable it. If you don't like this practice, you may wish to use an online auction site that allows auctions to end at a specific time.

Private Auctions

This type of auction is gradually appearing at more online auction sites. Until recently, I thought sellers typically used them when they thought bidders might not want their identities known to others, such as when adult material is up for sale.

Private auctions have another use—sellers want to discourage better offers made to their bidders. In Chapter 12, you'll read about bid siphoning and how it can take sales away from legitimate online auction sellers. Keeping bidder identities private prevents this type of auction site abuse. At the end of the auction, only the buyer and seller receive notification, and the bidding history is not available to anyone.

Privacy is an issue for some Internet auction users. At many auction sites, your contact information is usually available to other users. It's a risk you often take when you buy and sell online. In some cases, private auctions protect your customers from shady sellers who want to harvest their e-mail addresses for spam. Other sellers may want to undercut you. If you hide your bidders' identity, this won't happen.

Restricted-Access Auctions

Several auction sites restrict access to certain auctions. This category typically includes adult items and, at some sites, firearms. Any user with a valid credit card on file can access restricted listings. This is one way to ensure that the viewer is at least 18 years old.

If you list adult items or firearms on a site with restricted listings, only user IDs belonging to adults can view and bid on that listing. Be sure to enter the item in the appropriate category when you start the auction. If you want to see restricted auction listings, do a search for words you think would appear in such an auction. I'll forego listing examples. Some sites cancel auctions that contain such words; others don't. My advice—if you're browsing the auction listings at work or with children nearby, stay away from restricted auctions.

Fixed-Price Auctions

Instead of waiting for an auction to close that may only draw one bid, some sites let you sell the item to the first bidder. The minimum price the seller sets is actually the price he or she expects for the item and doesn't care to see if the bidding goes any higher. In this type of listing, the auction closes as soon as the first bid enters. The buyer and seller then handle the rest of the transaction off-line.

Amazon Auctions lets you offer the first bidder a 10% discount on the final sale price if he or she remains high bidder when the auction closes. eBay has its Buy it Now feature, and some sites have separate areas solely for fixed-price auctions. Overstock offers fixed-price listings, as do many other B2B or B2C sites.

Reverse Auctions

This is a new twist on the online auction process. Buyers post the price they want to pay for an item—a type of Request for Quote—and sellers bid the prices down. This makes it a buyer-driven auction and another accurate market determination. Many large corporations target reverse auction listings to sell products. Lucent Technologies is one corporation that has taken advantage of the RFQ-type of procedure. At a site called eBreviate (*www.ebreviate.com*, Figure 4.39), which is a B2B site that specializes in something called eSourcing, companies wishing to buy products from other companies can base purchasing decisions not only on price, but also on quality, delivery time, and customer service. Company representatives list what they're seeking, and suppliers "bid" on the sale to deliver the most competitive price.

Reverse auctions work well in B2B auctions by leveling the playing field for the contenders. Sites that offer reverse auctions are less common than the usual Internet auctions.

For small businesses targeting consumers, reverse auctions attract bidders who feel more in control of the transaction. If someone requests an item at a certain price and ends up paying less, who wouldn't be happy with that?

Sealed-Bid Auctions

While auctions are an efficient way to liquidate assets, not every client is an auction candidate. The sealed-bid process is a way to provide clients the opportunity to sell quickly and with a sense of urgency, while retaining control of the actual sales price. With sealed-bid auctions, your customers can only bid once and the person with the highest bid when the auction closes can buy the item for their bid price. In case of a tie, the earlier bid wins. Sealed-bid auctions are usually used when the auction accepts bids from both Internet users and those attending a live auction.

Now that you know how to select an Internet auction site, it's time to determine how your customers will pay for the goods they purchase from you.

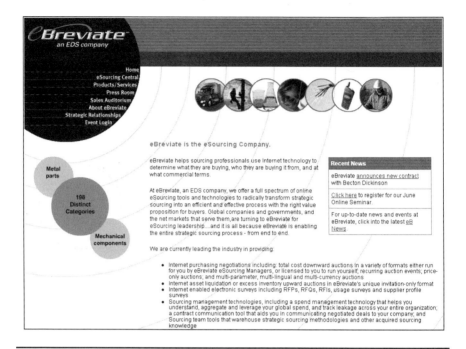

Figure 4.39. eBreviate's home page (*www.ebreviate.com*).

5

Payment, Billing, and Escrow

Step 3 of your Seven-Step Internet Auction Strategy is to identify the best billing methods for you and payment methods for your customers. Your Online Payment Service Worksheet will help you maintain an assessment of services that you research and use.

In this chapter, we'll discuss how Internet auction sellers receive payments from customers with whom the only contact is in e-mail, or occasionally by telephone. During the payment process, as the transaction comes off the Internet and into "real life," some of your customers may request that you agree to use an escrow service as an added safety layer in the transaction. Is this necessary? Here we'll discuss what you need to know to collect for the goods:

- How will your customers pay you?

- What's an online payment service, and how do you use it?

- What's the difference between an independent online payment service and one run by the auction site?

- How can you bill your customers?

- What is a third-party escrow service, and is it necessary?

- What are the benefits and drawbacks of using escrow?

- How is an escrow transaction handled, and how much does it cost?

How you handle your transactions during the payment process is crucial to building a good Internet auction practice. This chapter helps you understand your options.

What Types of Payments Should You Accept?

With Internet auction transactions, it's still common to close the sale the traditional way, where the buyer sends a check to the seller and the seller sends the item to the buyer. However, this method still poses the potential for problems and worries. Suppose the check bounces? What if the item never arrives? What happens if the item isn't what the seller promised in the auction description? Concerns such as these deter some consumers from buying anything online.

And what about auction sellers' concerns? According to Internet Fraud Statistics for January through September 2000 reported by the National Consumers League *(www.fraud.org)*, online auctions account for 79 percent of reported Internet fraud. Most of this comes from fraudulent sellers, but bogus payments account for a fair share. The table below compares fraudulent online auction payments to those occurring in general merchandise sales.

Online Auctions	General Merchandise Sales
Money Order 49%	Credit Card 27%
Check 32%	Check 25%
Cashier's Check 7%	Money Order 25%
Credit Card 7%	Cashier's Check 6%
Cash 2%	Trade 5%

From the National Consumers League
(www.fraud.org/internet/lt00stat.htm).

Several reliable methods exist for accepting payments from customers across the miles. In addition, e-business has brought with it several methods of reliable payment for goods purchased through Internet auctions. The table below ranks by volume the most common payment methods for Internet sales, including online auctions.

Jan.-Sept. 2000 Top 5 Payment Methods	
Money order	44%
Check	31%
Credit card	14%
Cashier's check	6%
Cash	2%

*From the National Consumers League
(www.fraud.org/internet/lt00stat.htm).*

These statistics don't consider two other payment methods that gained in popularity during 2000: online payment services and electronic funds transfers. We'll cover both of those in this section also.

Prepaid Checks

The buyer pays for these types of checks in advance, so there is little chance that they won't clear when you cash them unless they end up being fraudulent or stolen. Several types are available:

- **Bank check**—Most financial institutions issue checks in the amount you specify for a nominal fee. You pay for a bank check with cash or automatic account withdrawal.

- **Postal money order**—The U.S. Postal Service issues these for a small fee and cash-only payment. You can redeem them at any post office if you produce the required identification.

- **Other money orders**—Most work just like a bank check. You specify the amount of the check and pay cash for it along with a small fee. You can purchase money orders at many places: currency exchanges, grocery stores, department stores, and even convenience shops.

The National Consumers League reports money order fraud to be the top fraud involved in Internet auctions, but it also lists money order payments to represent 44 percent of Internet auction payments. This could explain the elevated percentage of reported fraud.

Personal Checks

Second to online payment services as the easiest way for a seller to shell out for his or her high bid, personal checks are iffy for many sellers. Most established businesses accept them and ship the item before verifying that the check clears. If you're a small business or an independent seller, that's not advisable. Be sure to wait until the check clears the bank before shipping the item. This takes a minimum of 10 business days. Unfortunately, it can also take longer.

Accepting personal checks makes the transaction easier for the buyer, but does hold some risk for the seller. Some sellers report finding out about bounced checks as much as 30 days after they've processed the check. On the other hand, sellers report that in the majority of cases, the checks clear and the seller usually receives the payment sooner than if the buyer must purchase a bank check or money order. It's your call whether you want to take the risks involved with accepting personal checks.

Credit Card Payments

Although most transactions paid for by personal check go off without a hitch, one way to remove a whole layer of potential problems is to encourage your customers to pay with a credit card. But can you do that? The typical independent seller isn't set up with a merchant account to accept credit card payments, but your business most likely is.

Credit card payments eliminate the hassles associated with bounced checks, and they're a boon for customers who want to buy now, pay later. Additionally, consumers who pay with credit cards have a built-in protection against fraud, should the need arise. As the seller, you're paid as soon as you can verify approval of the customer's credit card purchase. Cases of credit card fraud, such as an unsavory buyer using a stolen card, are transparent to your business. The issuing company usually handles the matter.

Note: If you accept credit card payments, bill the buyer's credit card account only when you're ready to ship the product.

Cash

Discourage people from sending cash through the mail. There's no easy way to trace it if it's lost. Some international buyers, however, may not be able to pay any other way. If you receive a cash payment through the mail, include a receipt with the shipment. Retain a copy.

Note: If you know in advance that cash is on the way, be sure your buyer knows which country's currency you're expecting. Most U.S. banks won't sing a song of sixpence, and francs won't cut the mustard.

Online Payment Services

In early 2000, Internet auction users in the United States received e-mail notification of a new service called PayPal, which offered a way to make paying for online auctions as easy as bidding. It also opened the door for independent sellers not set up with merchant accounts to accept payments from credit card users. The Internet-based application, now known as an online payment service, supported that premise.

Electronic Fund Transfers

These are normally used when funds exchange between financial institutions, such as when money from one account transfers into another. It's not advisable to give out your business (or personal) bank account information to your Internet auction buyers, but there are a few less intrusive ways for your customers to pay you with EFTs.

Western Union

You read about this company and its history in Chapter 1. They remain a reputable business today, and some folks pay for their online auction purchases with money "wired" through Western Union (see Figure 5.1). It's not common, but it's bonafide and secure.

If you wish to allow your customers to pay you via Western Union, it's a much simpler—and faster—process than it was in 1898. Your customer will send you money online, and you'll pick it up at a Western Union agent location near you.

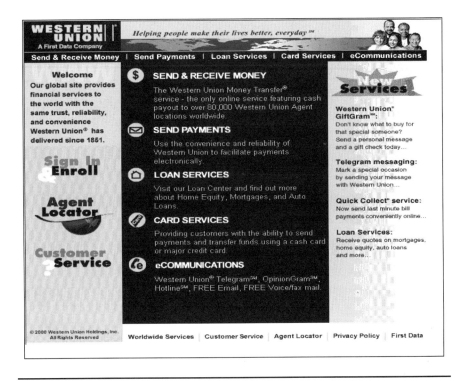

Figure 5.1. Western Union's home page (*www.westernunion.com*).

Figure 5.2 shows Western Union's MoneyZap, which is an online payment service that Internet auction users can register for and use to pay auction sellers.

Once you register, you can send, request, and receive money online. Your account, known as your Wallet, is where your MoneyZap funds exist. To get started, you need to add financial accounts to your Wallet or receive money into your MoneyZap funds. You'll access your Wallet to add, edit, or delete your financial account information. There are a few specifications:

- The accounts you enter must be with U.S.-based financial institutions.

- You can use either the MasterCard or Visa debit cards.

Figure 5.2. Western Union's MoneyZap (*www.moneyzap.com*).

- Traditional PIN-based ATM cards will not work.

The MoneyZap service supports business checking accounts. You send funds like you would with any online payment service, and the site notifies the recipient in e-mail. In order to withdraw the funds, he or she must first register a MoneyZap account.

Debit Cards

When a customer pays you with a debit card, the funds come right out of his or her bank account and transfer into a merchant account. Some merchant accounts can accept debit cards, and most online payment services accept debit cards issued by MasterCard, Visa, and several other issuing companies. The transaction is usually no different from a credit card transaction. Once the issuing company approves the debit, which is usually as fast as a credit card approval, you can proceed with processing the customer's shipment.

Independent Online Payment Services

An **online payment service** allows individuals to electronically send and receive money and request payments via the Internet, to anyone with an e-mail address. By way of an SSL server, you'll register an account with your name and address, and then enter a credit card number and/or a bank account number. You can also send funds to the online payment service via U.S. Mail to replenish your account. Then you can send funds to another user's account. The funds you send will debit from whichever account you specify. Most online payment services charge a small fee per transaction and offer special rates for business accounts. People can also send personalized electronic bills that can be paid online using the payment service.

A few Internet auction sites have online payment provisions built into the site, and there are numerous independently run online payment services as well. In this section, we'll cover a few of the most well known ones.

PayPal

Founded in December 1998 by Peter Thiel and Max Levchin, PayPal is a privately held company headquartered in Palo Alto, California. PayPal has repeatedly been named among the top Internet businesses by numerous publications and marketing services.

Considered the largest Internet based payment network, PayPal claims to have over 6 million members. Launched in November 1999, they report handling more than $7 million in sales every day. Figure 5.3 shows the screen that members see when they call up PayPal.com.

PayPal was the first well-known instant and secure online payment service. They promoted themselves by sending e-mail to registered Internet auction users, touting their free online payment service. They enticed prospective users with a $10 bonus for registering, and another $10 for each registered referral. The bonus money appeared in the user's online PayPal account. After a few months, the registration and referral bonuses lowered to $5.

PayPal now claims to constitute over 10% of all Internet traffic in the financial service category. The service is increasingly used at e-commerce sites. Your business Web site, for instance, can offer customers the option of online payments via PayPal. Their service can be used

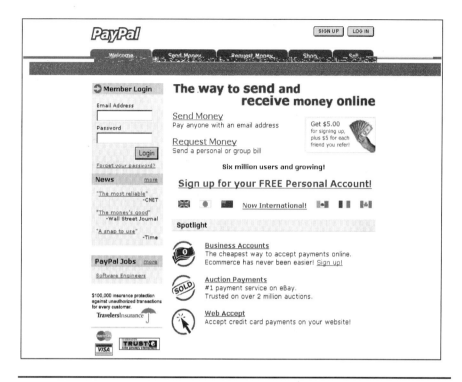

Figure 5.3. PayPal's home page and member login screen (*www.paypal.com*).

from PCs or Web-enabled mobile phones. Originally open only to users residing in the United States, PayPal eventually accepted customers who live in certain non-U.S. countries.

BidPay

BidPay has an interesting procedure. With a simple click on the Purchase Money Order button, your buyer (winning bidder) can pay for a money order online and have it sent via U.S. Mail directly to your business address. Instantaneously, both parties receive a confirmation e-mail letting them know that the order is being processed. Within 24 hours, a second e-mail arrives assuring both parties that the money order is in the mail. Figure 5.4 shows BidPay's home page.

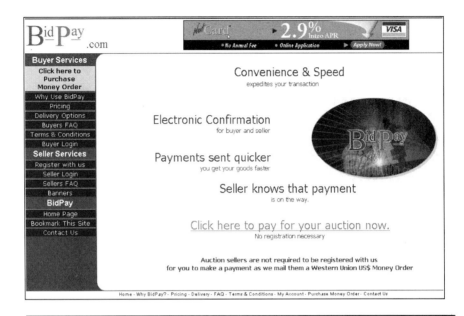

Figure 5.4. BidPay's home page and login screen (*www.bidpay.com*).

To appease online auction buyers, BidPay encourages sellers to ship goods within 24 hours of receiving payment confirmation via e-mail from BidPay. The idea is to urge sellers to ship promptly. Registration at BidPay is fast and easy. You'll enter your name, address, and user account information by way of their SSL server.

The information that you see requested in Figure 5.5 is all that's required. You won't have money on account with them, and you don't have to provide a credit card number or bank account information. When your customer transmits your payment, BidPay sends you a confirmation e-mail to let you know that you'll soon receive a Western Union money order, which you can deposit or cash as you would any money order.

Achex

Achex, Inc. *(www.achex.com)*, started out as IncuBay, L.L.C., a company formed by four entrepreneurs in January 1999. IncuBay's Managing Directors developed the concept for Achex, and chose it as their

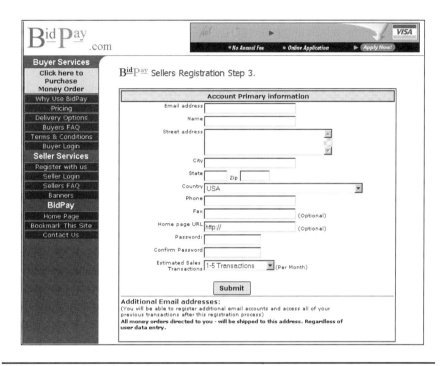

Figure 5.5. BidPay's seller registration page (*bidpay.com/ SellerRegistrationStep3.htm*).

first new venture to launch. Drawing on well-developed networks and existing relationships in the industry, the Achex cofounders recruited 15 leaders knowledgeable in essential areas of financing. The company's current advisory board is composed of payments experts, security experts, online merchants, venture capitalists, and angel investors. Figure 5.6 shows the login screen that users see when they call up the Achex home page.

Achex allows Internet payments for buyers and sellers via an SSL server. You can use your checking account, if it's active at any U.S. bank, to make payments through your Achex account.

Ecount

The online payment service called Ecount *(www.ecount.com)* presented something a little different from the others. They offer the usual fea-

Figure 5.6. Achex's home page (*www.achex.com*).

tures—the ability for any seller to accept credit card payments via their service, automatic checking account withdrawals, online billing, etc.—and another handy feature for registered users. With your very own Ecount Card, you can spend the cash in your Ecount anywhere offline and make withdrawals at ATMs. You're able to go shopping anywhere that you want on the Internet with an Ecount, and e-mail actual cash payments back and forth. Figure 5.7 shows the Ecount home page. Here's a rundown of some of its more notable features:

- Request cash from someone. You send an e-mail request for payment through Ecount, and your recipient clicks on a link and pays you.

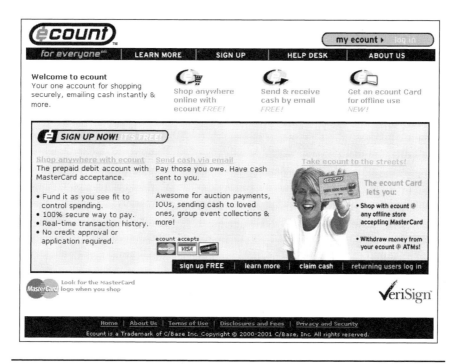

Figure 5.7. Ecount's home page (*www.ecount.com*).

- Send payments to people who don't already have Ecount. They get the payment and simply go to Ecount to claim it. After a quick sign-up process, they have access to the money.

- Set the exact date of your payment and request payment deliveries.

- Use images saying "Pay me with Ecount!" in your auction description.

Online Payment Service Fees

There's no need to publish site fees here that may go out of date by press-time. The Online Auction User's Association maintains a comparison list of online payment services, as shown in Figure 5.8.

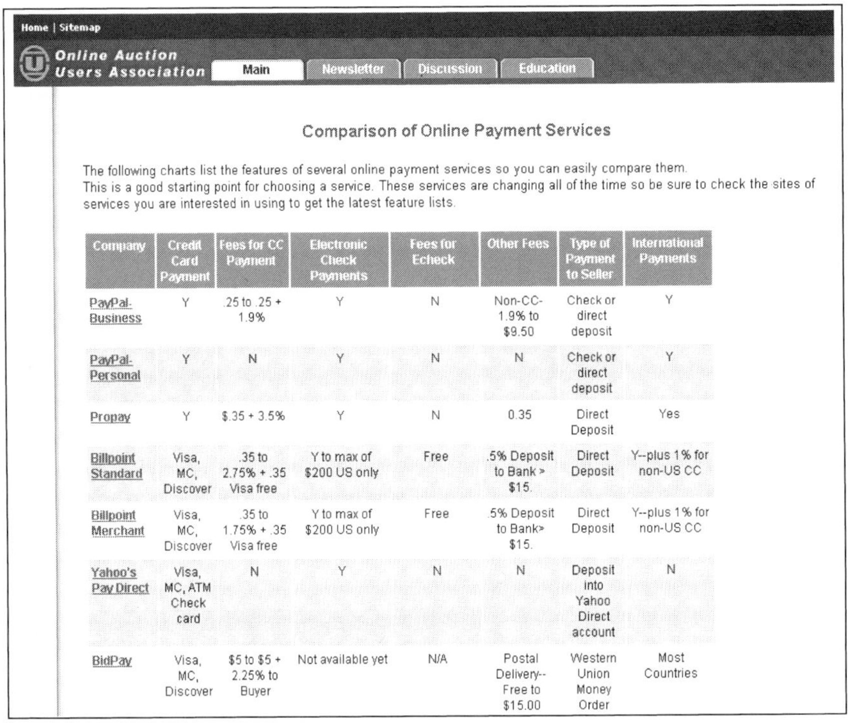

Home | Sitemap

Online Auction Users Association

Main | Newsletter | Discussion | Education

Comparison of Online Payment Services

The following charts list the features of several online payment services so you can easily compare them. This is a good starting point for choosing a service. These services are changing all of the time so be sure to check the sites of services you are interested in using to get the latest feature lists.

Company	Credit Card Payment	Fees for CC Payment	Electronic Check Payments	Fees for Echeck	Other Fees	Type of Payment to Seller	International Payments
PayPal-Business	Y	.25 to .25 + 1.9%	Y	N	Non-CC- 1.9% to $9.50	Check or direct deposit	Y
PayPal-Personal	Y	N	Y	N	N	Check or direct deposit	Y
Propay	Y	$.35 + 3.5%	Y	N	0.35	Direct Deposit	Yes
Billpoint Standard	Visa, MC, Discover	.35 to 2.75% + .35 Visa free	Y to max of $200 US only	Free	.5% Deposit to Bank > $15.	Direct Deposit	Y--plus 1% for non-US CC
Billpoint Merchant	Visa, MC, Discover	.35 to 1.75% + .35 Visa free	Y to max of $200 US only	Free	.5% Deposit to Bank> $15.	Direct Deposit	Y--plus 1% for non-US CC
Yahoo's Pay Direct	Visa, MC, ATM Check card	N	Y	N	N	Deposit into Yahoo Direct account	N
BidPay	Visa, MC, Discover	$5 to $5 + 2.25% to Buyer	Not available yet	N/A	Postal Delivery-- Free to $15.00	Western Union Money Order	Most Countries

Figure 5.8. Online Auction User's Association comparison of online payment services (*www.auctionusers.org/eval/onlinepay.shtml*).

This valuable OAUA chart is worthy of a bookmark, since it's a good starting point for choosing an online payment service for your business Internet auction transactions. The chart is updated periodically. You'll read more about the OAUA and the benefits it provides Internet auction sellers in Chapter 12.

Will Your Customers Use Online Payments?

The online payment services are relatively new. People are still getting over their apprehension of buying at Internet auctions, let alone typing their personal information (Social Security number, credit card information, and bank account numbers) into an input form on a Web site.

One stark reality is that most of the online payment services are not banks. Citibank backs a newer online payment service called c2it *(www.c2it.com)* that works very much like the other services and offers financial institution security. Many payment services, though, are privately held companies, and their accounts are not insured or covered by any government agency or system like the FDIC. Online payment services fall under the auspices of the Better Business Bureau and the Federal Trade Commission, which take seriously the issue of regulating these services. On a positive note, despite the occasional complaint, rumor, or touchy-situation story that pops up in the Internet auction discussion forums, the online payment services work very well, and thousands of folks use them every day with satisfactory results.

Auction Site Payment Services

With the resounding success of independent online payment services, many Internet auction sites leaped at the concept and developed comparable services of their own. These auction site payment services run almost the same way as PayPal or any of the independent services. The main difference is that the Internet auction site that sponsors them receives the fees. This could be one reason why some sites make registering for their payment service mandatory for sellers.

Nonetheless, they are easy to use and allow your customers to make fast, secure payments when the auction closes. Note that in most cases, you can only use the auction site payment service for transactions resulting from auctions or sales at the host site. In other words, you typically can't pay for an auction at one auction site with another auction site's online payment service.

Amazon Payments

The Amazon Auctions site offers an online payment services program called Amazon Payments. Using their service enables your customers to use the credit card they have on file with the main Amazon.com site to pay for your items. There's a small fee for sellers—25 cents per transaction plus 2.5 percent of the selling price. For Amazon Marketplace sellers, you do not pay an additional fee because it's already included in your commission rate.

Amazon Payments uses an SSL server, which means that any information you enter while using the secure server is encrypted before being transmitted. In an unprecedented business move, Amazon announced in February 2000 that Amazon Marketplace sellers are *required* to accept payment for every sale using Amazon Payments. Amazon Auctions sellers are not required to use the service but may be some time in the future.

When Amazon receives the payment from the buyer, they immediately credit your seller account for the full payment amount and debit your account for the payment fee. Once every two weeks, they'll automatically transfer any payments you received directly to your checking account. This account transfer completes within five banking days. Users in many different countries, not just the U.S., can use the service.

eBay's Billpoint

The Internet auction pioneer, eBay, also has an online payment service. Register as a Billpoint seller to accept credit cards or electronic checks online. You can access the Billpoint registration screen shown in Figure 5.9 through eBay's site map. Just enter your eBay user ID and password and then click the "Apply Now!" button.

When a buyer sends you a payment with Billpoint, they'll send you e-mail to let you know. You're paid automatically within three business days via direct deposit into a checking account that you enter when you register with Billpoint. You do not keep funds in an account as you do with a service like PayPal.

Your high bidder can pay you right after the auction closes directly from the auction listing page with the Instant Purchase link. Or you can send an eBay invoice to your high bidder or send a general invoice to any buyer with an e-mail address outside of eBay.

Yahoo! PayDirect

Yahoo! PayDirect is a service that lets you register and set up an account that you fund with your credit card or checking account (if you plan on buying as well as selling). When you sign up for Yahoo! PayDirect, you save time because you don't have to mail a check or wait for a check to arrive to complete your auction (see Figure 5.10).

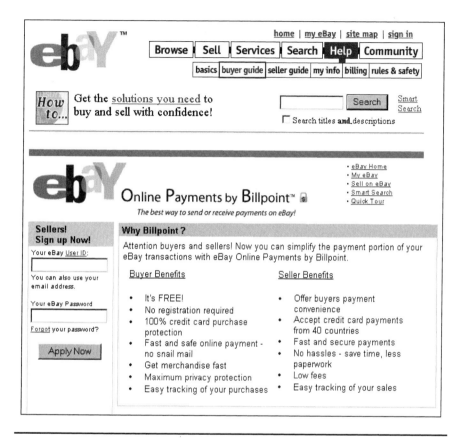

Figure 5.9. eBay's BillPoint information screen (*http://pages.ebay.com/help/ buyerguide/bp-overview.html*).

Once you have enabled Yahoo! PayDirect, every auction you submit will show that you accept Yahoo! PayDirect as a form of payment. A link to the PayDirect site and a special little icon appear on your auction listing pages.

Billing Methods

You've already read that most of the online payment services have a feature that allows you to send an online invoice, or bill, to your high

Figure 5.10. Yahoo's PayDirect information page (*auctions.yahoo.com/phtml/ auc/us/promo/paydirect.html*).

bidder. Some sites offer a feature that sends the e-mail notification automatically, with messages that you customize. You can also employ other methods of letting your customers know how and where they should direct their payments to you.

Online Billing Services

Most online payment services also have provisions for billing. PayPal lets you click on the "Request Money" link from the main login page, and you can send a request for payment to someone in e-mail. Here's the process:

- Enter your customer's e-mail address in the space provided.

- Enter the amount you request the person to send you.

- Select the transaction type: Service, goods-auction, goods-non-auction, Quasi-Cash.

- Enter a subject line for the e-mail the service sends your customer.

- Enter a message to go along with your request.

After you enter the requested information and click on "Continue," you'll see a confirmation screen with the information you specified. If you click on "Request Money," your customer will receive an invoice via e-mail containing the instructions for paying you via PayPal. Most of the online payment services have a very similar procedure for sending requests for cash to other users.

Your End-of-Auction Notice

You'll see end-of-auction (EOA) notices mentioned throughout this book. As you'll read about in Chapter 10, when using most Internet auction sites, you must contact your high bidders when the auction closes to arrange for payment. This is a fundamental step in the auction transaction. The EOA e-mail that you send can serve as your customer invoice. Here's a sample e-mail message that provides your high bidders with all the information they need in order to send you their payment. Send this right after the auction closes:

Subject: Gallon Size Terra Cotta Flowerpot—Auction #123456789

Dear (high bidder's site ID):

Thank you for being the high bidder on our Gallon Size Terra Cotta Flowerpot auction. Your high bid was $15.00, and Priority shipping is $3.50 for a total of $18.50. Please send a money order or personal check for that amount to:

Hix Communications
PO Box 54321
Auctiontown, IL 65432-0123
Phone: 630-555-6789

Please note that personal checks will delay shipping for 10 business days so the check can clear the bank. If you prefer to use PayPal, our e-mail address is OurName@email.com and our account name is HixComm. Please reply to this e-mail and let us know which payment method you will be using. Thanks for bidding on our auction!

Note: Please include the auction number with your payment.

—Nancy Hix

This message serves as your customer's bill. You'll see another sample EOA e-mail message in Chapter 8.

What's an Escrow Service?

You may occasionally encounter a buyer who asks that you complete the transaction by way of an escrow service. An **escrow service** is a third party that holds money for an online transaction until the buyer agrees to release the funds to the seller. Instead of sending the payment directly to the seller, in a typical escrow scenario the buyer sends it to the escrow service. Meanwhile, the seller ships the item to the buyer. If the buyer is satisfied with the item, he or she notifies the escrow service, which then forwards the payment to the seller. If the buyer does not wish to accept the item, he or she notifies the escrow service and then returns the item to the seller. When the seller receives it, he or she contacts the escrow service, which then returns the payment to the buyer.

That's many extra steps, and might be cumbersome for a high-volume seller. Do you feel the extra effort to put your buyer at ease is necessary? You know you're an honest seller, but should you have to prove it to everyone who wins your auctions? That's up to you to decide. Remember that the buyer gets more protection than the seller does, but since you're concerned with customer satisfaction as part of good business practice, it might be worth the effort in order to appease the buyer—especially if the transaction involves more than $100. Some auction sites that specialize in high-ticket items consider escrow a mandatory part of the transaction. Most consumer auction sites don't, but they do provide information on how to go about setting up a transaction with an escrow service.

Because of the high sales turnaround, many online escrow services cater to Internet auction users. Since it involves extra effort and a delayed payment for the seller, some are reluctant to agree to use escrow. Others agree to use escrow if the customer requests it, especially for big-ticket items where they stand to be scammed if the customer returns the item damaged.

Note: Using an escrow service is not a regular part of the auction. It's a service typically separate from the auction site, and costs extra.

Here we'll discuss the pros and cons of escrow services, when you should agree to the buyer's request to use one, and how to go about conducting the transaction with a third party involved.

How It Works

Instead of sending payment directly to the seller, the buyer sends it to the escrow service. The escrow transaction takes place via U.S. mail or a carrier the service specifies. The buyer's payment remains in an escrow account until he or she tells the service to release it to the seller. Then the service sends a check to the seller. Several online escrow services handle the transaction for a small fee. This section covers a typical escrow transaction and profiles one very popular online escrow service.

Escrow Transaction

The seller's part of the transaction runs one of two ways, depending on what the service requires:

1. The seller waits for the escrow service to indicate they received the buyer's payment. Then the seller sends the item directly to the buyer.

2. The seller sends the item to the service, which then forwards the package to the buyer after inspecting and repacking the piece. This is the typical operation of a service that provides both escrow and item authentication.

In both cases, once the buyer indicates that he or she is satisfied with the item, the escrow service drafts a check to the seller for the amount the buyer and seller agreed upon when the auction closed (minus any fees, if the seller is paying or sharing them). The buyer does not pay the seller directly.

Tradenable

Formerly iEscrow, award-winning Tradenable *(www.tradenable.com)* is based in Redwood Shores, California. Tradenable provides complete transaction services, including:

- Shipping (quoting, scheduling, tracking)

- Letter of credit

- Trade credit

- Currency exchange

- Escrow service

Tradenable's escrow service is of special interest for Internet auction sellers. Both buyers and sellers can view the status of a transaction at any time during the payment process. Tradenable provides transaction services to registered users to facilitate the purchase and sale of products or services. They don't partake in any negotiations between users unless such disputes arise directly from and relate to the performance of their services. Figure 5.11 shows the Tradenable home page.

Escrow fees are typically comparable to Internet auction site commission fees. The table below lists Tradenable's escrow fees as of June 2001, showing fees for both cash and credit card payments.

Transaction Amount	Escrow Fee (Credit)	Escrow Fee (Cash)
Up to $100.00	$2.50	$2.50
$100.01 - $25,000.00	4%	2%
$25,000.01 - $50,000.00	4%	1%
Over $50,000.00	Currently not accepted	1%

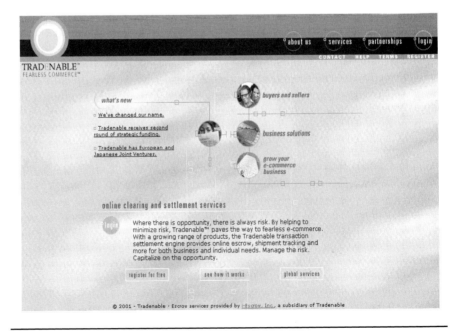

Figure 5.11.   Tradenable's home page (*www.tradenable.com*).

Who Initiates Escrow?

Typically, the buyer requests to use escrow. After both parties agree to it, the buyer contacts the escrow service and establishes an account. The service usually assigns a tracking number to the transaction that both parties must reference when sending the service anything related to the transaction, such as payment, parcels, or e-mail.

Similar to Tradenable, some services let you check the status of your transaction online.

Who's Protected?

The escrow services protect both the buyer and seller during an Internet transaction by acting as a neutral third party that handles the transaction. Here's the implied benefit:

- The buyer can inspect the item before the escrow service sends the payment to the seller.

- The seller won't have to deal with bounced checks or worry that the buyer will pull a "buy and switch" and keep the seller's good item and return an identical one that's damaged.

The escrow service holds payment until the buyer approves or declines the merchandise, or until a specified inspection period ends. The service sends payment to the seller after the buyer gives the okay, or if the inspection period expires—whichever comes first.

The buyer usually has two days to inspect the item after it arrives. This prevents the buyer from delaying payment to the seller. If the escrow service doesn't hear from the buyer within the allotted time, they send the payment to the seller and consider the transaction successfully completed.

What if the Buyer Wants a Refund?

Your customer may decide that he or she doesn't want the item after inspecting it, and must then notify the service of the intent to return the item. If this happens within the inspection interval, they will instruct your customer to pack and return it directly to you. You'll notify the escrow service when it's received in satisfactory condition. The service then sends the buyer a refund, minus the service fee. The buyer pays shipping and insurance for the returned item.

Fraudulent Payments

Bounced checks are the most common type of fraudulent payment a seller needs to worry about. An escrow service normally deposits the buyer's payment and sends you a check drawn off its business account, so you won't have to deal with an overdraft if the buyer's personal check made out to the escrow service ends up being rubber. If you encounter a service that simply forwards you the customer's personal check after holding it pending the customer's okay, then you receive no benefit from using the escrow service, only your customer's peace of mind. Be sure to find out in advance how the service drafts the payment that they send you.

Escrow services don't offer many safeguards that sellers can't do on their own, but they do add validity to the transaction.

Note: We'll cover fraud protection later in this chapter.

Don't Mention It if You'd Rather Not Use It

In their auction descriptions, sellers don't usually mention willingness to use escrow. Why should you, if your feedback record shows a history of good Internet auction business practice? Any potential customer who feels strongly about using escrow for payment should ask you about it in e-mail before bidding on your item. Escrow is not a requirement simply because the buyer wants to use it. Only auction sites that exclusively handle high-end, costly items like fine art and jewelry where closing bids are tens of thousands of dollars have mandatory escrow. Under those circumstances, I'd want to use it too—especially as the seller, to ensure that the transaction is final once I receive the payment.

One Seller's Approach to Escrow

A friend of mine sells gold and silver coins on eBay that often close at several hundred dollars. She has over a thousand positive feedbacks, but occasionally receives a buyer's request to complete the transaction by way of an escrow service. She'll agree, but warns the buyer in advance that she does not enter user feedback for escrow-assisted transactions.

"I feel that user feedback should serve as a statement of how well both the Internet auction seller and the high bidder can be trusted based on their previous transactions," says the e-mail message she sends to buyers who request to use escrow. "Since using escrow lessens the reliance on trust, I do not leave feedback for transactions carried out through it."

This is an interesting approach. As an Internet auction seller, how you handle similar requests is your option.

Who's Liable for Damage or Loss?

In most cases, the seller must insure the package on its way to the buyer and the buyer must insure the package if he or she decides to return it to the seller. The service should cover any losses incurred if the payments they send are lost or stolen before they reach the recipient. If you're considering an escrow service, ask in advance about liability. You may not find a telephone number on their Web site, so read the "fine print" carefully. Find out if the service is licensed and bonded.

The Benefits of Online Escrow

An Internet search for escrow services returns plenty of links, so it must be a successful business. That doesn't mean the service is always necessary. Let's take a closer look at who gets what out of it.

For the Seller
The seller does benefit somewhat from an escrow transaction, especially when the sale involves a hundred dollars or more. Here are a few seller benefits:

- Less chance of buyer's remorse

- No chance of unscrupulous buyer requesting a refund and then sending a different item back

- Seller does not have to hassle with bounced checks

- Seller can accept an indirect credit card payment without having a merchant account or using an online payment service

The most important benefit for the seller is knowing that once payment is received, the sale is final.

For the Buyer
The buyer benefits too, mainly from peace of mind in knowing that he or she will receive something in return for the payment. Here are a few specific benefits:

- Inspection of merchandise before payment releases to seller

- Coverage if item is lost or stolen before the customer receives it

- Assurance that the item received is the one advertised in the auction

- Ability to use a credit card for the purchase

- Hassle-free refunds if the item is unacceptable for any reason

There is a downside for buyers, however. Escrow services will accept credit card payments. So do many Internet auction sellers. Most credit card purchases ship the next day. When using an escrow service, though, there's a delay between when the escrow service receives the payment and when they notify you of it. And then, they allow you up to two days to ship the item to the buyer. Your customers end up waiting longer for the goods than if they'd deal with you directly—and they're paying for the delay.

When buyers use an escrow service, they know they'll get something in return for their money. That's a nice assurance, but your seller feedback can also attest to your good Internet auction practices.

The Down Side of Escrow

I'm not a huge fan of online escrow services for transactions involving moderately valued goods. Escrow is fine when you're buying a Swiss chalet or sinking hundreds of thousands into John Lennon's piano, but probably not when dealing in track shoes or pooping pig keychains. A typical consumer Internet auction site isn't exactly Sotheby's (although they do have their own auction site now).

Only under specific circumstances is using online escrow necessary or justified. I'd never advise an experienced seller to offer it in the text of an auction description. Nobody should ever be that desperate for bids. If you cultivate good Internet auction selling practices, no bidder should talk you into using escrow if you don't want to. In some respects, escrow services can detract from private Internet commerce. Here's why.

Why Make People Afraid of e-Commerce?

People may not realize the escrow service is a moneymaking venture— *not* a safeguard based on a history of fraudulent transactions at that site. If this were true, the auction sites wouldn't have millions of registered users and as many active listings at any given time. Scary messages won't make people comfortable with e-commerce. They hurt sellers.

Some folks come to the Internet ready and willing to get the most out of it. Others proceed cautiously, but relax after their first few successful transactions. That's exactly as it should be. Buyers should learn through their own experience that it's far better to develop their own strategies than depend on a third party for hand-holding.

Credit Card Disputes

If you own a credit card, you probably know that your credit card company will assist with merchant disputes. If you need to return the item for any reason, they will, in most cases, reverse the transaction for you. There's a slight catch when it comes to escrow services. Suppose you're the buyer and you paid the escrow service for the auction transaction with your credit card. You receive the item and it checks out fine on a cursory glance, so you give the escrow service permission to pay the seller. A week later, you realize that the product has a serious defect. You contact the seller, but he or she refuses to issue a refund. Will the escrow service cover the loss? Probably not.

Your credit card company may not be able to help you either since you purchased a *service* from the escrow provider—not the item itself. You can't dispute a service once it's been properly rendered. Even if it's not properly rendered, the credit card company may only reimburse you for the escrow service fee, not for the amount of your purchase.

At least one online escrow service I researched makes very clear their release from liability once the transaction completes, credit card purchase or not. If your customer couldn't examine the item until after the inspection period expired and then found a problem, he or she would be out of luck unless you, the seller, agreed to reverse the transaction—and you'd have the right to refuse under those circumstances.

Is Escrow Right for Your Business?

Using escrow is not mandatory, and nobody should talk you into using it if your feedback file reflects good practice. Unless you specifically state in your auction description or in your listing options that you will agree to use escrow, you can refuse.

It's not necessary if you have a merchant account for accepting credit card payments. Most experienced sellers would rather not use escrow because it adds another layer to the transaction. It's easier to receive the buyer's cleared check or money order and then ship the goods. Buyers who insist on using escrow will not be favorites among sellers. If they plan to establish a lasting relationship with you, they won't mention escrow.

When You Might Need It

A few Internet auction situations might make third-party involvement viable during the payment and shipping phase of the transaction.

- **Hidden Feedback and Warnings**—Some auction sites let you conceal your feedback. Users may do this if they don't want others to view negative comments others left for them. Suppose a bidder has hidden feedback, but you let the bid stand because you wanted the sale. In this situation, you might consider using an escrow service to handle the transaction. It's one case where a seller would request it, and pay for it.

- **Your First Sale**—If you're listing your first auction, a potential bidder doing his or her homework can read your feedback and notice that the comments you have so far all relate to you being the buyer—not the seller. If the auction bids up to an amount that the buyer isn't comfortable sending to a new seller, he or she might request that you use escrow. In this case, you have everything to gain from agreeing.

- **Big-Ticket Items**—Some items sold at Internet auctions these days can close for tens of thousands of dollars. Unless you're dealing with someone you know from past transactions, using escrow to handle the transaction isn't a bad idea at all. Just be sure to research whatever service you use to be sure you're comfortable with their method of operation. Check with others who had good results from the service.

Fraud Protection Guarantee

Some escrow services take responsibility for the item if it's lost or damaged when both parties deny responsibility. There's usually an additional fee for fraud protection—typically a percentage of the purchase price.

Here are some situations where this type of insurance would apply:

- The buyer receives eight trading cards instead of the expected 10, but the seller claims he sent 10.

- The buyer claims the piece is unsigned, but the seller insists she sent an autographed figurine.

- The buyer examines the product and then decides to return it. When the seller receives the package, the box is empty.

- The buyer returns the item. The seller receives it and finds a lesser-valued product in its place. The buyer claims to have returned the original item.

In each case, someone is lying but nobody knows whom. An escrow service that offers fraud protection will pay for the loss. Read the fine print for restrictions, fees, or limitations.

Escrow on the Web

There are many well-run escrow services in operation. Folks who use them will usually get exactly what they pay for—a third party handling their transaction. If you want to use escrow, many fine services in operation will gladly handle your business with integrity.

Several private escrow services on the Internet specialize in auction transactions. You can check these out for yourself:

- Tradenable *(www.tradenable.com)*

- Escrow.com *(www.escrow.com)*

- Safe Buyer *(www.safebuyer.com)*

- Escrow Guardian *(www.escrowguardian.com)*

Note: Research any online escrow service you plan to use to make sure you like the way it operates.

What They Expect of Buyers and Sellers
In order to operate in the best interest of both parties, the escrow service expects buyers and sellers to follow certain procedures in order to guarantee that the transaction eventually completes.

The **buyer** is responsible for a few things during an escrow transaction:

- Contacting the escrow service to initiate the transaction

- Agreeing to all terms and conditions of the escrow service

- Sending payment to the escrow service within a predetermined time

- Inspecting the item after receiving it

- Notifying the escrow service within the inspection period whether the item will be accepted or returned

- Packing and shipping the item back to the seller, if necessary

The **seller** has a few responsibilities as well:

- Shipping the item to the buyer

- Insuring the package

- Reporting the tracking number and date of dispatch to the service

- Accepting the item if the seller returns it

Typically, the seller has no margin of dispute if the buyer returns the item within the specified time.

Canceled Transactions
Some escrow services will refund your fee if the transaction is canceled before they act. Either party can usually cancel the transaction at cer-

tain times:

- Before the seller has shipped the merchandise, by a request from either the buyer or seller.

- After the seller shipped the item, and before the examination period ends, by a request from the buyer. Also by a request from the seller, but only if the buyer agrees.

The buyer usually can't cancel a transaction after the examination period ends. The service, however, can cancel under certain circumstances:

- If they don't receive payment from the buyer

- If the seller doesn't send the shipping or tracking number by the date the service specifies

- Any other reason the service feels is appropriate

Now that you're familiar with the payment options open to you and your customers, it's time to prepare your trial auctions and list them online.

6

Listing Your Auctions

To help you carry out Step 4 of your Seven-Step Internet Auction Strategy, this chapter introduces you to the elements involved in preparing an auction listing and putting it online. By the end of this chapter, you'll be open for Internet auction business and ready to let your customers know about it. Here's what we'll cover:

- Getting ready to sell

- Presenting your item for auction

- The auction title and description

- Including photographs with your auctions

- Writing your auction ad

- The importance of keeping it simple

- Starting your auction

- Using page counters to measure your traffic

- Tracking your listings

- Managing multiple auctions

- Getting in touch with your bidders

Even though you may end up using an auction service provider and auction-management tools to list and track your auctions, it's best to learn the business from the ground-up before you automate. What you'll learn in this chapter will help you generate auctions that win.

Getting Ready to Sell

With your Item Description Worksheet from Appendix C, you'll have a checklist of everything you need to know about your product before you start listing. You can keep track of what you're selling and how many of each item you have. In addition, you should be familiar with the tools you'll need to be an auction seller.

Tools of the Trade

This book assumes that you have a personal computer and ISP at your disposal, and that you're comfortable using both. It's still necessary to provide at least a rudimentary review of the hardware you'll need to access the Internet. If you're an experienced Web surfer, you can probably just skim or entirely skip this hardware review.

Hmm, they have the Internet on computers now! –Homer Simpson

Copyright © FOX Network

Computer

Unless you use and are comfortable with a system like WebTV, where you access the Internet via your television with a special keyboard, a personal computer would be a wise investment. You'll have more functionality and flexibility. Use a Pentium or something faster, and recommend the same to your customers who ask about buying your products on the Internet. Here are the minimum requirements for an auction seller's computer:

- Pentium II chip (or equivalent)

- 32 MB of RAM

- 3GB hard drive

- A modem that supports 56 Kbps

Programs
Once you have your computer up and running and you know how Windows 95 (or later) operates, familiarize yourself with these Microsoft Windows programs:

- **Notepad**—This is your practice and review area where you'll prepare and format your auction description. To call up Notepad, click on the Start button, go up to Programs, and then over to Accessories. You'll find Notepad under Accessories.

- **Browser**—You can use Internet Explorer or Netscape. They vary somewhat in format and function, but it won't make a difference when you list your auctions. It's also good to have both of them available so you can check how your customers will see your auctions with either browser.

- **Day/Time Properties**—This sets the clock. Double-click on the time of day marker at the bottom right of your Windows screen. This brings up a clock with a second hand. Set the clock to match the auction site, only in your time zone. If you want to time your auctions to start or end at a specific time, your computer clock will come in handy.

If you want to set your computer to the exact time in your time zone, access Time Ticker *(www.timeticker.com)*, which is shown in Figure 6.1. You can use a program that will set your computer clock to be within milliseconds of the exact Greenwich time.

Hardware

In addition to the software programs, your computer should come equipped with some essential hardware components.

- **Modem**—When you pick up the telephone while someone's using the computer, you'll hear some screeching, warbling noises. That's the modem. A standard dial-up modem converts digital information to analog signals (modulation), and then converts analog signals back to digital information (demodulation). Your computer produces digital information. A modem enables your computer to communicate over the telephone lines by converting digital signals from your computer into signals your telephone system recognizes. Many newer computers have built-in modems. If yours doesn't, you'll probably use a modem that's about the size of a credit card and four times the thickness.

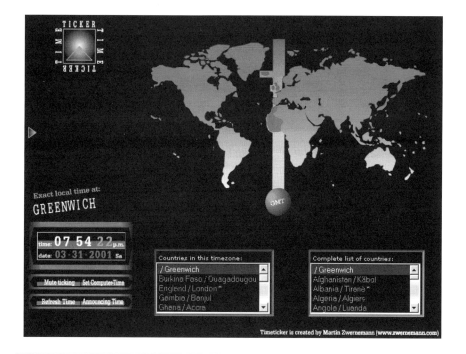

Figure 6.1. Time Ticker's home page (*www.timeticker.com*).

- **Cable Modem**—This type of modem connects your computer to the same coaxial cable used for your cable TV service. A cable connection is up to 50 times faster than dial-up but costs more. If you're interested in accessing the Internet over cable lines, check with your local cable company for information about their service.

- **Keyboard**—A keyboard is an input device for your computer. You'll use your keyboard mainly for entering text. If you want something better than the one included with your computer, you can upgrade and buy keyboards with fancy options and ergonomic key placement.

- **Mouse**—This is another input device for your computer. A mouse allows you to use graphical user interfaces for making selections. When you move your mouse arrow over one and click a button on your mouse, something happens. Moving the mouse across a flat surface controls the mouse cursor, usually shown as an arrow. You can control the speed of your mouse with the Mouse Control Program found within the Windows 95 (or later) Control Panel. Some computer mice come with separate control programs.

- **Printer**—You'll need a printer to produce your shipping notes. You can probably get an adequate color Inkjet printer for between $150 and $200, or higher if you want better resolution. If you're buying your Internet auction equipment as a package deal, be sure to include a printer in the bundle when you ask for a quote.

Imaging Tools

Further in this chapter, we'll discuss the importance of including images with your auction descriptions. Here we'll cover what you need to produce quality photographs to include with your auctions.

Digital Camera

A digital camera records photographic images in much the same way a traditional, or analog, camera does. An analog camera stores an image by using the incoming light to cause a chemical change in the camera film. A digital camera stores the incoming light in the form of a description of the image one horizontal line at a time. The lines are made up of picture elements called **pixels**. A binary number represents each pixel.

The picture file is a series of numbers representing the color of each dot. When you open the picture file in a graphics program or send it to a printer, the picture redraws one pixel at a time.

Digital cameras rank by resolution, or by how many pixels are in a typical picture. The more pixels per inch, the sharper or more realistic your pictures will be and the more lifelike they'll appear. Common resolutions for digital cameras start at 640 x 480. A better camera takes pictures at 1024 x 768. The more money you spend, the higher the resolution goes. Digital cameras with resolutions of up to 1600 x 1200 will typically sell for around $1,000. Some with resolutions of up to 3040 x 2016 sell for $3,500. Digital cameras store information in a number of ways, depending on which model you prefer.

- **Memory cards**—These devices store information in one of several formats. Smartmedia cards are small, thin, and hold up to 128 MB. Compact Flash cards are somewhat thicker and hold up to 256 MB. IBM Microdrives are small hard drives that come in sizes from 170 MB to 1 gigabyte (GB). Microdrives are made in the compact flash type II physical format. Some of the newer Sony cameras use a proprietary card called a memory stick that comes in sizes up to 64 MB. Some digital cameras will store images in non-removable memory. They're convenient because you don't have to worry about having extra cards with you. The downside is that once you take your limit of pictures, you can't take any more until you download the pictures to your PC. With this type of camera, you typically download images to your PC using either a serial cable or an infrared link.

- **Floppy disks**—You can store fewer images on a diskette than you can with internal memory, but this has one obvious advantage. As long as you have plenty of floppies, you'll never run out of space to store new pictures. The diskette is your film; you slip it into the side of the camera, then pop it out and slip it into the disk drive on your computer. From there, you can copy it to your hard drive and finish the image in a graphics program.

Scanners

A scanner captures images from regular photographs or printed matter and converts them into digital format. The most common scanner is the flatbed type, where you lay the picture face down and close a cover on it. Scanners usually come with software that lets you resize and otherwise modify the digital image. The device attaches to your computer with a cable. While you'll get the clearest images with a digital camera, you can scan photographs for your auction descriptions. You can also place items directly on the scanner for a passable image.

A Graphics Program

A graphics program is the software package that lets you alter digital images. Your digital photographs or scans probably won't be right for an online auction listing without a few modifications. The file is usually too big and you'll need to crop out the background. You'll read more about finishing your photos and image file formats further in this chapter.

To try out or select from many different graphics programs, go to Cnet's Download (download.cnet.com) and click on "Multimedia & Design." Then click on "Image Editing." As Figure 6.2 shows, you can choose from an on-screen demo, paid shareware, or freeware for many different imaging programs. You can also use the search box to find downloads for Paint Shop Pro, or another graphics program you've heard about and want to explore on your own. Paint Shop Pro is also available from your favorite software dealer.

Getting on the Internet

Once you have your computer and modem set up, you'll need a few tools for accessing the Internet auction sites. I assume you have or are about to have the services of an Internet Service Provider (ISP) that offers Web access. You can access the Internet any number of ways, depending on what kind of computer you own and how much you want to spend for your connection. Some Internet connections are split-second, while others can be agonizingly slow. Time is money on the Internet, which means the faster you connect, the more you can expect to pay for the service.

In Chapter 10, where I address Internet auction entrepreneurs who conduct their auction selling from their homes, I include a few ways to access the Internet on a limited operating budget. Here you'll read about a few other ISPs.

The Internet Fast Lane

You can access the Internet without using a phone line. The advantage of these alternate methods is that your connection speed will be fast and dependable. They may not all be available in your location or with your

Figure 6.2. Cnet's Download.com home page (*download.cnet.com*).

computer setup, and you can count on them being considerably more costly than a phone-line ISP.

Here are some of the premium ways to the Internet:

- **LAN Connection**—This connects you to the Internet at speeds of up to 100 megabits per second (Mbps) in both directions by way of a computer network. Instead of a modem and phone line, you just need a network interface card in your PC. Talk to your organization's system administrator if you need help getting Internet access.

- **Cable TV**—Many cable TV providers also offer access to the Internet. The Internet data is transmitted over the same cable that your TV programs come over. You use your own PC and a cable modem provided by the cable carrier to access the Internet. The connection is very fast and may be worth the higher price. Your cable TV provider can offer you more information.

- **ISDN**—If you want a faster connection than what's available (or possible) over regular phone lines, consider getting an Integrated Services Digital Network (ISDN) link to your ISP. You might be able to acquire an ISDN connection from your telephone company, but it's probably more costly than cable service and not as fast.

- **Satellite Connection**—Hughes Network Systems offers a service called DirecPC *(www.direcpc.com)*, which supplies 400 kilobits per second (kbps) download speed and requires a separate modem connection for uploading. The initial cost of around $300 includes an antenna and a special card installed in your PC. Monthly rates start at $29.99 per month with an ISP included, and increases depending on how many hours you spend online. In the very near future, two-way satellite Internet connections will be available that eliminate the need for a separate phone line.

- **T-1 Connection**—T-1 is a high-speed access method that connects one or more computers to the Internet. A T-1 connection operates at 1.544 Mbps. It can cost anywhere from $150 to $1,000 per month (or more).

- **ADSL Connection**—Asymmetric Digital Subscriber Line (ADSL) uses standard telephone lines and provides download speeds of up to 7 Mbps and upload speeds of up to 500 kbps. It requires a special ADSL modem on both the customer end and the ISP end. This makes it somewhat expensive. The price may drop as this system catches on throughout the country.

Internet Service Provider

Most people who have Internet access at home use one of the more common ISPs, such as AOL, Mindspring, Earthlink, or Microsoft Network. The major ISPs will send you an information packet and a start-up diskette if you call and request information about their services. Most ISPs provide unlimited usage at rates from $12 to $30 per month, depending on the plan. You'll need a dedicated line for your Internet connection so that other lines can be used for voice calls.

Almost every ISP provides you with an e-mail address and the ability to send and receive e-mail, which you'll need to operate your Internet auction venture.

Site ID and Password
In Chapter 1, you read about registering at an Internet auction site with a user ID and password. You can also register at several auction sites at the same time using a B2E auction site like AuctionWatch or GoTo, as explained in Chapter 4. When you get ready to launch your auctions, be sure you know your unique user ID and password for that particular Internet auction site.

Inventory

You'll prepare your auction title and description in this step, so take a close look at your inventory and any accompanying product information from the manufacturer. Have this nearby. Know what you're selling so you can concentrate on creating auction listings with titles and descriptions that entice bids.

Since it's best to start slowly, concentrate on one lot of goods, and be sure that it's a group of identical items. If there are any variations, you might not be able to sell that lot with one listing at some Internet auction sites. Generally, the variations that would necessitate a separate listing would be differences in form, fit, or function.

Seeing Is Believing
The best way to describe any item is to examine it in detail to learn about it. It's difficult to accurately describe an item without seeing it. Take one of the items from the lot and place it right in front of you while you prepare your auction listing. Having it physically nearby will help set the mood for writing your auction ad. If you try to describe something from memory, you risk leaving out important information about the product, or you might exaggerate some features.

Product Information
In addition to visually inspecting the item, you can get product information from several places in order to write a clear and accurate auction description:

- Manufacturer's specification sheet

- Catalog entry

- Company or manufacturer's Web site

- Order confirmation, either in e-mail or actual hard copy

Any of these might provide you with product information so you can let your customers know what they're bidding on. You can find out the part or model number, the name of the item, its dimensions, and the date of manufacture. Remember that a good item description doesn't have to be lengthy, but it should be complete.

Starting Price

Refer to Appendix C and your Pricing Worksheet to know whether you're setting your minimum bid or your fixed price, depending on what type of auction you're using. You'll need to have pricing information handy when you list your auction. Don't rely on being able to edit your listing to change the price once the auction begins. An eager buyer might place a bid as soon as you enter your auction. If you need to change the price, you'll have to cancel the buyer's bid and re-start the auction to adjust an incorrect price.

Work Space

You need an office. What's more, you deserve one. You're embarking on a product-selling venture that's going to result in record sales for you. I'm not suggesting prime office space in the World Trade Center—you just need adequate space for your computer, printer, and any hard copy or diskette-stored auction sales records. If your business has an inventory and shipping facility, then you don't need to shelve your products in your office. If you're a small business or independent auction seller, you'll need a staging area for your inventory, a way to organize it, and room for packing items for shipping.

Your Office

It helps to keep all of your auction "tools" in one place. Here's an Internet auction seller's office checklist:

- **Desk or tabletop space**—Dedicate enough surface area for your computer and printer equipment. If you're doing your own packing and shipping, you'll need room.

- **Access to your ISP**—Have a dedicated phone line or cable line in order to connect to the Internet.

- **Voice line**—You may have the occasional need to phone your business contacts, or your customers to clarify shipping or address information. You might also need to call the auction site, your auction service provider, your ISP, your online payment system, or your material suppliers.

- **Ergonomic comforts and lighting**—Be sure you have a supportive chair and footrest, and that your mouse and keyboard setup doesn't induce repetitive stress problems. Be sure the area is well lit so you can comfortably operate without eyestrain. As an aside, consider the need to get up and move around after long sessions at the computer.

- **Ventilation**—Your incense and peppermint candles might not be meaningless nouns if they prevent you from the oxygen you need to write brilliant auction descriptions. Also, airborne contaminants cause any number of health problems and they're not good for your computer equipment.

- **Hazel**—Be sure she dusts all the corners. If she's not available, be sure someone keeps your area tidy and dust-free. Not only will it keep your computer equipment operating efficiently, but also a semi-sanitary workspace will help keep you organized and ensure that you send your customers clean merchandise.

Merchandise Staging Area

Consider how you'll organize your goods if you do your own inventory management. Once you have items listed for auction, you need to keep them secure so they aren't damaged or don't mysteriously walk off before you can send them to your customers. Dedicate some space for merchandise handling and packing. Consider this your **staging area**. Here are a few important uses for it:

- Shelve your merchandise so it's easy to locate when it's time to photograph or pack it for shipping.

- Set up a mini photo studio to take your auction pictures, which you'll read more about later in this chapter.

- Store your shipping supplies, such as cartons, packing material, labels, tape, and markers, in a way that allows you easy access to them.

- Maintain accurate inventory control so you don't list more items than you have in your possession.

Your staging area can be in your office or in another location that you designate, as long as both areas can interact easily when managing auction transactions and shipping goods to your customers.

Presenting Your Item

For successful online auctions, presentation is an important spoke in the online auction success wheel. If it were a toss-up between selling your item and losing potential bids, which would *you* choose? This section will help you create attractive auction descriptions that will entice bids, and you'll read some hints and tips for putting your buyers at ease when they read your description.

How Do I List an Item?

Most Internet auction sites are self-explanatory and you'll be a pro auction lister in no time. Just be sure that you read any directions included on the auction-listing pages. A few other information resources exist in case you get stuck on any step of the listing process.

Note: Remember that an auction listing is an agreement with the auction site *and* your potential customer. You must sell any item you listed that successfully closed.

A well-run Internet auction site should have a Help page containing frequently asked questions (FAQs) to help get you through any rough spots during the auction-listing process. Some even have a help search function, where you can type in keywords pertaining to your question and then see a list of links to information sources to help answer your question.

Avoid Pre-sells

Occasionally, sellers list items they don't have in their possession. If the item sells online, they'll order or manufacture it after the auction closes. This risky practice is called a **pre-sell**. Some sellers don't call it anything, and conveniently forget to mention in their auction descriptions that they don't actually have the item in-hand. This can cause some problems.

Suppose the auction closes, payment arrives, and you find out that the item isn't available after all. You'll have to issue a refund to a disappointed buyer. You can end up with lots of justified negative feedback if you list items for auction that you can't ship right away.

Some Internet auction sites prohibit pre-sells, but eBay allows them under certain conditions. For instance, a seller must specifically state in the auction description that the item is being pre-sold, and he or she must promise to deliver the merchandise within 30 days. The 30-day period is in place in order for buyers to be covered by feedback and insurance. Any longer and the auction may drop out of the system, making any further site interaction impossible.

When's the Best Time to List?

It's important to time your sales. You probably won't get as much for the bocce ball set in the dead of winter as you will when the sunny courts are open and players are sipping mint juleps and polishing their pollinas. Sell your items when the demand is high in order to earn the best profits from them. Keep a few things in mind to get the best results:

- **Is this item seasonal?** Those sets of indoor/outdoor Christmas lights usually won't do as well in the spring as they will in late autumn.

- **What's happening this week?** List baseball items during the World Series. Use current events to your advantage.

- **How popular is the product?** If it's the hottest item on the market for holiday buying, it probably won't matter what time the auction closes, but you still want to schedule the auction to close at a reasonable time of day.

- **Don't be morbid.** Listing gag items intended to capitalize on publicized tragedies might make you a few bucks, but your image will suffer. Be sure that you don't do this inadvertently, either. Consider how any novelty items might be received in light of any current events.

How Long Should My Auction Run?

This depends on what you're selling. If you plan to sell something featured in thousands of other auctions, choose a short duration. A three-day auction quickly tickles to the top of the listings where you'll attract impulse buyers. They bid on auctions about to close. Others bid on those listings to nudge the competition out at the last minute. A seven-day auction will be too far back on the list for these folks. There's a good chance nobody will even see the listing until the last day it's running.

However, if your item is rare or unique, you'll want it exposed to the bidding pool for a longer amount of time. In that case, a seven-day auction is best.

Auction Features

Know in advance which of these attention-getting features you'll want to use to set off your auction listings. Remember that these features tend to cost extra, so be sure that what you're offering for sale is exciting enough to generate enough sales to cover the additional auction site fees.

Home Page Featured Item

When you read Chapter 4 and saw the various Internet auction site home pages included in the figures, you may have noticed that some sites feature links to certain auctions right on their home page. These auction sites typically use a rotation program that brings up listings at random for the home page. You'll usually pay an additional fee—upwards of a hundred dollars—for a home page featured listing.

In Figure 6.3, you can see some of the featured listings on ePier's home page.

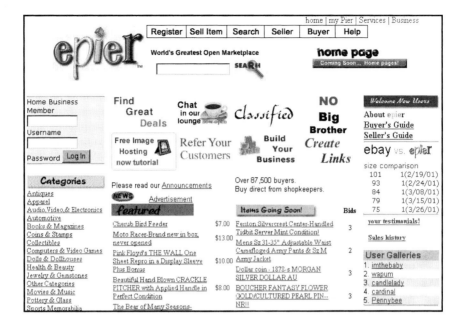

Figure 6.3. Home page featured listings visible at ePier.com (*www.epier.com*).

Category Featured Listing

For a more reasonable fee, you can opt to have your auction appear at the top of the page when a bidder does a category search (see Figure 6.4). Sometimes the category featured listings will change when you click your browser's "Reload" button because the program brings up category featured listings on a rotational basis. These are usually not as costly as home page featured listings.

Bold-Faced Title

Notice in Figure 6.4 that the category listings show up in the same type style. If you want your auctions to stand out among the rest, you can select a bold-faced title. This will show your auction title in bold-face type when it comes up in category or text searches.

In Figure 6.5, notice that one auction in the list appears in a bold typeface when compared to the others on the list. The seller paid extra for this feature. You can opt for other special features—check the auction site you're using for information about what they offer.

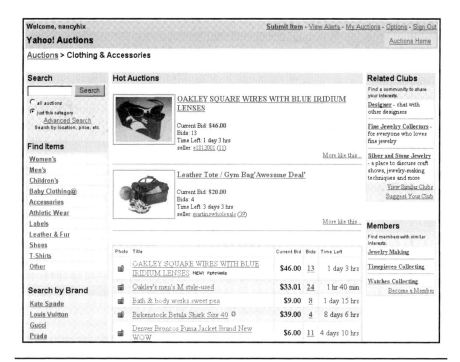

Figure 6.4. A category search at Yahoo! Auctions showing category featured listings at the top.

The Title and Description

The two most important elements of your auction listing are the auction title and the item description, or simply the **title** and the **description**. The title will help your customers find your auctions, and the description entices them to bid.

The Auction Title

On the auction-entry form of most B2C and B2B sites, the title is separate from the description area. For something with very few words, the auction title can make or break the success of your auction. It's the first thing potential bidders will see when your listing comes up in a search. From there, your potential customers will decide if they want to view your item.

Figure 6.5. A bold-faced title from a search at eBay, Inc.

Space Is an Issue
A typical title-entry line allows 40 to 45 characters, which, if you have my luck, is usually about three characters less than you need for the title you've planned. Sometimes it takes a little bit of word-maneuvering to create a good title that fits into the allotted space. When you reach the space limit, the cursor stops and won't go any farther. Figure 6.6 shows you what the title-entry line on the auction-input form might look like.

What to Include
Does your item have a particular make and style? If so, be sure you include that information in the auction title, if space permits. You definitely want to give your viewers the impression that you know what you're listing. You need to show them you're a confident, knowledgeable seller. Here's an example of a good auction title:

GardenGlad Elite Terra-Cotta 22" Flowerpot

This tells the manufacturer (GardenGlad), the style (Elite), the item's size (22 inches), and what it is (flowerpot). The more information you can squeeze into the title, the better.

Title (no HTML):	

Figure 6.6. Sample title-entry area.

➤ Note: Don't put the word "photo" in the auction title to indicate you've included one. This takes up too many characters needed for important information. Most sites put a little icon next to the listing if the seller entered the URL to an image.

Watch What You Abbreviate

Writing a good auction title is a lot like cramming a catchy phrase on a seven-character license plate. But on license plates, you can abbreviate. In your auction title, you *don't* want to abbreviate certain things, like the item name and style. If someone does an auction search for a GardenGlad Elite terra-cotta flowerpot, that's exactly what he or she will type into the search box. Search programs match characters, so this particular title won't list with the results:

GardenGlad Elt. TC flowerpot

Your GardenGlad Elite flowerpot won't get many bids if people don't know it's for sale. When in doubt, spell it out (and hope that it fits).

What You *Can* Shorten

You can abbreviate anything that isn't the brand name or style of the item. It's fine to use an ampersand (&) in place of the word "and" to free up two characters as long as the word "and" spelled out is not part of the item name.

➤ Note: Avoid using special characters like an asterisk (*), tilde (~), or quotation marks in your auction title. Some of them interfere with searches.

Writing Your Description

The item description is the most important part of your auction. This is why ASP sites that offer tools for formatting auctions are so popular.

The descriptions must read well and contain enough information to inform, educate, and entice people into bidding on the item.

Instilling Confidence

If you obviously know a lot about the product, you'll come across as a reputable seller. Consumers like to purchase items from vendors who know the product line, as long as the price is right. Here's an example of two auction descriptions. Which of these appeals to you more? They describe the same piece:

Description 1:

We're not sure who makes these clay flowerpots but they're a real pretty orange color. The rim has a flowery design that looks carved into the pot. They're huge pots that you put a big plant in.

Description 2:

These special design GardenGlad terra-cotta flowerpots were only produced for a few years. GardenGlad no longer makes pots this large. These are a deeper orange color, not commonly found in GardenGlad pots. This is the Elite model, which includes GardenGlad's bas-relief floral design around the rim of the pot. The pot is 22" in diameter and 25" tall. It holds 5 gallons. These pots are perfect for a large floor to near-ceiling plant, such as a mature schefflera or dieffenbachia. The GardenGlad logo appears on the bottom of the flowerpot. These pots are in excellent condition with no chips or cracks. This is a Dutch auction for 50 pots. Lucky high bidders pay shipping and insurance. Seller prefers payment with a money order; otherwise, item will ship after personal checks clear. If you have questions, please e-mail the seller.

Even if both included the same photograph, the seller in Description 2 obviously knows much more about the flowerpot. Description 1 left me wondering if the seller had any clue what she was selling. Will her customers be interested enough to bid?

Give Us the Facts

Offer information about your products, such as the manufacturer or crafter, and the general design and recommended use. If you're listing items that came in a lot with no manufacturer or product information available, then ask around in your circle of business contacts, make some phone calls, or surf the Web for information. Time spent now will pay off later if your auction titles come up in more searches and your explicit item descriptions entice bids.

What's So Great About It?
Tell people why they should bid on your item. Transfer plenty of information about it to your potential buyers. Entice them with descriptive phrases, as they apply to your product:

- Very limited production. You don't see many of these for sale.

- Heavy-duty fabric will last for years, and can withstand plenty of abuse.

- Here's a great item for someone seeking a true bargain.

- These ceramic mugs have classic prestige.

With persuasion like that, how will your customers be able to resist bidding on your auction?

Word It Up a Bit
Convince your buyers that they can't live without the items you're selling. It's not just yellow. It's a rich, buttery yellow. It's not just a chair. This ergonomically pleasing chair will cradle the contour of your body. And this is the notebook computer you could only dream about before, which can now be yours for an incredibly low price—in blue.

➡ **Note:** Remember when you wrote your last résumé? You didn't say you were okay for the job. You said you're an innovative self-starter who'd be an asset to any organization. Sell the item as you'd sell yourself to a company.

Provide enough information about the product to make it attractive to customers, while not crossing the line from truth to falsehood. While you need to present as much information as you can about the item, there is a difference between "wording it up" and "writing a novel." This is not the time to wax poetic.

Your Timbre and Attitude
Be friendly. Try to come across as someone easy to work with. You don't want to put people off or make them afraid of you, or they won't bid on your auctions. Combine a good, personable style of writing with

a touch of humor to put your buyers at ease. Then include all the important information into a few easy to read paragraphs.

This sample title and auction description touches on all the right stuff:

Title:

GardenGlad Elite Terra-Cotta 22" Flowerpot

Description:

These special design GardenGlad terra-cotta flowerpots were only produced for a few years. GardenGlad no longer makes pots this large. These are a deeper orange color, not commonly found in GardenGlad pots.

This is a Dutch auction for 50 of the Elite model flowerpot, which features GardenGlad's trademark bas-relief floral design around the rim of the pot as seen in the photo here. The pot is 22" in diameter and 25" tall. It holds 5 gallons. These pots are perfect for a large floor to near-ceiling plant, such as a mature schefflera or dieffenbachia. The GardenGlad logo appears on the bottom of the flowerpot (see smaller photo). These pots are in excellent condition with no chips or cracks. Lucky high bidders pay shipping and insurance. Seller prefers payment with a money order; otherwise, item will ship after personal checks clear. If you have questions, please e-mail us at seller@email.com.

Modest reserve to protect seller from site malfunction. The photo here shows a flowerpot from the actual lot up for sale in this auction.

Buyer pays shipping and insurance, seller reserves the right not to sell to anyone with excessive negative feedback. We leave positive feedback for all successful transactions. Payment with money order. Personal checks accepted if you have a 50 or higher positive feedback rating. Check out our other auctions to save on shipping. Thank you for checking out our auction!

Watch Your Spelling!

If you want the respect of your potential buyers, call the item by its proper name and spell it correctly. Always use care with your spelling and grammar. This is crucial when you list an auction, *especially* in the title. Spelling an item or company name wrong can also make you look foolish. Stay in good graces with your potential buyers and get the name right.

State Your Guarantee

Make your customers feel good about bidding. There are plenty of possibilities, as long as you're honest:

- Never used—still in original packing

- Would make an ideal gift for someone special

- Photo can't capture the beauty and color definition

- Stored in a smoke-free environment

- Starting price is well below current market value

- Item still has that new "sheen"

- Will blend with any decor

Obviously not all of these statements apply to every item you list. You'll know which ones do and I'm sure you can add a few "teasers" of your own. They'll help put your customers at ease.

Truth in Advertising

Remember that your auctions not only sell your product, but they represent your business ethics. There's a difference between eccentric, enthusiastic item descriptions and blatant lies. If you claim an item's in mint condition when it's actually flawed, that's a lie and the buyer has a right to be upset when a less-than-perfect product arrives. If the flaw is obvious, such as mismatched pockets on a pair of shorts, your deception appears intentional and you may find yourself with some very damaging negative feedback.

Be truthful about what you're selling. People are apprehensive enough about buying things on the Internet sight-unseen. Most auction sites take complaints about false item descriptions very seriously. You could lose your user ID, and your business could suffer.

State Your Terms

Just as your buyers have certain expectations of you, you'll want them to cooperate too. Include details in your auction description that prepare both you and the high bidder for the upcoming transaction.

Payment

Be clear about how you expect payment. If you mention this now, you'll have less chance of trouble later. Your terms of sale should include:

- Who pays for shipping and insurance

- How soon you expect to receive the payment before you'll relist the item

- Payment method you prefer—personal checks, money orders, or payment through an online payment service

- Length of time you hold personal checks to clear the bank

- Your return policy

Disclaimers

As a seller, watch out for your own interests. You have the right to protect yourself. In the auction description text, some sellers discourage users with excessive negative or hidden feedback from bidding. They prefer that problem users mend their ways at someone else's auction.

Note: You may be able to refuse bids from anyone you had problems with in the past. eBay and Yahoo both allow you to block certain bidders from bidding on your auctions. You'll read more about blocking bids in Chapter 12.

With a few standard disclaimers, you can protect yourself from a potentially bad situation. Here are a few examples:

- Seller reserves the right not to sell to anyone with excessive or recent negative feedback.

- Payment is due within 10 days of auction close.

- Personal checks accepted from bidders with 50 or more positive feedbacks and no negative comments.

- Seller cannot honor requests to end the auction early.

- Any items not paid for within 10 days of close of auction will be re-listed.

- Seller prefers not to work through an escrow service. Excellent feedback record should suffice.

While some bidders don't read auction descriptions all the way through, there is little they can do if you've clearly stated your terms up front.

Including Photographs in Your Auctions

Auctions with photos close higher than listings with just a text description. *Always* include a photo with your auction. Even if you're selling a common item that everyone has seen, a well-composed photo will help sell it. It might mean unpacking one item in the lot so you can get a photo, but your auction will do better if customers can see what they're buying. Even the most inane thing I ever bought on eBay, a Pooping Pig key chain, drew my attention because of the effective double photo (see Figure 6.7). There was no way the seller could have described this item accurately with just words.

Photos lend an aura of authenticity to your auction because the buyer can actually see what he or she is bidding on. In addition, it's implied proof that you actually *have* the item. People do wonder about that.

Note: It's better to include a photo you produce rather than a picture you borrowed from a Web site or a scan from a catalog page. And don't ever steal another auction seller's photo.

Image Files

Your photo must be in digital format before you can use it in your auction. The best file format for photographs is something called JPEG

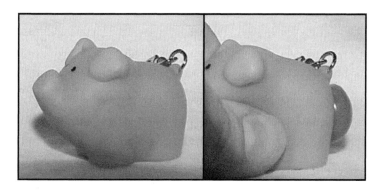

Figure 6.7. Pooping pig key chain—no justice without a photo.

(pronounced "jay-peg"). JPEG stands for Joint Photographic Experts Group. They designed the file format. A JPEG file has the extension "jpeg" or "jpg," as in *sweatsocks.jpg.*

Another common image format is GIF (pronounced "jiff"). GIF stands for Graphic Interchange Format. CompuServe developed it to establish a standard. Photographs can be GIF files, but they aren't as clear as JPEG files because the manner of compression for the image is different. GIF files, on the other hand, are far better for non-photographic images such as arrows, drawings, or animated icons. A GIF file has the three-letter extension "gif," as in *necklace.gif.*

Though other image formats exist, JPEG and GIF are the two most commonly used on the Web.

Going Digital

There are several ways to produce an image in a digital format:

- Use a digital camera.

- Scan a regular photograph.

- Place the item directly on the scanner and capture its image.

Once you have your digital image file, you'll need to put it on the Web so you can include it with your auction listing. We'll cover that further on in this chapter.

Electronic Photo Services

If you don't have a digital camera and don't plan to buy one, an electronic photo service will let you send your film in to have the images transferred to digital format. One such service is PhotoNet (*www.photonet.com*), whose home page is shown in Figure 6.8. You can also try Kodak PhotoNet Online at *www.kodak.com*.

Once the service processes and develops your film, a technician uploads the images to an Internet site that you can call up in your browser with a special password. From there you can save them to your hard drive and finish the images.

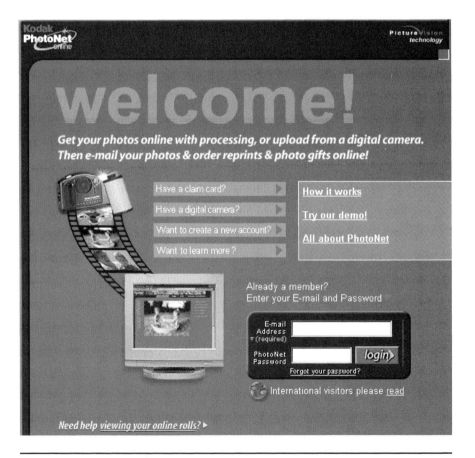

Figure 6.8. PhotoNet's home page (*www.photonet.com*).

Shooting Pictures

You don't need an elaborate studio. Find some cloth to use as a background drape, or create a seamless background with sturdy paper. Have a few different colors handy for backgrounds that will balance the colors in your products. Figure 6.9 shows a crude but functional area for producing quality Internet auction photos.

Note: The halogen lights shown in Figure 6.9 are called Ott-Lite Task Lights, from Ott-Lite Technology *(www.ott-lite.com)*.

We've used two halogen lights and a piece of thin blue tag board for the background. I clipped the paper onto a cardboard display like you'd use for a school science fair. In the finished photo, the water bottle will appear to be floating, like the sports water bottle in Figure 6.9.

Figure 6.9. Example of an amateur photograph production area. It works!

Cropping and Re-sizing the Photo

Most digital cameras produce images that are too large for auction description pages. The buyer doesn't need a poster-sized view of your cutlery sets up for auction. Resize your images so they take up no more than one-third the width of your browser. Unless it's necessary—if the item is huge, for example—less is more when it comes to an auction image. Just be sure the picture adequately portrays the item.

For photo finishing, I get the best results with Paint Shop Pro. Earlier in this chapter, I explain how you can download a copy of the program from download.cnet.com that you can preview to see if you want to purchase the program.

Once the image is on my hard drive, I can crop and resize it with minimal distortion in a few easy steps:

1. From the Paint Shop Pro File menu, select "Open."

2. Browse to the image file and double-click on it. The image will open in the Paint Shop Pro window.

3. From the tool bar on the left side of the screen, click on the crop tool. It looks like this:

4. Click inside the image and drag your cursor to draw a box around the item. Position the outline around the image by pulling the little squares with your mouse to crop out any unnecessary background.

5. Place your mouse cursor inside the crop area and double-click. Only the area you selected will remain. If you need to start over, go to the top of the Paint Shop Pro window and press the Undo button, which looks like this:

6. Once you've cropped the image, check the size. Most images taken with a digital camera should be reduced by at least 50 percent to

be practical for publication on the Web. To reduce the image, select "Resize" from the Image menu.

7. Select "Percentage of Original" and enter "50" in height and width.

8. Click on OK. Your image is now 50 percent smaller. If it's still too big, click on Undo and select a smaller percentage for reduction.

9. To save the file, go to the top of the Paint Shop Pro window and click on the Save button, which looks like this:

10. Now add a border.

Note: You can also download a helpful image re-sizing utility at *www.davecentral.com/imgcomp.html*. DaveCentral Shareware (see Figure 6.10) has many interesting shareware programs that you can explore.

Adding a Border

You don't need to have your picture surrounded by color, but it adds a nice touch and it's easy to do, so you might as well. Just be sure the border color enhances your photo and goes with the color scheme you'll use when you format your item description.

Here's how to add a border in Paint Shop Pro:

1. Open the image file in the Paint Shop Pro window.

2. At the far right side of the Paint Shop Pro window, you'll see a tool button that looks like this:

3. Click once on the lower square. A color chart will appear.

4. Click on the color you want for the image border by clicking in the colored square in the chart, and then click on "OK."

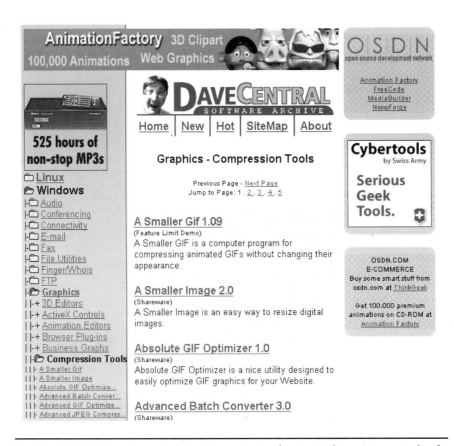

Figure 6.10. DaveCentral's home page. (*www.davecentral.com/imgcomp.html.*)

5. Select "Add Borders" from the Image menu at the top of the Paint Shop Pro window. The "Add Borders" dialog box appears.

6. If you want the border to be the same width on all sides, select "Symmetric." Then select a thickness in pixels for the border. If you don't want it to be symmetric, you can choose how thick you want the top, bottom, and sides by entering the appropriate number in the spaces provided.

7. Click on "OK." Your image now has a border.

8. Click on the Save button menu at the top of the Paint Shop Pro window. If you want an additional border, repeat the process and use a different color.

Now you're almost ready to put your photo on the Web. But first, you'll want to be sure that nobody steals your work.

Copyright Your Photo

With a swift right-click of his or her mouse button, a dishonest seller can steal your image and use it in a bogus auction. Also, another seller could use your own photo to compete with you. Don't let anyone steal your photos. Let each seller carry out the auction preparation steps. With a graphics program, insert copyright text where nobody can crop it out. Here's how you add text to a photograph in Paint Shop Pro:

1. Open the image file in the Paint Shop Pro window.

2. Go back to this tool button and click on the top square. That sets the text color.

3. You'll see the color box again. Select a color that shows up against your photograph but won't distract from the image. Light gray is usually subtle. That's a good color to use against a dark background. You may have to experiment. Click on "OK" once you've selected a text color.

4. From the tool bar on the left side of the screen, click on the text tool. It looks like this:

5. Position your mouse cursor inside the image, and left-click. This brings up the "Add Text" box.

6. At the top of the text box, you can select the font style, size, position (center, left, or right) and effects (underscore, etc.). Pick a size and style that's appropriate for your image.

7. At the bottom of the text box you'll see a field labeled "Enter text here." A standard copyright statement is the word "Copyright" and the copyright symbol (©) followed by the current year and your name. For example:

Copyright © 2001 Chris Colucci

8. Enter your copyright statement in the text area and click on "OK." The text will appear on your image.

9. Click on the Save button.

➤ **Note:** To get that copyright symbol, hold down the ALT key and type 0169 on the numeric keypad on the right side of your keyboard. Mac users, press option+g. You can also use the Microsoft Windows Character Map, which you'll read more about further on.

10. With your mouse cursor, position the text where it's readable and doesn't interfere with important details in your image. Make sure nobody can crop out the text and reuse the photo. Once you have the text where you want it, click the right mouse button and it locks in place. Figure 6.11 shows an example.

If you're satisfied with your finished picture, save it to a directory on your hard drive so you can retrieve it later when you upload your image to the Web. Just select "Save as" from the File menu.

➤ **Note:** Remember—use the "Undo" button to reverse any action you perform on the image if you don't like the results. You can undo all commands in reverse order since you last saved the file.

Scanners

There are two types of scanners. One is a specialized piece of equipment made to scan photographic slides, and the other is a flatbed scanner, which is the most popular. Flatbed scanners have three types of interfaces (the connection between the PC and the scanner).

- **Parallel port**—By far the slowest

- **Universal serial bus (USB)**—Moderate speed

- **Small computer system interface (SCSI)**—Definitely the fastest

Scanners that use the SCSI interface are fastest but also the most expensive. The USB and parallel-port models are the least expensive. All three scanners will do a good job. The main difference is in how much time you want to wait for the scanner to complete its duties. Some scanners are available with two interfaces, most often USB and parallel port.

Figure 6.11. Photograph with well-placed copyright information.

If you plan to use your scanner to capture images for use on the Web, a good middle ground is a scanner that uses the USB interface. USB is the latest innovation in the computer world and many new devices use this interface. If you don't already own a scanner and are thinking of buying one, make sure your PC has a USB port before you buy a USB scanner. Most new PCs have them.

Scanning a Picture

The basic procedure to scan a photo is the same no matter what type of scanner you have. The biggest differences come in the software that controls the scanner. I kept the procedure as generic as possible so it works with just about any scanner on the market.

Note: If you have scanner problems, refer to the manuals that came with your scanner. If you didn't receive any software manuals, refer to the Help function in your scanner software. You can also pay a visit to the scanner manufacturer's Web site, if one exists. Hewlett Packard has a great Web site at *www.hp.com*.

Here's how you'll scan a photo:

1. Open the scanner cover and place the photo face down on the glass scanner bed. Most models have rulers running across the top and down one side. Position the photo so that one of its corners is at the corner of the two rulers, if your scanner has them.

2. Carefully lower the cover while trying not to move the photo.

3. Start the scanner software if you haven't already. Select "Scan" or "Start New Scan" from the appropriate menu or button. This starts the warm-up period of the scanner lamp. When it has warmed up, you'll see it scan the entire bed of the scanner. This is the preliminary scan. Some scanners will only scan whatever you put on the glass bed of the scanner.

4. Check the software settings. You'll want to use the best setting for color photos. This happens when you adjust the resolution. For photos you'll use on the Web, limit them to around 75 dots per inch (dpi). If you go any higher, the photo will be too large.

5. Select the area you want to scan. Move the mouse cursor over the scanned image. If it turns into a crosshairs, or a plus sign, you're ready to continue. If not, look in the menus for an item such as

"Select area to be scanned." When you have the crosshairs, move the cursor to the upper left area that you want scanned.

6. Hold the left mouse button down and drag a selection area around the part you want to save.

7. Once you've selected this, click on the "Scan" button, or look for a menu item that says "Final Scan."

The device will scan the area you selected and you'll see it on your monitor. To save the image, click on the "Save Scan" button or select that option from a menu item. You'll see a dialog box where you can type a file name for the new image and select a directory in which to save the file. The scanner software usually lets you save the picture in several formats. Use JPEG for auction photographs. Once you've saved the file, you can open the photo in Paint Shop Pro and finish it.

Scanning the Item

Scanning the actual product is not very practical, especially if you're listing Shop-Vacs. However, if your product is small and somewhat flat, it does work sometimes. The procedures are the same as for scanning a photo except you won't be able to close the cover on the scanner.

When you are ready to scan the item, open the cover to the scanner and gently place it on the glass, somewhere near the top. Carefully close the scanner cover. Since you don't want the picture to appear washed out by the light leaking in from the sides, place a towel or a blanket over the scanner. Now follow the steps for scanning a photograph. You may have to experiment a few times before you get the results you want.

Image Hosting—Putting the Picture on the Web

You have to move your photo from your computer to a place where others can access it. It needs its own URL so that you can use it in your auction.

When you put a picture on the Web to use temporarily, such as for an auction, this is **image hosting**. If you have a home page on the Web, you can usually use that area as your image host, although some of the free Web hosting sites no longer allow you to host photos for auctions. If you can host photos where you have your business Web site, upload your picture to the directory in which you keep your Web page picture files, and make note of the directory path to the image. This will form the image's URL. For example:

> *http://www.yourserver.com/birdhouse.jpg*

Your Company's Server

If you're running auctions for an established business, chances are you already have a Web server on which you can host your images. If so, you can skip through the parts about finding an image host because you already have one. Be sure you talk to your systems administrator and set up a means of uploading the images you prepare for auction, and know what your unique image URLs will be.

Finding an Image Host

Most ISPs offer free Web space to their subscribers. Check with your ISP to find out how much Web space you have and how to access it. If you'd rather use an image hosting service, you'll find a table that lists many of them a little further in this chapter. Uploading images from your hard drive to your Web host is relatively easy.

Uploading Images

Image hosting sites have built-in, easy-to-use file-uploading capabilities. Figure 6.12 shows the file upload utility at Honesty.com.

You can upload five images at a time. Click the button to browse your hard drive. When you find the image file, double click on it. When you have up to five images selected, then click on "upload" and the file copies to your Web directory.

Here's what the URL to one of my image files at Honesty looks like:

> *http://images.honesty.com/imagedata/h/070/56/30750689.jpg*

Notice that with Honesty's system, there's an "Upload to" function where you can create sub-directories for your images to help you organize them.

Fee Plan for Image Hosting

Image hosting services have different rate plans depending on how many images you host and how much space they take up. Honesty, for example, charges for image hosting based on how much space you use. As an example, here's what Honesty charges to host images:

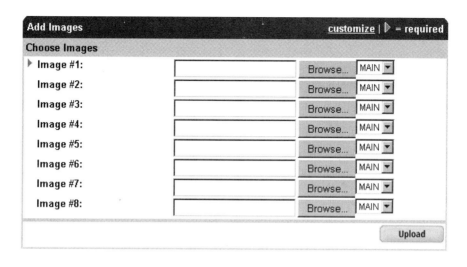

Figure 6.12. Image upload screen at *(www.honesty.com)*.

Honesty.com's Image Hosting Fee Schedule

Space:	Fee:
0-3 MB	$3.00/month—each additional MB (up to) $1.75/month
5 MB	$5.00/month—each additional MB (up to) $1.50/month
10 MB	$10.00/month—each additional MB (up to) $1.25/month
20 MB	$20.00/month—each additional MB (up to) $1.00/month
50 MB	$37.50/month—each additional MB (up to) $.75/month
100 MB	$50.00/month—each additional MB (up to) $.50/month
150 MB	$65.00/month—each additional MB (up to) $.40/month

Image Hosts on the Web

An image host stores your picture and makes it accessible to anyone using the Internet. A hosting site usually charges a small fee to host your image file. You might want to check out a few of these.

Site Name	Web Address
Photo Point	*www.photopoint.com*
Honesty	*www.honesty.com*
Images "R" Us	*www.imagesrus.net*
Picturebay Image Hosting	*www.picturebay.com*
Image Hosting at AuctionWatch	*www.auctionwatch.com*

Site Name	Web Address
ImageHosting.com	*www.imagehosting.com*
WeppiHeka	*www.weppiheka.com*
PixBay	*www.pixbay.com*
ImageHost	*www.imagehost.com*
Pongo	*www.pongo.com*
TraderJax	*www.traderjax.com*
MyItem	*www.myitem.com*
PixHost	*www.pixhost.com*
Bay-Town Action Tools	*www.bay-town.com*
Web Digger Auction Image Hosting	*www.webdigger.com*

There are many more out there. Appendix A includes information about Web sites that offer image hosting and many other Internet auction services.

Most Internet auction sites now offer an image-uploading feature. You can upload an image from your hard drive and the site hosts it for you, either as an auction service included in the listing fee or for an additional charge. Check at the auction site that you plan to use to see if they'll host your images.

Your Auction Ad

Your auction description is the advertisement for the item that you're selling. Previously in this chapter, we discussed what the ad should include. Once you have your description written, you need to decide how to format it. Most of the consumer auction sites allow you to use HTML to format your description. Some of the business sites prefer to have uniformity to their listings, so they format the description based on the text that you enter.

If you can use HTML to format your auction ad, you should. It will help make your auctions stand out from the rest.

Decide on a Method

How do you want to produce your auction description? You can create your own, or you can use an auction ad creation utility provided by some auction service providers.

Code Your Own

In Appendix B, you'll find a short HTML tutorial and one example of a coded auction description. You can create your own HTML files in Microsoft's Notepad, or another word processing program where you can save the file in plain text format.

Automated Auction Creation Tools

In Appendix A, you'll find a list of ASP sites, many of which include tools for formatting your auction descriptions. Most of the auction managers also provide auction creation assistance. When you check out the ASP sites, be sure to look into the tools they offer for helping you produce great-looking auction descriptions.

The Auction Description Field

Figure 6.13 demonstrates the area, or "field," on the auction entry form where you'll enter your HTML auction description code.

Although the text-entry area looks small, it expands to fit whatever you type there. The field doesn't get any bigger, but once your text exceeds it, a scroll bar appears at the right side. If you drag the scroll bar up and down with your mouse, you can view all your text. Figure 6.14 shows an example of the text entry form with a scroll bar.

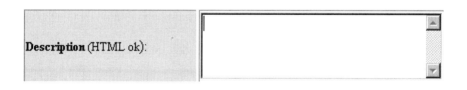

Figure 6.13. Sample auction description text entry area.

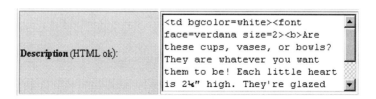

Figure 6.14. Sample auction description entry with scrolling text.

Some Internet auction sites set a character limit for the auction description field. The auction entry form will usually indicate what the limit is. If it's very limited, such as under 500 characters, you may have to settle for plain text formatting instead of HTML. However, most of the auction sites I tested didn't have a character limit for the description field. Either that or my auction description HTML text didn't exceed any limits that existed.

When you're formatting the description, choose colors, fonts, and images that go well with the photograph you include. This adds comfort and distinction to your listing that the potential bidder may not overtly notice—but will sense.

Be Professional

No matter how nicely you word your description, it won't sell your item if nobody can read it, or if nobody wants to read it. With all the auctions to choose from, you could easily deter a buyer if he or she has to work hard to read important details about your item. You need to use care in certain areas.

Don't Use ALL UPPER CASE!

Please PLEASE don't enter your auction description in all upper case. If you type that way, break the habit now. It's very hard to read. See for yourself which of the following blocks of text reads better:

> **Example 1:**
> BUYER PAYS POSTAGE AND INSURANCE, AND SELLER RESERVES THE RIGHT NOT TO SELL TO ANYONE WITH EXCESSIVE NEGATIVE FEEDBACK. PAYMENT WITH MONEY ORDER SHIPS RIGHT AWAY. PAYMENT WITH PERSONAL CHECK SHIPS AFTER 10 BUSINESS DAYS.
>
> **Example 2:**
> Buyer pays postage and insurance, and seller reserves the right not to sell to anyone with excessive negative feedback. Payment with money order or bank check ships right away. Payment with personal check ships after 10 business days.

Our eyes are used to reading standard upper- and lower-case text. You want your potential buyers to read your auction description. Make it easy on their eyes.

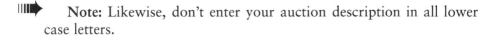 **Note:** Likewise, don't enter your auction description in all lower case letters.

The Fonts

The HTML tutorial in Appendix B shows you how to alter your text font. Be sure you use a common font that's likely to be available on everyone's PC. If not, the font will revert to plain old ordinary text.

Limit your use of gaudy typefaces. Those gothic and wedding-invitation typefaces might be more distracting than appealing:

> *Buyer pays postage and insurance. Seller reserves the right not to sell to anyone with excessive negative feedback. Payment with money order or bank check ships right away. Payment with personal check ships after 10 business days.*

If you want a serif typeface (letters with short stemming lines, as used in textbooks), don't set a font. Most browsers will default to Times New Roman, which is a serif typeface. Instead, change the size of the font or make it bold so certain essential points stand out. If you want a sans-serif typeface (letters with no stemming lines), use Arial, Helvetica, or Verdana.

If you want a whimsical typeface that's very easy on the eyes, use Comic Sans MS. I'm sure you'll recognize Comic Sans—it's that typeface that looks like the neat printing in comic book dialog balloons. Microsoft created it and it's all over the Web these days.

Diacritics

Also called accent marks, some languages require them over or through letters to indicate a variation in pronunciation, like in the word Lladró. Given the global reach of the Internet, e-commerce is rich with words that use diacritics. Use them if they're part of the item name or style.

Both Netscape and Internet Explorer recognize most diacritics, but you probably won't find them on a standard QWERTY keyboard. You can copy them from the Character Map that's included with Windows 95/98/NT. From the Start menu, select Programs, then Accessories, and then Character Map. You'll find all types of letters and symbols. You can click on the letter that has the diacritic you need, then on Select, and then on Copy. Then paste the character into Notepad where you want it to appear in your description.

Notice in Figure 6.15 that there's a character in the "Characters to copy" field. It's the letter S with the inverted circumflex diacritic called a *hacek* (pronounced HA-check), which is used in the Czech language to alter the sounds of certain letters. Over the letter s, it creates the "sh" sound. I selected the Š character by clicking on it and then on Select, which made it appear in the copy field.

Also, the bottom right corner of the Character map shows the key-strokes that will create the character that you have selected. In this case, to bring up the Š character, position your cursor in your document, hold down the ALT key, and enter 0138 on your numeric keypad.

Don't Overdo It

Annoying ads don't sell products. On any popular consumer auction site, your bidder has a lot of browsing to do. If he or she spends time reading your description, it should be because your description is interesting and informative. Don't make anyone wait too long for the page to load. The Internet has enough of its own naptimes—those days when every site you visit takes forever to load. Do what you can to speed up the page-loading process and entice viewers:

- Don't use unnecessary images, like cartoons or pictures that don't pertain to the item you're selling.

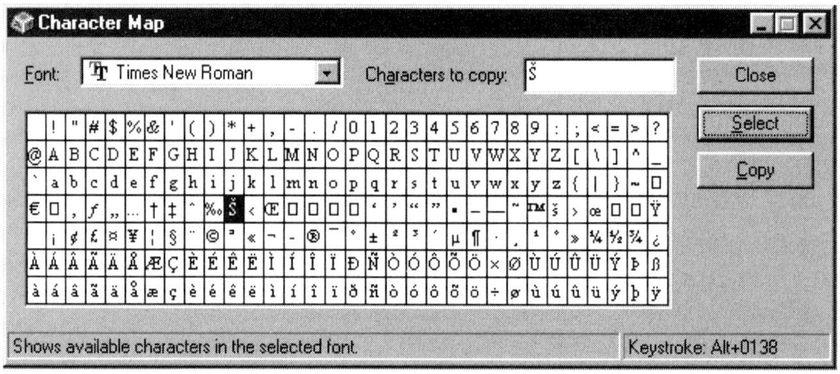

Figure 6.15. Microsoft windows character map.

- Don't use background images.

- Skip the background music entirely.

- Resize and crop your photos appropriately

The Colors

The Internet has more in common with television than it has with paper publications. You can get away with certain things in print because light shines toward it, not you. With a CRT, or cathode-ray tube like your monitor has, the light comes from behind the source right into your face. This is why long hours in front of a monitor strain your eyes more than reading a book does.

Keep this in mind when you're designing auction descriptions or any Web page. Too many different patterns and bright colors on one screen may cause people to lose interest.

Avoid Complements

Complementary colors—colors opposite each other on the spectrum—as shown in the following diagram—appear to bounce or vibrate when placed side by side. If you choose a background color for table cells in your auction description, be sure your font color doesn't complement the background. Avoid using these complementary colors side by side on any Web page:

- Red and green

- Orange and blue

- Yellow and purple

Use Good Contrast

If your background is a dark color, use beige, gray, or white text. Bold colored text works fine on light or pastel backgrounds. Avoid combining bright shades. Also, remember that light text on a dark background is usually harder to read than dark text on a light background.

Photo Too Big

One of the biggest culprits when it comes to slow page loading is a photograph that's larger than it needs to be because of excessive background. Who wants to wait for a photograph to load that's 80 percent wasted pixels? With your graphics program, trim as much as you can without disturbing the subject of the photo. As long as it's in focus and shows accurate color and detail, the photo doesn't need to be very large at all.

Photo Too Big

One of the biggest culprits when it comes to slow page loading is a photograph that's larger than it needs to be because of excessive background. Who wants to wait for a photograph to load that's 80 percent wasted pixels? With your graphics program, trim as much as you can without disturbing the subject of the photo. As long as it's in focus and shows accurate color and detail, the photo doesn't need to be very large at all.

Start Your Auction

Start your auction. List your auction. Launch your listing. They all mean the same thing—to get the auction up and running. Click on "Start" and the auction is ready to rock and roll—and draw bids from eager customers. By now you have the tools you need to present your collectible item for auction with tasteful pizzazz. Let's get that auction running!

Listing Checklist

Before you put your item up for auction, here's a rundown of what you need to do:

- Have the description completed and opened in Notepad or another plain-text word processing program.

- Choose an item category for your product from the selection.

- Know where you want to set your minimum bid.

- Have your auction image stored in a Web directory and know its URL.

- Know how to complete the auction-entry screen at the site you're using.

If the auction site has listing fees, be sure you've activated your account and have enough credit to cover them. If you have a credit card number on file or you've pre-paid your account with a check, you're all set.

The Description Text

By now you have your auction description coded in HTML and you've opened it in your browser to make sure it looks the way you expect. The text is open in Notepad and you know how to copy it into the description area. Look it over one more time:

- Is your auction title correct?

- Do you explain the item in a way that encourages bids?

- Did you spell everything correctly?

- Are your terms of sale and return policy defined?

- Is the photo positioned properly?

- Do your hyperlinks work?

- Can you read the text against the background color you're using?

- Is the text a reasonable size? Paragraphs in huge text don't read well. Only use large text for short phrases.

If everything's there, then it's time to launch your listing.

Pick a Category

Most auction sites offer category levels, especially in the varied world of collectibles. Be sure to list your item in the most specific category possible.

Here's a pared-down example based on eBay's vast category choices:

Girls' Clothing ➜	Toddlers ➜	General
	Girls ➜	Accessories
	Teens ➜	Dresses

If you're listing girls' clothing, you can select the most definitive category for your item.

Follow the Bouncing Ball

Once you're satisfied with the description, it's time to start the auction. Leave your Notepad window up so you can copy the text when you get to the description-entry area. Call up the Internet auction site in your browser and access the auction-entry screen. Enter your user ID and password wherever the site asks for them.

Most auction-entry programs are similar. Some of them contain less information and others may ask for information that isn't included here. If so, refer to the site tutorial.

Figure 6.16 shows a typical Internet auction entry screen.

The Image URL Field

The Web address, or URL, of your picture goes in the **image URL field**. When you enter a Web address there, some auction sites add that little picture icon by your listing to let folks know there's an image that goes along with the auction.

But suppose you code the description so the picture appears right in with the auction description. You don't want to repeat the same picture just to put something in the image URL field. That takes up unnecessary space on the auction-listing page. However, you need something in that field to get the little "image included" icon by your listing. People look for titles with the picture image and view those auctions first. Some folks don't even view auctions unless that little icon shows up by the title.

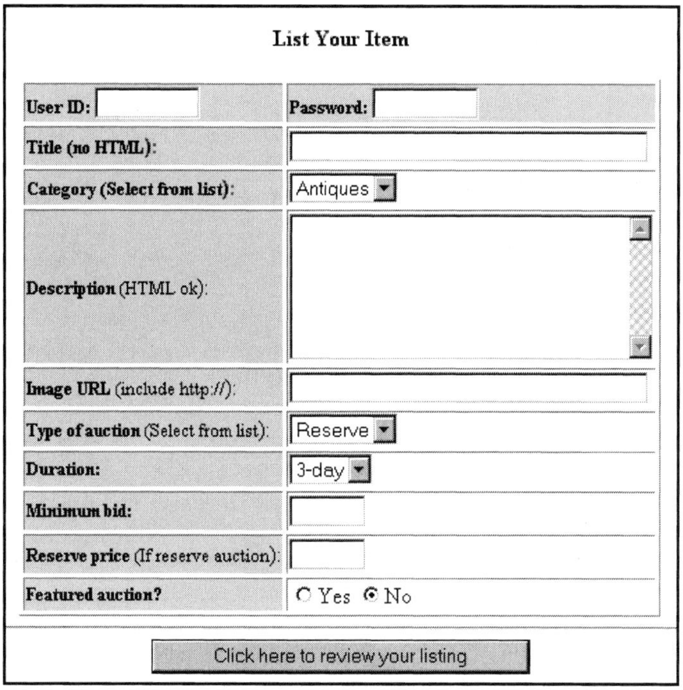

List Your Item

User ID:	**Password:**
Title (no HTML):	
Category (Select from list):	Antiques ▼
Description (HTML ok):	
Image URL (include http://):	
Type of auction (Select from list):	Reserve ▼
Duration:	3-day ▼
Minimum bid:	
Reserve price (If reserve auction):	
Featured auction?	○ Yes ⊙ No

Click here to review your listing

Figure 6.16. Typical auction entry screen.

If you don't need to add another picture to your auction, use this space to add a very small icon you grabbed from another site and copied to your directory. It can be an animated icon, a flower, a smiley-face, or whatever you want. Just make sure you have the correct URL and it's a pleasant picture. Use one that's tiny and doesn't take long to load.

Note: Some sellers use the image entry area to add those little "We take VISA" icons. If you do that, be sure your auction description contains a picture of the piece you're selling.

Here's the Step-by-Step

This is a good list to read before you actually start an auction at one of the consumer sites. It might seem like a lot of work just to list an item for auction, but it does get easier after you do it a few times.

Here are the typical steps involved in the auction-listing process:

- **Enter a title**—Try to use the name of both the item and its manu-facturer in your title. This will ensure that bidders see your auction when they do a text search. Remember—you're limited to the number of characters you can put in your title and you can't use HTML tags. Choose your words wisely.

Good Title	Not-so-Good Title
GardenGlad Elite Terra-Cotta 22" Flowerpot	Big giant flowerpots

- **Pick a category**—Highlight or use a pull-down menu to select your item's category. Since some auction sites have sub-categories, try to narrow down the category as much as possible. If your product has its own grouping, great. This will make it easier for your buyers to find your auction with a category search. If there isn't a category for your item, find something close.

- **Copy and paste your description**—Click over to your Notepad screen. From the Edit menu, click on "Select all." Go back to the Edit menu and select "Copy." Go back to your browser and click inside the box where you enter the item description. Go to the Edit menu on your browser and select "Paste." Your description will load into the text-entry area. Proofread the text after you load it into the description-entry area to ensure that everything copied over.

- **Add the picture URL**—There's usually a field for the image URL. Enter it into this space and don't forget to include http:// unless the site clearly indicates you don't need it. It might be assumed.

- **Enter the type of auction you're running**—Use Dutch auctions if you have a multiple of the same item and clearly understand how they work. There's usually no need to use a private auction unless you think your bidders would prefer to not have their identities known to other registered users at that auction site.

- **Enter the duration of the auction**—Decide how long you want the auction to run. Since most bidding happens at the end, use a three-day auction for popular items.

- **Enter your minimum bid**—The bidding starts at this amount. Start your auctions with a low minimum that's at or just above your price, or with the current selling price at auction. This attracts buyers.

- **Decide if you want any optional features**—If you want your auction to attract attention, make it featured or showcase. The additional fee appears on the auction-entry form.

- **All set?** Click the "Enter" button.

- **View the auction**—You'll usually have the option to preview your listing. Review it carefully. Does it look right? Is the title okay? Did you select the right category? Is the minimum bid correct? Did you format your description right and do your pictures show up? If not ...

- **Edit if necessary**—Hit the Back button on your browser and return to the auction-entry page if you need to correct anything. You might have to re-enter your user ID and password because some browsers erase them when you hit your Back button. When you're done, preview the auction again to be sure it's correct this time.

- **Hit the start button and let the bidding begin!**

Once you start the auction, the program usually takes you right to the auction page or to a link for it. Check it out, and see how it looks now that it's live.

Auction Hit Counters

Page counters, or hit counters, allow you to see how many times your Web page has been viewed. Several sites exist that help you add counters to your auction-listing pages. It's very helpful to be able to see how many viewers saw your auction page—even if many of the hits are from the same person—for a few reasons.

Honesty.com

Scott Samuel, Chief Community Officer of Ándale, Inc., and founder of Honesty *(www.honesty.com)*, had the idea for Internet auction-page counters (Figure 6.17) one evening when he was checking his auctions. He set up a working prototype on one of his eBay listings and then went

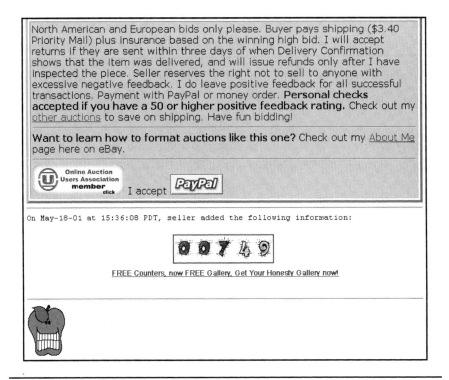

Figure 6.17. Example of an eBay auction with an appended Honesty hit counter.

to the eBay board and knew from his auction counter that users were viewing the page. He explained the counter and its use, and people asked him if they could use them, too.

Within moments, he had 20 people using the counters and within a week there were 100 users. This number grew to 300 within a few weeks. "Since this was running off one of my home PCs," Scott said, "I had to restrict registrations because we were full."

In late 1998, Scott accepted new registrations and soon had 10,000 auction sellers using his auction-page counters. Scott's friend Brian Deloria handled all the technical aspects of the endeavor in terms of the server. "Our ISP was starting to get upset since we were taking up a ton of their server capacity," Scott continued. "So, we bought another computer and brought it over there, and everything just continued to grow."

In 1999, Web advertisers approached Scott and Brian about advertising at the Honesty Web site, which then consisted of one page and a link to add a counter. Honesty.com was born. Several more developers and programmers joined the effort, working out of a small office in Grayslake, Illinois. In July 1999, USA Today listed them among the top 25 Web sites (based on traffic). In early 2000, Honesty purchased the Online Trader's Web Alliance (OTWA) and adapted the design of the auction user's message forum to match Honesty's motif.

Eventually, Ándale approached them. In June 2000, the two companies merged to became one entity. They currently employ approximately 100 people and their office is located in Mountain View, California. Over 70 percent of auctions run on eBay use Honesty counters.

Advantages of Knowing the Hits

Here I'm referring to Hits of the New Decade—auction-page hits. With a small dynamic image coded into your auction description, you can track how often your page loads in someone's browser. The image contains digits that increment with every page hit. It's important to know how many views your auction listings get for a few reasons:

- An auction with plenty of hits obviously comes up in title and category searches.

- Auctions for popular items also receive many hits. If you have more of these, plan to list them because buyers have found you.

- A low hit amount means that you may need to list the item in a different category or tweak the title a little.

For eBay auctions, you can add an Honesty counter right on the auction-entry page. If you use another type of counter or list at another site, you can add the counter once your auction is running. Honesty lets you add counters to auctions at the popular consumer sites. If you use another site, they'll provide you with cut-and-paste HTML code for a hit counter that you can add to your description. The table below includes a few sites that provide hit counters for Internet auction users.

Site Name	Web Address
Honesty	*www.honesty.com*
AuctionWatch	*www.auctionwatch.com*
Ruby Lane	*www.rubylane.com*
Digits	*www.digits.com*
BeSeen	*www.beseen.com*

Tracking Your Listings

There are many reasons to keep track of your auction listings:

- Check your listings to monitor their progress.

- Review your closed auctions to be sure the transactions completed. Did the buyer pay? Did you ship the item?

- Ensure that you left feedback for the other user.

This helps you manage your auction activity. If you're well organized and ethical in your dealings with others, it will show in your feedback ratings.

Search Your Activity

Some auction sites let you search by user ID so you can track your own activity. You can also check your billing information to see how much you paid in listing fees and site commission. You'll usually enter your site ID and password before the search retrieves that information.

Bookmarks

Both Netscape and Internet Explorer let you bookmark your favorite sites. When you find the page with your auction activity, select "Bookmarks" from the Netscape browser or "Favorites" from Internet Explorer. The browser lets you add the page URL to a list of sites you can easily return to later.

When you visit the page next time, you'll see updated information, possibly changed from the last time you saw it. At some sites, you'll search differently for bidding, selling, and feedback. Bookmark the pages with the results so you can check your auction activity.

Winning Through Volume Sales—
Managing Multiple Listings

Monitoring and managing the multiple-listing process can be time consuming and confusing, especially when you have several hundred listings running at one time. If you intend to be a successful Internet auction seller, you'll need some kind of assistance in launching and managing your listings.

Auction Service Providers

Here's where Auction Service Providers (ASPs) become not only helpful, but necessary. When the transaction progresses to the post-auction phase, which you'll read about in Chapter 9, the ASP tools can assist you in many ways. Here, we'll talk about services provided by some of the most well known and widely used ASPs.

Ándale
According to Scott Samuel, "Ándale (pronounced AHN-da-lay) is the premier auction management service, with an array of products and services geared toward all ranges of online sellers." Ándale offers these tools for volume auction sellers:

- Ad creation

- Listing tools

- Easy relists

- Live sales tracking

- Automatic e-mail

- Online checkout

- Sales organizer

- Shipping and payment tools

Figure 6.18 shows the Ándale home page.

AuctionWatch

Sellers who use AuctionWatch can market thousands of products by listing and scheduling auctions across multiple exchanges, complete the post-sale process with automated tools, and manage their customer relationships. Here are a few of the services that this popular Internet auction portal offers:

Figure 6.18. Ándale's home page (*www.andale.com*).

- Inventory management

- Bulk listing over the three major consumer Internet auction sites

- At-a-glance summaries of total inventory and item value

- Customized e-mail notification to winning bidders

- Packing slip and invoice printing

- Electronic payment acceptance

AuctionWorks
In September 1999, CEO Alec Peters created this Web-based auction management tool to allow businesses to efficiently manage inventory. Many of eBay's top sellers use AuctionWorks to manage their listings, including shooting-star user John Hannon. Figure 6.19 shows the AuctionWorks home page.

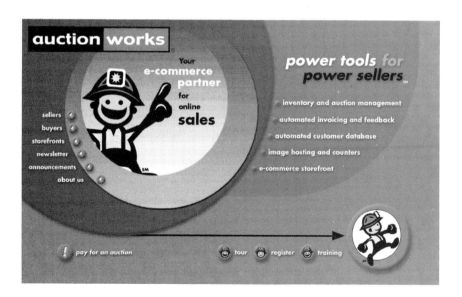

Figure 6.19.   The AuctionWorks home page (*www.auctionworks.com*).

AuctionWorks also provides image hosting for its users, including 100 MB of storage space, bulk image uploading, and an image monitor. You'll also find storefront management tools, post-sales tools, and miscellaneous services such as a newsletter, online training, and personalized support. The feature page at AuctionWorks is *huge*. It's an excellent auction-management site for high-volume sellers.

Large Businesses and Sophisticated Uploading

Sun Microsystems uses a sophisticated method of managing its Internet auction inventory. With an HTML-compatible program called XML, inventory data stored on a mainframe system can be uploaded and converted to HTML. This inventory management system saves the considerable time and expense that would be involved in converting incompatible data into compatible formats.

Now What?

Now that your auction is running, you need to think about how you'll get the word out to your market that your products are on the auction block. The next chapter will help you promote your auctions.

7

Promoting Your Online Auction Listings

To help you carry out Step 5 of your Seven-Step Internet Auction Strategy, this chapter will give you some ideas about how to promote your auctions. You'll find the information necessary to complete your Promotional Plan Worksheet in Appendix C.

As you know, more visits to your auctions means a better chance that your products will sell. Naturally, you want to do whatever you can to attract as many viewers as possible. While your products are actively listed, you can do several things to promote them.

Besides the extra frills that the auction site offers, such as listings in bold-face text, highlighted item lines, featured listings, and little gift icons, there are other tactics you can use to attract views. Some of these promotion methods will help you reach potential customers who may not be a regular visitor of your chosen Internet auction venue. With a few well-placed icons and hyperlinks, you can lure them there.

Here we'll discuss why it's vital to your success to promote your auction listings, and what facilities exist to make sure your auctions get as many views as possible:

- Why promote your auctions?

- Your business Web site

- Links to your auctions

- Auction sellers' online malls

- E-mail lists

- Banner ads

- Product-promotion sites

- Affiliate programs

- Paid advertising

- Free plugs on the Internet

Being online can be better for your business than many other mediums. These promotion tips, tools, techniques, and resources will help spark your customers' interest in your new way of doing business.

Reaching Your Customers via the Internet

The Internet has changed the way we do our jobs, conduct research, communicate, and get information. People turn to the Internet to complete their most important tasks, such as filing income taxes, paying bills, and grocery shopping. Some of your customers spend so much time online that it's obviously an excellent place to advertise. Large and small businesses alike are aware of this. The Internet is already a multi-billion dollar advertising industry, and you can accomplish a great deal without shelling out a fortune.

Getting Your Brick & Mortar Customers Online

Are all of your customers online? No, of course not. Maybe some or even most of your existing customers are, but certainly not all of your potential ones. Some people are still apprehensive about using computers. When you start chatting about "being online" and speaking with unbridled excitement about your new online auction venture, be prepared for some of your customers—or colleagues even—to wave off the whole idea of using a computer to buy and sell stuff. You may have an even harder time convincing certain computer-phobic people to register at an Internet auction site and bid on something. Some folks still hope this whole Internet thing goes away and leaves them alone. However, you can assuage these fears and possibly make Internet e-believers out of them with a few sneaky sales maneuvers.

If They Aren't Online by Now...
With the right incentive, they could be very soon. According to the U.S Department of Commerce's *The Emerging Digital Economy*, some 100 million people worldwide (including 62 million Americans) are online. Every 100 days, Internet traffic doubles. If your customers haven't gotten the Web bug yet, it's not too late for you to talk them into "going cyber." You might have a wooden cross or clove of garlic shoved in your face, but it's worth a try, and it's likely to be profitable.

Yack It Up in Person
Visitors to your Brick & Mortar store are great prospects. When you're writing out receipts or waiting for a Visa approval, toss around some chatter about your exciting new Internet auction venture. Get your customers interested in the concept of bargain shopping in their pajamas. With a graceful *pliét*, kick up your foot and show them the new shoes you got for a steal at Overstock.com and comment on how quickly they arrived at your house—only two days after you placed the order online. Let your excitement show.

Have a Computer Available
Even if your customers' initial reaction is a loud guffaw, any reaction short of them turning heel and bolting out of your store is an open door for you to invite them over to your computer to see what all the fuss is about. Some of them will recoil from the device, and some might opt to watch you work it from a comfortable distance, but it's worth a try. Can you get people excited about Internet auctions by showing them how they work? Probably. After all, someone got you excited about it, right?

Let Them Know It's Secure
They've all heard the horror stories about how all of your neighbors can see your bra size right there on the Internet once you type it into

your computer. You're bound to hear some of these urban legends when you encourage your customers to shop with you on the Internet. Try not to laugh, but do let them know that the stories are made up and silly. If you encounter customers who are afraid that their credit card numbers will end up on washroom walls, have Chapter 1 of this book handy and show them the section on Secured Sites. Explain SSL encryption protocol and show them the icons of the lock in both positions. Then point out where they should look for it in their browsers.

If people express worry about entering personal information over an SSL server, taste the wine before they drink it by telling them that you had to enter a valid credit card number to be a seller and with all you have at stake, you still trust it.

Do Your Customers Know About Internet Auctions?

"Internet auctions—everybody's doing it" may seem like the slogan *du joir*, but it's not true. Yes, millions of people visit Internet auctions. But no, not all of your customers do. If you want to turn them all into regular visitors to your listings, it's up to you to show them the way.

Make Sure They Know
Create some brochures or post cards with instructions for accessing any auction sites you're using, and include your site ID so that customers can locate your auctions. Write a systematic guide for using the site, in simple terms (see the sample in Figure 7.1). Be sure that each customer who visits your Brick & Mortar shop receives a copy with a purchase. Save the instructions in plain text format so that you can send them to other customers in e-mail.

Demonstrate How Auctions Work
Once you've successfully coaxed your customers to your store computer, sit them down, call up your favorite Internet auction site, and show them your auction listings. Demonstrate how to access an auction site on the Internet. Walk your customers through the site's registration process, even if it means setting them up with a Web-based e-mail address to get them started. Explain how a search function works, and then point out the different parts of an online auction listing—one of yours.

Then show them how to bid. With any luck, they'll be caught up in the excitement and you'll make yourself an Internet auction customer.

We've Docked at ePier!
GardenGlad Products Now at Online Auctions!

www.epier.com

Shop with us online! Now you can purchase our products from the privacy of your own homes, and get in on the excitement of Internet auction bidding!

GREAT VALUES!

Here's how to access our ePier online auctions:

1. Connect to the Internet from your home, school, library, or place of business.
2. Call up **http://www.epier.com** in your Internet browser. This brings up the ePier home page!
3. Click on "Register" from the navigation links at the top of the ePier home page.
4. Complete the online form and then click on the "REGISTER" button.
5. Click on "Search" from the top row of navigation links, and then click on "By Seller" from the main search page.
6. In the "Username or E-mail" field, enter "GardenGlad" and click on the "Search" button.
7. View our Internet auctions — and bid for some great deals!

Questions? Call 630-555-1234 or e-mail us@gardenglad.com.

Figure 7.1.   Sample Internet auction promo and site guide handout.

If they leave your store as the high bidder on an item, they'll most likely be compelled to want to check up on the auctions on their own.

Do Your Customers Know Which Auction Site You're Using?

While eBay might be the Internet auction giant, a business site might better suit your marketing plan, or you might use one in tandem with eBay. This is especially true if you list surplus or overstock items at a site like XSLots or B2Bstreet, or if you list auctions at a B2E multiple listing site. Let your customers know where your auctions are.

Business Cards and Flyers

Printed advertisements for Web sites are okay if the URL is short, because the customer must type it exactly into the address line on their browser in order to reach the correct page. Yahoo Auctions gives you a moderately short URL for your auction listings, as shown below:

user.auctions.yahoo.com/user/nancyhix

Anyone with good to moderate typing ability can handle copying that into a browser. At an Internet auction site such as eBay, though, the URL is a lot longer and has special characters that result from CGI and other programs that create the search results. Below is a typical URL to a seller's auction page at eBay:

*http://cgi6.ebay.com/awcgie/BayISAPI.dll?MfcISAPICommand
=ViewListedItems&userid=marble*

This is quite a handful to type. It might not even fit on one line of your printed matter, leaving your customers confused as to whether they need to enter a return through half of it. An easier way to lead customers to your auctions by way of print media is to include the site's home page URL, which is usually short, and then your seller ID. If you don't have enough room for the level of detail shown in Figure 7.1, include only the information they need to find your auctions. For example:

Visit our auctions at eBay (*www.eBay.com*). Search for auctions listed by "marble."

Auction URLs in Your E-mail
If you send e-mail newsletters to customers, always include the URLs to your auction listings for any site you regularly use. You don't have to wait until you have auctions running. Encourage them to bookmark your listing pages with the incentive of special offers from time to time.

Your e-mail messages can also include instructions like the ones shown in Figure 7.1. (page 272). Customers who have Web-enabled e-mail can click on the links you provide. Others will need to copy and paste the link into the address line of their browsers.

Use the Auction Site's Personal Web Page Feature
As you read about previously, many auction sites allow you to create a personal page to which you can direct their customers. eBay calls it an

"AboutMe" page, and SellYourItem calls it "My page." Both sites make them available to any registered user. You can select from several different formats that you can tweak with HTML, and you can specify the information that you want to include. Here are some of the benefits of having a personal page at an Internet auction site:

- You can design your page to include your active listings and most current feedback comments.

- Your customers will see only *your* listings.

- It's a great way to let your customers read a brief description about your merchandise.

- You can link to it from your business Web page or any other place on the Web.

Some business sites offer storefronts also, where you can display your listings with thumbnail images alongside your product descriptions.

Promoting Your Auctions on Your Business Web Site

This section will help you let your customers know that you've opened a new branch of your business at the Internet auction sites and you're receptive to answering any questions they may have in e-mail—you're just a click away! With a few tweaks to your business Web site, you'll have your customers visiting your online "Internet auction center" with ease and confidence.

Your Contact Information

Be sure that your customers have a way to get in touch with you if they want to ask questions about your online auction selling. Some of the auction sites will only give out your contact information to the high successful bidder on a recently closed auction. At other sites, it's a two- or three-step process before the person finally reaches a screen where they can type in a message to you. This arrangement sometimes deters potential customers from asking you questions about your auctioned items. It's better to allow potential customers a way to contact you outside of the Internet auction site boundaries if they have product questions.

In Appendix B, you'll learn how to make your e-mail address an e-mail hyperlink with some simple HTML code. Since most Web surfers have access to e-mail, you don't need to include a telephone number if you're not comfortable with that. An e-mail address will suffice.

Your Web Site as Your Internet Auction Advertiser

Some of the promotion tips in this chapter will lead customers to your business Web site, which will take them to your auctions. This is why it's important to include a link to your auctions in a prominent place on your Web pages. Each hit to your Web site means a possible visit to your exciting new sales.

Promote the Online Auction Industry
Don't be shy about adding a plug for the OAI. After all, it's your new selling medium, so you might as well do whatever you can to get your customers excited about it. Include links to pages where they can become familiar with Internet auctions, such as auction portals or auction-site directories. Once you have your customers eager and enthusiastic about the OAI, direct them to your auctions.

Note: Be sure that these sites open in a new browser, so you don't lose your viewers.

Links to Your Auctions
Place them prominently where your visitors will see them. As you can probably guess, the top of the page is the best place, as long as the link is unobtrusive. Set it off to one side so it doesn't dominate the page, while at the same time it invites your customers to your auction listings.

A plain-text hyperlink will work, but it might not stand out very well. You can use the icons that some auction sites provide. eBay offers you a "Shop eBay With Me" icon and will give you the HTML code to make it a link right to your eBay seller page (Figure 7.2).

With a graphics program, you can create your own Internet auctions icon that will take your visitors right to your listings at whatever auction site you're using.

If you keep the link icon generic enough, you can use it to direct your customers to any auction site you use (Figure 7.3). Just change the URL in your hyperlink HTML code to the correct auction site URL.

Hyperlinks

You need to master at least two essential HTML techniques. One is how to add an image to a Web page with the <IMG SRC> tag, which you'll learn in Appendix B. The other is how to create **hypertext**. When you pass your mouse cursor over certain text on a Web page, the arrow turns into a little hand, letting you know that if you click a button on

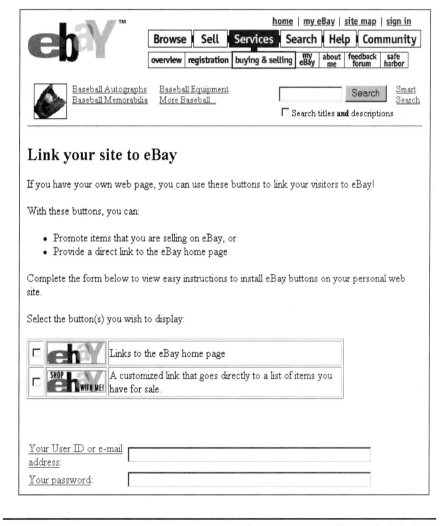

Figure 7.2. Link your site to eBay (*pages.ebay.com/services/buyandsell/link-buttons.html*).

Figure 7.3.   Sample "Visit Our Auctions" link icon for your business Web site.

your mouse, a new page appears in your browser. This special text is called hypertext, and it functions as a **hyperlink** to another Web page specified in the HTML code. Appendix B includes instructions for creating hyperlinks.

Direct Your External Links to a New Browser

If you include links to Web sites that are external to yours (in other words, pages that are not part of your site) make sure that the link opens in a new browser, leaving the current browser (with your Web site in it) undisturbed. You can have multiple applications of Internet Explorer or Netscape open at one time, and view different Web pages in each one. You can create hyperlinks that will open the linked page in a new browser window. For HTML coding instructions, see Appendix B.

People generally like it when links open in new browsers because it cuts down on loading time if they want to go back to the original page. Plus, having two browsers open means that your customers can keep track of your auctions while they do other surfing.

Promoting Your Web Site

First, read *101 Ways To Promote Your Web Site* by Susan Sweeney, C. A. (Maximum Press, 2000). Sweeney stresses the importance of attracting potential customers to your business Web site using numerous tips, tools, and techniques. The book targets entrepreneurs, corporate marketing managers, small-business owners, and many others who use the Web for marketing. It's an excellent resource to increase traffic to your business Web site.

Help Search Engines Find You by Using <META> Tags

Search engines direct the lion's share of Web traffic. Most Internet surfers will eventually use search engines to find Web sites, so it's important to make sure that the search "bots" find you. If you place well in search results, your site (and therefore your auctions) will receive plenty of visits.

One way to help get your site indexed is by use of the <META> tag in your HTML code. You can read more about the <META> tag and its use in your favorite HTML reference guide, and you'll see the HTML coding technique in Appendix B.

Note: Including <META> tags doesn't guarantee that search engines will index your site, but it will boost your chances.

Make the Search Engines Find You

Most search engines provide an online submission form to add your Web site to their search engine or directory. They usually ask you to fill in several form fields for your site including the URL, title, description, and keywords. There are several online resources where you can submit your Web site to many search engines at once. Some are free, and others charge a fee:

- Search Engine Registration: *www.siteadd.com*

- Add Me: *www.addme.com*

- Submit Plus: *submitplus.bc.ca*

- Malaysia Web Hosting: *www.hileytech.com/freesub.html*

Offer Incentives for Repeat Business

You have to give your customers a reason to visit your site regularly. A special discount to your online customers goes a long way to get them to respond to what you are offering. It also makes them come back again in the future for other special discounts and offers.

Advertising Doesn't Have to Be Costly

Carol Angelo, who markets inspirational and spiritual items through her Internet-based business called Angel Lights *(www.angelights.com)*, creates an advertising novelty that businesses operating on a fledgling budget can easily produce. Since most of Carol's customers are private consumers, she advertises her Web site where she knows they go several times a day—to the refrigerator.

"I bought a large pack of magnets and business card stock from Office Max, and created my own business cards with a special PC program," she said. "The magnets are business card size, with a peel-off label on one side that exposes a very strong adhesive. You place a business card on the sticky side and you have a refrigerator magnet to enclose with your customers' shipments."

Strategic Placement of Links to Your Auctions

In addition to your business Web site, there are many other places on the Web where you can insert links that will help increase traffic to your Internet auctions. Here we'll discuss where to put links within your auction description, and ways to arrange reciprocal links with other Web site owners.

Within Your Auction Descriptions

Always include a link to your other auctions within your auction descriptions. Bidders can save on shipping charges if they buy several items from you at the same time. You'll also sell more stuff.

Note: When you include a link to your auctions within an auction description, make sure the link takes visitors only to auctions on the same site. Many sites have restrictions for that.

Reciprocal Links

The whole point of the World Wide Web is "webbing" pages together so everyone's connected in some way. Links should be a reciprocal process, where you include a link to other sites in return for a link to your Web page. It's a little tough to agree to link to your competition, but you can always link to other business pages that only slightly cross markets with you. You specifically want links to your auction listings, but if the best you can get is a link to your business Web site, that will do.

Check out *www.virtualpromote.com*. This tutorial site covers how to promote traffic to your Web site with reciprocal links. It's a free service for all Web-site developers who want to learn more about announcing and increasing the visits to their Web pages. Once you get potential customers to your Web site, your Internet auctions are just a click away.

Auction Sellers' Online Malls

In Chapter 4, you read about the B2C Merchants Square Internet Malls at XSLots. These organized groupings of Internet auction listings are excellent opportunities to promote your auctions. You don't need to hunt for an established Internet mall, however. You can always start one up yourself as part of your business venture, like one particular group of independent Internet auction sellers. They coupled an idea with some Web-design talent and cooked up one of the first Internet auction malls for independent sellers.

SoupGirl

Several OAUA members thought it would be useful if all of their online auction listings could be linked from one site. It would be like an Internet auction exchange, but for private sellers.

"We're sellers, but we're also buyers. If we had one site where everyone could display their auction wares, we could browse each other's listings as if we were at a private mall," says Serenity Long, a veteran Internet auction user and professional Web-site and auction-description designer. OAUA member Gail Hotchkiss was in the midst of working on such a site, and Leon Herr was underway in developing a Merchant Plaza for OTWA.

"He had the same idea I did in a more straightforward approach without the 'SoupGirl' gimmick part," says Gail. "We decided to merge the duplicate parts of the two sites, and combined our efforts to create SoupGirl.com. (Figure 7.4). I wanted a way to feature the different sellers and give everyone a chance to showcase their items." This brainstorm gave birth to the Auction Seller's Online Mall.

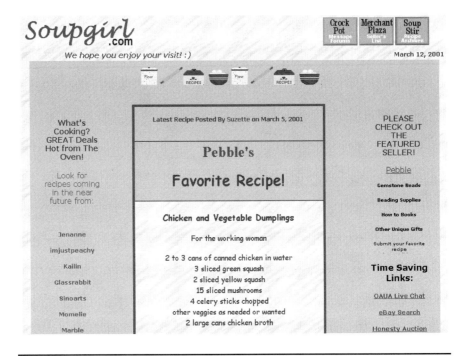

Figure 7.4.   SoupGirl.com, one of the first independent auction sellers' online malls (*www.soupgirl.com*).

"I hope we can pull more and more sellers into the group," says Gail, "and I will be thrilled the day I see people post in the auction forums saying 'I made a sale because someone saw my name as the featured seller on SoupGirl.com.'"

SoupGirl featured sellers change every week or so. The requirement is to have a reciprocal link from your Web page (or auction descriptions) to the SoupGirl.com site.

PayPal Shops

PayPal collaborated with Ándale to help you build an online storefront that's accessible to PayPal's multi-million registered-user network. Deanne Summer, an Amazon Auctions seller, says "I like anything that's free and brings customers. They offer the use of Humanclick, which is a free program that lets you chat in real time with customers at the site." She made a sale within the first week that she set up her PayPal shop.

The PayPal Shops area serves as a directory. The merchants listed on PayPal Shops operate independently from PayPal, and PayPal does not endorse any merchant or assume responsibility for transactions conducted with them. That aside, this is marvelous exposure for your products and auctions.

E-Mail Lists

If you know your customers' e-mail addresses, you can send one message to all of them with a single effort. Creating a group of e-mail addresses in order to keep your customers apprised of your business promotions is known as building an **e-mail list** (also called an **e-mail alias**).

If you predict that you'll receive more e-mail than one person or even a small staff can handle, then you may want to research the possibility of using **mailbot autoresponders** or **listservers**. An autoresponder will automatically send an e-mail response to anyone who sends e-mail to a certain address. A listserver is slightly more sophisticated, in that it responds to a specific request. For example, if you advertise a listserver address such as information@gardenglad.com, the listserver can send a newsletter to anyone who sent e-mail to this address. The newsletter might contain instructions on how folks can subscribe. Once they do, they're added to another mailing list that systematically sends out the newsletter.

You can employ some sophisticated e-mail marketing systems for your large business needs. *Marketing on the Internet* by Jan Zimmerman (Maximum Press, 2001) contains valuable information on using mailbots and listservers to handle large volumes of e-mail.

Marketing via e-mail is widely practiced these days, often with great results. The object is to encourage your customers to sign up as subscribers for your business e-mail, so you know that they're willing to receive commercial e-mail messages. It's important to distinguish between e-mail—messages you send with your computer to someone at another computer—and what's now called snail mail, or letters sent through the traditional post-office or mail-carrier channels. Both are important marketing channels, and we'll discuss how the two forms of communication should differ.

How Can You Build E-mail Lists?

Anyone who willingly lets you include their e-mail address in your e-mail list is a **subscriber customer**. They have given you permission to send them updates and news about your business. You can create e-mail lists in numerous ways, from simple hand building to list-building services that you can purchase.

Note: Be sure to provide a way for your customers to unsubscribe from your mailing list.

Starting Out

For a small-to-midsize business, a few channels exist for creating e-mail lists without the help of special programs or services:

- Have your Brick & Mortar customers write their e-mail address in a store guest book that's by your checkout counter.

- Include e-mail addresses of current and previous online customers.

- Save addresses of your Internet auction high bidders.

- Have your business Web site developer include a field where customers can indicate if they want to be on your mailing list for promotions.

Once you have your e-mail list, learn how to send e-mail to numerous addresses at once, depending on how your e-mail service provider works. Then compose your message, and send it.

Sophisticated E-mail List Marketing

Several e-mail list channels exist for businesses that need a much wider circulation than manageable by hand-built e-mail lists. You can subscribe to online public mailing lists, or you can build e-mail lists with the help of your ISP. You can subscribe to numerous mailing lists and make use of e-mail management tools on the Internet.

Site Name	Web Address
Liszt	*www.liszt.com*
List Universe	*www.list-universe.com*
List-Advertising	*list-advertising.com*
Lyris E-mail List Hosting	*www.lyris.com*

Before you send advertising e-mail to a mailing list at any of these sites, however, read carefully the terms and conditions of the service, and study any FAQs. Posting an unsolicited ad can get your toenails torn out—or so says Liszt. Know the community before you throw caution (or your tender feet) to the wind. You can use a subscriber mailing list to network and build clientele in private e-mail, or in mailing groups that don't have restrictions for business advertising. Also, make wise use of your e-mail signature file if you contribute e-mail to a subscriber list.

One very handy online e-mail list service is List-Advertising (*list-advertising.com*). They're a digest-only moderated discussion list for e-mail list advertisers. You'll find all kinds of valuable e-mail list advertising opportunities when you visit their site.

Your ISP may offer facilities for establishing e-mail lists. Expect to pay an initial fee and a monthly service charge to keep the list current. You can find more information at your ISP's home Web page.

What Should Your E-mail Include?

Business e-mail messages should not be as detailed or lengthy as your snail mail advertising letters. Learn how to translate your sales pitch into the lighter, briefer messages that comprise today's e-mail. Here are a few tips for your message content:

- **Be original**—Don't make this promotion sound just like your last one, or like an ad run by another marketer.

- **Take some risks**—Advertising should be bold, so aim for the creative high. Use trendy, catchy phrases without being corny or trite.

- **Forget business writing**—This isn't the time for formal openings and salutations. E-mail is a friendlier form of business communication, so take advantage of it.

- **Keep it light and simple**—Save the details for your business Web page, which your e-mail should always include a link to.

The following sidebar is an example of an e-mail message announcing your Internet auction venture. You can customize it to fit your business. Notice the links to your Internet auctions. Two other

Dear Valued Customers:

Win with us! We're thrilled to give you the new, exciting option of purchasing our products at a few well-known Internet auction sites. Enjoy several advantages of being our winning online bidders:

- Buy our products at a huge discount.

- Shop from the privacy of your own home.

- Browse our auction listings for the most current product information.

- Save money!

   Now you can use that exciting new venue that everyone's talking about, and get in on the fun. All you have to do is register at the auction sites—it's free! Then you can bid to your heart's content. Visit our auctions by clicking on the following links:

- Our Auctions at Yahoo

- Our Auctions at eBay

- Our Auctions at XSLots

important components of your e-mail messages are the subject line, and what comes last.

Your E-mail Subject Line

Just like the auction title, your e-mail subject line is the first thing your customers will see when they receive your message. With the rivers of junk e-mail cascading into the average user's electronic inbox, there is a growing tendency to just delete messages without opening them. According to Forrester Research, the average response for e-mail advertising is around 3.5 percent. If you want a better average, here are a few tips for your subject line:

- Avoid subject lines like "Hey, how are ya?" when the contents of the message is an introduction to your online auction venture. A subject line such as "Check us out at SellYourItem.com!" is truthful and well intended and won't invoke a grimace of disgust when your customer opens the e-mail.

- Avoid using characters or symbols in your subject line. They're annoying and, depending on your customer's ISP, they may translate into another kind of character. If you're excited about your Internet auctions, convey that in the text of your message—not by overusing exclamation marks, asterisks, and tildes in your e-mail subject line.

- If you're offering your customers an incentive, such as purchase points or a sweepstakes, it's perfectly all right to mention this in the subject line of your e-mail, as long as it's truthful. Incentives are wonderful ways to promote your business.

It's great to be original and take some risks, but do that in the content of your e-mail message. An outstanding promotion is based on something memorable. You can surprise, shock, delight, or awe your customers with your Internet auction campaign. Just don't tick them off with misleading or annoying e-mail subject lines.

Your E-mail Signature File

A signature file, or **sig file,** is one to six lines of text you create that automatically append to your e-mail message by way of an option accessed through your e-mail program. The sig file is a very powerful marketing tool. It's free advertising. Here's what you can pack into those extra lines of text:

- Your name and company

- The URL to your business Web site

- The URL to your Internet auctions

- Details about your product or service

- How to contact you immediately

- Options for reaching you (telephone number, e-mail, fax, etc.)

▥▶ **Note:** When including your business telephone number, be mindful of your international customers. They cannot use your toll-free number. Be sure to include your direct-dial number beginning with 1+.

The tail end of your message is your last chance to drive home the message that you've taken your business to Internet auctions.

Spam—Your Transport to Unpopularity

The act of sending unsolicited and unwanted e-mail to a multitude of users at one time is called **spam**. Another form of spam is cross-posting the same message to hundreds, even thousands of Usenet newsgroups at once. Spam is always unpopular, and can get you in trouble.

Mass e-mail is costly and ties up the network. If you spam Usenet, you could lose your newsgroup access since most ISPs are eager proponents of spam prevention. Additionally, Usenet folks detest spam posts. Offenders often find thousands of copies of the newsgroup FAQ clobbering their e-mail inbox, disabling the receipt of other important e-mail. This could cost you a lot of business and have you dropped by your ISP.

Limit your e-mail promotion recipients to those folks on the e-mail list you created from your own business contacts and professional resources.

Banner Ads

The most common type of advertising on the Web right now is **banner ads**. The most common banner ads are 60 × 450 pixels. They aren't always long and narrow, though. You'll see square banners, tall banners, round banners, and button banners. The term is used so much that "your Web ad" and "your banner" have come to mean the same thing. Banner ads are designed to entice the viewer to click on the ad, which then hyperlinks to the advertiser's site.

You'll see banner ads on business Web sites, Web shopping sites, and on any Web site that offers a free service. For an example of a banner ad positioned at the top of the Web site, see Figure 7.5.

Creating a Banner Ad

If you employ an advertising company, they'll usually provide you with several different banner ads in GIF format that you can use for your online advertising. You can hire Web designers to create your banner ads, or you can make your own. Guess where? On the Web, of course. Several sites exist where you can create your own banner ads free of charge. At a site like The Banner Generator, you'll follow a few simple instructions and create a banner ad that you can save to your hard drive, upload to your Web directory, and submit to banner exchanges.

You can also create your own banner ad with a graphics program. It's not as complicated as it sounds. Figure 7.6 shows a banner ad that I created using Corel PhotoPaint, with my sorely limited artistic abilities, for the fictitious GardenGlad Company.

Figure 7.5. The Banner Generator (*www.coder.com/creations/banner*).

Figure 7.6. Banner ad created with Corel PhotoPaint.

I could have done a lot more with it such as including a telephone number, information about our services, or the URL to my Internet auctions.

Banner-Ad Placement

Studies reveal that the average Web surfer—if there *is* an average Web surfer—will typically look two places on any Web page. One is the top, because that loads in the browser when he or she accesses the page. The next tendency is to scroll down the page and pause at the bottom. This is why many banner-exchange services specifically request that their banners "appear in a prominent place on your Web page—either the top or the bottom."

Given this information, it stands to reason that positioning the banner ad in either place will generate the most clicks. So, what type of ad goes where on *your* business Web page?

- If a visit to the site linked from the banner ad will generate business for you, place it at the top of your page.

- If the banner will generate business for someone else, place it at the bottom.

You may be bound by your banner-exchange service to place the banner in a specific area on your page. Be sure it doesn't obliterate important information on your site.

Link- and Banner-Exchange Programs

Now that you have your banner ad created you can privately exchange link banners with other Web site owners, just as you would reciprocal links. Instead of just a text link, though, you're placing another business's banner ad on your Web page in return for having yours placed on theirs. This works fine if you're dealing in a very small network of businesses. However, the whole idea behind taking your business to Internet auctions was to reach a much wider audience than you would otherwise. Try to exchange banner ads with as many businesses as possible.

Take part in a widespread banner exchange such as Microsoft Network's LinkExchange Banner Network, as shown in Figure 7.7. They're an association of Web sites that trade banner advertising space on over 400,000 Web sites. It's a free service in which users will share ad space with paid sponsors. When you submit your ad and site URL to a banner network, your banner will appear on a rotational basis on other participating Web sites in the market you select. The following table includes a few banner- and link-exchange networks.

Site Name	Web Address
Internet Banner Network	*www.banner-net.com*
Exchange-it	*www.exchange-it.com*
ClicksXchange Banner Network	*www.clicksxchange.com*

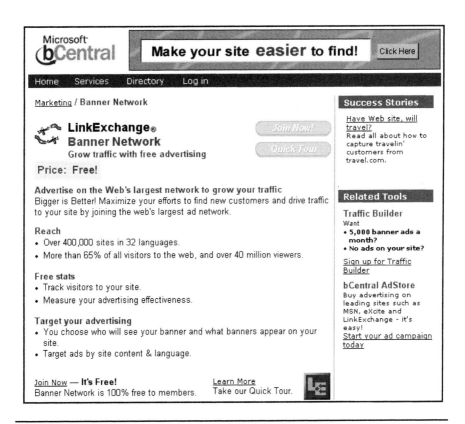

Figure 7.7. Microsoft Network's LinkExchange Banner Network (*adnetwork.bcentral.com*).

Product-Promotion Sites

One of the Internet's drawing features is the availability of "freebies" on the Web. Hundreds of sites let you register and accrue points for visiting certain sites, buying products, or providing feedback. You can then redeem these points for cash or prizes.

These sites are excellent places to advertise your business, which will in turn promote your Internet auctions. You'll pay a fee to have a link to your site included, and potential customers will be enticed by the incentives offered by the promotion site. Additionally, you can opt to have your business spotlighted as a click-through site, from which participants can gain points for visiting and making purchases.

The gold mine of these sites is that they ask users who sign up to fill out a questionnaire in which they offer information about themselves. When a user logs in, ads that are appropriate for that visitor's target market will appear.

Qool

Qool *(www.qool.com)*, Figure 7.8, offers free auctions for folks who register with a site ID and visit the site regularly. The online consumer-rewards company known as NetProspect, Inc., founded Qool in 1998 in San Francisco's South of Market (SOMA) region.

How It Works

You'll accumulate "coins" for logging in, viewing ads, referring friends, and shopping at the linked sites. You can then use these coins to bid on various different items. Members can download the QoolCatcher, a free desktop application that pays members in QoolCoins in return for Web-surfing activities. QoolCatcher enables members to receive additional discounts when they click on the sites of Qool's merchant affiliates. User profiles are never connected to individual identities. While surfing, members automatically receive QoolCoins, which can be redeemed in all auctions hosted at Qool.

To bid, you enter your site ID, the amount of QoolCoins you want to bid, and click on an ad banner. You'll visit the site and get 10 QoolCoins up to 10 times per day.

Partner, Merchant, and Advertiser Information

The free auctions are a cooperative business initiative where Web-site owners pay Qool to reward members for visiting their sites. More than

Figure 7.8. Qool's home page (*www.qool.com*).

400 merchants have signed up as affiliates of Qool. To find out more about advertising at Qool, click on the "Partners" link at the bottom of any page at the site. Depending on the type of business you have, your business Web site link will come up for members of your target market. It's a direct hit.

MyPoints

A leading provider of member-driven Internet direct marketing services, MyPoints (*www.mypoints.com*) features a database of more than 16 million members and provides advertisers with an integrated suite of media products (see Figure 7.9). Your business can target, acquire, and retain customers.

How It Works
Once users register and complete a questionnaire, they earn points that can be redeemed for airline miles, fine dining, gas cards, and other merchandise from many different companies. You can earn points in a few ways:

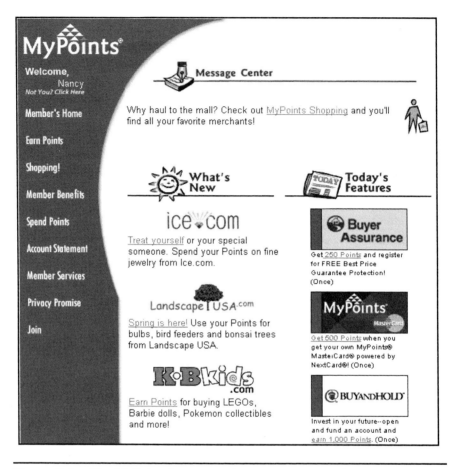

Figure 7.9. The MyPoints home page (*www.mypoints.com*).

- Visiting sites

- Trying out products

- Membership referrals

- Purchasing products from partner sites

- Responding to e-mail promotions from MyPoints

Advertising with MyPoints

MyPoints offers media-based direct marketing techniques in order to deliver qualified customers to your business Web site. When you register as an advertiser, you can take advantage of a Web advertising campaign on MyPoints to motivate consumers. It's a premium way to promote your Web site, and another direct hit to your customers. Visit *www.corp.mypoints.com/home.html* to find out more about advertising at MyPoints.

Affiliate Programs

The idea behind an affiliate program is to pay a premium to people who include a sales-producing link to your business on their Web site. For example, if you become an Amazon Associate and include a properly coded link on your Web site, you receive a small percentage of each resulting sale. Other sites have initiated similar programs. You'll see them called affiliates, associates, or referral programs, which mean the same thing—that you get a small commission if your Web site link results in a sale for the affiliate host.

The biggest benefit is increased sales. A secondary advantage is that every Web page that participates in your affiliate program provides a link to your business Web site.

Types of Affiliate or Referral Programs

Depending on your business model, you can determine which type of affiliate program you can manage. Since you're paying commission based on business produced by the program, your selection will depend on how much your business can afford to pay.

Pay Per Click

Pay Per Click is a term given to an affiliate program where you pay your associate for every time a visitor to his or her site "clicks in" a link to your business Web site. The link can be a banner or a text link. You pay for every visit to your site generated by the associate's link, regardless of whether the click resulted in a sale.

Pay Per Lead

If your site requires users to register, you pay your affiliate a flat fee for every new registered user that their link brings to your site.

Pay Per Sale

If the link results in a sale, you pay your affiliate a certain percentage of that sale. If you offer your affiliates a 1 percent commission on click-through sales, you'd pay them one dollar for each $100 in sales resulting from their link to your business Web site.

Starting an Affiliate Program

An affiliate program can increase your site traffic, create business leads, and generate profits through sales. If you want to coax buyers to your business Web site, you can start up your own affiliate program using services and software provided by service providers such as ClickTrade *(www.clicktrade.com)*, which is shown in Figure 7.10.

You can create a ClickTrade affiliates program without any special software on your end. You select from several different program types, such as pay per click, pay per lead, or pay per sale—depending on what your business can support. ClickTrade handles all of the tracking and time-consuming payments to your affiliates, and provides you with an online setup program to get you up and running quickly.

You can also check out Affiliate Marketing and Associate Programs by I-revenue *(www.i-revenue.net)* for many different affiliate marketing ideas.

Paid Advertising

We have already discussed several ways you can pay to promote your auctions, such as expenses involved in creating banner ads and affiliate programs. I won't attempt to cover all methods of Internet advertising that you can pay for. There are just too many, and to list them all would require a book the size of Sweeney's. What I will do is touch on some of the more common ways you can promote your auctions through paid advertising.

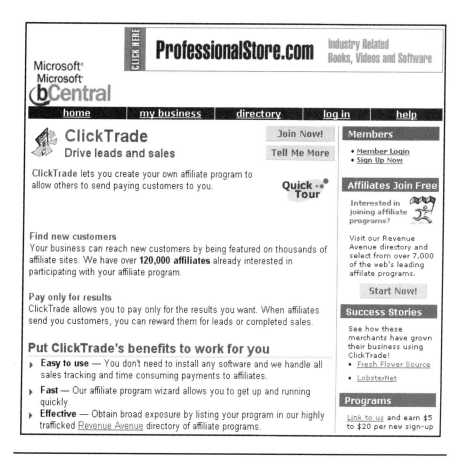

Figure 7.10. Microsoft bCentral's ClickTrade (*www.clicktrade.com*).

Classified Ads—In Print and Internet

You can take out classified ads on numerous Web sites on the Internet. Some of them are free, and others charge a fee based on your ad's length, duration, and graphical content. Once you've written an auction description that draws attention and bids, paring it down a bit to fit a smaller space as a classified ad will be a breeze for you. Just use the same good business sense. Make your ads entice and educate the reader. If you have the flair for it, make them entertaining too.

Many Web sites dedicate themselves to just classified ads. Check out a few of these to see if they look like sites that would generate interest in your Internet auction sales.

Site Name	Web Address
Excite Classifieds	*www.classifieds2000.com*
Yahoo! Classifieds	*classifieds.yahoo.com*
The Ad Net	*www.theadnet.com*
Trader Online Classified Ads	*www.traderonline.com*
A- Z Free Classifieds	*www.freeclassifieds.com*
Alana Jordan Publishing	*www.ajordan.com*

Some of them offer freebie ads to private parties but charge for business ads. Many Web portal sites allow you to list classified ads, and some sites cater to just classified ad placements. You can also get different levels of advertising in addition to classifieds.

Internet Advertising Terminology

The most significant difference between Web advertising and print advertising is the dynamic nature of Web ads. Print ads are static. They just sit on the printed page and never change no matter how long you look at them, shake your head, or stamp your feet. Web ads tend to flip slowly like a slide show. Each flip usually brings up an ad from a different sponsor. This is called **ad rotation**. Another form of ad rotation is when a different banner ad comes up each time someone views the page. This type of rotation gives more sponsors the chance to have their ad seen by potential customers.

Impression
Each time your ad comes up on a page, it's called an **impression**. The fee is usually based on the number of impressions. So, four visits to a banner ad will result in four impressions. If your ad is in rotation, it only generates an impression when it cycles into the page for viewing. If it's an animated rotation, where the ad in the space on the page keeps changing while the visitor is at the page, it's one impression if your ad is included in the animation.

CPM—Cost Per Thousand Impressions
Now a standard term in e-commerce advertising, **CPM** is used to calculate the cost of banner advertising. If a 60 x 468 pixel-wide ad sells for

$10 CPM and the ad had 3,000 impressions in one billing cycle, then the total cost would be $30.

Click-Throughs

You read about pay-per-click associate programs. Click-throughs are the same concept. Whenever someone clicks on a banner ad and visits the advertised site, it generates a **click-through**. Sometimes you can pay for ads based on the number of click-throughs.

Keywords

You can tie your banners to search engine results by "purchasing" certain words. If you sell alexandrine jewelry, for instance, you could purchase the word "alexandrine." When someone searches for alexandrine, your banner will appear in the page of links that result from the search. This is an excellent way to reach your target market. Figure 7.11 shows Keyword Advertising.com, one of several sites that will set you up with this type of advertising.

Web Site Ads

If you look closely at the bottom navigation links at many commercial Web sites, there will be one labeled "Advertise With Us" or something similar. If you think your ad would do well at the host site, find out who you should contact and how they base their fees—CPM, click-throughs, or some other calculation. To advertise on commercial sites, you'll usually supply your own banner.

Here are a few commercial Web sites where you might want to consider placing a banner for either your business Web site or your auction listings:

- Auction portals

- Web portals

- Product manufacturers

- Companies that sell products that supplement, but do not directly compete with, yours

- Search engines

- Internet bulletin boards or discussion forums

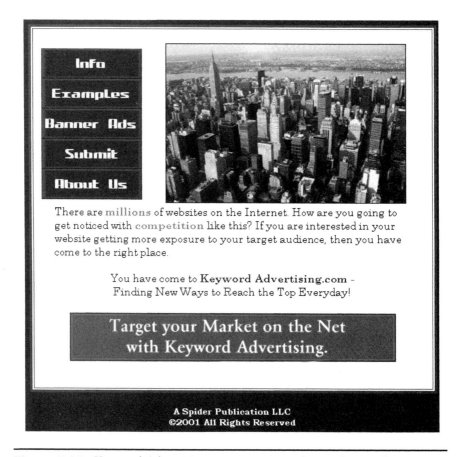

Figure 7.11. Keyword Advertising.com (*www.arvada.com/keywords*).

- Sites that offer free services, such as e-mail, auction tracking, banner ad creation, etc.

- Any sites that target your customers

Free Plugs on the Internet

You can sneak advertising into plenty of places free of charge. Using what you know about HTML tags and UBB code to create links, you can subtly direct people to your auctions wherever it's allowed. In this section, we'll discuss two media where users can post messages and discussion topics. You may discover other places on the Internet where you can slip in a plug for your auctions.

Bulletin Boards and Message Forums

Bulletin boards and message forums, also called message boards, are threaded discussion groups accessible via the Web. By allowing multiple participants to post messages, message boards allow folks to communicate as a group. Web portals and companies use message boards to provide customer support. They're all over the Internet, created for cyber-chatting devotees of every topic from the care and feeding of geckos to coupon clipping to building computers.

Internet bulletin boards have been around since the days of UNIX-based Bulletin Board Systems (BBSs). Look for bulletin-board-type discussion groups at AOL, or you can check out a few of these:

Site Name	Web Address
Web Communities in MSN	*communities.msn.com*
About.com	*www.about.com*
Forum One Communications	*www.forumone.com*
TalkCity Online Communities	*www.talkcity.com*

Many Internet auction portal sites offer discussion forums for auction buyers and sellers. You can ask other sellers for hints and tips, or for help if you encounter sticky situations with your bidders.

Figure 7.12 is a threaded discussion started by an Internet auction seller with concerns about a bidding pattern on one of her auctions. Other sellers respond with helpful advice and insight.

Ultimate Bulletin Board (UBB)

Many Internet discussion groups run on UBB programs. UBB, a product of Infopop (*www.infopop.com*), created a simplified version of "Web code" to enable users to create hyperlinks, add images to posts, create bullet lists, and several of other formatting options that would normally require using HTML code. UBB code is a collection of HTML tags made simple. UBB forums allow folks to use either UBB or HTML code, depending on how the options are set. Here is a sample of the simplified UBB codes:

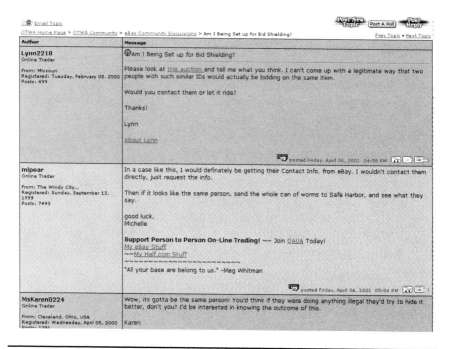

Figure 7.12. A discussion thread in UBB at the Online Trader's Web Alliance (OTWA).

- [url]http://www.maxpress.com[/url]—Makes the URL a hyperlink.

- [url=http://www.maxpress.com]Maximum Press[/url]—Displays the words "Maximum Press" as a hyperlink

- [img]http://www.domain.com/vase.gif[/img]—Sources the image at the specified URL onto the current page.

- [email]Marble90@aol.com[/email]—Brings up a mail window addressed to Marble90@aol.com when clicked (e-mail hyperlink).

- [email=Marble90@aol.com]E-mail me[/email]—Displays the words "E-mail me" as an e-mail hyperlink.

- [list]

- [*] Item

- [*] Item

- [/list]—Creates a bullet list. Each line preceded with [*] will start with a bullet.

- **[b]Bold text[/b]**—Sets text between the two tags in boldface.

- **[i]Italic text[/i]**—Sets text between the two tags in italics.

- **[u]Underlined text[/u]**—Sets text between the two tags in underscore.

- **[center]Centered text[/center]**—Centers text on the page or with the table cell or frame.

- **[quote]Text here[/quote]**—Shows included text as a quote that is set apart from the rest of the text.

A few other UBB codes change the text color and style. You can also insert little faces called **emoticons** to convey your attitude, which is otherwise difficult when communicating in emotionless text. Figure 7.13 shows a sample of typical UBB emoticons.

Discussions on UBB boards take place in what is called threads. One user starts a topic, and others respond to it in what becomes a topic-related discussion. Some message boards discourage **drift**, which is off-topic posting, but others allow it in moderation.

Note: You'll read more about message board use and protocol in Chapter 12.

Know Their Restrictions

Don't post a link to your business Web site, or endorse your Internet auctions, if the bulletin board or discussion forum prohibits it. This will make you look bad. It's a lot better to join the discussion, become part of the community, and work your Internet auction business venture into

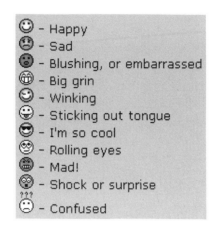

Figure 7.13. Typical UBB emoticons (Courtesy of OTWA).

the discussion slowly. Read for awhile before you post to get a feel for the atmosphere.

Protocol! Protocol!

An online discussion forum dedicated to users of products you're selling might be a stocked trout pond, but going about your business the wrong way can backfire on you.

Subject-focused Internet discussion groups are *not* the place to blatantly advertise your goods. Don't burst onto the scene with pronouncements of your great sales. It won't go over well. Enter the discussion as an interested participant who contributes to the discussion with the objective of making business contacts. You can work your message in gradually as you get to know the other participants.

Your Signature File

Some of the OTWA participants have links to their auctions in their sig files. Most bulletin board sites let you use a sig file similar to the one you can use in your e-mail messages. These files can include hyperlinks coded with HTML or UBB. Don't let this opportunity pass to include a link to your business Web site, and to your auctions. If you can only include one hyperlink, take them to your business Web page. This will raise their interest in your product and they'll see the prominent link to your Internet auctions on your page.

Auction Link Image

Figure 7.2 (page 275) showed a graphical link that eBay provides for you to direct people to your eBay auctions. If the bulletin board allows it, you can include this link in your post with either UBB or HTML code. You can also create your own image—perhaps a smaller, unobtrusive one—to direct potential customers to your Internet auction listings.

Open Your Own Discussion Forum

If you have enough regular visitors to your site, you might consider starting your own discussion forum where you can determine the guidelines and make the rules. You can purchase bulletin-board software that your Web designer can incorporate into your site. You'll also find numerous places on the Web that offer free bulletin-board programs in return for their own series of banner ads that will appear on your bulletin boards (Figure 7.14).

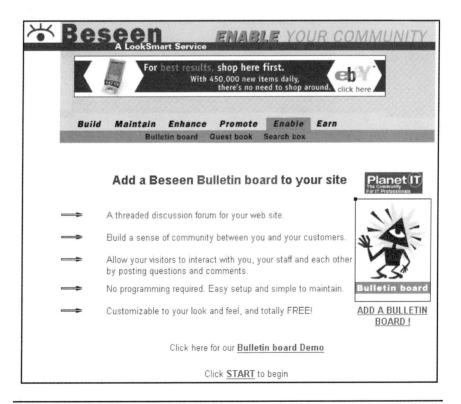

Figure 7.14. Beseen's Bulletin Board Service (*www.beseen.com/board*).

The following table lists several Web resources for bulletin boards.

Site Name	Web Address
Beseen's Bulletin Board Service	*www.beseen.com/board*
Nexus Web Development	*www.nexwebsites.com*
Ikonboard	*www.ikonboard.com*
Ultimate Bulletin Board	*www.infopop.com*

Some of these services let you download the software and use it on your Web page. Others host the bulletin board for you on their server, and you provide a link to it from your Web page. The transition is seamless for your customers, since they reach the board from your business Web site, and return to it via a "back" link that you can code onto the bulletin board page.

The next chapter explains your requirements as an Internet auction seller as you prepare to complete the transaction offline.

8

The Internet Auction Transaction—
A Seller's Responsibilities

This chapter will help you complete the Internet auction transaction, which is the element of Step 6 in your Seven-Step Internet Auction Strategy. In addition to keeping the customer satisfied with great customer service, you must operate within the terms and conditions of the Internet auction site you're using. Moreover, don't let anyone take unfair advantage of you or your business. You should know your rights as an Internet auction seller:

- You have the right to expect the high bidder to pay you.

- You have the right to insist that your high bidders comply with your seller terms, particularly if you included them in your auction description.

- You have the right to refuse to accept payment after a reasonable amount of time has passed.

- You have the right to refuse to do business with any particular user, provided you have just cause.

From a seller's perspective, it's important to know the steps involved in the Internet auction transaction. This will help ensure that you comply with the auction site and give your customers the best Internet auction service possible:

- The Internet auction transaction—what is it, actually?

- Your responsibilities during the auction

- What to do when the auction ends

- Packaging your items—individually wrapped, boxed, etc.

- Secure packing and shipping

- Determining postage

- Selecting a carrier

- Insuring the shipment at the customer's option

- Entering user feedback

- Avoiding underhanded tactics

- Keeping your personal Internet auction activity separate from business

This is an important chapter to read before you actually begin listing auctions. If you take the necessary measures to ensure that you cover all of your Internet auction transaction bases, your customers will trust you and appreciate your good business practices. Here you'll read about what your customers, the auction site, and Federal trade laws expect from you as an Internet auction seller.

The Internet Auction Transaction

The Internet auction transaction starts when you list your auction, because that's when you establish your intent to sell. However, you should be aware that the exchange of payment for goods is not the whole papaya in the online bidding jungle. The Internet auction transaction is typically a six-phase process, as shown in Figure 8.1.

We'll discuss these transaction elements throughout this chapter, along with what's expected of you as an Internet auction seller during each phase.

Your Responsibilities During the Auction

Auction sites usually expect you and your business to be solely responsible for the content of your auction description. This holds true both while the auction is live and after it closes with a successful high bidder. You have legal as well as ethical obligations, and common business sense dictates that you should strive to operate with stellar practices in order to retain your customers.

A Seller's Legal Obligations

Federal trade laws cover Internet auction transactions. As a seller, you must uphold these laws. Most Internet auction sites have them written

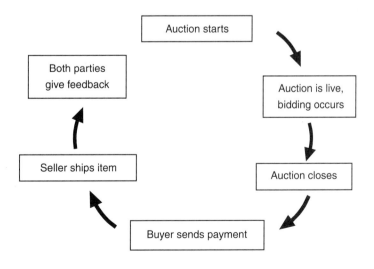

Figure 8.1. The typical six-phase Internet auction transaction.

into their Terms and Conditions. Figure 8.2 outlines an Internet auction seller's must-do's, according to the Federal Trade Commission.

If you uphold Federal trade laws, you have a better chance of being a successful (and long-term) Internet auction seller. If you run into a problem during your auction transaction, try to work it out directly with the buyer or with the auction site. If that doesn't work, file a complaint with the Federal Trade Commission by calling 1-877-382-4357 or by visiting the FTC's Web site at *www.ftc.gov.* You'll read more about dealing with Internet fraud in Chapter 12.

Presenting Your Items Accurately

In Chapter 6, you read about dolling up your auction descriptions with colorful words and phrases. You also know the importance of being honest about your product. This section includes some essential item presentation guidelines that you should consider when planning your Internet auction sales strategy.

Your Legal Obligations

- Federal laws prohibit deceptive or misleading acts in commerce, including Internet auctions. You are required to advertise your product or service and the terms of the sale honestly and accurately.
- Sellers are prohibited from placing "shill" bids or false testimonials. Some sellers improperly create a fake identity and bid on their own auctions to drive up the offers. Likewise, some sellers place glowing testimonials about themselves in the comment section of Internet auction sites. These practices are not only unethical, they're also fraudulent.
- Sellers are prohibited from offering illegal goods through Internet auctions. While many auction sites monitor their sites and attempt to delete illegal items, the ultimate responsibility for ensuring that a sale is legal rests with the seller and buyer. Some auction sites post a list of prohibited items as a guide.
- After the auction closes, sellers are required to ship the merchandise within the time frame designated during the auction or, if no time frame is specified, within 30 days. If you can't meet the shipping commitment, you must give the buyer an opportunity to cancel the order for a full refund or agree to the new shipping date.

Figure 8.2. Federal Trade Commission's Web site (*www.ftc.gov/bcp/conline/pubs/online/auctions.htm*).

Truth in Advertising

The law prohibits false and deceptive advertising. **Deceptive advertising** is the practice of making product claims that mislead, confuse, or deceive your customers. Consumers are used to advertisers making outlandish claims about the superiority of their products, and it's usually all right as long as we're not really expected to believe it. Many advertisers get away with exaggeration. For instance, has anyone ever proven that things really go better with Coke, or that nobody doesn't like Sara Lee?

While certain product statements surely don't apply to everyone in the world, companies are allowed to puff up their advertisements as long as their claim is an obvious overstatement. Within Internet auction ads, you'll see hype and puffy claims such as these:

- Best deals on eBay!

- We have the lowest prices on the Web.

- You can't beat our service.

- You'll love dealing with us.

The slogans above are blatant advertising terms and generally permissible business practice even if you don't have the best deals on eBay, the lowest prices, above average service, or if your customers don't end up in love with you.

However, you cannot make precise product offerings that you don't uphold. You can't offer free shipping on orders over $100 and then charge your customers to ship any size order. You can't offer a free wrench with a tool kit and then refuse to include it, unless you've specified "while supplies last." Use care with what you claim, and be sure you can make good on it.

Item Details

Describe your item or service as fully and accurately as possible, including whether it's new, used, or reconditioned. Here are some ideas about specific details to include:

- Does the item require batteries, and are they included with the purchase?

- Is assembly required?

- Are all parts included? Is anything shown in the photo *not* included?

- Does the item come packaged?

- Is the item banned anywhere?

- Will the item be appropriate for all ages?

- Do the colors vary, and can your customers choose the colors they want?

These may not apply to what you're selling, but if you study your product, you'll be able to come up with specific information that the customer should know. State these details up front. If you're selling chairs, are they leather, cloth, or wooden? Are your buckets galvanized steel? Do your tennis balls come three to a can? I'm sure you get it.

Truthful Photos

Specify whether the photo is of the actual item being auctioned, or if it's one of many you have listed in a Dutch auction or other multi-item listing. Clearly state whether the photo is the actual item, or a model. This protects you if problems arise later. You can include a phrase like this in your auction description:

> "Please note that the item pictured is not the actual item for sale, but is one from the lot being sold. Your item will be of identical coloration, style, and quality."

Many Internet auction sellers don't include this statement, and assume that if a product appears in a multi-item auction, customers will know that the item pictured can't possibly be the one they'll receive. It's your call.

State Your Terms

You have the right to state up front certain terms that you have as an Internet auction seller. These are your **transaction terms**. Include them in the auction description so that potential bidders know your policies before they bid. You also have the right to expect your customers to comply, as long as your transaction terms are reasonable and agree with those in force at the auction site. This protects you and your business in case a buyer has an issue with you and decides to complain to the auction site. Your terms should cover these areas:

- Payment

- Returns

- Feedback policy

- International sales

There is no guarantee that your bidders will read your terms, but they should be aware that bidding on your auction indicates their agreement to comply with them.

Your Payment Terms
State in your auction description how and when you expect to be paid. You can include a payment policy like this one, tailored for your business:

> *"Payment is expected within ten days of auction close. We accept personal checks, money orders, credit cards, or BidPay."*

Here again, you're covered if any problems arise with slow-paying bidders. You may occasionally encounter **deadbeat bidders**, or those who never pay for the items they order. Decide on a procedure for handling that situation. Will you relist items that aren't paid for within 20 days after the auction closes? Will you e-mail the buyer one reminder, and then consider the transaction canceled if payment still doesn't arrive after a specified time? You need a clear process, but it's not advisable to include your deadbeat bidder policy in your auction description. Based on a buyer survey I conducted, it's viewed by some potential bidders as an implied threat. Save your deadbeat policy for the e-mail you send late-paying buyers right before your patience runs out.

Note: You'll read more about handling slow-paying and deadbeat bidders in Chapter 12.

Your Return Policy

It's probably the last thing you want to think about when you list an auction, but a stated return policy can benefit the transaction in several ways:

- Instills bidder confidence

- Guarantees customer satisfaction

- Protects against unreasonable requests from the buyer

- Up-front statement of policy if a complaint is filed against you

A seller's return policy should get right to the point:

"I accept returns if you notify me within three days after receiving the item. I will issue refunds within 30 days, and only after I've inspected the returned merchandise."

Internet auction sellers who offer a clear, understandable policy for returns put potential buyers at ease. It's an implied guarantee of customer satisfaction, and reassuring for those still leery of buying merchandise through online auctions. Sellers should include their return policy in the auction description. Buyers have more confidence in a return policy stated in the auction rather than at a linked site, since they know you usually can't change the auction description once an auction closes. You can change your linked site any time. That doesn't mean you would, but you *can*.

Payment for postage depends on who made the error. If you agree to accept the return of an item accurately described in the auction description, then the buyer should pay all shipping costs involved with the return. If the auction description wasn't accurate or the item is incomplete or not working, then you should pay the postage. In either case, whoever ships the package is responsible for its safe arrival.

Your Policy on Feedback

This has been a subject of debate in many Internet auction user forums—when should Internet auction sellers enter feedback for their paid customers? These are the two most common attitudes:

- A seller should enter feedback for the customer as soon as the customer's payment is received and cleared.

- A seller should wait until the buyer receives the item and reports satisfaction with it, and then enter feedback.

It's up to you which option you choose, but under no circumstances should you expect a customer to enter auction-site feedback for you first. That's not good practice.

Your Policy on Escrow

If you're willing to accept buyer requests to use escrow to complete the transaction, you may wish to include this in your seller terms. A statement such as this makes very clear your policy on using escrow:

> *"I will honor requests to use escrow on items over $500, if the buyer pays the escrow fees."*

You can set the price limit wherever you choose. This may also serve as a confidence-boosting element of your auction. Hopefully, it will also keep bidders who are still suffering from e-commerce paranoia from asking you to use escrow for a $15 transaction, and expecting you to pay for it. It's easier to refer such a request to your auction description than it is to maintain a customer-friendly attitude while declining such a ridiculous request.

International Sales

Specify in your auction description whether you'll ship internationally. You may be bound by auction site restrictions, because some of them only allow residents of their operating country (United States, Canada, Australia, England, etc.) to register with a user ID. However, if the site is open to everyone who can meet the user requirements, you need to decide whether you'll accept bids from customers outside of your home country. Consider first the pros and cons, which can include:

Positive:

- Widen your customer base

- Increase the chance of bidding competition, which drives the price up

- Diversity and cultural enrichment for both parties

Negative:

- Possible language barrier hindering communication

- Shipping takes longer and there's more paperwork

- Elevated postage costs and convoluted claim procedures

If you decide to include provisions for international customers in your transaction terms, be sure to specify that you expect payment in U.S. dollars (assuming that's your preference). Also, decide whether you'll accept returns from international customers. Many sellers choose not to, fearing some well-publicized international fraud cases involving product returns. Be sure your policy on international sales is clear in your auction description.

Handling Returns

We discussed including your return policy within your auction description. Naturally, you want to serve your customers' best interests, but you don't want to jeopardize your business in the process. Remember that people buy things via the Internet because it's convenient. Returns should be a smooth process.

- Provide a direct address to which the returned goods should be shipped.

- Credit an immediate refund once you or your returns department inspects the product.

- Let them know promptly when you've credited their account or issued them a refund.

To retain your Internet auction customers, make the return process as easy as it is at a Brick & Mortar store. Remember that returns are not always a bad thing. Occasionally, a buyer will return an item and request one of higher quality for an additional cost. Any online transaction that remains pleasant for the customer could lead to more sales in the future.

Auction Site Policies on Returns

Some B2B and B2C auction sites determine the return policy and expect sellers to uphold it no matter what. A standard return policy reads like this:

> "Any returns must be sent postage prepaid in and with original containers and packing materials, and received by the seller in undamaged condition within 30 days subsequent to the date of original shipment by the seller. Freight, insurance, handling fee and/or delivery charges are non-refundable."

In some cases the business auction sites won't accept returns. Instead, they direct the customer to the product manufacturer, and only if the item is defective. The C2C sites generally expect sellers to accept returns after a 3-day inspection period.

Your Rights Where Returns Are Concerned

Product-return fraud has been a problem for many e-tailers. Since the person issuing the refund isn't always the one who inspects the product, some Internet auction sellers ultimately refund money on a large rock placed inside of an otherwise empty product box. As an Internet auction seller, you should be aware that you have specific rights when it comes to product returns:

- The right to inspect a returned product before issuing a refund

- The right to require customers to pay shipping charges on returned items, unless you made the error

- The right to declare a time limit from date of purchase on returns (such as 30 days)

- The right to deny a refund on items you did not sell the customer

- The right to deny a refund if the item is defective due to improper use or wear by the customer

You may wish to incorporate these statements into the e-mail message you send to a customer who has informed you that he or she wishes to return an item. Your message should also include specific return instructions. Many consumers judge businesses by how easy it is to return items.

Communicating with Your Bidders

In Chapter 11, you'll read about e-mail etiquette and how to communicate during the various situations that may arise throughout the Internet auction transaction. This section addresses when you would need to be in contact with your bidders while the auction is running.

Questions from Prospective Bidders

Always answer e-mail from potential bidders promptly and include all of the information the customer requested (and more, if you feel additional information is relevant to the question). Be sure that the customer has time before the auction runs out to decide whether to bid.

If you receive any questions from potential bidders in e-mail, keep track of when you received them and how long it takes you to respond. You'll use this information during your evaluation process in Chapter 9.

Associate Customer's E-mail with Auction Number

An eBay user known as StormThinker *(www.StormThinker.com)* reports having problems knowing what auction his customers are referring to when they e-mail him with questions. To help solve the problem, he creates an e-mail hyperlink that populates the user's e-mail subject line with the auction number, and customizes it for each auction.

"Before I started doing this," StormThinker explains, "it was nearly impossible to tell which auction each question pertained to, since bidders seldom provide adequate information by themselves. They sometimes believe that you only have one auction up at a time, and can't imagine that it may be just one of hundreds of items on auction. The coded e-mail links solved this problem for the most part."

When the Auction Ends

Once the auction closes, the transaction moves into e-mail. Your customer's user ID becomes an actual name, and you get to present your business practice with something other than creative HTML. You're about to meet the bidder who devoted online time to winning your auction. He or she is probably just as eager to get the Internet auction transaction under way.

End-of-Auction E-mail

The e-mail message that you send your high bidder when the auction closes is called the **EOA message**. This is the first step in making direct contact with your customer. Use this time to make a good impression so that the transaction runs as smoothly as the online auction did.

What to Include in Your EOA E-mail

Always assume that your buyer has made purchases from different sellers and will need to be able to reference which auction you're requesting payment for. Think about what you'd want your customers to include with their payment so you know what items to send, and this will give you a good idea of what your EOA message should include:

- Internet auction site name

- Auction title

- Number of the auction

- Date the auction closed

- Total amount the customer owes you (high bid + shipping + optional insurance)

- Your site ID

- Your address and telephone number

- Your preferred methods of payment

- Your seller terms and conditions

Many buyers include a hard copy of a seller's EOA e-mail message when they mail payments. The more information your e-mail includes, the easier it will be for you to identify what the customer is paying for.

EOA Message Subject Line

Always include the auction number in the subject line of your e-mail messages. That way, both you and your customer know exactly which transaction the e-mail references. The auction number will carry over into any subsequent e-mail you exchange. If you need to hunt for a message later, you can find it by browsing e-mail subjects. You won't have to open all of your old mail to find the right one.

Another important reason to include a reference to the auction in the e-mail subject line is the spam and junk mail people receive every day. People tend to delete messages from users that they can't readily identify. Others fear computer viruses sent in e-mail from unknown accounts. You don't want your EOA message deleted by mistake. You'll find instructions for coding a subject designation into your e-mail link in Appendix B.

How Soon Should You Send It?

Send the EOA message as soon as you can after the auction officially closes. This may be when the clock runs out on a timed auction, or it might be when the Internet auction site informs you that someone has placed a bid on one of your fixed-price auctions. For good customer service, try to send your EOA notices within one hour after the auction closes. Keep track of how soon you send them out. This is another checkpoint for your customer-service performance.

Some eager buyers may contact you when the auction closes, asking how they can make payments. You can reply to this message with your standard EOA message, taking care to thank the person for his or her prompt communication.

Sample Message

When you send the EOA message to your high bidder, remember that this person is about to buy something from you and may feel a bit apprehensive. Be polite and friendly and include everything your customer needs in order to call in a credit card number, mail the payment, or pay through an online payment service.

Figure 8.3 shows an example of an EOA message you can send to your high bidders. This includes all of the necessary information and adds a nice personal touch. It will help the buyer feel more confident about sending payment to a stranger, or to a company he or she has never dealt with before.

Hi!

Congratulations on being the high bidder on auction #1885068 for the GardenGlad Elite Terra Cotta Flowerpot, which closed on April 3, 2002. Your high bid was $65. Please add $9.50 for shipping and insurance for a total of $74.50.

We offer several payment options:

PayPal: Our account is xxx@xxx.com and our last name of record is Hix

VISA or MasterCard: Please call with your card information: 630-555-1234

Check or Money Order: Please send payment to this address:

GardenGlad
1234 Auction Drive
Flowerpot, IL 57432

We hope you enjoy your purchase. If you are not satisfied with it for any reason, we accept returns after a three-day inspection period starting with the day the item is delivered to you. The buyer is responsible for return postage. We appreciate payment within 10 business days of the auction close.

Be sure to include the auction number and item name (or a copy of this e-mail) with your payment so we can leave feedback for you and ship your item. Please let us know what payment method you will be using and send us your shipping address so we can get your package ready. Thanks for bidding on our auction!

—GardenGlad ("marble" on eBay)

Figure 8.3. Sample EOA e-mail message.

Post-Transaction Correspondence

You might occasionally hear from your customers weeks or even months after the transaction completes. Your customers could have many reasons for contacting you:

- Questions about the item

- Requests for information about your company

- Orders for additional merchandise

- Inquiries about your current sales

Again, always answer e-mail from your customers—especially customers in good standing. Provide whatever information they're seeking. The buyer might also send an acknowledgment of your fine service or concerns about the item. You can use this opportunity to ask if you can add them to your e-mail list for future offers.

When the Buyer Isn't Happy with the Item

If the buyer contacts you within your specified inspection period, refer to your return policy and proceed as you would under "Handling Returns." If the customer contacts you months later with a complaint, you have a few options that could appease the buyer and end up working in your favor:

- Offer a replacement at a discount

- Suggest another item he or she may like better

- Send an electronic coupon for 10 percent off his or her next purchase with you

Do whatever it takes to keep your customers happy. And when you respond to their e-mail, don't forget to append your sig file that has links to your Internet auctions.

Ask If You Can Add Them to Your E-mail List

Here's another opportunity to add customers to your electronic-distribution list. Internet auction customers are part of your target audience by simple virtue of the fact that they purchased your product. It's good practice, of course, to ask before you add someone's e-mail address to your list. Once you've made your customers happy with proven and reliable products and customer service, they aren't likely to say no.

Packaging Your Items

It's important to distinguish between packaging and packing. Here, **packaging** means the typically decorative or descriptive product housing in which the product delivers to the consumer. Later you'll read about **packing**, which is the act of getting an item ready for shipping.

Unlike traditional Brick & Mortar store displays, your on-line auction customer will see your photos of the unpackaged product with your auction listing. Aside from the usual "MIP" designation in your listing, the product package doesn't need to appeal to the eye as much when you sell on-line. You need to decide whether to sell your products packaged in multiples, individually packaged, or loose (no packaging). Your item packaging depends on who your customer is. If you're selling multiples of items, a lot will depend on what your customers plan to do with the item. There are three possible types of customers:

- End-user, or consumer

- Resale business

- Wholesale business

Each type of customer will have different expectations where item packaging is concerned.

Packaging for Consumers

If you are targeting the end users—the consumers ultimately using the item—they will be more interested in the product itself rather than fancy packaging. They'll only see that for a few seconds before they unwrap it when the product arrives at their home. However, consumers sometimes want items that are in their original packaging in certain cases:

- If the item is intended as a gift

- For the item to have a "newness" appeal

- If the item is purchased as an investment or a collectible

Knowing how to package your item depends on knowing your target market and your customers. In Chapter 3, you read about the importance of specializing in the products you sell at the auction sites. This includes how well you can predict whether your customers will want to see them packaged.

Product Enclosures

I recently bought a new leather office chair to enjoy some comfort during all the hours I spend at my computer. The chair came packaged in a corrugated box with a picture and some descriptive text on the outside. When my husband unpacked it, he found the components to assemble it, instructions, and a single-use metal wrench. The wrench is a **product enclosure.**

In a sealed polyethylene bag, he found an assembly instruction booklet and a separate sheet with the usual product warnings. Several hang tags affixed to the chair gave instructions on operating the chair itself, such as how to adjust the height and the lumbar support tension. These items are **product documentation**, and are part of the product packaging.

Pouches, Little Boxes, or Bags

If you sell items that you acquired unpackaged, or you're assembling products in gift-type arrangements, you'll probably need a source for packaging material. Numerous Web-based businesses can supply you with various items you'll need, depending on what you're marketing. The table below includes a sampling. You can find other Web-based businesses by doing an Internet search for packaging-material suppliers.

Site Name	Web Address	Items Offered
Merrifield's Tissue Paper & More	*www.merrifieldshomedecor.com*	Plain and printed tissue paper
Fire Mountain Gems	*www.firemountaingems.com*	Gift boxes, pouches, polyethylene bags
Mac Paper Supply, Inc.	*www.macpaper.com*	Wholesale gift packaging
Extreme Packaging	*www.xpackage.com*	Interior and exterior packaging supplies
Anchor Box Company	*www.anchorbox.com*	Packing boxes, gift boxes, packaging, bags

Packaging for Resale

If you're selling to another business for resale, you need to specify whether items sold in lots or multiples are individually packaged, and how they are packaged. Packaging is an expense that your customer will want to anticipate when buying for resale. If it's a large-scale purchase, you may consider offering the option to custom-package the lot. This could increase your product's appeal and net you a satisfied business customer.

Packaging for Wholesale

If you're selling to a wholesaler, there's a good chance that you can ship the items in an unpackaged lot. If this is how you plan to ship, you need to be very specific about this in your auction description. You'll need to communicate with the purchaser to work out the product-delivery details.

Packing and Shipping

Your customers expect their items to arrive in perfect condition. How you pack an item for shipping can mean all the difference in the world. Perhaps you pack items yourself, or maybe you'll employ a shipping manager. Either way, it's up to you to ensure that all items you sell through Internet auctions are packed well for shipping. If they arrive damaged, everything else was a waste of time. Use this section when you complete your Packing Worksheet in Appendix C. Here we'll cover the essentials of good product packing and shipping:

- The importance of prompt shipping

- Reliable packing methods and materials

- Your shipping note

- Enclosures

If you're shipping large items, such as dressers or refrigerators, you may need to consult a professional packing company for assistance, or farm out the packing and shipping of those items. Figure 8.4 shows the Craters and Freighters home page.

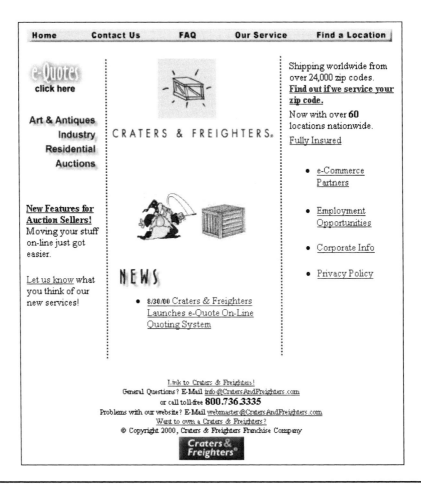

Figure 8.4. Craters and Freighters' home page (*www.cratersandfreighters.com*).

The Importance of Promptness

Once you receive payment and sufficient time has passed for a personal check to clear, ship the item within 24 hours. Notify the buyer immediately of any unavoidable shipping delay. When your customer has paid for an item, he or she owns it and you need to transfer the property to its new owner as soon as possible.

Don't Make the Customer Wait!

Your shipping policy should specify a business hour lapse of no more than 24 hours between acceptance of payment and the product going out the door. If you encounter delays in being able to ship the goods, inform the customer immediately, and include a time estimate of when you can ship. Be sure that your e-mail conveys that you regret the delay, and will do whatever you can to see to it that the item ships promptly. If it's delayed more than a week, include a little something extra—a discount coupon, a product sample, a bookmark ... whatever.

Your Shipping Schedule

Product shipping can be a vicious circle, especially for business sellers. If your shipper only picks up parcels two days a week, or you can only get to the post office on Thursdays, this means you have a limited schedule for when you can ship items. Be sure to include your shipping schedule (if you have limitations) in your auction description. Let your customers know that there might be a slight delay, and that an item they paid for on Monday may not ship until Friday.

Reliable Packing Methods

This is almost as important as describing the item well. The product must reach the buyer in the same condition it was in when you shipped it. If you're sending out items pre-packaged by the manufacturer, check that the item is adequately cushioned for shipping. If not, you'll have to reinforce it.

Use a box that's large enough to allow adequate packing material to cushion the item on all sides. Secure it sufficiently to withstand jostling. It's far better to over-pack and possibly pay a little more for packing materials than to ship an item without adequate protection.

Don't Damage the Item!

Your packing method should not damage the product you're shipping. It's bad enough when shop owners slap gummy price stickers on books and items of potential collectible value. As some adhesives age, chemical changes cause even more damage to certain surfaces. I often ask store clerks to remove price stickers placed on products before I will pay for them. If damage occurs to the product from removing the sticker, I won't buy it.

Unfortunately, some auction sellers commit the same commerce no-no. While wrapping the product in tissue, etc., they let adhesive tape contact it. Adhesive of any kind can do nasty things to paper-based items. You're responsible for any damage item caused by price stickers, adhesive tape, or anything you've added to the product that would damage it when removed. Your customer has the right to expect a refund or a replacement. Employ packing methods that ensure the item arrives unharmed.

Double Boxing

Double boxing extremely fragile items helps protect them. Pack the item securely in one box; then float that box in a slightly larger box by surrounding it with more packing puffies. Make sure the product won't jostle inside the container once it's sealed. The carrier usually won't stamp it "fragile" if something bounces around inside when the package is shaken.

Bubble Wrap®

The term "Bubble Wrap" is actually a trade name registered by Sealed Air Corporation of Saddle Brook, New Jersey *(www.sealedaircorp.com)*. Its technical term is **air cellular cushioning material**. The manufacturing process is credited to Marc Chavannes and Al Fielding, who developed the process back in 1957. Layering two sheets of thin polyethylene while extruding uniformly placed trapped-air pockets in one layer makes it look like one sheet of polyethylene with bubbles on one side. It can be cut with scissors and taped around fragile items for shipping. It's available in different thicknesses and with large or small bubbles and can't be beat as a reliable packing material. Any business that ships items should have a plentiful supply of it on hand.

It's also fun to pop. Check out The World's Best Bubble Wrap home page, shown in Figure 8.5 *(fathom.org/opalcat/bubblewrap.html)*.

Bubble Wrap has replaced abrasive paper products for packaging material, as those don't adequately cushion heavy or delicate items.

Packing Loose Items

Depending on how you received the items you're listing for auction, you may find yourself shipping loose pieces. If it's breakable, wrap it in Bubble Wrap, secure it with packing tape, and nest it in plenty of puffies. If the item has several parts, such as a lid and a base, wrap each one separately. Wadded newspaper can help fill in larger spaces. These prod-

Figure 8.5. The World's Best Bubble Wrap's home page (*fathom.org/opalcat/ bubblewrap.html*).

ucts might take longer to unwrap, but the buyer will be far more upset if the item breaks.

Note: Save packing puffies from shipments you receive. They can be reused.

If the item is bendable, be sure to secure it so it won't crease during shipment. Use a shipping container big enough for the item, the product packaging, and a secure layer of puffies. Be sure the carton has adequate room for the item to "float" in the center of all the packing.

Manufacturer's Packaging—Is It Adequate?

Manufacturers may package items adequately for one shipment, but will the packaging withstand two or more trips across the miles at the mercy of unknown hands? It's always better to double pack items that shipped to you already in some type of packaging. To be on the safe side, follow the procedures for double boxing.

Reliable Packing Material

Years ago, my grandfather in Czechoslovakia packed items in sawdust and then nailed them into a wooden box that he shipped to us here in the U.S. The box and sawdust usually comprised nine-tenths of the package's total weight. Many times, the treasures he sent us arrived broken. Modern packing materials, such as Bubble Wrap and packing puffies, cushion items for shipping like no other products can, without adding much weight to the package.

Earth-friendly folks can order packing puffies made out of a cornstarch material that biodegrades. You can also use recycled paper shreds. Both are a lot less messy than sawdust. Check with your shipping supply company to see if they're available.

Some private Internet auction sellers rinse out recyclable soda bottles, re-cap them, and use them as packing material. I advise against using air-popped popcorn or any other edible item as packing material. Who wants to receive anything packed in stale food?

Where to Buy Shipping Supplies Online

Do a search on any C2C or B2C Internet auction site for whatever shipping items you seek. You'll find many sellers who specialize in selling them. The table below lists a few Internet businesses where you can request a catalog and purchase items right from their Web sites.

Site Name	Web Address
Gator Pack Shipping Supplies	*www.gatorpack.com*
ShippingSupply	*www.shippingsupply.com*
Bargains Galore	*www.bargainsgalorestore.com*
BrassPack Packing Supply	*www.brasspack.com*
FetPak, Inc.	*www.fetpak.com*
BubbleFAST	*www.bubblefast.com*
123Pix	*www.123pix.com*
3Pak	*www.3pak.com*

A Word of Advice to Smokers

It's your business if you smoke, or if you allow smoking in your shipping department, but your customers might not appreciate it when their package arrives. Cigarette, pipe, and cigar smoke has a way of permeating porous items such as fabric and packing material. Most non-smokers can tell right away if a smoker shipped an item by the way the package smells when it arrives.

Keep your auctioned items and especially packing material in a well-ventilated area so they don't reek when they reach your customer. This is another adverse result of being around too much smoke. End of sermon.

Your Shipping Note

Include a note with your shipments that identifies the contents of the package. Corporations should include the paid invoice and a letter of thanks for the sale. Smaller businesses and independent sellers can create their own shipping note so the customer can reference the transaction. Shipping notes also help sellers keep their shipments straight. You won't be as likely to send a customer the wrong item if you pack it with a piece of paper that tells you what should be in the box.

What It Should Include

Your shipping note is a printed record of the Internet auction transaction. It should reiterate the auction information. The buyer may want to save it for later reference, if necessary. Retain a copy for your records. The note should also contain the essential information about the item enclosed:

- Item name

- Auction number

- Ship date

- Your user ID

- Your phone number or e-mail address

Here's an Example

If you're creating a shipping note for your new Internet auction business venture, Figure 8.6 contains a sample to get you started.

Tuck the shipping note where your customer will see it when he or she opens the package. This is also a chance to promote good karma—and maybe more business—by enclosing a few other items with the shipment.

Enclosures

Another way to promote your auctions and your business! Include some printed matter with the shipment that will lead your new customer right back to you for future purchases. You can bundle and toss in a product

Your Item has Arrived!

Enclosed you will find your:

_____

Auction site: _____

Auction number: _____

Today's date: _____

Please Let us Know When it Arrives!
Send email to GardenGlad (xxx@xxx.com) and let us know that
you got the package. If you encounter any problems or you need
to reach us sooner, please call us at: 1-630-555-1234

If You're Happy with Our Transaction:
Please post positive feedback for our user ID (marble). We already
left feedback for you when your payment arrived. If we didn't, let
us know ASAP!

If You're NOT Happy with Our Transaction:
Please notify us right away. We will take whatever measures necessary to be sure we're all satisfied with the outcome.

Thanks!

(Name and Signature)

Figure 8.6.   Sample shipping note.

brochure, order form, new product announcement, discount coupons,
or a small product sample.

Business Card or Brochure
Including a business card or brochure with your shipment is a great
way to generate more sales. Your customer will see it when he or she
likes you the most—the day the item arrives! If you're sending a catalog
or something with volume, be sure you don't charge the customer for
the additional postage.

Mail-in Order Form for More Products

Your customer may be so thrilled with his or her item and your business ethics that he or she may jump at the chance to do business with you again. Here's your chance to include a price list for items that you're selling offline. You can also include the URL to any auction sites where you regularly list merchandise.

Follow-up E-mail

When you ship the item, let the customer know so he or she can be on the lookout for it. Send e-mail notifications to your customers to keep them apprised of the status of their shipment. You should also request that your customers notify you via e-mail when their package arrives, so you can assess their satisfaction.

Determining Postage

Include the cost for shipping in your auction description unless you're paying for it. You need to determine postage before you actually take the package to the carrier. One Web site you'll want to bookmark is the United States Postal Service home page, shown in Figure 8.7.

Even if you select another carrier, the USPS site is a wonderful shipping information resource. You can verify zip codes and locate address management services, and reference countless information pages and links to Web sites that provide information for frequent shippers. You'll also find a chart for determining postage, and how to classify a package as standard, large, or oversized.

Figure 8.8 shows the results returned when I did a query on shipping a 3-pound standard-sized package from Chicago to Phoenix. The origin and destination zip codes determined the results. A similar tool helps determine international postage.

Necessary to Own: A Postage Scale

A postage scale will increase your business's mailing efficiency and prevent you from under- or over-charging your Internet auction customers for shipping. For an explanation of postage scales, check out BuyerZone

Figure 8.7.   The United States Postal Service's home page (*www.usps.com*).

Domestic Calculator

To add special services such as insurance or Delivery Confirmation, select one option below.

Service	Estimated Delivery Time	Rate	Help
Express Mail	Overnight to most areas	$18.85	Express Mail Help
Priority Mail	2 Day(s)	$5.15	Priority Mail Help
Parcel Post	6 Day(s)	$4.71	Parcel Post Help
Bound Printed Matter Restrictions Apply. Click for Details	6 Day(s)	$2.35	Bound Printed Matter Help
Media Mail Restrictions Apply. Click for Details	6 Day(s)	$2.20	Media Mail Help

Click here to back up or edit data.

Click here to start over

Figure 8.8.   USPS postage calculation results from on-screen query (*postcalc.usps.gov*).

(www.buyerzone.com). With their search feature shown in Figure 8.9, look for "postage scale" and you'll find the information you need.

How to Weigh an Item with Packing Material

One handy way to estimate the shipping charge is to take a Priority Mail box, fill it three quarters full with whatever packing material you use, and set the item on top of it. Weigh this. You'll get a ballpark idea of how much it will cost to ship, and you can include this in your auction description.

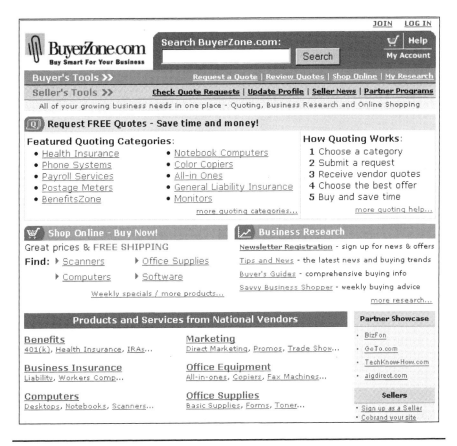

Figure 8.9. BuyerZone's home page *(www.buyerzome.com)*.

Selecting a Carrier

A few pages back, you read about the United States Postal Service (USPS) and the informational Web site they provide. You can select from other carriers too, as long as your customers can receive shipments from them. Here we'll discuss a few other leaders in the shipping industry.

UPS

The need for private messenger and delivery services in 1907 inspired 19-year-old James E. Casey to establish the American Messenger Company in Seattle, Washington. From Jim's office under a sidewalk, he established strict policies for customer courtesy, reliability, 24/7 service, and low rates. In 1913, Jim merged with a competitor, and the company changed its name to Merchants Parcel Delivery. Together they pioneered the concept of consolidated delivery—sending packages addressed to a certain neighborhood in one delivery truck. In 1919, they changed the company name to United Parcel Service in order to describe their mission clearly.

By the early 1950s, they had branched into nationwide service and acquired the rights to deliver packages for both private and commercial customers. Later, they offered two-day service to major cities on the East and West coasts. The UPS Blue Label Air service took off and by 1978 was available in all 50 states. By 1985, UPS Next Day Air service served 48 states and Puerto Rico. UPS later branched into international air package and document service, serving the U.S. and several European countries.

In 1988, the Federal Aviation Administration (FAA) authorized UPS to operate its own aircraft and by 1990, UPS provided service to Asia and Mexico. UPS Airlines is presently the ninth largest airline in North America. Figure 8.10 shows the UPS home page at *www.ups.com.*

From the UPS Web site, you can determine rates, schedule shipments, order shipping supplies, and track shipments.

FedEx

Originally called Federal Express, FedEx delivers nearly 5 billion shipments every business day (see Figure 8.11). Five major operating companies comprise FedEx Corporation:

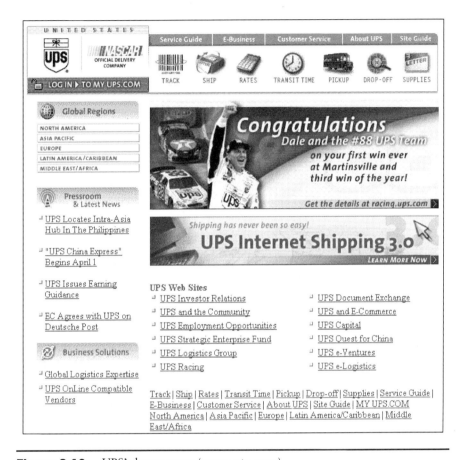

Figure 8.10. UPS's home page (*www.ups.com*).

- **FedEx Express**—Delivery of documents, packages, and freight shipments each business day.

- **FedEx Ground**—Small-package B2B ground delivery.

- **FedEx Custom Critical**—Time-specific delivery of critical and special handling shipments.

- **FedEx Logistics**—Global transportation-management services, integrated logistics, consulting, and other professional services.

- **FedEx Trade Networks**—Full-service customs brokerage, trade consulting, and electronic clearance.

Figure 8.11. FedEx's home page for U.S. customers (*www.fedex.com/us*).

Each company operates independently, focused on its market segment. Their virtual networks handle over 100 million electronic transactions a day.

FedEx offers a rate-calculation tool on its Web site. You'll enter the origin and destination zip codes, specifics about the package, and the type of service you're seeking. You can also manage your FedEx account, contact their Customer Service department, and track both FedEx Express and FedEx Ground shipments from one screen.

Avoid COD Shipments

For the seller, COD demands a lot more work from you than conventional shipping and puts most of the risk right back in your lap. The seller should avoid having both the item and the payment out of hand. Receive and process the buyer's payment before you ship the item.

Shipping packages via COD is more costly and it takes much longer for you to receive your payment. If the customer refuses the item, you must pay the return postage on top of the high COD shipping charge.

Insurance

All major parcel carriers allow you to insure shipped items for their full value. UPS parcels are automatically insured up to $100, and you can purchase additional protection up to $50,000. The USPS offers optional insurance for the item's full value. The coverage includes the value of the contents (less depreciation) at the time of mailing, if lost or destroyed, or the cost of repairs. It does not cover spoilage of perishable items. The coverage will not exceed the amount of coverage you paid for. In other words, if you insured an item for $85, the USPS only pays that amount even if the item's actual repair or replacement value is more than that.

When Is It Advisable?

Always recommend insurance, and provide it at the customer's request. Never deny your customers the option of insuring a package at their expense.

Who Pays?

Unless your auction description specifies that you'll pick up the tab for shipping and insurance, the buyer should pay for both. That's standard procedure. You'll find that some sellers insist on insurance, and others refuse it. If you didn't calculate insurance into your postage fee, be sure to ask your buyer if he or she wishes to pay for shipping insurance. You can specify that the buyer is responsible for recouping any loss incurred on an uninsured item if he or she declines the coverage.

Insurance Provided by the Auction Site

A few auction sites offer insurance coverage to protect users against loss or fraud. It exists mainly to protect buyers, and helps draw customers to an Internet auction site that provides it. It's available free to all registered users and only covers transactions made through the issuing site. Although it can be a valuable service, it hasn't quite caught on yet. Amazon Auctions and eBay are two Internet auction venues that provide auction insurance; not many other C2C and B2C auction sites do.

Covered by Lloyd's of London, eBay will reimburse buyers as much as $200, with a $25 deductible, if Lloyd's deems them to be a victim of fraud once they investigate the claim. This means that eBay's coverage applies only to expenditures of more than $25. For smaller claims, it's still between the seller, the buyer, and SafeHarbor if they'll get involved.

At Amazon Auctions, defrauded buyers can receive as much as $250 of the listing's final closing price. If the buyer used the Amazon Payments service, the coverage leaps to $2,500 with no deductible. The lifetime limit for each unique user is three claims.

Now that we've covered packaging, packing, and shipping, we can move on. Customers are typically happiest with you when their item arrives in the condition they expected. This helps when the online auction transaction progresses to the final phase.

Entering User Feedback

After you transact with another user, you can enter a one-line comment about how it went. Some sites let you judge on a scale from one to 10; others, like eBay, simply have you declare the feedback comment as positive, neutral, or negative. The comment becomes part of that user's permanent record at the site. Typically, leaving feedback is not required. It's an acknowledged courtesy, much like tipping an attendant.

Some B2C and B2B sites, especially those where the auction site has possession of the goods and ships them out, don't offer buyers the option of rating them. Feedback is most important when sellers with reputations and practices unknown to the auction site can list items and sell through that venue. The site wants to protect itself by allowing prospective bidders a chance to check out the seller's performance record. The same holds true for buyers and their payment habits. There's no better way to judge someone's method of operating at an online auction site than by the testimony of someone who did business with the person. Many people read a seller's feedback comments before deciding to bid on his or her auctions.

Types of Feedback

Each site has a slightly different system. Some are more effective than others are, while some types are subject to abuse. There appears to be an OAI movement toward developing a standard, trustworthy user peer rating system. Currently, the process still varies from site to site.

Open Feedback

When eBay first started its feedback system, you could leave any type of comment for any other user. The only restriction was that only one comment you left the same person would count toward his or her overall rating.

This means that someone you never dealt with could post a negative comment about you and it would stay on your record as long as that user ID was in the system. Feedback misuse was a problem at times. Most Internet auction sites, including eBay, no longer allow open feedback.

Transaction-Related Feedback

Many auction sites only let you leave feedback for someone with whom you did business. Unless you and the other person were the buyer or seller for the same successful auction, your comment won't register, or your comment will appear on the person's feedback page but won't count toward his or her overall rating.

With this method, you know when you review someone's feedback file that the rating number represents actual auctions in which the person participated, as either buyer or seller. There are certain drawbacks to only allowing transaction-related feedback. If your high bidder backs out and the next highest bidder buys the item, you can't exchange feedback with that person no matter how well the transaction went.

It's Usually Permanent

Once you enter feedback, it's typically there to stay. Most sites won't erase or edit it for you. From the onset of the feedback system, sellers have complained that undeserved or retaliatory negative comments damage their business reputations. At this writing, some of the sites will, under certain circumstances, remove negative comments if both the author and the recipient agree. Other sites allow the author of the comment to edit the text and change the classification after it's been entered.

Regardless of this, most auction sites advise you to enter neutral or negative comments only as a last resort. Knowing the remarks are permanent, users should carefully consider what they post about another person, especially since their own user ID stays attached to the comment forever.

Character Assessment?

No online auction site can guarantee that a positive rating means you won't have any problems with a particular user. A person could have a positive rating as a buyer, yet operate poorly as a seller. Use feedback as a tool to help you make an informed decision about whether you want to accept a person's bid if you have any doubts.

Will Auction Sites Remove Feedback?

Most of the auction sites will remove a feedback comment in certain situations:

- If the comment is obviously vulgar, obscene, racist, or threatening

- When the comment includes personal information, such as the recipient's home telephone number, an e-mail address, or a Web site URL

- In cases where the author is found to have misused the feedback tool, such as by egregiously winning many auctions with no intent to pay, and then flooding the seller's feedback profile with negative comments

If you receive feedback that you feel should be removed, contact the auction site's customer service or complaint department and explain the situation.

The Rules

Most of the auction sites apply certain rules to their peer rating system. Here are some examples:

- You can't post feedback for yourself from a secondary user ID.

- You can't leave negative feedback if a user fails to perform some action outside the scope of the auction.

- You can't transfer your user feedback from another site.

Too much negative feedback can cost a user his or her auction-site privileges. The same applies to users who are caught misusing the feature to discredit other users or to pump up their own rating. They'll be subject to investigation and may be booted from the auction site.

How to Enter Feedback

From the feedback entry-page, you'll enter a brief comment explaining how the transaction went and then click "Enter," or something similar. Your comment and your user ID append to the person's feedback file, which any registered site user can read.

Note: Some sites let you hide your feedback. Most sites advise against this, though, because it raises suspicion about what you're keeping quiet. If someone enters feedback containing slanderous, obscene, or personal information, you may want to set your feedback to "private" until the auction site can deal with it.

Finding the Feedback Page

The first place to look for the feedback entry page is on the site's home page. If you don't find a link there, check the site map, if one exists. Still nothing? Then continue your hunt by clicking on the rating number after the person's user ID. If that doesn't take you to the right place, go back to the auction listing and see if there's a link there. You might also find it under Customer Service, Help, User Services, or Auction History.

It's often a challenge, but once you find it, follow the instructions the site provides to enter the feedback comment. That part is typically very simple.

Wording the Feedback Comment

Be as specific as possible within your character limit. With a little practice and by reading comments left for others, you'll get the hang of it quickly. Phrases like these get right to the point:

> Fast pay, good communication, easy to deal with.
>
> Paid right away with PayPal! Hope to do business again soon.

Some of the Internet auction service providers let you upload feedback for multiple customers with one effort. They'll also store your comments, so you can compose an effective one and re-use it by selecting it from a drop-down menu. Check with your auction service provider to see if they offer this feature.

Negative Feedback

Like the first dent in a new car, receiving a negative feedback comment is aggravating and even painful when it happens. Don't let one negative feedback comment spoil your Internet auction business venture. Keep up your stellar business practices and the comment will fall further back in your feedback file with every new positive comment. If you have 5,432 positive comments, will your customers care if some misanthrope left you a negative comment three months ago? Probably not.

You have the right to be treated with dignity and respect, and this includes interaction on the Internet. When it comes to the complex world of online auctions, people are bound to make mistakes at first. I did, and maybe you will. When you're an experienced user and a new user wreaks unintentional havoc with one of your auctions, it's better for both parties if you explain the proper procedure to the person and try to make the best of it. You may earn a new customer in the process.

When Negs Are Necessary

Be sure any negative feedback you submit reflects only *your* experience with the bidder. Since you can't withdraw comments, enter negative feedback as a last resort. Always try to settle the matter first on the telephone or in e-mail. Here are some instances where posting negative feedback about a winning bidder is necessary to warn other sellers:

- Buyer never pays

- Buyer receives your perfect item and tries to get a refund for a broken one

- Buyer becomes a harassing, threatening, annoying pain in the assets

By the time the situation reaches the negative feedback stage, you should have already reported the user to the site and requested a non-paying bidder refund.

Wording the Negative Comment

State the facts without making assumptions or accusations. Those can harm your business reputation. For example, if several weeks pass and a promised payment never arrives, a negative comment like this will suffice:

> Waited 1 month and no payment arrived, only promises. Re-listed item.

Avoid any "beware" or "caution" statements. Let others make their own judgments based on the facts you provided.

Responding to Negative Feedback

At some sites you can respond to comments entered about you. Not many people respond to positive comments because there's no pressing need to. However, negative comments are another story. It's critically important to respond to them, if the site has the option. Why? Because your potential customers will direct their attention to your negative feedback when they assess you before bidding on your auctions. When responding to a negative comment, keep your cool, remain professional, and state the facts. The following table offers some suggestions.

Negative Feedback Comment	Suggested Response
This guy never contacted me after the auction closed so I couldn't pay him!	*Sent two end-of-auction messages, waited a month, buyer never responded.*
Beware! Seller overcharges and then sends fake items!	*Untrue. This neg is retaliatory for one I left after filing a nonpaying bidder complaint.*
This transaction was the worst experience of my life. Avoid this seller.	*Buyer e-mailed that she was pleased with item. I had no problems with this deal.*

These types of responses can actually make the negative comments work in your favor. Your prospective customers may judge you by how you handled an unreasonable customer. They'll also check the grouch's file to assess his or her record, and will hopefully realize that you were not the party at fault.

Avoiding Underhanded Tactics

It's your business reputation, so keep it clean and avoid giving in to certain temptations. The OAI is light-years ahead of where it was in 1997, and buyers have learned to be wary of sellers attempting to operate with questionable ethics. Most, if not all, of them will report you, and the consequences can quickly put an end to your exciting new business venture. Why risk it? Using Internet auctions to sell products offers lucrative opportunities for business success when used properly. There's no need to misuse it.

With that said, let's rewind to 1997 when eBay was new and the first books being written about it were still in outline form. Many of us early users approached the whole concept with trepidation and building excitement over its incredible potential as a marketing tool. Just the fact that it was available on the World Wide Web made our hearts leap, and for millions of people it was yet undiscovered. eBay had site rules, and most of us followed them (of course). However, other folks found ways to avoid site fees and hinder other sellers. Since some of these tactics had no governing rules, they shirked their ethics and kept up the dirty work.

When eBay threw away its training pants and went into an initial public offering, it focused a lot more attention on preventing fee avoidance and general site misuse. They developed very strict policies and suspended users who violated them. Their competition did the same thing. Unfortunately, some users got away with violating the rules and found ways to "beat the system." What follows is an explanation of unsavory seller tactics that may seem tempting, but can cost you your site privileges.

⇒ **Note:** As Internet auction buyers become more perceptive, it grows increasingly unwise to attempt any kind of deceptive practice as a seller.

Shills

When someone bids on an auction for the sole purpose of altering the high bid, this is **shill bidding,** or **shilling.** It's also called **bid padding.** The most common form of Internet auction shilling is bidding up auctions from a secondary user ID, or asking someone else to nudge up the price.

Bidding on your own item to inflate the final bid amount is against the rules at all Internet auction sites. Some sites allow you to place an outlandishly high bid on your item to deter bids if you want to cancel the auction, but none of the well-known sites use that method.

Bid Siphoning

Many thousands of non-participants watch auctions. In some cases, they can access auction listings and check e-mail addresses without being a registered user. Bidding on an item indicates an interest in buying it. This makes your customers likely targets for online solicitation, or spam.

A sneaky seller might contact the bidder and offer to sell the same item off-line for less than your minimum bid. He or she avoids paying listing fees and site commissions. This is **bid siphoning**, and registered users can lose their site IDs for doing it.

As you know, buyers have become wise to this. Some of them feign interest, ask for the person's Internet auction site ID to check his or her feedback. Once they know the person's site ID, they promptly report the offender. If one of your customers lets you know that they've received a "better offer in e-mail," encourage them to report it to the auction site administrator if the offender contacted them by way of your auction listing.

Auction Interference

Whenever an Internet auction user contacts another user in an attempt to dissuade them from bidding, this is **auction interference** and it's against the rules at almost every consumer Internet auction site. Even if you fiercely believe that your claim is founded, don't become a "Net Cop" and interfere in anyone's auction activity. This holds true in these types of situations:

- Sending e-mail to a seller, encouraging him or her to cancel a bid from a particular user with whom you had a bad experience

- Sending e-mail to a bidder to warn him or her about a seller whom you feel is engaged in dishonest practices

If you must warn other users about a deadbeat bidder or hostile participant that you've dealt with, use the feedback forum for that, and keep your comments professional and factual. If you've never dealt with the person but notice a pattern of rule infractions, report it to the site. Let the auction site handle problem users.

Your Personal Auction Activity

You may want to bid on other sellers' auctions, such as for your shipping supplies. As you peruse the Internet auction sites, something might catch your eye that you'd like to purchase for personal use. I bought a few items myself while doing research for this book. If you stumble upon a great deal for bath towels, or simply can't resist bidding on a hand-made king-sized quilt for your guest room, then go for it. Remember, however, that you'll want to keep your business and personal activity separate from one another.

Keeping It Private

In Chapter 1, you read about searching for auctions by user ID. Everyone with access to the online auction site who knows your user ID can see what you're bidding on and how much you've spent. For this reason, you may want to consider using another user ID for auction activity that you wish to keep private.

Note: If you have more than one user ID, they must never interact with each other in the same auction. This is shilling, and it's a no-no.

Remember Who's Watching

At most Internet auction sites, users can monitor your activity. Just as this book offers hints and tips for sellers, other books exist that tell Internet auction buyers what to watch out for when they plan to bid on items up for auction. Here's an example:

> Watch for the same user ID showing up repeatedly in the bidding history of a seller's auctions, especially for items that greatly differ from one another. While this could be a loyal customer, it could also be the seller using a secondary ID to shill.

It would be wise to conduct your business with an ID you use only for that purpose, and any personal buying and/or selling with another user ID. You'll need a different e-mail address for each site ID you register.

You never know when one of your competitors may want to screw up your feedback record. Someone could list an item he or she knows you'd be interested in, draw your bid, and once the auction closes leave you an intentional neg on your record. If you have a personal site ID, the seller won't even know it's you and even if he does, he can't touch your business record.

Once you've completed the auction transaction, it's time to look back on your Internet auction activity and determine just how successful you were.

9

Assessing Your Internet Auction Success

Wow—you made it to the final step in your Seven-Step Internet Auction Strategy. Where the first six steps involved preparation and production, Step 7 is your evaluation step. This is where you examine the results of your completed Internet auction transactions and measure your success. Here's what we'll cover:

- Assessing your Seven-Step Internet Auction Strategy and how it effected your results

- Evaluating your goals

- Re-listing items that didn't sell

- Maintaining good auction transaction records

- Deciding whether Internet auctions are right for you and your business

By the end of this chapter, you'll be ready to return to Step 1 and begin the process again. You'll assess your test Internet auctions in terms of satisfactory transactions, profits earned, expanded customer base, and practicality for your business. You can also use this chapter to assess auctions that you listed during your ongoing auction business.

Did Your Internet Auction Strategy Work?

As you read this section, you may want to have your Worksheets handy so you can update them as you arrive at certain conclusions based on your experience. Here you'll examine the essential components of each step by quizzing yourself about the results of your auction trial.

Did You Market the Right Products?

In Chapter 3, you assessed your products for salability through Internet auctions. You determined your target market and the best ways to reach your customers. You also examined how to tailor your selling style to avoid some common marketing mistakes. Now let's review your newly acquired experience with Internet auction marketing.

Did You Have Adequate Stock on Hand?
One way to determine if you needed more stock is if you ran a Dutch auction and ended up selling every item in the lot for more than your starting bid. This means you could have listed more and sold more. If you sold all that you had on hand, congratulations! Your auction was a huge success and you're ready to do it again.

The same applies to single auctions. If your item sold much higher than what you determined to be a market-compatible starting price, then you need to list any that you have left in stock—soon.

Were You Able to Write an Accurate Description?
While the auction was running, did you receive many e-mail messages from potential bidders asking the same or similar questions? If so, you know to incorporate this information when you update your descrip-

tion for the next round. You'll also be able to anticipate questions and include the answers in advance.

Does Your Sales Pitch Need Improvement?

If you sold less than one-third of your lot, the answer is yes. Further along you'll read about taking another look at your auction to decide what you need to improve. Since folks will buy virtually anything at the Internet auction sites, there's no reason why your products didn't sell if you put enough effort into your listing and timed your auction to be consistent with current market demands. It may take a few tries to get it down—and that's perfectly all right. Don't give up if your first attempt isn't a resounding success. Make the best of what you learned and keep going. You have a chance to even out your profits as you get the hang of planning your Internet auction sales.

Was Your Price in Line with the Market?

Product pricing is another component of Step 1. Now that your auction has ended, check your closing bid against that of auctions that your competitors listed for the same product. Were your starting bids all within range of each other? If yours closed under the average, you have room to price the products higher next time. If your auctions closed higher than your competition, keep doing whatever it is you did during your trial. You're an Internet auction natural if customers were willing to pay more for *your* stuff. Either way, it's important to analyze your results. And be sure to calculate your profits!

How Many of Your Auctions Closed Successfully?

Suppose you ran 10 trial single-item auctions and six of them closed successfully. Take a close look at the four that didn't result in sales and consider the following possibilities:

- Incorrect listing category

- Unsearchable auction title

- Errors in title or description

- Attempted sales during an off-season

- Starting price too high

- Lack of market interest

- Insufficient information in the description

- Uninviting description composition

- Unrealistic seller terms

Review Chapter 3 and your Step 1 worksheets to see how you can adjust your sales pitch (via your title, description, and timing) to improve your results. Remember, too, that there is also a chance that the market just wasn't "on" for your item during that particular week. Many items sell after one re-listing. I have listed items with starting bids of $10 that close with no bids, so I re-list them and they close for over $20 the second time around. I find this amazing, since the same items would have cost $10 the week before. But that's the nature of online auctions. If at first you don't succeed, then list, list again. Or something like that.

How Many Bids Did Your Trial Auctions Draw?

If your lot of 10 items drew 20 bids, your auction was a huge success and you should list another lot the same way as soon as you can. Don't change a thing. If your reserve-price auction didn't successfully close but drew one or more bids, then your price was probably out of line with what customers will pay. Try again with a lower starting bid, as long as it's not below your price floor.

Did You Use the Right Type of Auction Site?

If you opt to list at more than one site to widen your market, go back over Step 2 in Chapter 4. With your Internet auction experience fresh in your mind, you can make an informed choice about what type of venue you plan to use for your future online auction business.

Which Type of Auction Site Did You Use?

If your test auctions were successful and you're satisfied with your earnings, then you know you've targeted the right market via the right site, or type of site. If you feel bold and wish to branch out, then you can decide if you want to list at more sites either exclusively or in conjunction with another type of Internet auction site. It all depends on your business goals and expectations, and whether you have the resources available (such as time or adequate staff) to increase your auction efforts.

Will Another Type of Site Fit Your Business Model?

Do you meet a B2B site's qualifications to list at their venue or sell on consignment through their channels? Selling to other businesses usually means you'll have customers with deeper pockets placing larger orders. You need to decide if your business is ready for that kind of expansion and if it can handle the extra volume. If not, continue building your momentum slowly.

Should You Use a Bigger or Smaller Site?

In Chapter 3, I recommend running your test auction at an established C2C Internet auction site like eBay or Amazon Auctions. Determine if your success at one of them was sufficient to meet or exceed your goals. You may want to consider listing at more than one of them, or at a newer site like SellYourItem.com. You can also try listing at a B2B site if it fits your business model.

Was the Site Easy to Use?

If your auctions succeeded and you made a satisfactory profit, it probably doesn't matter if the site was easy to use because with practice, you'll be able to list auctions by rote no matter how convoluted the process is.

However, if your auctions were only marginally successful and launching them was a headache-producing venture, try another site. There are too many of them available to find yourself stuck at a site that's not user-friendly. Also, consider using an auction service provider with auction-listing software that works with the auction site that you're using.

Did Your Requested Payment Method Work?

Step 3 helped you decide on the best payment methods for your customers. During your test auctions, you most likely opted to accept several different forms of payment so you could assess each one's effectiveness for your business. You may not have had an opportunity to experience each option, but you can assess the method by which your customers *did* pay you.

Did Your Customers Mail in Payments?

If you asked your high bidders to mail payments to you in the form of a personal check or money order, check your records to see if you received them within the interval you specified in your seller terms. Did waiting for personal checks to clear hold you up too much, or did you consider that it helped your business by making it easier for your customers to pay you?

How Was Your Experience with an Online Payment Service?

Many businesses swear by the ease at which online payment services allow them to complete transactions and get products out to their customers. Market predictions indicate that some of the major credit card companies will soon offer online payment services backed by financial institutions. The idea has definitely caught on and will be a boon to helping many businesses offer instant turnarounds when shipping products to their customers. If using an online payment system didn't work for you for some reason, the best advice is to isolate the problem, and then resolve it. Here are some possibilities and suggestions:

Problem	Recommended Solution
Customers were not registered at any online payment service.	Send them a link to the payment site's registration page and extend their payment deadline by a few days so they can become familiar with the site.
Customer is registered at another popular online payment service and you're not.	If it's that popular, consider registering an account there, or offer the customer an alternate payment method.
Site charges excessive transaction fees.	Look into establishing a business account with the payment site. Or, check the fee schedule at a competing site to see if it better fits your needs.

To nurture customer relations, you must accept that some customers will be reluctant to use an online payment service. Whether it's been warranted or not, sites like PayPal have received a fair amount bad press. Continue to offer other payment methods for customers who are leery of the online payment services.

Did You Opt for an Online Billing Service?

If you used an online billing service to dispatch your end of auction e-mail messages, were you satisfied with the level of interaction it allowed you to have with your customers? If not, you may want to check out an online billing program that allows you to personalize your EOA messages. You definitely want your EOA e-mail message to be effective.

Did Anyone Request to Use Escrow?

Most Internet auction customers aren't as likely to request using escrow from auctions run by a business unless they're purchasing a big-ticket item and you have low feedback or recently registered. People are more inclined to request escrow when they're buying something very expensive from a private auction seller. If your auction description reflected a business-run sale, it's doubtful that anyone requested escrow.

If any of your customers did request third-party intervention, use it to your advantage. Examine your auction from a potential bidder's point of view. Does something sound "fishy" in your product claim? Try to determine how your description can better instill a potential bidder's confidence in your business practices. Maybe you need to re-vamp your auction ad a little.

Did the Auction Listing Process Run Smoothly?

In Step 4, you read about the tools you need in order to list auctions, and how to launch your listings once you registered at an Internet auction site. Then we discussed writing your auction description and including an image. You started your auctions, and then kept track of them. You watched as your customers found them and bid while the clock ticked away. Did each phase of this process work for you? Let's find out.

Did Your Tools Work?

PCs and their associated hardware components are typically user friendly, and there's plenty of tech support available for any part of that process that may become problematic. If your mouse bites you, someone either a phone call or e-mail message away can give you help and advice. You can even find answers to your hardware questions on the Web, if you do a search for "computer hardware tutorial." Check your bookstores for comprehensive manuals. And do something about that cranky mouse.

Was the Auction Site Tutorial Helpful?

All user-friendly Internet auction venues provide instructions on how to list auctions and bid. If you had to e-mail the site with questions one too many times, though, the tutorial probably wasn't as effective as it should be. If you liked everything else about the site (including your sales results), make your own set of crib notes to use next time you list an auction there.

Were Your Title and Description Accurate?

The best way to determine this is by using page counters on your auctions, such as the ones provided by Honesty. If an auction page counter indicates more than 35 hits for a 5-day listing, this is a fair indication that your title came up in searches. If your page counter was low, then you need to adjust your title to contain words that your customers are likely to use in their searches. Check out what your competition uses, and make a few adjustments when you list the products again.

The same logic applies to your auction description, but it goes a little further than just having it come up in searches. Let's say your auction listing had plenty of hits (good title) but a measly amount of bids. This could mean that potential bidders viewed your auction but weren't turned on by your description. Here are a few possible reasons:

- Did you provide enough information about the product, and make it sound attractive?

- Big orange letters on a bright purple background may have sent your viewers running for aspirin. Did your auction formatting detract from your listing?

- Bad spelling and grammar lessens your credibility as a seller. Did you proofread before you went live?

- Did you overuse special effects, such as slowly loading background images, annoying music, and unnecessary Java Applets? Remember that there's a difference between "adding nice touches" and "grossly overdoing it." Your lost customers would probably agree.

These checkpoints mainly pertain to the overall composition and appearance of the auction—maybe you can call it "auction housekeeping." If your auction description was a Web page developer's dream, other reasons could have made bidders shy away from it.

Did You Successfully Create and Upload Your Images?

If your listing image came up as a broken link and you didn't get around to fixing it, the result was probably disastrous. You most likely lost out in favor of competitive listings with photographs. If your image host experienced a lengthy site outage that prevented your photos from uploading into your auction listings, let the site administrators know that they cost you valuable time and money—especially if you're paying for the service. If you don't get a satisfactory response, consider changing to a different image host.

If your photos did appear but your auctions had only marginal success, be sure the images were effective:

- Did you crop out extraneous background?

- Was the picture in focus?

- Was the photo too dark or washed out, not representing the item well?

- Did you shoot the photograph from the best possible angle?

- Were there too many other items in the picture?

If you think you could have done a better job with your images, review the guidelines presented in Chapter 6 for preparing eye-catching auction photos. With the right presentation, you'll have an edge over your competitors.

Did You List Auctions via a Bulk Uploader?

Most full-time auction sellers I know swear by auction uploaders because they save so much time. With stored descriptions and images, the seller schedules the auctions to start at a particular time and can do something else while the program does the work. If you plan to have many Internet auctions active continuously, you should consider using a tool that lets you launch numerous auctions at one time.

Did You Time Your Auction Well?

Those of us who spend a lot of our free time logged onto the Internet know how hours slip away unnoticed. Before we know it, it's one in the morning and we're still plugging along. An eager Internet auction seller may work a few hours on his or her auction descriptions, proofread and check the results, and then list them without realizing that it's 2 A.M.—which means that the auctions will close at 2 A.M. a few days later. This might be great for bidders in Tibet, but not if you're trying to target customers on your home continent. Did this happen to you? If so, you've most likely learned your lesson and will shoot for a better time when you list auctions in the future. Unless, of course, your auction managed to entice two insomniacs into a bidding war. But don't count on it.

Were Any of Your Auctions Closed by the Site?

Oops. If the Internet auction site notified you that they closed one of your auctions because the content violated their Terms and Conditions, be sure that you consider this action very carefully. You should always operate within the site's guidelines. Violations can have severe consequences, even it they were unintentional. You'll read more about auctions closed by the site in Chapter 12, along with how you should handle the situation.

Did You Promote Your Auctions?

Chapter 7 helped you develop a plan to promote your auctions, as called for in Step 5. We discussed e-mail lists, banner ads, paid advertising, cost-effective ads, and where you can sneak in freebie plugs. Even with a limited budget, there's plenty you can do to let potential customers know that your business is alive and your products are out there right now, coaxing bids.

What Promotional Methods Did You Use?

Did you make refrigerator magnets like Carol Angelo's, or purchase a banner ad on a popular Web portal for $10,000 CPM? Whatever meets your business needs and gets you the results you want—more customers and tidy profits—is worth the time and effort. Keep track of how well your auctions did during specific advertising campaigns so you can see if there's any connection. Stick with a winner.

Which Ones Drew Bidders to Your Auctions?

The best way to find out is to ask your high bidders how they found your auctions. You can incorporate a question like this into your end of auction message. Ask your high bidder to let you know how he or she found your auctions from a list of choices. Here are some suggestions:

- Auction title search

- Title and description search

- Link from your business Web site

- Business e-mail

- Banner ad

- Bulletin-board post

- Store handout

- Refrigerator magnet

- Subway graffiti

Okay, so that last one is stretching it a little bit. But asking your customers how they found your auctions lets you know where to concentrate your promotion efforts in the future. This is especially helpful if you have a limited advertising budget.

Assess New Customers Gained from the Venture

How many of your high bidders were new customers? Since you increased your market to include anyone with Internet access in countries you designated in your listing options, there's a very good chance that all of your high bidders were new customers. Hopefully, their e-mail addresses now appear on your e-mail list for product offers and newsletters.

Did the Transaction Complete Smoothly?

Step 6 is the final production step in your Strategy, and deals with completing the six phases of the transaction that you read about in Chapter

8. Here you'll assess how well you carried out your seller's responsibilities. You'll examine how effective your product packaging and shipment packing was, whether you chose the best carrier for your business needs, how well the exchange of user feedback went, and if you were able to accomplish all this in keeping with good business ethics.

Did You Receive Any Questions During the Auction?

In Chapter 8, where you read about responding to potential bidders' requests for information about the product you had up for auction, I encouraged you to keep track of your response interval. This record is part of your customer-service audit. Did your response arrive in time for the users to place a bid, if they chose to? You can't control how fast your e-mail response transmits once you send it, but you can control the timeliness of your response. Any clarification request from a potential bidder that you receive while the auction is live should be given top priority.

How Soon After the Auction Did You Send Your EOA Message?

Most Internet auction sites—even the high-end B2B movers—notify the high bidder right after the auction ends. In this case, "right after" means within minutes of the auction closing. The auction site's EOA messages reach both the seller and the high bidder by way of computer-generated e-mail, so the speed of the message depends on how well the network is moving and if the e-mail program is oiled up and running optimally. It usually does, but sometimes it doesn't. It's best not to rely on auction site-generated EOA messages to let you know when your auction closed. Watch your listings as they close, if you can, and then send your own EOA message to your high bidders.

So, using the records you kept from Chapter 8, how many of your EOA messages went out within one hour of the auction closings? Strive for 100 percent.

Did You Include All Necessary Packaging?

Here's a packaging checklist:

- Did you ship the item in the manufacturer's packaging?

- Did you re-package the item with custom materials?

- Did you include any product enclosures?

- Did you include all associated product documentation?

These may not all apply to the products you sold, but you should be mindful of any packaging that should ship along with your goods.

Did You Pack the Product Securely for Shipping?

The best way to find out if you adequately packed a shipped item is if it arrived intact at the customer's location. If not, you most likely know about it already from the customer's complaint or return. If all of your shipments arrived intact, keep using whatever packing method you used during your trial. It obviously worked.

Did You Select the Best Carrier?

Here again, if the customers received their shipments timely and intact, your shipper did the job well and you picked a winner. If you had any claims to file on lost or damaged shipments, here's how you can assess the shipper's performance:

- Was the claim form easy to complete?

- Did their Web site give you the information you needed to determine the shipping rate?

- Did the shipping company's representative treat you (or your customer) respectfully?

- Did you experience anything that you'd consider a "hassle" when filing the claim?

- Was the claim paid? (You may not know this for a few months.)

You can make an overall assessment of your shipper's performance based on rates, usability of their Web site, and shipping performance.

Did You Give and Receive Feedback?

We discussed the two prevailing attitudes among sellers about when to enter feedback. After deciding which policy to adopt, did you post feedback once the buyer met the obligations as a paying customer? Here are several business tips on feedback etiquette:

- As a seller, always post feedback first. Never expect the customer to. This shows that you have faith in your business ethics.

- Always post positive feedback for promptly paying customers.

- Enter negative feedback as a last resort only, to warn other users.

- Use neutral feedback for situations where the customer brought undo duress to the transaction but did eventually pay you.

Double check now to see if you've entered feedback for all of your completed auctions during your trial.

Did You Play Nice?

At this point, we gather all of the Internet Auction Honors Candidates to the podium for their final dissertation, during which we ask these questions:

- Did you treat your customers with dignity and respect?

- Did you refrain from gouging customers with excessive shipping and insurance charges?

- Did you send the customer the item you advertised in your auction?

- Were you able to resist the temptation of foul play behind the Internet auction scenes?

If you answered yes to all of these, then consider yourself inducted and about to be sworn into the Internet Auction Seller's Honor Society. You may go forth and multiply your success. If you answered no to any of them, please get off the Internet and find yourself a different pastime.

Did You Meet Your Internet Auction Sales Goals?

This may be hard to tell after only running a test auction or a test campaign of auctions, but you can still determine whether you made a profit. As you progress, your assessments will increase in accuracy. This section contains some important things to consider when making the calculations.

Sales Estimates

Estimating your sales from Internet auctions is definitely not an exact science. It takes some research and you may not always be able to come up with an accurate estimate of how well a product will sell when listed at an online auction. You'll look for sales records in a few places:

- Closed auctions for the same item

- Sales for the same product generated through your Web site

- Sales results for the item as shown in business or trade journals

To estimate your future Internet auction sales, you'll have to rely on the results of your test auctions.

Operating Expenses

In addition to your essential business expenses, you'll need to allocate funds to cover the following Internet auction selling expenses:

- Upkeep on your computer hardware

- Necessary upgrades for your operating software

- Charges related to your Web-page development and maintenance

- Monthly access charge for your Internet Service Provider

- Auction-site fees

- Membership fees for your Internet auction service provider (image hosting, auction tools, etc.)

- Fees associated with your merchant account

- Fees associated with your online payment services account

You should also consider additional fees associated with IAO growth. One rule: if an online service you rely on is free, be sure you have the funds set aside to pay for it because it won't be free forever.

Cost of Inventory

In order to maintain a steady supply of items to list at Internet auctions, you need to invest in the products you're selling. You need to keep track of how much you spend on the goods you sell and how much it costs you to store the items. Some of the Internet auction service providers offer programs to help you keep track of your inventory. This is essential if you're stocking thousands if items.

Adequate Manpower

If your objective was to carry out your Internet auction business while maintaining a profitable Brick & Mortar business, carefully asses whether you or your Internet auction manager carried out the new venture without jeopardizing the whole business by spreading too thin.

If your business suffered because running Internet auctions took more time than you anticipated, you have a few options that will keep your Internet auction business running:

- Hire additional staff to run your auctions.

- Decrease the number of auctions you run per campaign.

- Shop around for an auction site with a less time-consuming process.

- Look into auction assistant software, or use an Internet auction service provider.

All of them depend on your business model, and your financial situation. You will have to choose the option that's best for your business.

Auction Site Fees

When you calculate your operating expenses, you must include Internet auction site fees. The C2C and B2C sites charge similar amounts for listings and site commissions. The B2B sites have a slightly different fee schedule.

Typical Fees at C2C Sites

At a site like eBay, sellers pay fees associated with the listing:

- Insertion fee

- Commission

- Optional display features (bold title, featured auction, etc.)

- Optional fees associated with special services

- Instant-purchase option fee

- Optional reserve-auction fee (applies only if item does not sell)

This table is an example of what you'll pay for listing auctions. You'll pay an insertion fee for every auction you list. Ordinarily, the fee varies according to your auction's opening value and multiplies based on the amount of items you offer.

Opening Value or Reserve Price:	Insertion Fee:
$0.01–$9.99	$0.30
$10.00–$24.99	$0.55
$25.00–$49.99	$1.10
$50.00–$199.00	$2.20
$200 and up	$3.30

Don't expect these fees to stay constant. They will increase periodically. Also, remember that the insertion fee is usually non-refundable if your item doesn't sell.

Note: Some sites offer Free Listing Days, so be sure to take advantage of those.

Here is what you can expect in terms of commission, or what eBay calls Final Value Fees. The site final value, or commission, is five percent of the sale amount up to $25, plus 2.5 percent of the amount above that. This table of Final Value Fees is from the eBay site:

Range of Final Price:	Final Value Fee:
$0.00–$25.00	5% of the closing value
$25.01–$1,000.00	5% of the initial $25 ($1.25), plus 2.5% of the remaining closing value balance.
$1,000.01 and up	5% of the initial $25 ($1.25), plus 2.5% of the initial $25-$1000 ($24.38), plus 1.25% of the remaining closing value balance.

For Dutch auctions, the fee depends on the amount of the minimum winning bid multiplied by the quantity of items sold.

Fees at B2C Sites

Since most C2C sites are also B2C sites, the same rates apply. However, at sites that only allow businesses to list items, the fee schedule may be slightly different. You may pay a flat monthly fee to list auctions, or a per-auction percentage. The plans differ at each site, which means you'll need to use an Auction Site Fee Calculation Worksheet from Chapter 2 in order to compare site fees and commissions.

Re-list Items that Didn't Sell

If your item doesn't sell the first time around, don't get discouraged. There's probably a customer looking for your item now who wasn't looking for it before. Most of the C2C sites offer free re-listing. Some of the B2B sites that offer timed listings will re-list your auctions automatically over the course of six months until the products sell.

Be sure that you understand the auction site's re-listing policy and that you know how the process works. Also, find out if you can change your title, description, starting price, and listing category when you re-list an item without being charged an additional fee. You might want to make a few adjustments that could encourage more bids.

Cross-market at a Different Site

If your products aren't doing well at consumer sites, try marketing them in lots at a B2B site. They may be hot products for a reseller to grab up in a large quantity. Likewise, if you listed one auction for a large quantity, you may want to split the items up into smaller quantities or singles, and go for the individual sales at a C2C or B2C site.

Use a Different Type of Auction

Maybe you need to get rid of that reserve price and adjust your starting price to be appropriate with the current market. Many bidders are put off by reserve auctions, and it's dubious whether business sellers should use them anyway, especially if you're marketing multiple items. Also, if you have your items individually listed, try using a Dutch auction where you list quantities of identical items. Perhaps your customers would rather buy your items in pairs or even larger quantities and would rather not have to track six or seven of your listings to make the purchases they want. This will also serve to keep your customers from buying some products from you, and the rest of the ones they need from your competition.

Keeping Good Records

Whether you maintain a photocopy of your shipping and payment notes or chronicle them in an accounting ledger, accurate records come in handy if you need to refer to the transaction later. One way to keep track of your auctions, whether you're the buyer or the seller, is to print the main auction page to keep on file. That page usually has the winner's name and the amount of the high bid in case you need to look it up once the auction ages out of the site's database. In addition to assessing your profits, you'll need to keep your auction descriptions, photos, and records of correspondence.

Determine Your Earnings

In Appendix C, you'll find your Monthly Earning Worksheet. Complete one line for each auction that successfully closed in the current month. For Dutch or other multi-item listings, use one line for each item sold in that auction.

Your Monthly Earning Worksheet will help you calculate your profits (or break-evens), but it will also help you calculate market trends for certain items. You'll know by checking your earnings which items do better at certain times of the year, or during certain events.

Keep Auction Descriptions on File

Save your auction descriptions as HTML files. If you used Notepad or a similar word processing program, you'll indicate this with the file extension ".html" or just ".htm" if your operating system will only accept three-letter extensions. Create a directory on your hard drive just for your auction descriptions and name them by item, such as "flowerpot.html." This will help you retrieve the right description when it's time to list the same product again.

Managing Your Photos

Keep copies of all your auction photos. You never know when you'll need to refer to one. Plus, in certain cases you can re-use auction photos if you plan to list a multiple-item auction for the exact same item in the photo.

Store any auction photos that you're not currently using in an auction on your computer's hard drive. Unless you're listing the same item again, delete the photo from your hosting location. This saves space and lessens the chance that someone will reuse your photo, since it will be unavailable to the public once you take it off the Web. You can also save photos on a floppy disk, CD, or another type of portable data-storage device.

You may want to number the image files after the date you listed the auction, like this:

Image file:	Date auction listed:
10312001-1.jpg	October 31, 2001
01292002-1.jpg	January 29, 2002——first one
01292002-2.jpg	January 29, 2002——second one
04302002-1.jpg	April 30, 2002——first one
04302002-2.jpg	April 30, 2002——second one
04302002-2a.jpg	April 30, 2002——second one, side view

With this type of system, there's a better chance of finding the picture if you need to refer to it long after the listing ages out of the auction site.

Save All E-mail!

I save all e-mail that transpires from online auction activity. I keep it in special directories named after the auction site the messages result from. Saved e-mail is helpful for many reasons:

- Recalling an address or telephone number the person sent you

- Checking the date the person promised to send payment

- Referring to the original agreement if a dispute arises

- Remembering a transaction with a particular user if someone asks for a reference

- Providing any necessary memory refresher about the transaction

- Most sites want to see copies of e-mail that transpired when you are reporting a dispute.

Your customer may appreciate your saving the e-mail too, especially if it's the only record of the original agreement. Sometimes e-mail disappears accidentally. I save auction-related e-mail messages on my hard drive for 12 months. Then I download them to a floppy diskette to keep on file. You never know when you might need to refer to an old e-mail message months after a transaction completes.

Is Selling at Internet Auctions Working for You?

By now you should know if this new venture works for you, and if it creates profits for your business. You now know which type of Internet auction site brings you the best results, and you have a working knowledge of how to list auctions and complete the transaction with your new customers. This is where you decide if you plan to make Internet auctions a regular part of your business.

Did the Auction Trial Meet Your Expectations?

If you sold all or most of the products you listed, then of course it did, provided you priced your products in line with your earning expectations. Here are a few more important questions:

- Can you devote the necessary time to this venture?

- Do you have adequate staff to handle this new facet of your business?

- Can you maintain adequate levels of customer satisfaction with this type of marketing?

If so, then it's time to ask yourself the final question.

Are You Ready to Keep Listing?

If the answer is yes, then gather your worksheets, your products, your digital camera, and your auction description templates and return to Step 1 for your next round of profits. You're on your way to getting the most out of an exciting new Internet selling venue.

You'll also want to read Chapters 10 through 13 for information that will help you hone your Internet auction transaction skills. Chapter 10 is primarily for independent sellers, but business sellers can benefit from the goal-setting and record-keeping techniques that I recommend for individuals who earn a living on eBay, Yahoo, or any of the other C2C auction sites. Chapters 11 through 13 offer hints and tips on winning with your new customers, handling difficult situations that may arise, and making the best use of online resources available for Internet auction sellers.

Good luck, and may your auctions bid high and your earnings abound.

10

Becoming an Internet Auction Entrepreneur

The Seven-Step Internet Auction Strategy also applies to independent sellers who have decided to take their products online. The World Wide Web is open to everyone, and many folks make their living by listing items on eBay, Yahoo, Amazon, or any number of other C2C or B2C auction sites. Many of the seller IDs you'll see with high feedback numbers belong to full-time online auction sellers.

If you're an independent seller who runs a one- or two-person Internet auction selling business, this chapter will help you apply the Seven-Step Internet Auction Strategy to your minimal-staff marketing efforts. We'll cover some of the best and most economical resources that are available to you, and we'll discuss a few business elements that will help you maintain a profitable venture:

- Your operating business model

- Applying the Seven-Step Internet Auction Strategy to your independent operation

- Accessing and using the Internet

- Your presence on the Web

- You and your Internet auction business

- Comments from full-time Internet auction sellers

If you're already a winning Internet auction seller, this chapter will help you put your business venture in perspective and keep you on a flexible and profitable course. You may even pick up a few ideas. Internet auctions can help you establish an online marketplace for your products, and to help further your online marketing career—and perhaps your personal goals.

Your Modus Operendi

Many folks make their living or supplement their family income through Internet auction sales. There's money to earn, so you might as well get your piece of the action.

If you read the previous chapters that cover the Seven-Step Internet Auction Strategy, you know everything that it takes to create auction listings and launch them. You won't have to kowtow to investors and a board of directors. Your Internet auction business is your brainchild, and you'll decide how it develops and runs.

Your Business Objectives

Naturally, you want to earn money from this venture. Your incentive will depend on how you've earmarked your earnings; that is, what you're going to do with the money. Mad-money earners can usually operate in whatever way strikes the mood, but for those who need the money for a specific reason—such as to live on—a structured plan is in order. This will give you better control over attaining your goals. We'll discuss goals a little later. Here we'll determine your driving force.

Event-Specific Earning
Perhaps your goal is to earn enough money to pay college tuition for yourself or a loved one. Or, maybe you're raising money to buy a house, pay for medical expenses, or finance a car. If you're earning profits

through Internet auctions to cover these types of expenses, this is **event-specific earning**. If you plan to list auctions only until you meet these expenses, then you'll be able to calculate a date of completion when you determine your goals.

Use this formula to determine how long you'll be running your Internet auction business before you attain your event-specific goal:

> Money needed ÷ Monthly earning potential
>
> = Number of months to operate

You can also determine your monthly earning goals by changing the formula:

> Money needed ÷ Number of months to operate
>
> = Monthly earning goal

If you decide you want to keep up your Internet auction business once you attain your goal, you can decide whether you want to direct your profits toward another financial obligation. Re-evaluate how you'll use the money, and then adjust your goals.

Family Income

Working from home is a preferred option for many people nowadays. Parents of small children can save on daycare costs, those who prefer to set their own hours can work when they please, and disabled people can support themselves. These examples are neither presumptuous nor all-inclusive—people want to work from home for any number of reasons. However, many people don't have a long list of choices, and Internet auction selling is one of very few available options.

Supplementing Disability Income

"Twelve years ago I became a right hemiplegic after an on the job accident requiring surgery damaged my central nervous system," says Marjie, a disabled eBay seller. "Being a hemiplegic means that I don't have the use of my right arm or my right leg. After years of wear and tear on my left limbs, I have limited use in those now as well."

Marjie is now wheelchair-reliant and sells full-time on eBay to supplement her disability income. "Well, it's full time for *me*," she says. "The nature of the disability renders me incapacitated for long periods. If I can get a good three hours of productive time out of most days, I consider myself very lucky. In my case, those three hours might be 20 minutes here or 45 minutes there, but you learn to work with what you have." Marjie spends from 10 to 15 hours per week preparing and listing her auctions, and tries to keep between 30 and 50 running at all times. I asked her how she handles the tasks involved with listing items for auction online.

"If you mean, do my customers know I'm disabled and does it affect whether they do business with me? The answer to that is no," she says. "The greatest single thing about selling online for disabled people is that no one need ever know. To my customers I'm just another seller. No prejudices going in, no special treatment. I started on the same playing field as everyone else. The disabled online seller is really no different from an able-bodied seller." Marjie chose a product line to list and sell on eBay that she found both interesting and productive.

"My most popular selling items are the Charity Bears, which support things like breast-cancer research, AIDS, children's cancer, homelessness, organ donation, and the like." Clearly, Marjie does much more than just supplement her disability income. Selling on eBay lets Marjie extend a helping hand to others in need.

Business Springboard
Perhaps from your Internet auction business you hope to build an expanded e-business. Test-marketing your products by listing them at Internet auctions is an excellent strategy, as you read about in Chapter 3. You determine your market, set your prices, and gain a wealth of important data to build a bigger business.

What Are Your Goals?

You might be saying, "Why set goals? I left a job where I had to prepare forecasts and compile endless reports. I just want to list auctions and make money!"

That may sound good, but goals are an important part of any moneymaking venture, at least one that has any chance of being successful. This section will help you decide which goals you want to attain, and how to pace your Internet auction business in order to achieve them.

Goals? I Don't Need No Steenkin' Goals!

Yes, you do. Goal setting is especially important for you. Suzette Assink, auction seller and associate of Ron's House of Rocks *(www.house-of-rocks.com)*, feels that establishing and maintaining monthly seller goals is paramount to the success of any independent Internet auction seller.

"We don't have a supervisor or coworkers to work with every day asking about our progress or competing with us for a raise," Suzette explains. "We really have no accountability to list auctions, but we still have to in order to survive in the business. We need to supervise ourselves by creating a goal sheet that checks up on us every month, like a boss would."

Suzette claims that setting goals helps ensure that she'll be profitable. "By finding even one other person to compare my success with, or by setting goals, I have a target to reach. It keeps me focused on keeping my auction numbers up."

When asked how she tracks her progress, Suzette says, "I use Ándale for monthly sales and eBay current listings to track the number of auctions I have active. I don't look at how many auctions that I list in a month. I strive to keep 200 active at all times."

In the sections that follow, we'll discuss how to break down your goals so you can calculate what you need to do in order to achieve your earning goal.

Monetary Goal

The amount of money you wish to earn is your **monetary goal**. For event-specific earning, your goal will be a specific amount, such as $9,500 for a down payment on a car. For earning household income, the goal will be a set amount at intervals you choose:

- Per week

- Per four-week period

- Per month

- Per year

If you know your monthly desired income, divide the number by 4.33. This will give you your earning goal for a seven-day period, or one week. It's easier to calculate auction earning and listing goals on a weekly basis, since the average auction runs from five to seven days. This will help you define your forecast and later determine if your results met your goals. When you start your auction selling, plan a 12-week trial. If you can meet or at least come close to your goals, you know they're realistic.

If you run a few test auctions before your trial period, you'll have some idea of what you can expect to earn from the type of products you'll sell. This is your estimate of earnings, and it will help you determine how many auctions you should run every week.

Listing Goal and Earnings per Item

Your **listing goal** translates into how many new auctions (which include re-listings on items that don't sell) you plan to launch per week. In order to generate new sales, you need to acquire more products, create new auctions, and manage the transactions with customers in order to keep your production running. Figure 10.1 illustrates a typical production flow for an independent Internet auction seller.

You should base your listing goal on your monetary goal and how many auctions you can reasonably manage. Then you need to deter-

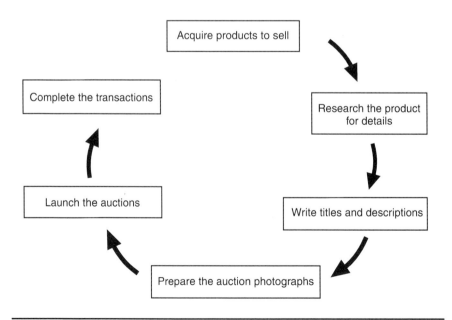

Figure 10.1. A typical production flow for an Internet auction seller.

mine how much you must earn for every item you sell. Some auctions may close higher or lower than others will, but the average price at which you must sell each item becomes your **earnings per item**.

Say, for instance, that you need to earn at least $3,500 every four weeks in order to attain your monetary goal. Your monetary goal should include your desired income, fees associated with online auction services, and what you pay for the products you sell. Suppose you decided you can manage 50 auctions per week, and we'll assume that all 50 of them close successfully. Here's a breakdown of how to calculate the average earnings per item in order to attain your monetary goal:

Monetary Goal per Four-Week Period	$3,500
Income needed per week ($3,500 ÷ 4)	$875.00
Listing goal per week (how many auctions you can manage)	50
Average high bid amount needed per item ($875 ÷ 50)	$17.50
Added listing fee and site commission (based on eBay's 2001 rate chart)	$1.18
Required average earnings per item	$18.68
Weekly earnings on 50 successful auctions at $18.68 each	$934.00
Minus site fees for 50 sales at $1.18 each	- $59.00
Weekly net earnings	$875.00

According to the chart above, you need 50 successfully closed auctions per week at an average earnings per item of $18.68 to attain your goal of $875 per week, and $3,500 per four-week period.

Note: If you list Dutch auctions or another type of multi-item listing, count each item you offer in the auction as one listing. For example, a Dutch auction for six items counts as six listings.

Completed Auctions Goal

In the forecast table above, you determined that you needed 50 completed auctions to attain your monetary goal if you attain your earnings-per-item amount. This makes 50 your **completed auction goal**. While the calculations assume that all of your auctions will successfully close, that doesn't always happen. Any number of factors can cause items to run for five days without a bid. The OAI is quirky at times.

To attain your weekly goals, you should list a higher number of auctions than your completed auction goal. If your completed auction goal is 50, strive to list at least 65. This will allow some leeway if some of your auctions don't successfully close, or if the average earnings per item on 50 closings falls below your requirement.

Week _____ / _____ to _____ / _____	
Monetary Goal per Four-Week Period	
Income needed per week ($_____ ÷ 4)	
Listing goal per week (how many auctions you can manage)	
Average amount per item ($_____ ÷ _____)	
Plus listing fee and site commission (based on eBay's 2001 rate chart)	
Average closing price goal per item	
Weekly earnings on _____ successful auctions at $_____ each	
Minus site fees for _____ sales at $_____ each	
Weekly net earnings	

Weekly Forecast and Results Worksheet

You can use the following table for your listing and sales goals. You can use the same worksheet to calculate your results, which you'll read about a little further on.

Keeping Records of Your Earnings

You need to keep track of your closed auctions and your earnings per item in order to assess your Internet auction selling plan and determine whether you need to work harder in any particular area. Here we'll discuss tracking your auction sales results, and adjusting your goals and sales efforts accordingly.

Auction Number	Date Closed	High Bid	Site Fees (insertion and commission)	Net Earnings

Record of Successfully Closed Auctions

Use the table below to keep track of your closed auctions and net earnings. If you use more than one auction site, you may wish to insert a column to record on which site the auction ran. Since this worksheet is ongoing and not broken down into seven-day or four-week periods, you can use it to calculate your results by calendar month. Then you can complete your monthly results worksheet.

Only record auctions that successfully close. Record the auction number, date of closing, and the high bid price on your worksheet. For Dutch or multiple-item listings, use a separate line for every transaction resulting from that auction, and count each sale as one listing.

Monthly Results Worksheet

From your record of successfully closed auctions, you can keep track of your earnings per month. Once you've completed your monetary and listing forecasts, you can transfer the results to a quarterly earnings worksheet. Here is a sample worksheet to help you measure the success of your goals.

Quarterly Listing and Earning Monthly Goals and Results				
First Quarter 2002	Goal:	Results:		
		January	February	March
Listings Active				
Successful Auctions				
Net Earnings				
Results:				

▌▌▌➡ **Note:** Some sellers also include goals for feedback received from satisfied buyers. While this won't directly effect your earnings results, it will effect your reputation as a seller, which could have an indirect effect on your results.

Adjusting Your Goals to Meet Your Needs

If your results meet or exceed your goals, you're a huge success and you have the option of raising the bar. Increase your goals and earn even more. If your results fell short of your needed earnings, you have the option of adjusting your goals. Here are a few other ideas:

- List items that sell higher.

- Launch more auctions for more items.

- Sell different products.

- Try another auction site.

- Review Step 1 to determine if you're marketing your products effectively.

With a few adjustments to your way of operating, you can run another trial to see if you have better results.

Should You Have Help?

The more successful your Internet auction business becomes, the more you'll be at it, and the more work you'll have. If you suddenly find that you can't ship all of your items to your high bidders during your specified interval or adequately manage your listing goals, this could mean that a helping hand or two is necessary. Since you'll be able to increase your earning potential by having more time to list auctions, this could easily offset paying someone minimum wage for a few hours a week.

Hire a Part-Timer
For some of the physical aspects of the job, such as packing items for shipping and dispatching them to the carrier, a part-time clerk or messenger could save you plenty of time. Using your stack of prepared shipping notices (see Chapter 8), he or she could prepare shipping labels, securely pack items for shipping, insert your shipping enclosures, and deliver the packages to your shipper.

Offer the job to someone you know who might need some extra spending money. Your local community center might be able to provide qualified candidates with references. Be sure to operate within your community's hiring laws. Check the Small Business Homepage at MyCounsel.com *(www.mycouncel.com/content/smbusiness)* for some important employer guidelines.

Get the Kids Involved!
If you have children, it might help to let them handle some of the tasks appropriate for their developmental level. Small children can fold your

shipping notices and put them in envelopes along with your other enclosures. Older children can retrieve and replace items for you as you take your auction photographs. They can also help you load your trunk with packages when you head for the post office. Teens of driving age can serve as porters to take packages for shipping, and check your mail for payments.

Involving your children in your Internet auction business can teach them about good business practice and responsibility. You'll also be spending quality time with them.

"As soon as your children are old enough, explain what you are doing and encourage their involvement. For example, let your toddler turn on your computer each day. As your children grow, they will learn how to use your equipment and begin to absorb business principles which will help them throughout their lives. When you have success, share it with them and let them choose a new toy or go out and celebrate in a special restaurant. If your children can see tangible benefits, they will want you to succeed at your work."

From "10 Ways to Have Happy Kids While You Work at Home," *www.homeworkingmom.com/kids.htm*

Applying the Seven-Step Internet Auction Strategy

Now that you know how to calculate your sales goals in order to achieve your desired income, you need to determine what you'll sell. You may want to decide on a theme for your business so you can target the right market. The Seven-Step Internet Auction Strategy you read about in the previous chapters provided essential details in setting up your business. For your independent Internet auction seller strategy, a few of the steps are more important to you.

The Essential Steps for an Independent Seller

For independent sellers, you need to pay special attention to these three steps, and their associated chapters, that contain essential elements of your independent strategy:

- **Step 1 (Chapter 3)**—Select your products and identify your market.

- **Step 4 (Chapter 6)**—List the products for auction.

- **Step 6 (Chapter 8)**—Complete the transaction.

From these three Internet Auction Strategy steps, you can develop a simplified process that you can follow.

Applying the Steps to Your Business

Here we'll map the essential components of the three Internet Auction Strategy steps to your independent seller activities and extract the most essential elements of them. This will serve to create some helpful guidelines for you when you customize your own selling strategy.

Step 1—Identifying Products to Sell

For independent sellers, deciding what products to sell is quite different than for business sellers. Business sellers typically have a somewhat-defined product line. Independent sellers have infinite choices of items to sell at online auctions, limited only by availability. Knowing your own capabilities and paying attention to current entrepreneurial trends will help you decide what type of products to sell. Your product focus might include these general categories:

- **Once over lightlys**—Sell second-hand clothing or items you pick up at thrift shops or garage sales.

- **Specific products**—Sell items you know backwards and forwards and build a reputation on it.

- **Handcrafted items**—Many crafters market their products on the C2C sites and do quite well at it. You'll see hand-crafted jewelry, polymer clay figurines, acrylic paintings, and even homemade cookies.

- **Your own patents**—Do you want to market one of your own patented inventions by selling them through Internet auctions? This will help if you later seek an investor for your idea because you can boast a sales record.

- **Anything and everything**—Sell whatever comes your way. Shop yard sales and thrift shops, clean your aunt's attic, and ask your friends to send you their castoffs. No limits.

Start slowly by running some trial auctions involving low-cost items to build up a user rating. The results of your trial will also help you determine your target market, what category to list your products in, and help you forecast pricing levels for your future auctions. Review Chapter 3 for detailed advice.

Step 4—Listing Your Auctions

Chapter 6 covers Step 4 and describes the tools you need to access the Internet and locate the C2C online auction sites. First, do you have everything you need to get online? Here's a checklist:

- **Hardware**—Computer, modem, keyboard, mouse

- **Software**—ISP program, graphics program

- **Imaging tools**—Digital camera, scanner, makeshift studio

- **Internet access**—ISP, auction site ID and password

- **Inventory**—Have enough product to cover your listings. Sell only what you have in your possession; avoid pre-sells

Now read about the finer points involved in preparing an auction listing. Plan to spend some time researching other sellers' auctions to get some ideas—and then do it better than they do. You can also get some great ideas and information by asking your "Internet auction coworkers" in a discussion forum to critique your listings for you.

- **Site tutorial**—Learn how to use the site.

- **Target hours**—Determine the day and time of day for your auction to close.

- **Title**—Write an accurate auction title that will come up in searches.

- **Description**—Present your products better than your competition.

You need to include an image with each auction you list, even if it's a stack of 10 cloth diapers. People still want to see them. This will take some preparation time if you want to do it right.

- **Digital images**—Produce your photographs in GIF or JPG format.

- **Production**—Set up a small photo studio, take the photos or scan your items with a scanner, and then crop and resize the pictures.

- **Image host**—Find a way to have your images hosted on a Web site.

You'll read more details in Chapter 6. Once you have all the necessary elements needed for your auctions, it's time to list them.

- **Auction-entry form**—Access it and enter your auction title.

- **Category**—It's important to select the one that best fits your item.

- **Description**—Copy your prepared auction description into the field provided.

- **Picture**—Enter the image URL in the appropriate space.

- **Click "Enter"**—Start your auction, launch your listing; it all means the same thing. Take it live and make it sell.

Step 6—Your Responsibilities During the Transaction

The Internet auction transaction starts when you launch the auction and ends when both parties leave each other site feedback. As a seller, you're responsible for knowing your rights and what's expected of you by the OAI.

- **Truth**—Present the item accurately, include any pertinent details, and include accurate photos of the item.

- **Terms**—Include your policies on payments, returns, feedback, escrow, and international sales.

- **Accurate postage**—It helps to have a postage scale. Check carrier's Web sites for rate charts.

- **Returns**—Know your rights if a buyer wishes to return an item, and watch for scams.

- **Communication**—Promptly answer questions from potential bidders, giving them enough time to decide if they want to bid on your auction.

When the auction ends, send out your EOA messages as soon as possible. When you're ready to ship the item, you need to be especially careful how you pack it for shipping to make sure it reaches your customer undamaged.

- **Be prompt**—Buyers want their items as soon as they pay for them, or once their payment clears.

- **Pack soundly**—Use reliable packing materials, such as Bubble Wrap and puffies, and double box if necessary. Be sure you don't damage the item when you pack it. Watch that adhesive tape dispenser.

- **Shipping note**—Include the item name, auction number, and date you shipped the item.

- **Enclosures**—Enclose your business card, or goodies to thank your customer.

- **E-mail**—Let your buyer know when his or her item has shipped.

Just a few more things:

- **Feedback**—*Always* enter positive feedback for customers who carried out their end of the transaction to your satisfaction.

- **Personal activity**—If you also use your seller site ID to buy items from other users, watch out for sellers that might mar your reputation with negative feedback. Many full-time sellers use a secondary user ID for buying.

That was a review of Step 1, Step 4, and Step 6. Be sure to carefully read the corresponding chapters when you plan your goals and selling strategy.

Business Tips

As an independent online auctioneer, you have certain advantages over midsize and large business online auction sellers. You typically won't have as much money tied up in your goods, which means it's easier for you to shift gears if you decide to change your product focus.

Remain Flexible

Allowing yourself to run test auctions lets you ascertain how certain products sell. The more items you have experience selling, the less chance there is that your earnings will suffer if your main product line suddenly loses popularity. A few years ago, one of my favorite pastimes was making knotted friendship bracelets out of embroidery floss. They were wildly popular with the neighbor kids. I had a ready supply of friendship bracelets in all colors and styles to dole out as rewards for doing my yard work. Over time, though, the friendship bracelets became passé. Now the kids were wearing colorful glass seed beads strung on elastic cord.

To stay current and keep my yard tidy, I put away the floss and stocked up on beads and elastic. If this had been my eBay business, the product switch would have kept my earnings up by shifting my product line to match current trends. Changing from knotting to stringing beads is an example of profitable marketing flexibility. To keep my earnings steady, I could have sold my remaining friendship bracelets as a lot. This may have produced a break-even point on the remainder stock, and it would serve to clear out excess inventory and make room for products with better earning potential.

Seeking Other Opportunities

You might specialize in selling handmade quilts and comforters, but that doesn't mean you have to pass on something available at a yard sale that you know might sell high. Here again you have an innate advantage over a Brick & Mortar business. How likely would you be to sell a silver salt cellar in a toy store? It could take years to sell it, and not many customers would be willing to pay top dollar for it. It's difficult and costly to switch markets for a one-item sale no matter how valuable it might be to the few buyers looking for it—unless you're online.

No matter how specialized your Internet auction sales are, you can list a hot item in another auction listing category while your usual product line continues to thrive. Your hot item reaches the right market, and sells for top dollar. Never pass up an opportunity to make an honest profit at the auction sites—especially if your livelihood depends on it.

Cashing in on Trends

You're doing some shopping at a toy warehouse and you see their recent shipment of a hot item that sells at online auctions for at many times the retail value. You're on your way over to grab one for a profitable secondary-market sale, but your steady online auction customers are used to buying note cards from you. Many of them have your auction page bookmarked and this toy auction will come up along with your other auctions. What will they think of you for cashing in on a trend?

In Chapter 8, I mention the importance of keeping your business and your personal Internet auction activity separate. If you plan to list an item to earn a quick buck but you worry that your income-producing customers might not approve, sell the item under your personal user ID. There's no reason you shouldn't cash in on a trend—especially one worth a few hundred dollars.

Going Internet

In the previous section, we talked about the tools you need in order to list online auctions, one of which is access to the Internet. Before you can operate successfully as an Internet auction seller, you need to take care of three important details:

- Access to the Internet

- A Web page

- An e-mail address

Getting on the Internet—Cheaply

You need access to the Internet in order to use it for anything, of course. Review the "Getting on the Internet" section in Chapter 6 if you're not online yet. Here we'll discuss some ways to access the Internet on a fledgling budget.

WebTV

This service, provided by WebTV Networks, Inc., requires the use of a "set-top box" that's about the size of a standard VCR. It allows you to access the Internet through a television set without using a computer. It sits on top of your television with one cable hooked into your set and another connected to a phone line. You must purchase the box and then pay a monthly service fee. The connection is somewhat less expensive than an ISP, but has a few limitations associated with it:

- The Web pages you access appear about 10 lines at a time, which means you'll have to do a lot of scrolling.

- The resolution on a typical TV screen is not as good as on a computer monitor, making small text difficult to read.

- Unless you plug a keyboard into the set-top box, you're limited to read-only, meaning that you can't enter data. Internet sellers need the optional keyboard.

- You can't download programs or view certain streaming video programs.

- You may have trouble participating in chat rooms run with the Java programming language.

Despite these, many independent auction sellers successfully use WebTV to list auctions.

Free Internet Access

Several sites offer free Web access and e-mail. To use one of these services, you need an active connection to the Internet in order to download the free site software, unless you have the program on diskettes or a CD. When you surf the Web this way, you'll dial a number provided by the service. Then, as you launch your browser, a little advertising window appears on your monitor screen. Throughout your session, you'll see continuous ads from companies that sponsor the site.

The table below includes Web sites that offer free Internet access:

Site Name	Web Address
dotNow! Free Internet Access	*www.dotnow.com*
NetZero	*www.netzero.net*
PowerChannel	*www.freepctv.net*
NoCharge.com	*www.nocharge.com*
Juno	*www.juno.com*

For more information about free Internet access sites in the United States, Canada, and several other countries, check out the Free E-mail Address Directory *(www.emailaddresses.com)*. From the "Free Stuff" directory, click on "Internet Access."

There are some drawbacks to free Internet access. Response time is typically much slower and less reliable than what you'll get with a paid ISP, and, of course, the free providers bombard you with ads the entire time you're online. You may also pay by the minute for calls to their technical support.

Getting a Web Page

You'll find many places on the Web where you can build yourself a Web page without paying a dime for it. These freebie sites offer other services as well as letting you build your own home page. They'll host your domain or provide you with a URL, let you establish your own Web address, and offer you the most important part of your independent auction seller business—an e-mail address. Sites that allow you to establish yourself on the Internet are called **Web Presence Providers** (WPPs). They're different from ISPs, as you need an existing Internet connection to use a WPP.

If you can afford it, you may want to look into a Web host that you pay for because the presentation is more streamlined than a free service. However, if your budget dictates that you make the most of free services (and can tolerate the sponsor ads), check out these WPPs:

- Angelfire.com

- Tripod.com

- Geocities.com

Your visitors may see pop-up windows when they access your page, but an independent auction seller's customers won't spend a lot of time there. We'll discuss why a little further along.

Getting an E-mail Address

You need an e-mail address for several reasons, including:

- Communicating with your customers and the auction site

- Registering at an Internet auction site

- Opening an online payment service account

- Setting up auction service provider accounts, if you decide to use them

Many free WPPs provide you with e-mail accounts for the same non-existent price. Your paid Internet service provider (ISP) typically provides e-mail and most of them will host your Web site.

Registering Your Internet Business

You'll need to come up with a name for your business in order to distinguish you from others. The name should be memorable and have something to do with your endeavor.

Naming and registering your business is important for several reasons:

- It comes in handy during tax time.

- It will help maintain your privacy.

- You can open a business bank account.

When customers address payments to your business, it's not as personal as when they address them to your first and last name. You won't even have to reveal your real name to your Internet auction customers if you only operate under your business name. This is very important for folks who don't like to reveal a lot of personal information. You can also set up your auction site IDs in your business name.

Since your business will probably be classified as a sole proprietorship, you'll need to register your business name as a fictitious or assumed name. This will prevent anyone else from using your business name to steal your customers or cash in on your good reputation. Before you can register the name, make sure it's available in the area where you plan to operate. If you'll operate from your home, then that's considered your area. Your county clerk will be able to tell you if your business name is already taken. It's best to have a few alternative names picked out just in case.

A sole proprietorship using a business name other than the owner's real name must be registered. Your county clerk can provide you with an application for a fictitious or assumed name with the county, and all the information you need to register and protect your business name. Be sure to specify that you'll be operating an Internet business and not setting up a Brick & Mortar store.

Open a Bank Account
Once you've registered your business name and you've fulfilled your local and state requirements for operating under that name, open a business bank account. This will allow your customers to make out checks and money orders directly to your business. You can also register an online payment service account under your business name, which will keep it separate from your personal accounts.

Hello, Uncle Sam
If you're in the United States, you need a Tax ID number on file with the Internal Revenue Service in order to file income tax. You're also responsible for paying taxes based on the revenue that your business generates. These may include federal income tax, state income tax, and property tax. Instead of attempting to include the information here, which is subject to change, I'll direct you to the IRS Small Business and Self-Employed Community *(www.irs.gov/smallbiz)*. That site contains the most current tax information for small business owners.

Register a Domain Name

Your own Internet domain, such as "www.YourBusiness.com," will call attention to you as a standout venture. If your regular Internet auction customers want to check out what you've got up for auction in any given week, they can call your site by your memorable domain name and see the links right to your auctions. Your business Web page will help you in number of ways:

- It adds dimension to the products you're marketing.

- It lends credibility to your selling venture.

- It provides a reference point for your customers.

To register a domain, you first need to find out if it's already taken. You can check a few places on the Web:

Site Name	Web Address
Network Solutions	*www.networksolutions.com*
Interland	*www.interland.com*
The Official United States Domain Registry	*www.nic.us*

Network Solutions allows you to search a database of registered domains (see Figure 10.2). If the one you request is no longer available, you'll see a list of suggestions that closely match your request. For instance, if you request *www.qwertyuiop.com* and someone already has it, Network Solutions will bring up a list of suggestions, such as:

- myqwertyuiop.com

- e-qwertyuiop.com

- aboutqwertyuiop.com

- qwertyuioponline.com

- qwertyuiopcentral.com

Prepare to pay between $25 and $50 for the domain name, per year. Once you've registered and paid for your domain, you'll need to have it

Figure 10.2. Search for and register a domain at Network Solutions (*www.networksolutions.com*).

hosted somewhere. Interland *(www.interland.com)* is both a domain registry and an Internet hosting service. After you design your site, which we'll cover next, you can upload it to a hosting service like Interland. Then it's accessible on the Web.

Can't Afford a Domain and Web Host Yet?

If the cost of registering a domain and hosting a site makes it prohibitive for you, don't worry. You can create a free Web page with a Web Presence Provider and use your business name as your identifier. They'll give you a URL that's a combination of the WPP's domain and your site ID. For instance, if you create and host your free page on Tripod, your business URL will be "*YourBusiness.tripod.com*," which is close enough to a dedicated domain for your customers to easily remember—and bookmark. You can register a domain later, when it becomes affordable for you.

Your Presence on the Web

You definitely need a presence on the Web other than just your auction site ID. You'll want to take full advantage of every free resource available to you for promoting your selling venture. Create an AboutMe page at eBay, a storefront at your online payment service's site, a free Web page at Angelfire—whatever you can grab, free of charge, to get noticed.

In addition to these freebies, you'll need an Internet auction Web page that draws people to your online listings.

Why Have a Web Page if I'm Just Doing Auctions?

Because your auction listings at a C2C site like Yahoo or eBay won't come up in search engine results. If you sell ergonomic pool cues, your potential customers can try every search engine from AltaVista to iWon to Yahoo and they probably won't find your auctions. They will, however, eventually find your Web page (if you're clever with your content) which will take them to your auctions. Here are plenty of advantages to directing people to your Web site:

- You can update it at any time.

- You can solicit direct sales.

- You can announce specials.

- You can link to any other site you want, unfettered by the auction site's regulations.

- You can present your products with fewer formatting limitations than auction sites impose.

- You can provide your own brand of customer support.

- You can try new ideas.

- You can wax poetic.

It's important to note that some auction sites, like eBay for instance, prohibit you from including links to Web sites where you're selling the same products. However, they cannot control where you link to your auctions *from*. So, your personal page can include links to your auctions, which your potential customers can view after they visit your enchanting Web page.

Another use for your Web page is if you plan to deal with international customers. Why restrict your market to the English-speaking world? Translate your Web site into a number of languages and offer a choice to users when they visit your page. Several sites on the Web will translate your page into a few other languages, such as Italian, Spanish, German, or French (see Figure 10.3). If you can capture the HTML code of the translated page (some of the translation sites make that possible), you can offer your viewers a choice of languages with a drop-down menu. Talk about service!

Now let's discuss the most important function of that Web page you're working on.

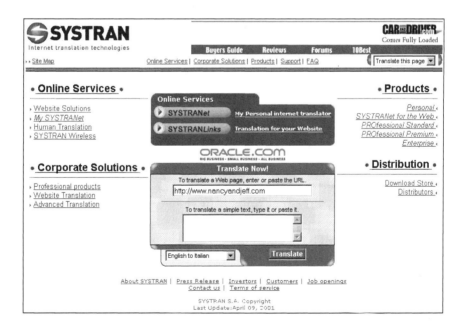

Figure 10.3. Translate a Web page at SYSTRAN (*www.systransoft.com*).

The Doorway to Your Auctions

Your independent seller's Web page should include a series of links to your Internet auction listings. This makes it your **doorway page**, because it opens a hypothetical door to the heart of your business. Whether it's part of an existing small-business Web site or a standalone page, your doorway page will tie your auctions to the rest of the Internet. You can model it to come up in keyword searches, and take advantage of link and banner exchanges to draw viewers.

Jeff Savage of Drexel Grapevine Antiques (*www.drexelantiques.com*) created his own doorway page that serves as an Internet auction marketing channel for his business. He uses thumbnail images as links to his eBay auctions. Figure 10.4 shows part of the page.

As you scroll down the page, you'll find more information about what Jeff sells, his important seller terms (as mentioned in Step 6), links to Jeff's eBay feedback, his contact information, and a link to his main business Web page. Potential customers have everything they need to view his products and then bid on them at the auction site he's using.

Essential Elements of Your Doorway Page

Here's what you must include in order to make optimum use of the page:

- **Your business name**—Include this so your potential bidders and customers can associate your business name to your auction listings.

- **A prominent link to your auctions**—This needs to be so prominent that if your visitors don't read anything else on your page, they'll see this. Your auctions are the essence of your business, so take them there as quickly as they want to go.

- **Your contact information**—This should include the business name you registered and use on the Web, and your business e-mail address. If privacy is an issue, use a P.O. box or a mailbox hosting service.

- **Your terms of sale**—It's good to have them on your doorway page. This way potential bidders will know in advance, if they read them, what you expect. Read Chapter 8 for suggestions about what to include.

Figure 10.4. Drexel Grapevine Antiques' Internet auction doorway page (*www.drexelantiques.com/auctions.html*).

- **Your auction seller's organization affiliations**—Include your OAUA icon and links to any online auction user communities you frequent. You'll read more about those in Chapter 12. These are great confidence builders.

- **A page counter**—They're just as important for your business Web page because it's the best way to see if the search engines pick up and list your page, or whether your link exchanges are working.

Some of the WPPs provide them. If you're creating a page for use on your own domain, check out Honesty.com or Digits.com for free page counters.

Content That Will Entertain, Educate, and Engage

A successful Web page of any kind must use the appropriate content strategies to encourage its target Web surfers to stick around, read a little, and then click over to your Internet auctions. Make your page fun to look at and your text entertaining to read. Include some history on the items you're selling so your visitors can learn something from you. And remember—the more complete your text content, the better chance you have of the bots indexing your page.

Eeny Meeny Mynie Meta

Be sure to use the <META> tags you read about in Chapter 7. Some search engines are rumored to ignore them and recommend that Web page authors rely on content, so be sure to use both. Some search engine specialists recommend that the first thing on your Web page should be text. If it's an image, the bots will pick up the HTML tag characters and not index your page correctly. You'll find instructions for coding your <META> tags in Appendix B.

Independent Business Web Sites That Work

This section shows examples of doorway pages for an independent seller's Internet auctions. Michelle's Knic Knac Nook, shown in Figure 10.5, directs her site visitors to her auctions. Further down the page, she includes links to her auction site affiliations.

The Web site in Figure 10.6 gets right to the point. That's all there is. The links take you to the seller's auction pages on Yahoo. The owner probably gets a lot more hits to his or her auctions with this page active than without it, because at least one search engine has indexed it. I know this because I found it via a Google.com search.

The page in Figure 10.7 belongs to Serenity's Treasures. It's actually her small business home page, but notice the prominent links to her eBay auctions. Her Web shoppers are aware that she also offers serene treasures on eBay.

These sites are examples of effective Internet auction sellers' doorway pages. The following table lists a few more.

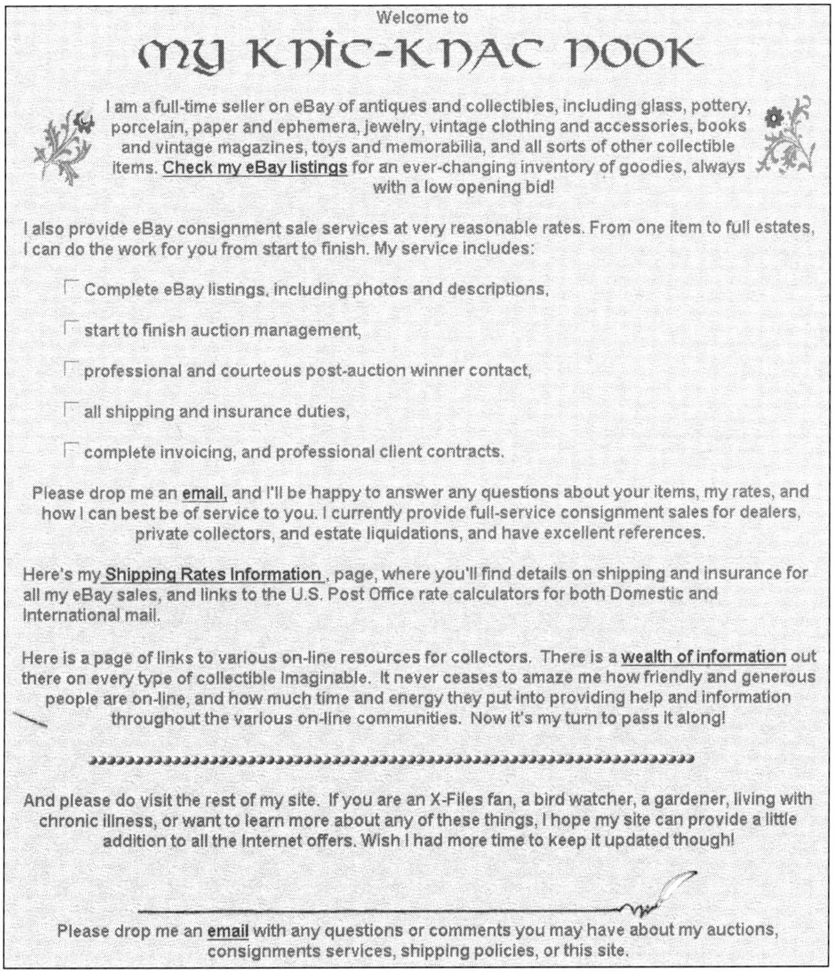
Welcome to

MY KNIC-KNAC NOOK

I am a full-time seller on eBay of antiques and collectibles, including glass, pottery, porcelain, paper and ephemera, jewelry, vintage clothing and accessories, books and vintage magazines, toys and memorabilia, and all sorts of other collectible items. Check my eBay listings for an ever-changing inventory of goodies, always with a low opening bid!

I also provide eBay consignment sale services at very reasonable rates. From one item to full estates, I can do the work for you from start to finish. My service includes:

- Complete eBay listings, including photos and descriptions,
- start to finish auction management,
- professional and courteous post-auction winner contact,
- all shipping and insurance duties,
- complete invoicing, and professional client contracts.

Please drop me an email, and I'll be happy to answer any questions about your items, my rates, and how I can best be of service to you. I currently provide full-service consignment sales for dealers, private collectors, and estate liquidations, and have excellent references.

Here's my Shipping Rates Information, page, where you'll find details on shipping and insurance for all my eBay sales, and links to the U.S. Post Office rate calculators for both Domestic and International mail.

Here is a page of links to various on-line resources for collectors. There is a wealth of information out there on every type of collectible imaginable. It never ceases to amaze me how friendly and generous people are on-line, and how much time and energy they put into providing help and information throughout the various on-line communities. Now it's my turn to pass it along!

And please do visit the rest of my site. If you are an X-Files fan, a bird watcher, a gardener, living with chronic illness, or want to learn more about any of these things, I hope my site can provide a little addition to all the Internet offers. Wish I had more time to keep it updated though!

Please drop me an email with any questions or comments you may have about my auctions, consignments services, shipping policies, or this site.

Figure 10.5. Michelle Pear's Knic Knac Nook (*members.nbci.com/mlpear/knicknac.html*).

Site Owners	Web Address
Elizabeth Hohns and Deanne Summer	*www.morevideogames.com*
Vicki and Thomas Bennett	*www.bennetts-bargains.bigstep.com*
Matt Ryan	*www.cardboardstars.com*
Bob LeFevre	*www.mrbucks.com*
Kelly Pound's Art	*www.pounddesigns.com*

I sell under three different names on Yahoo:

PaperHut
Selection of stocks, bonds and crate labels

PaperHutStocks
Main listing for stocks and bonds

PaperHutLabels
Main listing for crate labels

Auctions won under all names may be combined for shipping charge calculation.

Figure 10.6.   Collectible stocks and bonds (*www.paperhut.com*).

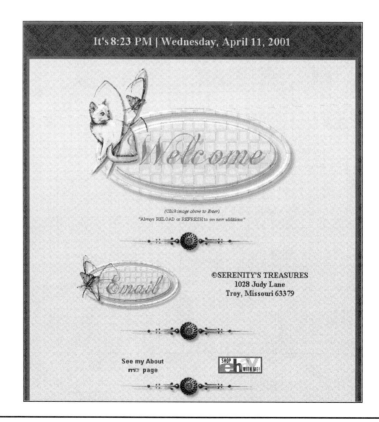

Figure 10.7.   Serenity's Treasures (*www.serenitys-treasures.com*).

You and Your Independent Internet Auction Business

You're probably aware of this, but you are the most important element in the success of your auction selling venture. As with any business, the first six months will require a lot of concentration, research, legwork, and Web surfing before you fall into a comfortable routine. At first, much of your effort will be one-time startup efforts, such as registering a domain name, locating a Web Presence Provider, registering at an auction site, and all of the other activities involved with Internet auction selling.

Eventually, auction selling will be the most natural thing in the world for you to do. When your family and friends ask you why you spend so much time on your computer or catch you clipping liquidation sale notices, you'll be able to say, "Hey, it's my *job!*"

Just like you'd be expected to afford your employees a certain amount of time to regroup and relax (coffee breaks, lunch hours, comp time, vacations, etc.), you must treat yourself with the same amount of consideration. You are, after all, worth it.

Managing Your Time

It might be tempting to work around the clock until you fall into bed, exhausted. Similarly, you may realize late in the day that tomorrow is your listing day and you must create 50 auction descriptions to achieve your goals. It's a lot better to budget your time over several days instead of knocking yourself out to get things done in a few hours. The following table is a sample independent auction seller's schedule for someone who specializes in selling discounted items from liquidation sales:

Week of ____/____	Monday	Tuesday	Wednesday	Thursday	Friday	Saturday	Sunday
Morning	Pack items for shipping	Attend liquidation sale	Pack items for shipping	Write auction descriptions	Send EOA notices, update doorway page	E-mail	E-mail
Afternoon	Take packages to PO, check PO box	Write auction descriptions	Take packages to PO, check PO box	Prepare and upload photographs	Attend liquidation sale, check PO box	Check auctions	Check auctions
Evening	E-mail	E-mail	E-mail	List auctions	E-mail		

This schedule allows the seller to pack and ship items on two days of the week, attend two liquidation sales to replenish stock, and make Thursday the auction preparation and listing day for seven-day auctions. On Friday morning, the seller sends EOA e-mail notices for the auctions that closed Thursday night, and adds the information about the new auctions to the doorway page. Notice that the seller can casually spend evenings and weekends reading and answering e-mail and checking the auctions for bids.

Taking Care of Yourself

You naturally want to sell as much as you can for the highest possible earnings, but if you're operating out of your home, or even a small office, it's imperative that you set yourself some boundaries. For instance:

- What hours will you devote to acquiring products and listing auctions?

- When will you be online and when will you be offline?

- Will your routine include enough physical activity?

Yes, your earning goals can include boundaries! If you don't set them, you run the risk of burning out, losing interest, and missing out on a wonderful opportunity to achieve some financial independence. So let's talk about *you*.

Your Business Hours

Checking your auctions and answering e-mail from prospective bidders is something you can do during your leisure time. One of the biggest advantages of using the Internet to make a living is that it's always open. You don't need a security guard to unlock the door to let you out or a parking lot attendant to walk you to your car if you select the night shift a few evenings a week. You can save your mornings for your personal time or your middays for watching the soaps, and do your packing and description writing in the late afternoon and evening. It's all up to you.

When to Be Online/When to Be Offline

You definitely need to schedule plenty of time away from the computer. If you can combine your stock replenishing missions and a pleasant outdoor walk with a friend, it's up to you to decide if this is sufficient. Anyone who does a lot of Internet auction selling—or has written a book about it—knows the importance of getting up, getting out, and looking at something other than a computer monitor. Spend time with your family, do some yard work, or catch up on your reading. Whatever you'd normally do on your personal time.

The Right Routine

Take time to fit your offline life into your online life. If you don't, it will get old really fast, and so might you. Fitness expert Anne Hawkins, founder of the Northern Illinois–based Bod Squad exercise club, estimates that the average adult between the age of 30 and 50 (prime Internet auction age) needs at least three hours of aerobic-type exercise per week. Besides the obvious health risks from a sedentary lifestyle, exercise helps keep your mind sharp and your spirits soaring.

So, try to work some recreational time into your schedule. Turn up some fast music, put on a happy face, and dance.

Tales of Full-time Sellers

For some, full-time Internet auction selling was a conscious decision reached after a few successful sales brought them impressive profits. For others, it was a last-ditch effort to stay financially afloat.

Given the relative newness of the Internet and online auctions, people who have come to depend on them are pioneers. In this section, you'll read about full-time independent auction sellers who are able to support themselves—and often thrive—by listing and selling at Internet auction sites.

Deanne and Elizabeth

When Deanne's employer went bankrupt, she didn't sit idle very long. She purchased a computer and told her family, "Somehow or other, I'm going to figure out how to make a living with it." Deanne and her partner, Elizabeth, got right to work. The first decision was what to sell. As with many fledgling Internet auction sellers, the first place they looked was at home.

"We cleaned out our basement and headed to the flea market to sell our stuff. We were amazed at the popularity of the old video games," says Deanne.

Next, they needed to find out which Internet auction site would generate the best sales for the biggest profits. After running a few trial auctions, they decided to list on Yahoo and sold there for a year before switching to Amazon Auctions.

They eventually registered the domain *www.morevideogames.com* and set up doorway Web page to their Internet auctions. The page is also a sales adjunct. Interested customers can contact them by Humanclick (a free live chat application), or by phone, e-mail, snail mail, or by visiting them at their local live sales booth. Their Web page includes contact information and prominent links to their auctions (see Figure 10.8).

"We started slowly at first," Deanne continues. "Our auctions were such a success that we decided to expand and sell them directly from our site. The response was fabulous. We went into this with such uncertainty and we had to put a lot of work into it, but it sure paid off." Deanne and Elizabeth try to keep at least 800 auctions running at any time.

"My mother still asks me if I'm going to stay unemployed," Deanne laughs, "even after showing her that we did over $42,000 in online sales during our first year!"

Their Operating Principle

With questionable success at eBay, Elizabeth and Deanne switched to Yahoo to take advantage of their free listings at the time. They feel that the more active listings they have, the better their sales average will be.

"I think that everything will eventually sell if I can leave it up until the right person finds it. With over 800 items listed, I can take two weeks off from listing auctions and my sales stay the same." They report having an average of $700 a week from online sales, which has been steady for the past year. "I plan to get some auction management software soon to help me with the mundane stuff. This will allow me more time for listing—our goal is to get it up to over 1000 active auctions and see if our earnings increase."

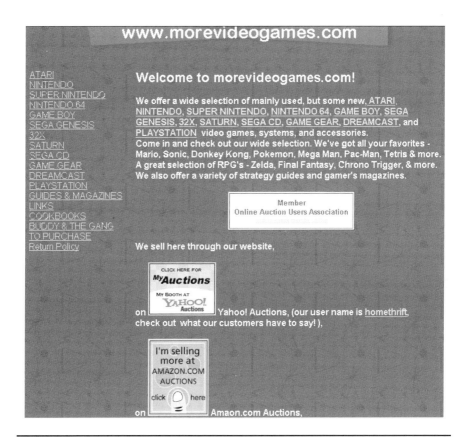

Figure 10.8.   Elizabeth and Deanne's Web page (*www.morevideogames.com*).

Getting the Word Out

Their Web page was all the advertising they needed at first. They included their URL in their auction descriptions as long as Yahoo allowed it. Sales went well and the payments rolled in. "I tried the 'pay me to list your site with 50,000 search engines' and got nowhere until I started manually submitting to the search engines myself," Deanne says. "Then I got this e-mail from PayPal that I almost deleted without reading. Good thing I did read it. They were offering me something called a Storefront that would help sell my goods. I set up a Storefront with the program they sent us." In the first week, Deanne and Elizabeth got three new customers through their PayPal Storefront.

"PayPal helped advertise for us," Deanne continues. "I believe that the more places our business name and URL appear, the better off we are. I'm not sure about the other sites, but the dodge for Amazon is that you can put the URL of your Web site, Storefront, or whatever into your description, as long as you don't make it a hyperlink. And, of course, we include a link to our Web site in all of our e-mail correspondence."

Deanne and Elizabeth recently learned that Yahoo's search engine finally indexed their Web site. They report that they're starting to get some significant Internet auction traffic that doesn't originate from the auction searches. While they're making plenty of direct sales from their site, Internet auctions remain their "bread and butter."

Serenity Long

In 1996, Serenity Long had a storefront. She and her husband built and sold computers, and taught classes in Windows95, Microsoft Word, and WordPerfect. Their storefront wasn't a typical Brick & Mortar store. It also functioned as an office. "I mostly sold our computer service," Serenity says, "which also included setting up Intranets. The only reason I started the business was because I was sick of being in real estate, and my husband was making too much money at his job. We needed a tax deduction." However, after her first year of paying the overhead for a storefront in a small town, she closed her shop and moved everything to her house. "I sold a lot of the office furniture since I wouldn't have room for it anyway," she said. Then she thought about setting up a Web page.

Designing Woman

In February 1998, she registered her first domain name and checked around for quotes on what others would charge to build a Web site to her specifications.

"Well, that experience absolutely *blew me away*," Serenity said. "One bid was even as high as $5,000 for about five of what I call 'basic yuck' pages. I wasn't about to pay that much for them. So, I decided I'd learn to design Web pages myself and use the money for something else that I'd need along the way. That's how I found myself getting very interested in using the Web to earn money." Soon after that, Serenity discovered eBay.

Selling at Auction

She started out slowly, at first listing auctions for custom-built computers and service. She then expanded her inventory to include items she always enjoyed being around, but never before thought about selling. She purchased at wholesale a supply of crystals, gemstones, jewels, collectibles, prisms, and medicine bags. Then she added a link to her eBay sales from her "Serenity's Treasures" home page (see Figure 10.7 on page 400).

"I was a lot happier—more serene—while surrounding myself with peace-enhancing items. So many computer companies were closing their storefronts, so I knew it was not promising for the future. I wanted to have something else, like my Web design work, my eBay sales, and my doorway Web site to sell my favorite type of merchandise on in order to stay in business."

She has since expanded her inventory. From her Web site and through her eBay auctions, she now sells her Web design work, custom logos, forms, business cards, jewelry, gems, carved stones, leather purses, leather medicine bags, and collectibles. She normally keeps between 30 and 70 auctions active, and earns approximately 25% of her income from Internet auction sales.

"My eBay sales allow me to deal with merchandise I love, and the earnings allow me to continue the Web design work I find the most rewarding," Serenity explains. To stay ahead of the competition, she offers her customers some extras:

- Free shipping on orders over $100 to her U.S. customers

- Small gift enclosed (such as a Swarovski prism) for her repeat customers

- Discounts to members of OTWA and OAUA, two online auction users' associations with which she is affiliated

- Free gift wrapping on request

"I'm not exactly doing this full time," Serenity says, "but it takes a *lot* of time. I do a lot more than just list items at eBay, but I have to admit that selling through Internet auctions helps me stay financially independent."

Alexis Forrester

"I didn't seriously consider selling on eBay full time until the company I worked for decided to shut down our center and put us all out of work," says Alexis Forrester, a divorced mother of two children, ages 9 and 3. "I got the idea from other sellers in the online auction users' forums who made tidy profits on items they paid little or nothing for."

Alexis works a part-time job between 40 to 80 hours a month in the early mornings, but the income isn't enough to cover her expenses. "I home school my nine-year-old daughter, Kiernan, and I didn't want to have to put my son John in daycare if I got a full-time job," she explains. "I knew that if I sold stuff on eBay (Figure 10.9) several hours a day, I could home school my daughter."

Product Specialization

Alexis sells mostly women's and children's clothes. She's familiar with many different exclusive clothing brands, and she can pick a treasure out of a castoff pile that others might miss. A St. John sweater she bought for $2.50 closed at $211 on eBay.

"I get my clothes from a lot of different sources," she says. "Some are just given to me. A friend I met through an online auction forum gave me a trunk load of clothes, and told me to sell them for whatever I could. She wouldn't take a dime for them." Alexis spends her offline hours preparing the goods. In order to meet eBay's requirements, used clothing must be advertised and sold as clean.

Alexis enjoys hunting for bargains at the Goodwill store, consignment shops, and yard sales. "As much as I love doing that, though, I am very cautious with my money," she explains. "Unless it's another St. John 'sure thing,' I think long and hard about buying something for more than three dollars." Alexis tries to spend less than $30 a week on items to resell.

Time Management

I asked Alexis how she manages her time, being a full-time eBay seller and caring for two young children in her home.

"Manage? You mean manage to keep my sanity, right?" she laughs. "With the way my home life is, there is no set time. I have an estimated schedule I try to stick to, and it usually works for me."

Here's the schedule Alexis worked out for herself:

imjustpeachy's clothing & collectibles

Welcome!

Let me introduce myself. My name is Alexis and I am a divorced mother of two. My "punkinheads" are Kiernan (Kiki), who is 9, and Baby John, who is 3. I homeschool Kiernan and has that been interesting! I must say, it is a challenge, but I think it is well worth it. I had been keeping a journal of our progress, but I have been very busy lately. If you are interested, take a look where I left off. (Journal)

I started selling on eBay in August of '99 as a way to make ends meet. As of January 31, 2001 eBay is one of two PT sources of income. I have a part-time job to supplement eBay just in case. I love working on eBay because of the different people that I meet from so many different places. I treat everyone with respect and courtesy because I consider this my "business." I was a retail Customer Service Manager for 7 years so I know what great customer service means to people. I am a member of the Online Traders Web Alliance (OTWA). This wonderful group of people have taught me so much, as well as given me many laughs. They are like a second family to me.

So with all that said, browse and enjoy. Maybe even bid, too. And please don't hesitate to email me if you have any questions.

Highest bidders agree to the following terms:

- Checks, "Postal" Money Orders, and Credit/Debit cards are accepted. Debit/Credit Cards are taken through secure servers at Yahoo PayDirect, PayPal, or Billpoint. Click a link below to sign up. If you would like me to try a different online service, email me and we can discuss it.
- Payment must be received within **ten** days of auction's end.
- All US items are shipped via **Priority Mail** unless otherwise stated.
- International orders will be shipped the most economical way possible. Please email me for shipping quote.
- Due to a hectic schedule, I ship twice a week, on Tuesday and Friday.
- Win more than one auction and *save on shipping*!
- Insurance is optional, but recommended, and is at the winner's expense.

Figure 10.9. Alexis Forrester (imjustpeachy) uses eBay's AboutMe page as her business Web page (*members.ebay.com/aboutme/imjustpeachy*).

- **Time at computer**—10-12 hours

- **Reading and posting at OTWA**—One hour

- **Updating auction templates**—15 minutes per auction

- **Time taking photos**—15 minutes per item

- **Packing and shipping**—For printing shipping notices and packaging, 10 minutes per package

An occasional trip to the nearby post office adds about five more minutes. Alexis tries to involve her children in her eBay selling whenever she can, somewhere between their home schooling and basic care.

"Kiernan is learning to use eBay and to print out invoices and labels, and sometimes she sends my EOA e-mail notices. She's very proud of having sold a few things of her own," Alexis smiles. "She took the photographs, wrote the descriptions, and was absolutely thrilled with the money she made. And John loves to help me carry packages into the post office. All that the postal clerk sees is the package and some little hands reaching over the top of the counter."

Whether you're an independent auction seller or manage Internet auction sales for a corporation (or somewhere in between), you'll want to use special care when dealing with those who keep the venture afloat—your customers.

11

Winning with Your Customers

Since the people who buy your products are the crux of your business, making sure they're happy with their purchase and content with the service you provide is very important. So is your communication with them.

In this chapter, we'll assume that you're dealing directly with consumers from either a B2C or C2C Internet auction site. The advice here applies to business and independent sellers. Both can benefit from learning effective customer-service techniques. We'll discuss how to ensure that your Internet customers find the Internet auction process as exciting and fulfilling as you do:

- The importance of customer service

- The customer is always the customer

- Effective e-mail messages

- Rating other users

- What your buyers expect from you

- Adding your personal touch to the transaction

All of these are components of an effective online auction business. Here you'll see examples of e-mail messages, shipping notes, and secure product-packing techniques.

Customer Service Makes or Breaks You

More than half of all orders placed over the Internet are abandoned in mid-purchase, maybe because the customer feels that the transaction is too risky. Successful e-commerce sites know this and provide increased levels of customer service for their Internet customers. This is important for you as an Internet auction seller. The results of a customer's first transaction with you will determine if he or she will buy something from you again.

Serving Your Customers via E-mail

Your primary means of communication with your Internet customers will be via e-mail. While e-mail is a powerful communication tool, it's also easily misunderstood. Treat your Internet auction customers with the same level of courtesy that you do when dealing with your Brick & Mortar customers. With a faceless, voiceless medium that relies on words alone to convey a message, you must adapt your communication skills for this new way of interacting.

You might be sending out 100 end-of-auction e-mails this week, and the task may seem droll after the first 10, but remember that typically, a unique customer will read each message. To them, it's not a form letter. It's a personal message from you that contains important information about how they should complete their purchase.

Imagine for a moment being a telephone receptionist who must answer a constantly ringing phone with the phrase, "Good day, this is Garden Glad Nurseries, home of healthy plants and happy yards. We also deliver landscaping gravel. How may I direct your call?" After eight hours of saying this same phrase repeatedly, your voice may lose that cheerful edge toward evening, longing to answer just one call with, "What!?" If that last call was a first-time customer seeking quotes for a corporate landscaping job, giving in to that tired temptation could be disastrous.

Sending EOA messages isn't a tireless task, but you can rely on a well-written template when you contact each of your customers. No matter how many EOA messages you send out in any given day, you can treat each high bidder with courtesy and respect. If you use an auction management service, you can select one that allows you to customize your EOA messages so they sound like *you*—not like a worn-out recording.

To Whom Are You Talking?

If you've studied your market, you know what types of people you'll be dealing with as your high bidders. You're also aware that for some products, your customers are of varied ages and backgrounds and all of them will rely on your e-mail for payment, product, and shipping information.

Take toys, for example. The Pooping Pig key chain fell under the "toy" classification, but it's not something I'd buy for a four-year-old. Many of them sold to older teens and young adults. I'm in my 40s and I bought one; so did my 25-year-old stepdaughter. My brother, a die-hard LSU Tigers fan in his 50s, has a room full of collectible plush tigers for which he's often engaged in a tug-of-war with his granddaughter. A cursory glance around any corporate office reveals toys of all colors and styles living peacefully in cubicles atop computer monitors. Even fast-food toys become targets of adults seeking a thrill, and let's not even talk about what Beanie Babies did to nice, normal adults.

Toys are one example of a product with a broad target market. If your chosen Internet auction product is a toy, you'll be dealing with just about anyone. When your auction for 50 teddy bears closes with 50 bidders, your EOA message should be understandable by anyone from 18 to 110, male or female, from all occupations and lifestyles. Can e-mail communication be that flexible? Of course it can.

Make No Assumptions

Don't assume that only men buy socket wrenches and only women buy women's clothes. Remember that it's your customers' business what they to do with their purchases. Your only concerns are that they pay you for them, and that they're content with them.

It's all right to be enthusiastic and friendly, especially when the transaction moves to one-on-one e-mail if the customer has questions or a special shipping request. Just stay away from personal questions, and don't make judgments.

Prepare to Adapt Your Interaction Style

When a customer sends you e-mail, read the message carefully before you respond. Watch for any clues to try to adapt to the person's level of communication. While you must always be able to answer questions about products you're selling, don't assume that your high bidder is a product expert as well. Be prepared to explain what the product is and how it works in simplified terms.

If the syntax of his or her e-mail hints that the customer may not have a natural command of the language, make sure your response isn't heavy with idioms and euphemisms. For example, the phrase "This item takes the cake" may confuse a customer who isn't familiar with that phrase. Why would a leather ottoman steal someone's dessert? A better choice of words would be "This is a new and exciting product with many useful features."

Stay in Contact During the Transaction

Customers often have questions. Even if these questions consist of daily queries about the status of their order, it's important to treat each question as though it's the most important one you'll answer that day. Always try to be accessible to your customers and smile when you type your responses, even if you have to chew gum to keep from gritting your teeth. Remember that they're sending you money and they don't want to be ripped off. They've heard the horror stories about Internet scams. This is your chance to set things right for the good of e-commerce.

Customer Service from Your Business Web Site

Always refer your potential bidders to your business Web site when you answer their questions in e-mail. Not just with a link in your sig file, but tell them directly that if they have any more questions, they can either contact you again, or find the information on your Web page. If you designed your Web site to offer quality customer service, here's what they'll find when they take you up on your suggestion:

- How to contact you (we've covered this, but it's important)

- How soon you'll respond. If you can't provide 24/7 coverage, then specify when the customer's off-hours e-mail will be addressed.

- Your policy on customer service

- Your product guarantees

Include as much of this information as you can in your auction descriptions. If your customers click over to your business Web site, though, or visit there from a search engine result, they'll want to know that real people exist who can answer their questions.

Customer Service—Be Easy to Reach

In Chapter 7, we discussed the importance of including your contact information on your business Web site, even if the site is mainly a doorway page to your auctions. If you have a sophisticated business Web site that contains an online ordering system, *always* include a prominent link to a customer service interface. Your customers can type their messages into a text field, enter their own contact information, and then click on "send." You can program this to generate an automatic e-mail response letting the sender know that your customer service department received the message and will respond within a certain interval.

If you can't provide an on-screen interface, include a customer service e-mail address. It should be an address set up on your business domain that's called CustomerService@YourBusiness.com, or something similar. Even if e-mail sent to that address ends up in the same e-mail inbox as every other message you receive, the "Customer Service" label makes very clear your confidence-boosting commitment to their satisfaction. If your company can provide 24/7 customer service telephone coverage, then include the number. A toll-free number is even better. All of these contact methods let your customers know that someone is ready to handle their inquiry. A business Web site without at least an e-mail contact address makes people wonder if it's legitimate.

Note: Your business e-mail link should always be easy to find. See Appendix B for instructions on how to make your e-mail address a hyperlink, and format it that way wherever you include your e-mail address on the Web.

For any Brick & Mortar operation, large or small, you should always include a business address on your Web site. This lets the customer know that it's an established business with a physical location.

Your Product Guarantees

State your product guarantees on your business Web site. This is similar to stating your Internet auction return policy in your descriptions. Your product guarantees should cover all of your products, including items purchased through your Internet auctions.

The Customer Is Always the Customer

When you deal with your Internet auction customers in e-mail or on the telephone, they are no less your customers than if they were standing across a counter from you. You know that standard business credo, "The customer is always right?" That slogan has been around for years, and while it's the right idea, it implies that whenever there's any discord between you and one of your customers, you're always wrong.

The customer is *not* always right. However, they have the right to have their complaints heard as long as they behave in a civil and constructive way. This includes how they word their e-mail. Some of the vilest words exchanged between vendors and customers in the past decade have transpired in e-mail. Hiding behind a computer monitor tends to bring out the worst in some people when they're angry.

The customer wants to be listened to, acknowledged, and understood. Any angry words you return in e-mail could end up working against you to a far greater magnitude than you imagined. E-mail is a text file that can be made into multiple copies in seconds. It can be posted on message boards and included on Web pages. Maintain your composure and never put your anger in writing.

This attitude will not only help to preserve your existing customer base, but it's a lot better for your self-esteem when you know you handled yourself in a dignified manner—and perhaps salvaged a business relationship with a customer.

Customer Complaints—Their Gift to You

A lot depends on how you treat an unhappy customer. A few tips in handling complaints may help you turn a dissatisfied person into a permanent customer.

Some people are more assertive than others. Assertive people will usually let you know when your customer service has fallen short of their expectations. Consider a customer complaint to be a gift that you can use to improve your service. This doesn't hold true for every complaint. Here's the difference:

- **Constructive complaint:** Customer informs you that the tape you used to seal the shipping carton peeled up during shipping and the box arrived partly open. From this, you'll know that you need to use a better brand of packing tape in order to ensure that your shipments arrive intact.

- **Non-constructive complaint:** Customer sends you an angry e-mail because the packing puffies you used to cushion the shipment were of several different colors and shapes. You can explain to your customer that when you recycle puffies, you store them in a large container where they tend to blend with other styles. Or, you can assure the customer that you'll try to get a better match next time.

The constructive complaint helped you improve your service, whereas the non-constructive complaint did little more than make you stare at your computer monitor for a few seconds.

Responding to a Customer Complaint

Read the customer's e-mail carefully before you respond so that you understand the problem, or at least know what the customer perceives as a problem. Then investigate the situation. Your response should include three essential elements, in this order:

1. **An apology:** "We're sorry that you were not pleased with the Hawk canister set."

2. **Restate the customer's problem:** "We understand that you were expecting black enamel canisters and that you received instead our silver tone Hawk stainless steel set."

3. **Suggest a resolution:** "If you return the set you received, we will replace them free with the black enamel Hawk set and credit your account for shipping charges."

Start every response to a customer complaint with an apology. The customer will know that you regret that he or she had to take the time to complain about your shipment. Then restate the customer's problem, as you understand it. This tells the customer that you understand his or her frustration. Lastly, offer a solution. If the fault lies with you or your company, then tell the customer how you plan to resolve the issue—such as in the previous example.

If the fault lies with the customer, you can still offer a resolution. Suggest what the customer could do differently next time he or she bids on one of your auctions.

> *"We're sorry that we can't accept returns on merchandise after two weeks have passed, but we invite you to take advantage of our three-day inspection period next time you buy from us."*

If the customer keeps sending angry, argumentative e-mail messages, then respond by restating your original position.

Make Right Your Mistakes

In Chapter 8, we discussed the seller's responsibilities during an Internet auction transaction. One of them is to be sure that you ship the products you advertised in your auction description within the specified period. If you can't do that for some reason, you must be prepared to explain what happened—and make it right. Here are a few examples of mistakes that would keep you from upholding your obligations as a seller:

- You misplaced the customer's order, thus delaying the shipment.

- You mixed up two shipments, causing customers to receive the wrong items.

- You didn't pack the item securely and it was damaged during shipping.

- You sent the wrong color, size, or style.

No matter who discovers the error first—you or your customer—you must act immediately to remedy the situation in a way that will uphold your obligations. If the customer reports the error, respond right away. How you handle your mistake will determine whether you'll earn yourself a repeat customer.

Here are a few examples of how you can win with your customers by making right your mistakes:

- Since you misplaced the customer's order and caused a shipping delay, ship the item via express mail and enclose a money-off coupon for the customer's next purchase.

- If you shipped the wrong item or mixed up two shipments, e-mail the customer and request that he or she return the item. Immediately after it arrives, ship the correct item. Be sure to credit the customer's account for postage on the returned item.

- Didn't pack the item securely and it arrived damaged? Ask the customer to return the damaged item. At the same time, ship a replacement that's carefully packed. Credit the customer's account for postage on the returned item.

Occasionally your mistakes might cost you—and rightfully so. If you want to keep your customers happy and make sure they stay your customers, don't fret over a few dollars lost in correcting one of your mistakes. Next time, you'll know better, and your customers will remember how quickly you remedied the situation. And once you've taken care of it, be sure to check back with them to find out if they're satisfied with the outcome.

Solving a problem to the customer's liking (reasonably, of course) will usually get you a repeat customer. The person might want to make at least one more transaction with you to set the situation right.

When the Customer Tries Your Patience

If the customer receives the wrong item, he or she may sit down and bang out a terse and cranky message about how you wrecked what would have been a nice day by sending the wrong item. Can you handle it? To be successful, you really have no choice.

If you lose self-control, then you've lost control of the situation and that's not good. If you mishandle angry customers, they may vent their frustration by telling others not to bid on your auctions. You might find a rash of canceled bids on your active auctions if someone decides to e-mail all of them with a warning about you. Most sites have rules against this type of auction interference, but angry people might find a way around it. In the time it takes you to report the problem to the site, the damage is done and you've lost business. It's best to diffuse their anger quickly without appearing to be minimizing their problem.

Count to Ten

When you receive a heated complaint in e-mail, think it over. Assess the situation. Check the order. Find out who really made the error, and then respond accordingly. One great thing about communicating in e-mail versus face to face or on the telephone is that you can take a minute, or several minutes, to compose and re-read your e-mail response to an upset or downright mean customer. Whatever you do, always remain professional. What follows are some do's and don'ts for communicating with knickers-in-a-knot customers.

Do's

- Change from "I" to "we." This implies that you're following a standard business policy.

- Acknowledge challenging questions and then redirect the situation to the goal of appeasing the customer. If he or she starts an e-mail message with "Why don't you just close down! You don't know what you're doing," your answer can be "Sir, we have no plans to close our business. Quite the opposite. We'd like to make this situation right."

- Read the customer's e-mail completely. Avoid responding based on the first few sentences. Sometimes people think as they type, and the person may have a different attitude at the end of his or her e-mail.

- Be sensitive to any communication barriers, such as language, learning challenges, or culture.

- Paraphrase any unreasonable statements and include them in your response. "Ma'am, you told us that you'd like a complete refund and your next 10 shipments free, but we find this a bit excessive. However, we'd be happy to exchange or refund the item that you're not happy with."

- Consider how you'd want to be treated in the customer's situation, and act appropriately.

- Use respectable phrases and salutations in your e-mail responses, even when you're tempted to write, "Listen you little slime-trailing maggot..."

Don'ts

- Don't make accusing statements. Give or at least imply the benefit of the doubt.

- Never mention a person's bad grammar, poor spelling, or lack of composure in your e-mail response.

- Don't be judgmental or aloof.

- Don't take anything the angry customer says personally, even if it was your fault. Let an imaginary third party at fault absorb the guilt.

Position Yourself as Mediator

When you're dealing with irascible customers, the goal is to diffuse the customers' anger while validating it, in order to appease them and not lose a customer. No matter how nasty or abusive a customer becomes, keep repeating the phrase, "I understand that you're upset, and I'll see what I can do to fix the problem." Then assure the customer that you'll find out what went wrong with the transaction.

If you're on the phone, let the customer know that you're listening, and try to get him or her to start the story from a less frustrating point, such as when the bid was first placed. Then work up to what happened. Repeat what the customer says to make it clear that you understand. Then agree to talk to the employee who is responsible for the problem. If you step out of your own role and take on that of a mediator, the customer will feel confident that a "third party" is handling the problem.

Invent Someone to Take the Blame

"I'm so sorry. Our order-fulfillment specialist obviously confused your order with someone else's." Your order-fulfillment specialist is, of course, you, when you packed the wrong item for shipping during a hectic day. However, your customer probably doesn't care how it happened—he or she just wants the correct item. You can diffuse the person's anger at you if you direct the blame somewhere else—in this case, someone abstract.

If you're a small business or independent seller, you can still direct the blame away from yourself while you agree to resolve the problem.

"The packer we hired must not have listened when I told her to use plenty of Bubble Wrap." If you imply that you'll have a stern talk with this person, the customer won't feel trivialized, but will instead know that you're going to act on the problem.

Mind Your Manners

Always remain courteous and professional and remember that you're representing your corporation or business, even if you're a one-person operation. This is especially important in this age of communication via e-mail. Remember—e-mail can end up in far wider distribution than you intended.

Customer-Satisfaction Surveys

Ask for your customers' opinions. They're your ultimate performance appraisal, especially during your first year of Internet auction selling. It helps you to know what your customers expect from you as a product vendor.

If you've decided to go the way of a market survey so you can complete your Customer Satisfaction Worksheet that we discussed in Chapter 3, find out in advance if the person would be willing to receive it. Ask your customers if they're interested in helping you provide the best customer service by completing the survey and returning it to you.

Wording Your E-mail Messages

Over any 12-month period, you'll deal with many different types of people, most of whom you'll communicate with only through e-mail. It's the best medium to communicate with your buyers because you can keep records of auction correspondence. That's difficult with telephone or in-person conversations.

For people just starting out with electronic communication, e-mail can be tough to get used to. It's still a "faceless" medium. We miss important components of human interaction such as body language, voice inflections, and even handwriting. All we have are words on a screen, so we must word our messages carefully to avoid misunderstandings.

If you follow a well-planned strategy, most of your Internet auction transactions will run smoothly. The e-mail that you exchange with your auction buyers will typically be very friendly. They have their own agenda for treating you well, particularly when they're about to send money to you and trust you'll uphold your end of the deal. Pleasant communication impresses your customers. They'll most likely mention it as part of your selling practice when they leave feedback for you.

Grammar and Spelling

Since communication on the Web is about 95 percent writing, you need to concentrate on the grammar skills that you learned in school. There was a reason why your teachers wanted you to learn the difference between a preposition and an adverb—so you'd be able to communicate effectively in 21st Century e-mail. Well, maybe they didn't have that much foresight, but it's always been important to be able to write well, especially when preparing business communication. Internet auction e-mail is definitely that.

Correct Spelling

Monumental business deals have been decided based on the clarity and correctness of the written communication that transpired during quote and proposal negotiations. Deciding which company gets the account might hinge on one misspelled word. Running across typos in magazine advertisements is an eye-rolling experience for many, and some of the classics end up immortalized in books about print media "bloopers." And, consider the amount—or total lack—of authenticity you place on tabloid articles riddled with careless typos. While some folks argue that "nobody shuld care how I spel," that attitude is foolish. Why risk your business on it?

Spelling is a hot topic for many. Here are some spelling rules you should apply to the e-mail messages that you send to your customers:

- **Always spell your product names correctly.** This will lend credibility to you as a product vendor.

- **Always spell the customer's name correctly.** Refer to the contact information that the auction site sent you, or check e-mail the customer sent you for the correct spelling.

- **Always proofread your e-mail for spelling.** Certain mistakes can be disastrous, such as leaving out the "r" in "shirt."

In Chapter 6, we talked about how important it is to be mindful of your spelling when you write auction titles and descriptions since it can effect your credibility as a seller. You should be just as careful with the e-mail you send to your customers, or when you send e-mail to the auction site, your online payment service, your auction service provider, or any others you contact.

Word Usage

Many people, especially in business, are particular about correct language usage. Avoid some common mistakes well known for hitting raw nerves with language perfectionists. Watch your spelling of "February," for instance, and remember that there's no such word as "alot." Here are a few more:

Common "Fingernails on Chalkboard" Word Usage Mistakes

Error:	Correct Use:
Confusing "your" and "you're."	"Your" is the possessive of "you." Examples: *Your* order shipped today. We received *your* e-mail. We appreciate *your* business. "You're" is a contraction for "you are." Examples: *You're* welcome. *You're* a valued customer. We hope *you're* satisfied with your item.
Using "should of" and "could of."	Correct use for both is "should have" and "could have." Misuse comes from the pronunciations of the contractions "should've" and "could've."
Use of "suppose to."	Correct use is "supposed to." Example: Your order was *supposed to* have shipped on Friday, but there was a slight delay.

Note: Most word processing programs, such as Microsoft Word, will highlight these errors when you perform grammar checks.

Use spelling and grammar checking tools. AOL has a spell-checker for e-mail, and so does Microsoft Outlook. Smart writers use them. Plus, it will be worth it when your customers feel comfortable communicating with you. Your writing speaks for your credibility.

E-mail Etiquette

Mark Twain once apologized to someone for sending a lengthy letter, explaining that he'd have written a shorter one if he'd had more time. It's funny, but true. It takes some thought to write short, polite e-mail. On the receiving end, it takes up your customer's valuable time to read a rambling message. Be kind to your e-mail recipients by getting to the point, and staying there. Here we'll discuss how you can win with your customers by sending e-mail that's clear and concise.

Including the Text of the Original Message

Not long ago I worked for a charitable organization and very often found myself at odds with a verbose officer I'll call Spike. Our communication transpired in e-mail and, per protocol, the other officers received copies of our point-counterpoint "discussions." When I replied to Spike, I only included the parts of her e-mail that pertained to my response. She soon demanded that I either include her entire, adjective-rich message, or quote none of it. Given the amount of e-mail that the board of officers exchanged in any given week, Spike was quickly admonished. They all read her original, so why see it again along with my reply? She apparently wanted to see it as many times as possible. Someone finally suggested that if she wanted to read it again that bad, she should review the copy in her e-mail outbox.

They were right, of course. If you're only replying to part of a person's message, you don't need to include the whole thing. It's important to include the text of the original e-mail and the date you received it, so the customer knows what you're referencing. However, you don't need to include information that doesn't pertain to your subject, such as:

- The customer's sig file

- Extraneous code contained in the customer's e-mail

- Lengthy e-mail header information

There's no need to bog anyone down with extraneous text that both the sender and receiver have already read. The exception is if you copy someone on the e-mail who didn't receive the original. For example, suppose a customer e-mails you a request for the status of his or her shipment. When you assure the customer that you'll have your ordering department check on it, add your ordering clerk's e-mail address as a copy-to recipient. Since the clerk didn't receive the original message, include the entire text of the customer's e-mail message so the clerk can adequately address it.

Stay off THE CAPS LOCK KEY

Never, ever, ever-never-never send e-mail in all capital letters. It might be easier to type, but it's a pain to read because our eyes are trained to read standard upper- and lowercase letters. Also, using all uppercase letters is typically perceived as anger or shouting. Take a little extra time to start sentences and proper nouns with capital letters, and put periods at the end of your sentences. Similarly, don't type in all lowercase letters. This might send the wrong idea to your customer: Can someone this lazy get my order right?

Always Mind Your Temper

As mentioned before, a furious insult intended for one person could end up being read by a much larger audience. Here are a few things to think about when sending e-mail, especially when tempers are flaring:

- If this message was displayed publicly, would it embarrass you?

- Would you say the same thing if the customer was across the counter?

- Remember that you're dealing with people of all ages and occupations. Is your message easy to understand?

- Did you proofread your e-mail? A small typo could cause a gross misunderstanding or make you seem foolish.

- Are you sending the equivalent of an electronic punch in the jaw? If so, expect a similar response.

- If an e-mail message provokes a strong emotional response in you, did you take time to read it over to be sure you clearly understood the intended meaning?

- Avoid sending messages that are "just kidding" with an included emoticon. This is not appropriate for business communication. :-)

- How would your e-mail sound if it were read in court?

Smile When You Say That

Be nice. Wording your EOA messages with pleasant, friendly overtones is the Internet equivalent of service with a smile. I've heard numerous comments from high bidders who receive EOA messages that are little more than threats of negative feedback if payment doesn't arrive exactly as the seller specifies. Here's an example of a dreadful e-mail message:

> Dear High Bidder,
>
> You owe me $25 for the item you bid on. Add $3.50 for shipping and another $1.80 if you want insurance. If you don't pay for insurance don't blame me if the item gets broken. You must send me a U.S. Postal Money Order. If I don't receive your payment within 10 days and it's in any other form, I'll leave you negative feedback. Don't even think of sending me a personal check, and I don't use PayPal nor do I care to sign up so you can get the five-dollar referral. Send the payment to the address below and include a copy of this e-mail or you might not get the right item. Don't write the auction number or the word "eBay" on the Postal Money Order, just make it out to me.

As horrible as it sounds, the above is an actual EOA message that an Internet auction buyer forwarded to me for comment. I only had one: Never bid on this seller's auctions again! What a horrible way to treat customers. How would this attitude go over in a Brick & Mortar store? Imagine being greeted this way as you walked in the door:

> "You just entered my store. Don't touch anything unless you intend to pay for it. We only accept cash. The cash had better not be dirty. Don't expect any favors from us if you buy anything. Wipe your feet."

How fast would you leave *that* store? The overall tone of your e-mail communication with buyers or sellers is crucial for building a good reputation as an Internet auction seller.

Normal Transactions

A "normal transaction" is one in which you're dealing with someone of an even, predictable temperament. Always assume that the person you're writing to is as nice as you are. If you're terse or rude, there's a good chance the payment will never arrive. Here are several instances when you should contact your customers in e-mail as a business courtesy:

- **Receipt of payment**—It's both important and courteous to let your customers know when their payment reached you. Be sure to tell the buyer when you plan to ship the item. If the buyer sent a personal check, indicate when you'll deposit the check and include a date that's 10 days later as your expected ship date.

- **Notification of shipment**—Always inform your customers when the product has shipped, so they can be on the lookout for it.

- **Credit card or money transfer issues**—Let your customers know immediately if a credit card transaction or EFT was declined by the financial institution. Remember that this is usually embarrassing for the customer, so be nice. Offer to attempt the transaction again in a few days, or suggest that they send payment via U.S. Mail.

Difficult Situations

Sometimes the transaction doesn't follow the plan. When unexpected events hamper the natural course of the Internet auction selling process, you'll need to contact the other party in e-mail. Remember that this is when it's the most crucial to maintain a level head.

Here are some "sticky situations" that necessitate sending e-mail to the customer that may put him or her on the defensive:

- **Payment never arrived**—Always initially assume that the payment was lost in the mail, or that the customer was much too busy with important things to remember to send it, or that it was processed in error. Assume that the buyer still plans to uphold the agreement and politely ask for the status of the missing payment. Don't accuse or admonish. After all, the error might be yours.

- **Buyer's check bounced**—Give the customer the benefit of the doubt and assume it was the bank's fault, but let him or her know that you expect another form of payment that should include any overdraft fees that your bank charged you. Don't ship the order until the payment issue is resolved.

- **The deal is off**—It's been over a month and still no payment. Let the customer know that you have canceled the transaction, and invite them to initiate another one if they wish. Avoid being harsh. You never know what's going on in someone's life.

- **Customer requested a refund and sent you a rock in a box**—Forget e-mail. Notify the authorities and nail the creep.

Now let's talk about the final phase of the Internet auction transaction.

Making Nice with Feedback

Wise Internet auction sellers make smart use of this very important and very *public* way to acknowledge customers. It's important to enter a nice comment about a successful transaction. Another important issue is *when* you should do it.

Who Goes First?

Most Internet auction users have their own policies about when they should leave feedback. A few of them take an unfortunately jaded approach. I've known sellers who refuse to enter feedback until the customer enters a comment first. The idea is to safeguard their own feedback rating against customers who might be unhappy with their shipments. At eBay, where you can't edit feedback you've entered, if the seller has already entered positive feedback and the customer then enters a negative one, the seller has no way to retaliate. To keep their sterling record, they want the customer to enter feedback first; then and only then will they reciprocate. This self-serving attitude on the part of a seller is an atrocious business practice.

The seller should always enter feedback for the customer first. Why? For the same reason your cashier says "thank you" before the customer says, "you're welcome." Once the customers have paid for their purchases, they have fulfilled their end of the transaction. It's then up to the seller to complete the transaction in a way that will earn him or her a positive feedback rating from the customer. Never, ever expect the customer to enter transactional feedback before you do. Whether you know this or not, many seasoned Internet auction buyers will check feedback records to see if the seller entered feedback before the high bidder did. This shows that the seller has confidence in his or her own business practices. You could lose a potential customer if feedback records show that your customer entered feedback before you did.

When Should the Seller Enter Feedback?

Sellers are split on this one. Some, including me, feel that once the customer's payment is received and cleared, the seller should enter positive feedback since the customer's part of the transaction is then fulfilled. Other sellers prefer to wait until the customer has received the item and is satisfied with it to enter feedback, so that the comment covers the whole transaction and not just the buyer's payment.

The second theory is acceptable, provided the seller ultimately enters feedback first. The problem is that not all customers will let you know that they've received the item. They'll just head for their computers, enter positive feedback for you, and consider their part of the deal over and done with. Sometimes you won't know that the customer received the item until you see his or her feedback in your file. The result is that the customer has entered feedback for you first, and this is very bad seller practice. It's up to you if you want to wait until the customer is satisfied before you enter feedback, but remember one thing. You should always rate a customer on how well he or she fulfilled the high bidder's obligations—not on how well they think you fulfilled yours.

Now let's talk about what's on a customer's mind when he or she contemplates bidding on one of your auctions.

The Internet Auction Buyer Psychology

Many books exist that tell people how to buy things at online auctions. The books are rich with sound advice, warnings, tips and tricks for getting a bargain, and what to do if the seller sends the wrong item or never sends anything. The sellers also know that Internet auctions present the caveat emptor, and that they must pay for any auctions they win. The art of bidding carries styles and techniques as the prospective customer attempts to get the best buy for the lowest price. In order to understand your high bidder's point of view, this section will cover the Internet auction transaction from the customer's viewpoint.

What Other Books Tell Buyers to Watch For

Once the potential bidders know what they're looking to buy, they'll read advice about how to locate auctions, how to place bids, deciding how much to spend, and a few tricks on winning auctions. They'll be cautioned to read the auction description carefully, and to ask the seller questions before placing the bid. They'll also learn how to spot a fraudulent auction and what to do if the seller defaults and then disappears (these are called **deadbeat sellers**). Knowing what advice is offered to buyers will help you cover all the bases and come across as a trustworthy seller.

Finding Auctions
Experts advise potential bidders to know what they want before heading to the Internet auction site in order to avoid "window shopping" or impulse buying. They're instructed to go right to the auction site search page, type in a text search for the items they seek, and then shop around for the best deal by reading the auction descriptions, examining the photographs, and perusing the terms of sale. This is all great advice.

Your job as a seller, of course, is to make sure that you catch any prospective buyers in the act of looking for what you're selling. The only way they'll bid on your auction is if they can find it. The best way to accomplish this, of course, is with well-planned titles and complete and accurate descriptions.

Setting a Maximum Price
The next bit of buyer advice is to decide in advance the most they want to spend on an item. They'll read about proxy bidding, which is a pro-

gram that incrementally advances their bid to the declared maximum if someone attempts to outbid them.

For sellers, if you've managed to time your auction so that you don't have a lot of competition (auctions for the same item closing around the same time), this may encourage your bidders to dig a little deeper into their pockets if some last-minute bidders attempt to beat them. It's important to study your competition and their Internet auction habits.

Interpreting the Auction

Some books break down the auction page and explain every bit of data in painstaking detail. Others offer advice on what to look for in the auction description written by the seller. Here's a checklist for a well-informed bidder:

- Read the description carefully.

- Examine the photograph.

- Compare the photograph to the auction description.

- Read and understand the seller's terms of sale.

- E-mail any questions about the item or auction to the seller before you bid.

Prospective buyers will compare your description to the photograph you included to see if the product has any flaws you didn't mention—or if you sneak the mention where it's likely to be overlooked. They'll also be on the lookout for double entendres and they'll glance over sales hype. It's vitally important for you to write straightforward, accurate, and honest auction descriptions that inform and engage the viewer. Okay, yours can *enchant* the viewer too. As long as he or she bids on your item, and not on your competitor's.

Sizing up the Seller

Any online auction book worth the paper it's printed on will advise prospective bidders to check the seller's feedback before placing a bid. Rest assured that well-informed, reasonably cautious bidders *will* look at yours, which is why it's so important to respond to any negative comments in a calm and professional manner. A few other checks can help a prospective auction bidder feel you out:

- How long you've been registered at that particular site

- Any other user IDs that you've used

- Other auctions you're currently running (and closed ones)

- User verification, if the auction site has that option

- Your "AboutMe" or equivalent page

If you followed your Seven-Step Internet Auction Strategy and planned your auctions carefully, all of these checks will work to your advantage and may help promote your other auctions. Many books tell bidders to check out the link you provide to your business Web site. Wonderful! Thank those authors. This is exactly what you want, as long as the auction site you're using allows links. The books continue with more great advice for buyers, most of which translates to great results for you.

Auctions to Avoid

Experts also caution auction users to avoid auctions that are obviously bogus or silly. Nobody should bid on joke auctions, even in fun. Joke auctions devalue the Internet auction site's integrity and take up space. To bid on one is a show of approval, and makes the bidder look as foolish as the loosey goosey seller does. Do you want to deal with someone dense enough to place a bid on Mt. Everest? Maybe his or her bid on *your* auction will be just as frivolous.

Here are more warning signs for bidders:

- **High minimum bid**—Don't bid if the starting price is more than you're willing to pay.

- **Unclear description**—If you can't envision it by reading about it, it's not worth the risk.

- **No photo**—Maybe the seller doesn't really have the item. Pick another auction that includes a photo.

- **Short description in all caps with spelling errors that reads as if it was written by Attila the Hun**—Let's not even go there.

Here's good advice for Internet auction buyers:

> "If your instincts leave you feeling unsure or uncomfortable about the item for sale, don't bid. Given the amount of Internet auction traffic on the Internet, a better opportunity is bound to come along."

That better opportunity is waiting at one of your auctions.

Bidding to Win

The advice for buyers is to wait until the last few hours and bid just before the auction closes. This keeps early bidding wars from driving the price up. But, you of course know this is lousy advice. With the new instant-win features, the item might be long gone by the time this ill-advised bidder comes around again looking for it.

Setting a "Buy it Now" or "First Bid Wins" price whenever it's practical may help you reel in the "bid to win" customers. The books warn bidders not to be impulsive, but you know they won't listen.

How to Beat Fraud

Buyers worry about Internet auction fraud. However, if they heed the sound advice about checking out the seller's feedback, reading the auction carefully, and asking any questions before they bid, they'll usually do all right. It's not to say that an eBay PowerSeller with over 10,000 positive feedbacks won't suddenly cut and run with his high bidder's money, but it's not likely. Nonetheless, bidders have the right to be cautious. They also have the right to ask you if you'll ship an item COD, or if you'll agree to use an escrow service for a low-money transaction, even if your description specifies that you won't. Buyers can ask.

And you should say no. Not only because your feedback record is excellent, your auction description and terms are clear, and you fully intend to complete the transaction. You should decline unreasonable requests that would cost you unnecessary time and money because you have every right to. Be polite, be firm, and say no. Some of the books recommend that buyers always request COD and low-money transaction escrow as definite safeguards against fraud, but don't buy it (the advice or the book). You're not going to defraud your customers. You have the right to expect your customers to abide by your terms of sale, and you deserve their trust. If you come across and operate as an ethical seller, your customers will catch on and they'll remain your customers. Loyal ones.

What It Means When You Get a Bid

A bid on your auction is a stamp of approval for you as an Internet auction seller. It means that a wary bidder checked you out and you successfully passed; you've set the stage to win with a future customer. That one bid represents the essential elements of your road to Internet auction success:

- Your auction title came up in searches.

- Your description is believable.

- You included a well-composed photograph.

- Your minimum bid is in line with the market.

- As a seller, you passed scrutiny.

- The bidder wants your item.

In Step 1, you determined your opening bid based on factors like your price floor, your price ceiling, and the product's going rate. A bid on your auction indicates that at least one person is willing to pay your asking price. Either you did an excellent job estimating what your customers will pay, or your auction was so brilliantly executed that your bidder doesn't mind paying more than the item is worth. Both work, but the first scenario works more often.

The bid also means that you effectively carried out Step 4 of your Internet Auction Strategy. Earning a satisfied and repeat customer depends on how well you carry out Step 6.

The Buyer's Expectations

The self-help books on interpersonal relationships typically tell us that the best way to win with someone is to find out what their needs are, and then fill them. Then they advise us to set limits and boundaries so the need-filling doesn't turn into codependent behavior.

A similar theory applies to the Internet auction seller and his or her customers. The seller fills the bidder's needs, which in the Internet auction venue are straightforward:

- Bidder wants the item.

- Bidder wants to pay a fair price.

- Bidder wants the item shipped when payment clears.

- Bidder wants item to arrive in the expected condition.

- Bidder wants positive site feedback.

You can fulfill all of these needs, provided the buyer meets yours: valid, timely payment. It's win-win.

Special Touches

While writing this chapter, the UPS driver pulled up to my house with a huge box. It was my 34-piece kitchenware set from a closeout auction site. I pulled out four different boxes, each containing the various kitchen items, and then found a fifth item in the bottom of the box. It was a complimentary set of plastic measuring cups. I was thrilled! These were probably worth very little and I already have two sets, but they'll be excellent for one of my kids.

Someone I don't know included this nice touch with my shipment. It was an appropriate bonus item in the same genre as the other items I ordered. Receiving it made my day. Next time I'm in the market for similar products, I'll buy them from that site. As an Internet auction seller, you have many opportunities to reach out and provide your buyers with a nice touch.

Bonus Items

The measuring cups were a **bonus item**, included with my shipment at no cost to me. They may have been a discontinued or surplus item, a new product sample, or something the seller fully intended to use as a gift item. The most important aspect is that the bonus item was appropriate. Here we'll discuss things that make good bonus items, and what to avoid.

Appropriate Items

Something related to the item. If the buyer ordered candles, send a sample votive candle to introduce a new line. With a shipment of men's slacks, you could enclose an inexpensive tie tack. Here are some other ideas for bonus items:

- Bookmarks

- Notepads

- Pens or pencils

- Refrigerator magnets

- Keychains

- Advertising novelty bearing your business name and URL

These are usually appreciated and seldom discarded.

What Not to Enclose

Don't include items that may have an adverse reaction from the recipient. Avoid enclosing anything perishable, because no matter how nice a bonus item is, it will have the opposite effect if it arrives moldy. Here are a few more items on the "not appropriate" list:

- Scented items, because the buyer might be allergic (unless the items ordered are also scented)

- Something that's personal or intimate, such as deodorant or underwear

- Candy, gum, or anything else that's edible

- An item totally unrelated to the product ordered, such as including a tampon sample with a pair of men's athletic shoes

Use your good judgment.

Send Clean Products

What if your stock sat on a warehouse shelf long enough to develop a filmy sheath of dust? The obvious remedy is to clean it before you sell it. Never ship a dirty item. Wipe down any product that has gathered dust or grime before it goes into the shipping carton.

Whenever possible, ship products in the original, sealed packaging. When we covered shipping items in Chapter 8, we discussed packing items to be sure that they arrive undamaged. It's also important to be sure that they arrive clean. If you've ever purchased pressed-powder makeup, you've noticed the protective paper between the compact and the little box it comes in. This gives the item an aura of cleanliness and newness. The items you ship to your customers should be just as clean and new.

Buttons and Bows for the Occasion

Depending on your business, you might offer special services for your customers, either free or for a minimal charge. Be careful that you don't end up assessing mandatory extra charges, such as fees over and above those associated with the auction transaction, because that's usually against the Internet auction site's terms and conditions. If you offer the services, specify that any gift-wrapping or special packaging is an *optional* extra charge. Make this offer in e-mail when you send your EOA notice and give definite rates for the special service you're offering.

Will You Gift Wrap?
If the customer requests it, and you're set up to do it, then why not. The special service could earn you repeat customers. One word of advice when gift-wrapping Internet auction purchases, though, is that you may want to leave one side undone so the customer can slip the wrapping off to inspect the item. Be sure to mention this if you agree to gift-wrap. It's always best to give your customers the option of ensuring that you shipped the right item, and that it arrived in the expected condition.

Enclosing Gift Cards
Similar to gift wrapping, this is a nice touch that doesn't take much effort on the part of the seller. If you have a supply of inexpensive gift cards, which are easily custom-made on your computer, ask the cus-

tomer what sentiment to put on the card and tuck it in with the item. If you know the item is intended as a gift, you can offer this special service, especially if the item is shipping directly to the recipient.

Shipping to Alternate Addresses

You might occasionally get a request from a winning bidder to ship the item to an address other than his or her own. This usually happens when the item is a gift. Most sellers don't mind, since it doesn't add any more effort to the transaction. Remember, though, to inform the customer that this may change your three-day inspection policy. You also need to specify that while you're shipping to a third party, the transaction is still between you and the winning bidder. If any problems occur during shipping, then he or she—not the third-party recipient—must communicate with you to resolve the issue.

12

Problems, Resolutions, and Online Support

Wouldn't it be great if there was a profitable business venture available that was easy, economical, and hassle free? Selling through Internet auctions is relatively easy and definitely economical, but sometimes it's not hassle free. This chapter will prepare you for some of the roadblocks you may encounter:

- When it feels like the auction site is working against you

- What to do when you encounter problems with other sellers

- Canceling a user's bid

- Blocking bids from particular users

- When the site cancels your auction

- Dealing with slow or deadbeat bidders

- Auction site outages

- When a bidder retracts a bid

- Feedback misuse

Most Internet auction transactions go off without a hitch and it's very unlikely that you'll ever face some of these problems. The information here will help prepare you for the unexpected. You'll also read about Web sites and auction portals that provide online support for auction sellers:

- Internet auction portals and support

- Auction service providers

- Information sites and e-newsletters

- Discussion forums

- Real-time communication media

No matter how successful your Internet auction business venture becomes, you'll spend a lot of time on the computer before you can handle your new selling venture by rote. These resources will provide plenty of information for you, some of which you may not yet be aware that you'll need to be a successful Internet auction seller.

Is the Auction Site Working Against You?

The Internet auction site is someone's livelihood. Site administrators, designers, and programmers may truly love the OAI, but running the site is their job. Successfully run Internet auction sites strive to earn the biggest profits possible to cover their own overhead without jeopardizing your service—or at least that's the theory. When you list auctions, your high bidders are your customers. When you sell at an Internet auction venue, *you* are the auction site's customer and you have the right to expect your money's worth.

Rate Increases and Fees for Features

Listing an Internet auction started out free and soon cost a dime. Later the insertion fee went up to 25 cents and seems to climb a little higher every two years. Are the auction sites gouging us? Maybe, but maybe not. Naturally they want to make a sound profit, but they also want to retain their customers—and that's you.

As more users register and list auctions, this puts an added strain on the servers that host the auction site. To keep the site operating takes software upgrades, additional servers, and an adequate work force. The support tools required to manage a site like eBay are complex and costly. Without upgrades and improvements, the auction site users will experience downtime, slow page loading, and many other annoying problems. Even routine maintenance can be costly, so they look for ways to increase their profits.

Additional Fees

Sometimes an auction site will introduce a new feature free of charge in order to see how well it's received before implementing it permanently. Once an introductory period passes, sellers pay a fee to use it. Some users complain that the site accustoms them to a free feature and then gouges them for it.

In most cases the feature was never free for the auction site to offer. The program that runs the feature, the customization and development of the program, and the maintenance required in keeping it operational are costly.

Charging for Features

In 2000, eBay started charging a fee to set a reserve price on an auction. This was necessary in order to prevent misuse of the feature. They discovered that some sellers were setting high reserve prices with low minimum bids, not intending to sell the item. The seller just wanted to see how high it would bid to get an idea of its value. This site had no chance to earn commission from the sale, and the listing took up space. To deter this, they started charging an additional 10 cents per listing to set a reserve price, and specified that the minimum bid must be at least 10 percent of the reserve price. This discouraged sellers from abusing the feature.

Poor Customer Service

Not many Internet auction sites display a telephone number, but most of them include an e-mail address or a "contact us" link. When the site administrators communicate via e-mail, they can send you automated canned responses, or "form letter" e-mails. These messages may only marginally address your issue.

Sometimes it's necessary to answer certain types of questions with canned responses, such as when the question is adequately answered by providing the user with a link to the site tutorial. If a million users all sent e-mail to an auction site asking, "How do I bid on an item?" it would take months for them to answer each message individually. Instead, they categorize questions by topic, and auto-respond with any one of numerous prepared responses.

You can avoid getting canned responses in a few ways. The best advice, though, is to at least peruse the form-letter e-mail you receive in case it does answer your question. If not, I have a few suggestions that might get you a personal response from a customer service representative at the auction site:

- Put "Second Request—Personal Response Requested" in the subject of your e-mail message.

- Include "Please don't send me a canned response" at the beginning of your message. Then restate your issue.

- Add "Attention: Supervisor" in your e-mail subject line. Reserve this for when you're reporting a site violation or something that requires an immediate response.

These messages usually go straight to customer service for attention, and there's a good chance that someone will respond to you personally.

Problems with Other Sellers

Free enterprise creates competition, and e-commerce has its share of it. Some forms of advertising allow companies to compare and contrast their product with another one on the market, and say theirs is better. For instance, remember the "Pepsi taste test," where the Pepsi Cola Company claimed that its product tasted better than Coca Cola? Burger King had a long-running campaign claiming that its Whopper won a taste test over McDonald's Big Mac. These were both acceptable advertising tactics.

It's different for Internet auction sellers. You usually have competition, but your auction description can't claim that your products or values outshine user so-and-so's. The auction site would pull your listing, possibly on the grounds of interfering with another seller's auctions. This doesn't mean that sellers won't compete with you. It means that if they do, they can't be obtrusive about it. Here we'll cover a few of these shady tactics and what you can do about them.

Auction Description Plagiarizing

There is little more annoying for dedicated auction sellers than to learn that a less-than-ethical seller has stolen their work. Most C2C and B2C sites will crack down on sellers who plagiarize auction descriptions. Writing successful auction descriptions should be an acquired skill for every auction seller.

Note: Auction description plagiarizing is another reason to check your competitors' auctions every now and then. Be sure that they aren't recycling your work.

"On certain high value items, I spend considerable time writing lengthy descriptions in order to better sell the item and to pick up as many relevant keywords as possible," says Steve, an auction seller who posts in the OTWA forums. "When my descriptions started showing up, word for word, in other sellers' auctions, I joined eBay's VeRO program in order to protect my work."

eBay is one of many Internet auction sites that will protect copyrighted information. They launched the Verified Rights Owner (VeRO) Program to help filter auctions for violations. The program ensures that items listed for auction do not infringe upon the copyright, trademark, or other intellectual property rights of others. VeRO participants may report and request removal of allegedly infringing auction listings. It's usually for product copyright infringements, but it does carry over to auction description text and auction photos.

"I really wouldn't care if I only sold one of a particular widget," Steve explains. "But on items that I have multiples of, the infringement hurts my future sales, which ultimately cuts into my earnings."

See Figure 12.1, eBay's VeRO Page, where you'll find guidance on how to report violations.

eBay's Verified Rights Owner (VeRO) Program™: Protecting Intellectual Property

In keeping with its status as the internet's largest venue for person-to-person trading, eBay does not and cannot verify that sellers have the right or ability to sell or distribute their listed items. However, we are committed to removing infringing or unlicensed items once an authorized representative of the rights owner properly reports them to us. eBay's Verified Rights Owner (VeRO) Program works to ensure that items listed for auction do not infringe upon the copyright, trademark or other intellectual property rights of third parties. VeRO Program participants may identify and request removal of allegedly infringing auction listings.

Any person or company who holds intellectual property rights (such as a copyright, trademark or patent) which may be infringed by eBay auction listings is encouraged to become a VeRO Program Member. It's fast and its simple to do so. Current Program Members include hundreds of individuals, local, state and federal law enforcement, and companies from a wide array of industries.

Program participation entitles you to the following benefits:

- Dedicated eBay staff to assist you in getting the most out of the Program
- Rapid response by eBay in ending auctions reported by you as allegedly infringing
- Dedicated priority email queues for reporting alleged infringements
- The ability to obtain identifying information about eBay users through your eBay Membership
- eBay member rights and privileges as described in the eBay User Agreement and Privacy Policy
- Automatic updates on new benefits available under the Program

How to Become a VeRO Program Member

It is fast and simple to join the VeRO Program. We require only that you fill out and fax to us a Notice of Infringement form specifying the allegedly infringing listings and infringed works, complete with an original authorized signature. The information requested by the Notice of Infringement is designed to ensure that parties reporting items are authorized by the rights owners, and to enable eBay to correctly identify the material or listing to be ended. After your first Notice of Infringement is received by us, you'll be able to transmit future notices to eBay by email. Click here to download the Notice of Infringement and explanatory materials. You will need Adobe® Reader to view and print these documents. Free downloads are available at Adobe's web site by clicking on this button:

Figure 12.1. eBay's VeRO page (*pages.ebay.com/help/community/vero-program.html*).

Contact the Infringing Seller

Sometimes, the auction site won't act as quickly as we hope they would under these circumstances. If that's the case, contact the infringing seller yourself. Include in your e-mail that you've reported the infringement (if you have) and that you'd like to see the auction significantly changed so it's not the same as yours.

In the case of Stephanie Lee, an independent Internet auction seller, the auction site didn't act as quickly as she hoped they would. "I found an auction that copied my description text word for word," she said. "I sent an e-mail to the seller letting him know that it was against the site's rules, and heard nothing back. I contacted the site and included all of the information I thought they'd need to know: the date of my listing, the URL to the offending listing, the seller's user ID, etc. Again, I heard nothing back." Stephanie finally convinced the seller to change his description.

How Far Should You Go with This?

Contacting the site and notifying the seller is about as far as you can go. Among other sites, eBay has rules about auction interference. Contacting bidders to warn them about a seller, regardless of the reason, falls under that category. The correct procedure, according to eBay, is to contact SafeHarbor@eBay.com or TimeSensitive@eBay.com and alert them to the infraction. One reason eBay enlisted this procedure is to protect sellers against "auction site vigilantes" who e-mail sellers on a whim, and end up being wrong about their hunch. The seller loses business, and eBay loses final-value fee commission.

Can You Prevent It from Happening?

Not easily. You can make your auction text part of an image so the text can't be copied and pasted, but then a buyer could claim that you changed the description or your seller terms in the image after the auction closed. Some fancy programs circulating on the Internet will prevent users from doing a right-click copy of text and images. However, it won't take long for users to figure out that these programs only work if the user has Java enabled. They can turn off Java and then copy and paste away.

When Another Seller Uses Your Images

Imagine your dismay when you discover that another seller is cashing in on your hard work by using one of your photographs in his or her auction listing—especially if the seller is stealing your business. This is the main reason I urge you to add copyright information to your images. But every now and then, you'll find a seller who is bold enough to use your photographs anyway. What then?

Notify the Auction Site

If someone reuses your copyrighted auction photo, I wouldn't bother sending e-mail to the seller asking him or her to change the image. What they've done is a bold infraction. You need to e-mail the auction site as soon as possible. Include the URL to your photo and the URL to the offender's photo so the site administrators can make a comparison and see that another seller has effectively stolen your photo. Include the auction number or the listing page URL. The auction site will deal with the offender.

Linking to Your Image Host

If you discover that another seller has been foolish enough to actually use an image linked from your image host, you can have all kinds of fun re-customizing that seller's auction. If you're not currently using the image in one of your auctions, upload a different image in that one's place, making sure that the new image has the same URL as the image being pirated. Imagine the viewer's surprise when an auction description for a set of delicately scented candles suddenly includes a photo of the local landfill. Hopefully, the seller will learn an important lesson about stealing another seller's images.

Auction Interference

Any attempt by any user to adversely affect the outcome of a seller's auction is **auction interference**. This can include any of these:

- Offering bidders on a particular auction the same product at a lower price

- Encouraging bidders to cancel bids on another seller's auctions for any reason

- Placing a high bid on an auction to deter other bidders, and then canceling the bid at the last minute

Almost every Internet auction site has strict rules against auction interference, and will revoke the user IDs of repeated offenders.

It's important to report this misuse to the auction site; however, it's up to the bidders to do that since they're the ones contacted behind the scenes. If your bidders let you know about it, encourage them to report it to the site administrators.

Fee Avoidance

Since most of the consumer sites offer bid history information, the user IDs of non-winning bidders are easily available. Another shoddy tactic called **fee avoidance** happens when unethical sellers contact non-winning bidders on auctions for items similar to one they have for sale. They offer the product to the non-winning bidder at their bid price. If they sell their items outside of the auction venue, they pay no listing fees or site commissions. Fee avoidance can be a form of auction interference if you lose bids because of it.

Canceling a User's Bid

Many of the consumer auction sites allow sellers to cancel bids on their items. In some situations, canceling a user's bid is amicable. If someone bids on your item and then decides to bid on a more expensive one you have listed, he or she may ask you to cancel the bid on the first item. In this case, you might as well. Bidders can usually cancel their own bids, but several sites make bid cancellations part of the bidder's viewable record. If the seller cancels the bid, there is typically no viewable record.

When It's Advisable

A few instances could cause a seller to want to cancel a user's bid:

- You've had bad experiences with the bidder in the past and would rather not deal with him or her again.

- You have sufficient reason to believe that the bidder is using a bogus account.

- The item you listed was destroyed or for some other reason is no longer available, and you must end the auction to avoid defrauding users. In this case, you must e-mail any bidders and explain the situation when you cancel their bids and end the auction.

Once you cancel bids, you usually can't reinstate them.

Consequences

When you remove a user's bid, the action withdraws all bids on your item from that particular user. If any of those bids drew proxy bidding from another bidder, those bids fall away as well. Canceling a user's bid reverts any bidding on the auction to the way that it would be if the user had never bid. The price on the item may drop lower than you realize. If you're going to cancel a user's bid, check the bidding history on the item so you can anticipate the impact it will have on your earnings. Then you can proceed after determining one of the following:

- Should you wait it out, and hope someone else outbids the questionable bidder?

- Should you cancel the bid and just take the lower price in order to avoid potential problems?

- Should you just let the bidder win the item and hope for the best?

The choice depends on whatever reasons you had for canceling the bid in the first place.

Bid Blocking

Some consumer auction sites allow sellers to block bids from certain users. Yahoo was the first major auction site to offer a feature called the "Blacklist," where a seller could specify user IDs that would be blocked from placing bids on their auctions. eBay introduced a similar feature in April 2001. If someone tries to bid on one of your auctions with a user ID that you have designated as "blocked," a message appears telling the user that he or she isn't authorized to bid on that auction.

Auction sites that offer this feature protect sellers from problematic users, and make things easier for themselves in the process. Allowing sellers to block unsavory users often prevents problems before they happen. The site has fewer complaints to deal with.

When to Use It

You'll block some bidders for the same reason a Brick & Mortar shop owner tosses out shoplifters and loiterers. It's the online auction equivalent of telling an Internet auction user, "We don't appreciate the problems you've caused us and we would rather not do business with you." Bid blocking protects sellers from certain unsavory users, such as:

- Bidders who are known for making unreasonable demands on sellers

- A user who has threatened to bid up all of your auctions and then never pays you

- Someone who gave you unwarranted negative feedback in the past

- User IDs that show a lot of recent negative feedback

- Users that you can't easily verify

If the auction site doesn't work fast enough to suspend a user who has caused problems for you, add that user ID to your blocked bid list. Remember, though, that these lists only go by user ID, not by a person's name. A user can register another site ID and bother you again until you add the second ID to your blocked bid list.

Sites That Allow It

At this writing, two of the major sites, Yahoo and eBay, allow sellers to block bids from specific users. Once sellers add a user to their blocked bid list, that user can't bid on any of that seller's auctions unless the seller removes the name from the list.

Yahoo Auctions' Blacklist

From Yahoo's "Options" link, you can select the "Edit Blacklist" link to block selected sellers from participating in your auction (see Figure 12.2). You'll enter the IDs of any users you want to ban from bidding. Adding and deleting users from your blacklist is done by way of an onscreen interface. You can blacklist users when you enter an auction, when you cancel a user's bid, or at any time when the auction is active.

eBay's Blocked Bidder List

By using eBay's Blocked Bidder List, you can set up a list of bidders who won't be able to bid on any of your listings. Using the input screen shown in Figure 12.3, you'll add user names one at a time as I did in the example, hitting your "Enter" key after you type each name. You can add or delete bidders at any time by returning to the input screen and backspacing through a user ID.

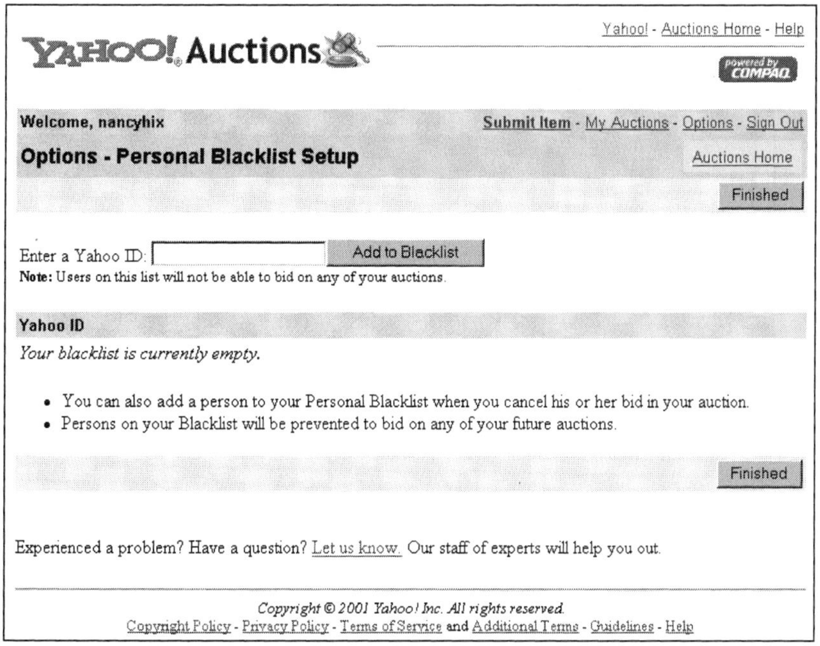

Figure 12.2. Yahoo! Auctions' personal blacklist setup (*user.auctions.yahoo.com/show/blacklist*).

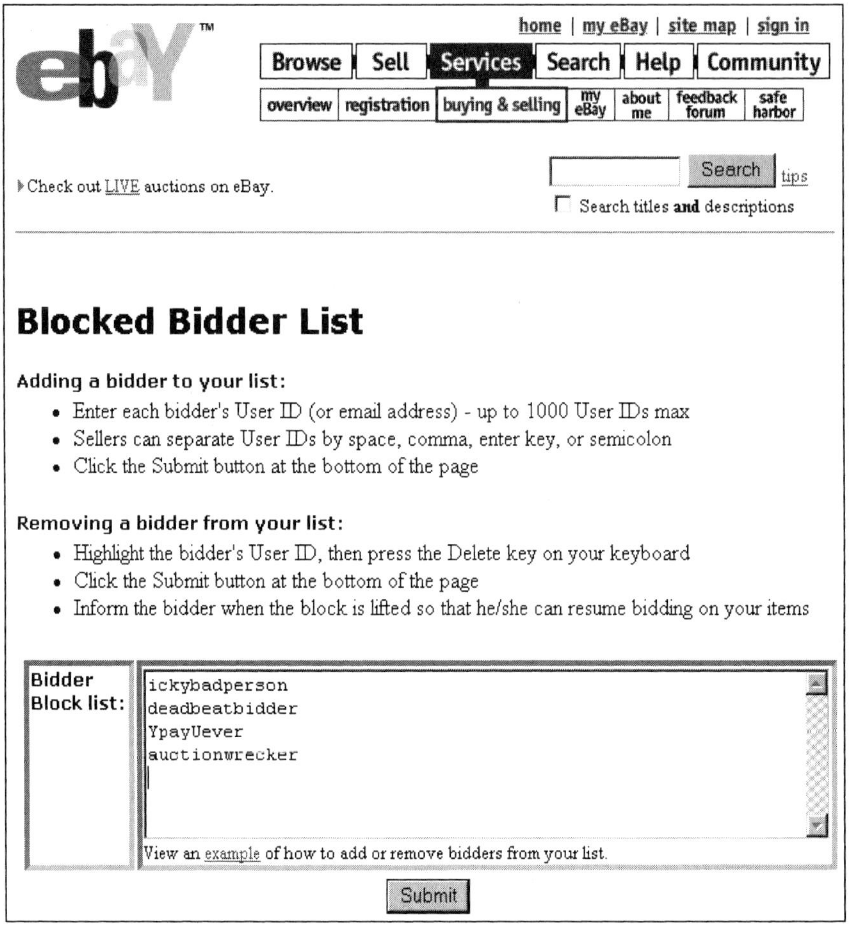

Figure 12.3. Adding user names to an eBay blocked bidder list (*pages.ebay.com/services/buyandsell/biddermanagement.html*).

Auctions Canceled by the Site

Knowing that auction sites earn money by charging you listing fees and commissions, imagine your surprise when you receive an e-mail from the site administrator informing you that they closed one of your auctions "due to a site terms and conditions violation." It does happen.

Why Was My Auction Canceled?

One likely reason is that someone reported your auction to the site administrator. Perhaps it violated either the site's terms and conditions, or the user felt that it was an infringement on his or her own copyrighted material. Following the report, the site administrator viewed your auction, agreed with the complaint, and canceled the listing. If the site closed your auction in error, you have to argue your case with them.

What Can You Do About It?

Unfortunately, not a lot. Even if the site canceled your auction in error, they won't re-start it where it left off. Any bids placed on your auction fell out of the system when they ended your auction. The site administrator cannot reinstate a user's bid once they cancel it. If they rule in your favor, they'll refund your listing fee and invite you to list the auction again.

If your auction *did* violate the site's policy, you have two options. Change the auction description to remove the offending text, or accept the fact that you can't sell that item at an Internet auction site. Find other items to sell that don't violate the rules.

Slow or Deadbeat Bidders

When you start listing tens or hundreds of auctions at a time, you're bound to encounter bidders who pay you slowly, and others who won't pay you at all. Sites such as eBay and Yahoo will send reminder e-mail messages to the delinquent bidders, but only after you let them know that you haven't been paid.

Dealing with a Slow Bidder

It's been 10 days since the auction closed and, despite smooth and pleasant post-auction e-mail correspondence, you haven't received payment from the high bidder. Standard procedure is to contact the bidder with a payment reminder. Depending on the size of your business and how much time you can devote to tracking down late payments, you can approach this issue from a few directions.

Be Gentle but Firm

If your bidder seems flustered and embarrassed about the delay, you'll have a lot better luck by being nice than by issuing threats of negative feedback. Harsh tones may drive a bidder away completely. Patience and understanding, coupled with a gentle-but-firm reminder that you expect to be paid, goes a long way.

You need to ask yourself which is more important to you:

- Cutting your loss and entering the negative feedback; then relisting the item. Who has time to wait? Apply for site credit and move on.

- Waiting it out and staying in contact with the person, with the possibility of receiving his or her payment and making a new customer.

If you're a small business operator dealing with private consumers, you need to interact with them a little more closely than if you're a mass-marketer. Use this to your advantage. If "gentle nudges" are within your operating comfort level, employ that method before giving up on the person. You may earn repeat customers and save the time involved in recovering your site fees, and you won't set yourself up for a retaliatory negative feedback comment in your profile.

If you're running Dutch auctions for a huge number of items, you can afford to wait a little longer for payments since you can list another lot and still put one item aside in case the late payment arrives. It's up to you how long you want to wait in that case.

Establish a New Deadline or Re-list

If the buyer missed the first payment deadline, consider negotiating one more. Let the buyer tell you what it is. If the payment hasn't reached you by that date, then e-mail the buyer to tell him or her that you've decided to re-list the item. Here's an e-mail sample:

> Dear Person,
>
> I contacted you two weeks ago about paying for the picture frame and I haven't heard back from you. The auction ended a month ago. I assume this means that you have changed your mind about the sale. I will leave the appropriate feedback for you and relist the item today. If you have unforeseen circumstances, I wish you well.
>
> Sincerely,
>
> -Seller

Since you're obviously not getting any money from the high bidder, you might as well re-list the item.

Handling a Deadbeat Bidder

I've encountered two types of deadbeat bidders. The worst will string you along by promising to send payment, but never do. In the meantime you can't re-list the item, nor can you close out your accounting for that trans-action. The best kind—or perhaps "less aggravating"—are those who just disappear after your auction closes. They don't respond to your EOA message, or your gentle reminder, or even the message you send letting them know that you've given up and re-listed the item. It's a little easier to deal with this type of phantom bidder because the most time you'll lose is about 10 days. The "stringers" might keep you waiting for weeks.

When to Apply for Credit
Yahoo instructs you to complete the Non-Paying Bidder form located on the closed auction page within seven to 45 days after the auction closes. If you don't receive payment within 10 days of completing the NPB form, contact the site again to arrange for a refund.

eBay also requests Non-Paying Bidder alerts filed within seven to 45 days after the auction closes. If 10 days pass and you still haven't received payment for the item, you can request a commission (final-value fee) credit.

Appropriate Feedback
The auction sites encourage you to leave "the appropriate feedback" for non-paying bidders. Once you've filed your complaint with the site

and re-listed the item, warn other sellers about a deadbeat bidder by entering a negative comment. Refer to Chapter 8 for information about what the negative feedback comment should contain.

Auction Site Outages

What happens to your active auctions when the Internet auction site you're using shuts down for a few hours? Some of the sites try to keep sellers happy by refunding fees and extending auctions, but other sites specify that you list at your own risk and overlook site outages if they occur.

Outage Policies

It's clear that eBay has the best site outage policy, probably because they have the most site outages, which is one downside of being the most trafficked online auction site. eBay's Outage Policy (see Figure 12.4) is clearly defined.

Some online auction sites make no amends for service gaps and expect sellers to accept system downtime as another tough break in the auction game. These sites clearly state so in their Terms and Conditions pages. For example, "This site cannot guarantee continuous, uninterrupted or secure access to our services and cannot compensate losses incurred as a result. Operation of our site is subject to interference by factors outside of our control." In other words, if the site goes kablooey, you're just plain out of luck.

What Can the Seller Do?

Aside from hoping the site doesn't experience unscheduled downtime as two bidders are "dueling snipos" as your auction ticks away its final seconds, there isn't much you can do if it happens. You can either take it in stride and accept your listing-fee refunds, or you can use some preventive measures to guard against site outages when you list your auctions. Wary sellers start their minimum bids at their

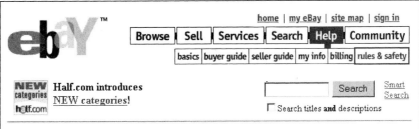

Outage Policy

Our highest priority is your trading success. However, eBay occasionally experiences outages during which bidders cannot place bids or cannot effectively locate items via our Title Search function. When these outages occur, we offer this Outage Policy to compensate for your inconvenience.

Title Search Outage of 1 or more hours:

- eBay automatically credits all associated fees for affected listings.
- The following listings will be eligible for credit:
  o Any listing scheduled to end during the outage
  o Any listing scheduled to end in the hour after the end of the outage
- Unlike our policy for Hard Outages of two hours or more, listings will not be extended

Hard Outage of more than 1 hour but less than 2 hours:

- eBay automatically credits all associated fees for affected listings
- The following listings will be eligible for credit:
  o Any listing scheduled to end during the outage
  o Any listing scheduled to end in the hour after the end of the outage
- Additionally, credit will be issued for the 10-cent promotional fee on any 10-day listing that is running during the outage (regardless of the time it's scheduled to end)
- Includes either of the following features:
  o View Item
  o Bidding
- Unlike our policy for Hard Outages of two hours or more, listings will not be extended

Hard Outage of two hours or more:

- eBay automatically extends listings for 24 hours
- eBay automatically credits all associated fees for affected listings.
- The following listings will be eligible for extension and credit:
  o Any listing scheduled to end during the outage
  o Any listing scheduled to end in the hour after the end of the outage

Figure 12.4. eBay's site outage policy (*pages.ebay.com/help/community/png-extn.html*).

absolute price floor, knowing through experience that the site sometimes goes down. Another precaution against downtime is setting a reserve price. Though unpopular with bidders, single-item auction sellers can sugarcoat it with a simple disclaimer in their auction descriptions:

> Modest reserve set to protect my investment in case of a site outage.

Hopefully, your bidders will understand. Those who have also been sellers will understand perfectly.

When a Bidder Retracts a Bid

Do bidders have the right to change their minds? At some online auction sites, yes. At other sites, bids are final and cannot be retracted under any circumstances, possibly because the site doesn't have the necessary provisions for it. If you list your Internet auctions at sites that allow bid retractions—and most of the major ones do—you need to get used to the idea that it might happen on one of your auctions.

Early in the Internet auction experience, some folks browsed the site, placed bids, and then retracted them if they changed their minds. This is known as the "shopping cart" syndrome, because it's similar to putting something into your cart and taking it back out if you change your mind. Recently, however, sites like eBay show bid retractions along with user feedback, so bidders are aware that the shopping cart syndrome won't go over well there.

When a Bidder Can Rightfully "Unbid"

There are a few instances where bidders can retract their bids and appeal to the auction site so the action doesn't show up on their "permanent record."

- If the seller adds something to the description that significantly changes the item's appeal, such as revealing that it's damaged or not in working order

- If the bidder detects and can reveal significant evidence of shilling

- If the seller appends additional shipping or handling charges to the auction after bids have been placed

Any of these cases are causes for justifiable bid retractions on the part of the bidder. The last two are shoddy seller practices anyway.

What Happens to the High Bid

Typically, a bidder can only retract a bid if it's the current high bid. A bid retraction will cancel all bids by that bidder on the item. Take, for instance, this active bidding for a single-item auction that started at $30:

> User1: $50 (current high bidder)
>
> User2: $45
>
> User1: $40
>
> User2: $35
>
> User3: $30

In this example, User1 is the high bidder at $50, with User2 the second high bidder at $45. If User1 retracts her bid of $50, her earlier bid of $40 also falls away. The current bidding would then appear like this:

> User2: $35 (current high bidder)
> User3: $30

Notice that since both of User1's bids were canceled, User2's bid of $45 became moot and dropped out of the system, reverting his earlier bid of $35 to the current high bid.

If the Seller Asks You First

If you cancel a user's bid on one of your items, it doesn't show up on the bidder's record. You might receive an e-mail message from a bidder asking you to cancel his or her bid. Based on the reason given for the request, it's up to you to decide if you want to honor it. It could work in your favor for a few reasons:

- If the bidder doesn't have the money to pay for the item, this will save you the hassle of re-listing the item and filing an NPB notice.

- Perhaps the bidder wants to bid on another item you have listed.

- The bidder may have made an error with a decimal point, and bid $3000 instead of $30 and wants to place a correct bid. Once a bidder retracts a bid, he or she usually can't bid on that item again so you can cancel the bid instead.

Agreeing to cancel a bid is typically the best action in any of these situations. It will save you problems later.

Note: At some sites, only the seller can cancel a user's bid.

Feedback Misuse

User feedback is an objective and powerful assessment tool, designed to help online auction users decide whether they want to do business with a particular seller or buyer. However, the system—like most systems—is far from perfect. Feedback can and has been misused.

Unfortunately, users have found plenty of ways to abuse feedback. Some feedback misuses are simply against the rules, while others push ethics to the limit. None of them will leave you in good stead with users who take feedback seriously—which is most of us.

Buyers Who Hold Your Feedback Hostage

You may encounter customers who refuse to enter feedback for you unless you carry out a specific function beyond what's expected of you as an auction seller. Be sure to save *all* e-mail correspondence from a buyer who makes an unreasonable request and refuses to enter feedback for you until you comply, and send it to the site with your complaint.

If someone wants you to operate outside the scope of the auction transaction and threatens you with negative feedback if you don't, this is **feedback extortion**. Don't act on threats and don't give in to the customer's unethical demands—let the auction site deal with it.

Retaliatory Feedback

A user with a genuine need to enter a negative comment does so, only to receive a totally unwarranted negative comment—often a complete lie—in return. This is called **retaliatory feedback**. Unfortunately, that's one risk of leaving a negative comment. Until the auction sites find a way to prevent or regulate retaliatory feedback, many users won't enter negative feedback to caution others. Will that retaliatory neg really tarnish your record that much? Not if prospective bidders read your calm and rational response to the comment.

Internet Auction Portals and Support

Any Internet auction seller can benefit from interaction with other sellers. The markets differ, but C2C and B2B Internet auctions have the same roots and often use similar tools. The main difference is the amount of money that changes hands. If you list auctions for midsize and small businesses, you'll find many other folks in a similar line of work who can answer your questions, comment on your auctions, and provide the level of support that most new Internet auction users need.

What Online Support Can Offer You

Some auction users claim that they've never picked up a reference book about Internet auctions because they get all the information they need from other users. While the books are helpful, the online forums can provide different viewpoints about unique situations.

Message Boards
You've probably heard about online bulletin boards, Internet message boards, chat boards, or discussion forums. They essentially serve the

same purpose. People all over the world can post messages and participate in discussions from wherever they can access the Internet. You can
access the boards 24 hours a day as long as the hosting site is operational. Auction users who stay current with the latest in OAI news often
post articles or news items on the auction message boards so that many
users can read and comment on them.

How They Work

A message-board system lives on a server that users access via the Internet.
Most of the boards associated with auction user forums are secured,
requiring users to register with a user ID (also called a login) and password. Many secured bulletin boards allow you to log in as a "guest,"
but you must register with a user name in order to post new messages or
respond to other messages.

When you register to use an online bulletin board, the information
you provide is usually available to other participants of the board unless the registration page specifically states that it's kept private. Look
for the locked lock indicating an SSL site if registration requires entering personal information.

Posting a Message

Figure 12.5 shows the post-entry screen at AuctionWatch. When I clicked
on "Post New Topic" from the message board, I was asked to log in
with my user ID and password. Then I saw the post entry screen shown
in the figure. You'll see a similar process used at most of the UBB-based
bulletin boards.

Enter the subject (rather like an auction title) of your post in the
field provided, and then type your message in the field below. When
you're satisfied with your post, click on "Post New Topic" or the equivalent. This sends your post to the bulletin board. The UBB-based boards,
and many others, allow you to edit your post.

Fitting In with the Crowd

When you join any online community, one of the first things you'll notice is that many of the people who post will seem like they know each
other. That's usually because they do. Many online friends meet at the
message boards, and many message board communities organize in-
person get-togethers. The Online Trader's Web Alliance eBay Commu-

Figure 12.5. Post entry screen for users logged in at AuctionWatch.

nity had its first convention, or "OTWAcon," in July 2000. Forum members from all parts of the United States met in the Chicago area. Many of them either drove or flew in to visit Honesty's headquarters, then in Northern Illinois, and spend a few days with folks they had previously only known through online posts and e-mail messages.

Initially, most of your communication with your new online coworkers will be at the message boards and in e-mail, so it's important to know a few points of protocol when you first enter an online discussion group.

Read First

Always spend some time reading a message board before you join the discussion. Get to know the attitude of users in the group. Some are more temperamental and defensive than others and don't like contradictory follow-ups to their posts. Others are friendly and helpful. Everyone has "on" and "off" days.

Be mindful of turf issues, and know who is considered an expert in what topic. The fastest way to unpopularity in an online bulletin-board community is to try to claim "expert" status over one of the long-term regulars. If that classification is rightfully yours, let it become evident over time. At first, join the discussion, ask questions, and share your experiences. There's a lot to be learned from seasoned Internet auction sellers.

Message Board Etiquette

Sometimes people who are unfamiliar with communicating on the Internet commit blunders that really annoy other users and get the person started off on the wrong foot. Such mistakes are easily avoidable if the person learns the basic bulletin-board etiquette before posting:

- **Show respect for others.** State your opinion rather than admonishing someone else's.

- **Don't post in all uppercase.** It's difficult to read and looks like shouting. Posting messages in all uppercase letters is extremely poor form on the Internet. If you need to use all caps for emphasis, do so sparingly.

- **Don't post e-mail messages.** Unless you have the originator's permission, it's always bad form to post the content of an e-mail message you received privately unless it was sent to many users as a general announcement of sorts. Some users argue that threatening or harassing e-mail messages should be posted to warn others in the forum, but in all honesty, most people would rather not see them.

- **Don't post large images.** Either reduce the picture so it doesn't take that long to load, or refer your readers to the URL of the image so they can view it later.

Your New Coworkers—The Internet Auction Water Cooler

At these portals and message boards, you'll meet other folks who sell products at the Internet auction sites. Just like coworkers in an office environment might consult with each other about business strategies, auction sellers do that by posting in the online forums. Here we'll discuss several cases in which communicating with other Internet auction sellers can be a helpful and supportive experience.

Advice and Critiques on your Auctions

Maybe your auction description looks to you like something's not quite right. If you post a link to the URL where you have your description HTML hosted as you get it ready for listing, some of your Internet auction coworkers might be willing to view it and post or e-mail you their critique. Sometimes all it takes is another person's ideas to make a difference in whether the auction will attract customers or not. You can get some helpful hints on your descriptive text, the formatting style you chose, or your auction photo. This type of help is extremely valuable, and there is no better resource for it than experienced Internet auction sellers.

Shared Joys

In December 2000, I received my 500th unique-user feedback on my eBay account and heard about it from an online auction friend in e-mail. Before Rob sent me the e-mail, though, he had posted a congratulations for me at the OTWA eBay community forum. By the time I checked the thread, some 20 people had posted congratulations for me, as they did for a user in the example shown in Figure 12.6. It was an emotional boost to have so many others share in this milestone.

Shoulders to Cry On

Are you certain you're about to get your first negative feedback comment from an unhappy user? Or, maybe you're dealing with a non-

Figure 12.6. Congratulatory OTWA post for a user who achieved a 500 star on eBay.

paying bidder for the first time and need to ask some opinions about an e-mail message you plan to send the person. Here again, it helps to present these types of situations to experienced users who can offer you some advice. In time, you'll offer coaching based on your own acquired knowledge as well.

Auction Service Providers

Most Internet auction portals are Auction Service Providers. Regardless of what they choose to be labeled, most of them provide Internet auction services as part of their anchor offerings. This section covers four Web sites dedicated to providing Internet auction users with a central operating center for their Internet auction selling venture. Some of them claim to not be portals in the exact sense, but would rather be known as information and action tool resources. They each have a unique set of online auction services.

AuctionWatch

AuctionWatch *(www.auctionwatch.com)*, according to their press materials, is a leading provider of software solutions that enable businesses of all sizes to efficiently sell large or small volumes of merchandise online through dynamic and fixed-price marketplaces. They have over 2.8 million unique visitors every month and thousands of registered users.

The site originated in July 1998 as a message board on cofounder Mark Dodd's home page. Dodd wanted so share his interest with other Internet auction users and thought they'd benefit from a central Web site where they could learn from each other. Dodd's message board soon attracted thousands of members. Through message board posts, they shared their Internet auction experiences and sought answers to questions. Then Dodd teamed up with Rodrigo Sales, a fellow Internet auction user. They incorporated AuctionWatch.com in January 1999, with the mission to provide information and services to help people buy and sell through Internet auctions (see Figure 12.7).

Dodd and Sales enhanced the Message Center and developed Internet auction services for sellers. These include image hosting, auction-launching capabilities, and auction-page counters. Before long, the company

Figure 12.7. AuctionWatch's home page (*www.auctionwatch.com*).

became a resource for casual Internet auction users and businesses that depend on buying and selling high volumes of merchandise through Internet auctions. Their services offer sellers the necessary tools to effectively sell merchandise and grow their customer base.

Auction Manager
At the Auction Manager, you can track your active auctions, pending auctions (those you have scheduled to list), and closed auctions. You can import your active listings from Amazon, eBay, or Yahoo by clicking on Track Auctions (see Figure 12.8). On one screen, you'll see all Internet auctions that you're participating in as a seller.

Universal Search
With one search, find current auctions at many different auction sites. Keep an eye on your market by searching auctions for the products you're selling, and then do your market and pricing research. You can

Figure 12.8. Auction Manager Control Panel at AuctionWatch, showing auction tracking.

select specific auctions to track from the Auction Manager Control Panel. Check what other sellers list the products for at the other Internet auction sites and see how well the products are selling.

Storefronts
Figure 12.9 shows a sample Storefront at AuctionWatch. Here you can create a showroom with your auction listings. You can establish an online business identity where buyers can bid on your eBay, Amazon, and Yahoo listings on one screen. It's like a business Web site that links to your auctions, and a good way to highlight your products.

Message Boards
You'll find bulletin boards for users of various Internet auction sites, and discussion groups for users of AuctionWatch services (see Figure 12.10). You can find out what's going on with the latest site outage, ask for critiques on your auctions, or ask other sellers for their opinions on suspected fraud or bargains.

Figure 12.9. Sample Storefront at AuctionWatch.

MESSAGE CENTER

Forum	Posts	Last Post
Auction Site Specific		
Amazon.com Auctions NEW! Discussions and issues regarding Amazon.com Auctions.	8398	March 21, 2001 7:35 PM
The eBay Outlook NEW! Discussions and issues regarding eBay.	127536	March 22, 2001 9:26 AM
Yahoo Auctions NEW! Discussions and issues regarding Yahoo Auctions.	18634	March 22, 2001 9:14 AM
Other Online Auctions ... NEW! Other auction site forums.	6241	March 22, 2001 9:24 AM
AuctionWatch.com		
AuctionWatch.com Services NEW! For general discussion or help with AuctionWatch.com's many services including Auction Manager, Auction Manager Pro, Image Hosting, Counters, and Universal Search.	9099	March 22, 2001 9:26 AM
AuctionWatch.com Partner Services NEW! For discussion or help with one of AuctionWatch.com's payment or shipping service providers.	5322	March 21, 2001 8:42 PM
The AW Round Table NEW! A place to kick back, relax, and have fun! Share a story, tell a joke, write a poem, make a friend...	51056	March 22, 2001 9:25 AM
AW News & Information NEW! General discussion and issues regarding AuctionWatch.com's daily editorial content.	2021	March 22, 2001 9:23 AM
Buyer Beware NEW! Experience trouble with an individual or company? Post your experience here.	1308	March 22, 2001 8:16 AM
Fraud and Illegal Goods NEW! For the discussion of fraud and illegal items found on online auctions.	353	March 21, 2001 3:19 PM
Wanted NEW! Looking for that special item? Let users know about it here.	1740	March 22, 2001 1:46 AM
Moderator's Corner NEW! A meeting place for moderator and user discussions.	245	March 21, 2001 2:11 PM
Bargain Hunt NEW! Share the buzz on the latest bargains.	1397	March 21, 2001 11:53 PM

Figure 12.10. AuctionWatch Message Center (*www.auctionwatch.com/mesg*).

News and Information

You can browse through the AuctionWatch News and Information pages shown in Figure 12.11 and read about Internet auction seller success stories. You can catch up on Internet auction news with specialized articles by the AuctionWatch staff and a variety of contributing writers.

The articles cover daily OAI news, Internet auction site profiles and reviews, tips and tactics for Internet auction users, a Collector's Beat area, and an editorial viewpoint column. Check out the AuctionWatch site for information about the other features offered.

Online Trader's Web Alliance

Jim and Crystal Turner-Wells started the Online Trader's Web Alliance *(www.otwa.com)* so that a few of their fellow Internet auction sellers could discuss the various aspects of the OAI (see Figure 12.12).

Figure 12.11.   News and Information page at AuctionWatch *(www.auctionwatch.com/awdaily)*.

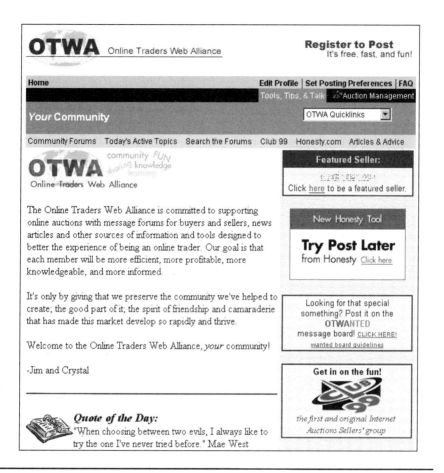

Figure 12.12. The Online Trader's Web Alliance home page (*www.otwa.com*).

"The intent was to provide a productive place," says Crystal. "We could discuss sales events and such for sellers to utilize in order to increase their business." The original OTWA was hosted at Honesty.com, although they were separate companies at the time.

"I thought we'd get a few posters; maybe a few regulars and a few people interested in forming online selling clubs," Crystal said. "Instead, almost from the beginning, we were just jamming with users, and more registered every day. It wasn't long before our expenses far outweighed our ad revenue, and I was selling stuff on eBay just to pay for server space." Soon after that, Honesty purchased OTWA and the two continued to support each other. OTWA presently has over 5,000 registered users, many of whom post regularly at the message forums. Others only read and rarely if ever post messages (which is called **lurking**).

Community Forums

Figure 12.13 shows part of the Community Forums listing. The list of forums is too huge to fit on a static page without a scrolling feature. OTWA offers discussion forums for users of each of the major consumer auction sites and most of the online payment services. You'll also find forums where sellers of glass, kitchenware, jewelry and gems, and many other items can posts photos and have other folks help with item identification.

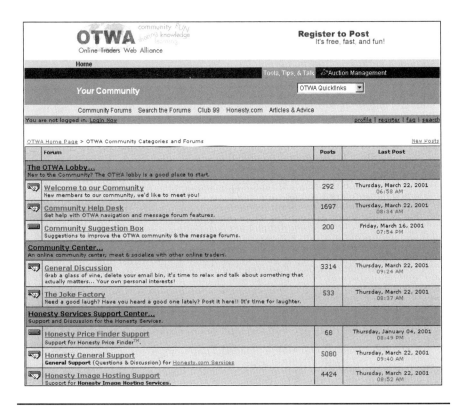

Figure 12.13. Community forums at OTWA (*community.otwa.com/3/ OpenTopic/a/cfrm*).

Club99

This association is an independent group of sellers that originated on eBay. The original purpose of Club99, shown in Figure 12.14, was to encourage bidding on Saturdays, which seemed to be the slowest day for sales. They currently run regular and special-event auctions to encourage bidding and sales. Club99 Regular Event auctions have an opening bid of 99 cents and no reserve. This activity offers several benefits for both auction sellers and bidders:

- Greater level of exposure for their auctions

- Opportunity for some great bargains

- Excitement of real auctions on the Internet

Check out the OTWA site to read about the other features they offer for Internet auction users.

Figure 12.14.   OTWA's Club99 home page (*club99.otwa.com/index.shtml*).

Online Auction User's Association

The OAUA *(www.auctionusers.org)* offers the latest in OAI news and information. According to Jen Hassler, President and Chairman of OAUA, "Our mission is to provide a collective voice for Internet auction sellers and buyers. Our vision is to enfranchise, educate, and represent the interests of Internet auction sellers, and to equip them with tools and training."

The OAUA supports online auction users in several ways:

- Identifies the shared issues of the online auction community and working together to improve the Internet auction emerging market

- Codifies and maintains the highest ethical standards for members of the association

- Provides training, educational, and support services to enhance members' abilities to buy and sell effectively

- Disseminates industry news, trends, and data of interest to community members

- Secures benefits and group deals that would not be available to individual users, as well as opportunities, such as trade shows and seminars, to bring community members together

- Lobbies to promote laws and regulations that benefit the community

- Supports members through counseling and advocacy

All sellers who are registered members of OAUA must uphold a posted seller's code of ethics.

Membership Requirements
The qualifications for membership in the OAUA are as follows:

- Members must be at least 18 years of age.

- Members must be a registered user of at least one auction site.

- Members must agree to adhere to the Association's Code of Ethics for Internet auction users.

- Members must provide the OAUA with identification.

The OAUA requires identification for several reasons, but mainly as an intent to flush out any unscrupulous traders and fraudulent sellers. Sellers who commit fraud typically register under false names and addresses to make it difficult for their victims to find them, so OAUA requires some way for applicants to prove that they are who they claim to be. You'll find more about joining OAUA and providing identification under the FAQ (frequently asked questions) link.

Scheduled Chats with Auction Site VIPs

You'll find Internet auction buyers and sellers in the OAUA chat room just about every day. Live chat can be one of the most valuable information resources for the online auction seller. OAUA chat (see Figure 12.15) provides a place to share Internet auction experiences, learn from others, and get the advice you need when a sale goes bad or you've decided

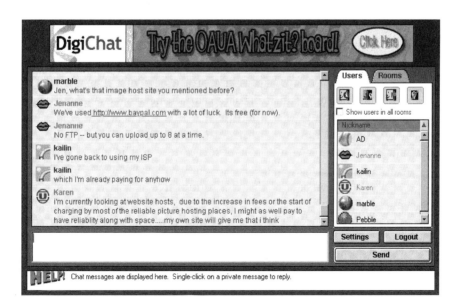

Figure 12.15. The OAUA chat room, with auction chat in progress (*www.auctionusers.org/chat*).

to branch out your business. They periodically invite auction site CEOs or other Internet auction VIPs to chat with auction users.

"Our chats can be a relaxing time, or they can be a learning experience," says Karen Siddiqi, OAUA Chat Coordinator.

"For instance, if you're having problems with a buyer and you've never dealt with that particular issue before, you can get an immediate reaction or response to your questions or concerns from other sellers. They may have more experience and can make informed suggestions about how you should handle the situation." Karen's goal for sellers is to embrace a certain kind of philosophy about what they do. "They are the people who remember what the word 'trust' means," she says. Karen has been hosting organized online chats for several years.

USAWeb

This auction portal is of a slightly different genre from those previously mentioned, as it targets both online and live auction enthusiasts. Since many folks who sell at online auctions also participate in live auctions, this auction portal is worth a look. Founded in February 1995, USAWeb, shown in Figure 12.16, offers several online events that help auctioneers promote their business. The biggest draw is the Internet Auction List *(www.internetauctionlist.com)*. The IAL is a comprehensive directory of auction-related information and events. This site was instrumental in helping traditional live auctioneers grow comfortable with selling through Internet auctions.

You'll find auction information and services for live auctioneers, online auctioneers, and consumers interested in any kind of auction information.

USAWeb consists of these communities:

* The Internet Auction List (*www.internetauctionlist.com*)

* Auction Web (*www.auctionweb.com*)

* FasTalker Directory (*www.fastalker.com*)

* AuctionTalk (*www.auctiontalk.com*)

* Auction Marketing Institute (*www.auctionmarketing.org*)

Figure 12.16. USAWeb portal to the auction community (*www.usaweb.com*).

To find out more about these USAWeb communities, visit the USAWeb home page and click on the "About" link.

Internet Auction Information Sites and e-Newsletters

Some of the Internet auction online resources provide information and news articles. You can usually register for an auction-related newsletter that you'll receive in e-mail. The sites in this section offer those types of informational services for Internet auction sellers.

AuctionBytes

Sign up to receive AuctionBytes-Update at *www.auctionbytes.com*. It's a free twice-monthly e-mail newsletter and a practical resource guide for Internet auction users. The newsletter contains articles on how to become more efficient and effective as an Internet auction seller, and it evaluates auction products and services.

Ina and David Steiner started AuctionBytes in 1999 after David sold some professional video equipment on eBay (see Figure 12.17). One violin and comic book collection later, they were Internet auction addicts.

Since starting the Web site, David and Ina have seen many products and services spring up to serve the Internet auction user, such as appraisal services, online payment services, auction management software, and many new online auction sites. AuctionBytes keeps track of them with its AuctionBytes-Update newsletter.

The Auction Guild Notes (TAGnotes)

Rosalinda Baldwin and three others founded The Auction Guild (*www.theauctionguild.com*) in March 1999. Rosalinda's partners provide technical and business advice and assistance. "We are completely self funded with no outside investors," she explained.

Figure 12.17. AuctionBytes' home page (*www.auctionbytes.com*).

TAG's mission is to help provide a safe trading environment for buyers and sellers, and to ensure that person-to-person online auction trading survives in cyberspace. They also claim to act as a watchdog for the Internet auction industry.

More Internet Auction Newsletters

The following table shows more Web sites that offer newsletters of interest to Internet auction sellers.

Site Name	Web Address
The Online Seller—Auctiva	*www.auctiva.com/tos/default.asp*
AuctionBuddie	*www.auctionbuddie.com*
Internet Auction List	*www.internetauctionlist.com*
AntiqueCAST	*www.antiquecast.com*
e-newsletters	*e-newsletters.internet.com*

Discussion Forums

In addition to AuctionWatch, OTWA, and OAUA, several other Web sites exist that offer message boards for Internet auction users. This section presents a few of them.

AuctionInsights

This site has a great menu of resources available to Internet auction sellers. AuctionInsights *(www.auctioninsights.com)* offers auction services, a very easy to use free auction ad creator, an image tutorial, links to auction sites, bidder and seller tips, and auction news (see Figure 12.18). You'll also find the AuctionInsights Community by clicking on the "Community" link.

Crock Pot at SoupGirl

Frequent Internet auction user Gail Hotchkiss created The Crock Pot discussion forum *(www.soupgirl.com/ikonboard/ikonboard.cgi)* for

Figure 12.18.   AuctionInsights' home page (*www.auctioninsights.com*).

members of OTWA and OAUA. You'll find message boards for and about Internet auction interests. Some interesting comments from users add a humorous, though starkly perceptive, perspective to the OAI.

Other Discussion Forums

The following table lists a few other Internet auction discussion forums available on the Web. Some are members-only, some are privately run, and others are adjuncts to Auction Service Providers.

Site Name	Web Address
Blackthorne Software Discussion Forum	*www.blackthornesw.com/discus*
eBay's Announcement Board	*www2.ebay.com/aw/announce.shtml*
Auction Opinion	*pub16.ezboard.comfauctionopinion auctionopinion*
BayPal Forums	*www.baypal.com/forums*

Site Name	Web Address
eBay For Beginners at Yahoo	*groups.yahoo.com/groupebay_beginners*
Yahoo's Announcement Board	*auctions.yahoo.com/phtml/auc/us/promo/ announcements.html*

Real-Time Communication Media

Any America Online (AOL) user knows about Instant Messages, or IMs. This type of communication medium appears as a small window on your screen and lets you "converse" with another user in real time. The messages appear as soon as they're sent. The window typically has two areas. You'll type in one part and the messages from the person you're conversing with show up in another part of the screen (see Figure 12.19). Here we'll discuss programs that allow you to have real-time conversations with your customers, provided they also have the program downloaded and installed on their computers.

AOL Instant Messenger

AOL Instant Messenger, or AIM, is one of the most well known real-time communicating tools available. AIM is available to AOL users and also those who don't use AOL as their Internet Service Provider. It has many different features that allow you to customize your real-time conversations:

- Designate a font style and color for the text you send

- Set an "away" message for when you're not at your computer

- Send photos, pictures, and sounds

- Create a "Buddy List" so you can see when your customers are online

- Set a profile with information about yourself

Figure 12.19 shows an example of the type of IM conversation that can take place between an auction seller and an interested potential bidder. User HKAuthor typed his comments into the bottom window

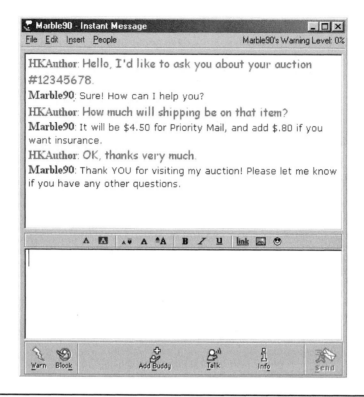

Figure 12.19. AOL Instant Message (AIM) conversation in progress.

and then clicked on "Send." The responses from Marble90 appeared on the top window along with HKAuthor's own part of the dialog.

HumanClick

The HumanClick service *(www.humanclick.com)* allows visitors to your business Web site to get immediate, real-time assistance from you (see Figure 12.20). It also enables Web site owners to track and communicate with visitors to their site. HumanClick, an Application Service Provider (ASP), uses eleven different languages in more than 60 countries all over the world.

Visit the HumanClick Web page and use the "Download it" link to download the program free.

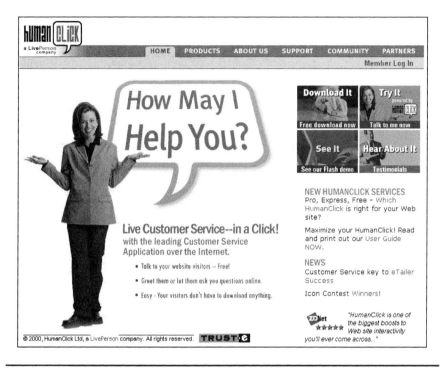

Figure 12.20. HumanClick's home page *(www.humanclick.com)*.

Yahoo Messenger

You can use the Yahoo Messenger *(messenger.yahoo.com)* with Yahoo Auctions bidders who have the feature enabled. Figure 12.21 shows what the message screen looks like. Click on the "Quick Download" link on the Yahoo Messenger home page to download the messenger client.

ICQ

ICQ *(www.icq.com)* is a user-friendly Internet tool that informs you who's on-line at any time and enables you to contact them whenever you want to. ICQ alerts you in real time when they log on. You can chat, send messages, transfer files, and share URLs.

ICQ lets you choose the mode of communication you wish to use. Figure 12.22 shows the popular ICQ home page.

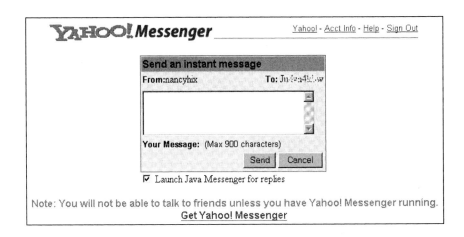

Figure 12.21. Yahoo Messenger message screen (*messenger.yahoo.com*).

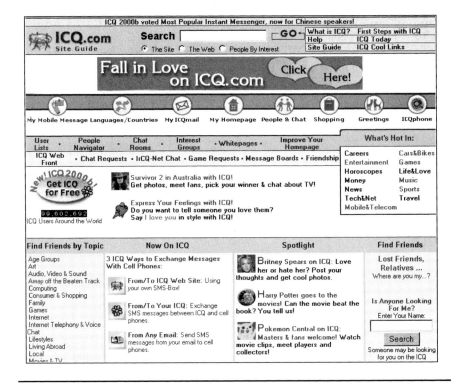

Figure 12.22. The ICQ home page (*www.icq.com*).

It's easy to use. When you install ICQ, the program asks you to register at a server, which is connected to a broad network of servers spanning the Internet. Once you've registered, you'll receive a unique ICQ number, also known as a UIN (Universal Internet Number). ICQ also lets you enter personal information along with your ICQ number so other users can recognize you when you log on. Once you've registered, you can compile a list of associates. Then when you log onto the Internet, ICQ automatically detects the Internet connection. It announces your presence to the Internet community and alerts you when associates sign on or off.

This chapter has described some of the more valuable resources available to Internet auction sellers. All of them will help you grow comfortable with your new selling medium, as you carry out your Seven-Step Internet Auction Strategy. It won't take long for you to be a successful Internet auction seller—in fact, I'm guessing that you already are.

Appendix A: Site Directory

Auction Sites

The tables in this section include auction site directories and various types of auction selling venues.

Auction Site Directories

These sites offer lists of Internet auction sites.

Site Name	Web Address
AuctionBytes Yellow Pages	*www.auctionbytes.com*
AuctionRiches	*www.auctionriches.com*
Gomez	*www.gomez.com*
OAUA Auction Site Directory	*www.auctionusers.org/links.shtml*
The Auction List	*www.theauctionlist.com*

Consumer-to-Consumer

The Internet auction sites listed here allow any registered user to sell to any other registered user. While that's the credo of most Internet auction sites, the C2C sites allow private consumers to register and sell to other private consumers. The major C2C sites also allow business sellers to register and sell to other users.

Site Name	Web Address
Amazon Auctions	*auctions.amazon.com*
AuctionoffStuff	*www.auctionoffstuff.com*
Bargain and Haggle	*www.bargainandhaggle.com*
BidVille	*www.bidville.com*
CityAuction	*www.cityauction.com*
DellAuction	*www.dellauction.com*

Site Name	Web Address
DutchBid	*www.dutchbid.com*
EasyNet	*www.easynet.com*
eBay	*www.ebay.com*
EPier	*www.epier.com*
GearBay	*www.gearbay.com*
JustBeads	*www.justbeads.com*
Lowest Bids	*www.lowestbids.com*
SellYourItem	*www.sellyouritem.com*
ToyFan	*www.toyfan.com*
TreasureHuntersInc	*www.treasurehuntersinc.com*
321Gone	*www.321gone.com*

More About Bargain and Haggle:

If you can devote time to letting your customers bargain and haggle with you, give this site a look. Bargain and Haggle bridges the gap between existing fixed price and auction models. While negotiating, your buyer has the choice to offer you your asking price, or an offer that he or she feels is fair. You can accept, stand firm, or meet somewhere in between. If the deal dissatisfies either party, either the buyer or the seller can walk away, and the user making the next bid can start negotiating. There are no obligations to close the deal until either the buyer or the seller accepts the current offer.

Business-to-Consumer

While many of the consumer-to-consumer sites also cater to business sellers, these Internet auction sites specialize in businesses selling goods to consumers.

Site Name	Web Address
AuctionMAX	*www.auctionmax.com*
CityBid	*www.citybid.net*
CyberAuctions	*www.cyberauctions.com*
DealDeal	*www.dealdeal.com*
Egghead/Onsale	*www.egghead.com*
FirstAuction	*www.firstauction.com*
Overstock	*www.overstock.com*

Site Name	Web Address
uBid	*www.ubid.com*
USBid	*www.usbid.com*
Ruby Lane	*www.rubylane.com*

Business-to-Business

These Internet auction sites allow businesses to sell products and goods to other businesses.

Site Name	Web Address
B2Bstreet	*www.b2bstreet.com*
BizAuc	*www.bizauc.com*
ComAuction	*www.comauction.com*
DoveBid, Inc.	*www.dovebid.com*
eDeal Marketplace	*www.edeal.com*
LiquidPrice	*www.liquidprice.com*
Overstock B2B	*www.overstock.com*
PurchasePro	*www.purchasepro.com*
SnapTrader	*www.snaptrader.com*
TradeOut	*www.tradeout.com*
uBid for Business	*www.ubid.com*
VenueBid	*www.vbiauction.com*
XSLots.com	*www.xslots.com*

More About SnapTrader:

SnapTrader is designed to target business-to-business surplus trading. Users may sell to any business (small to large), or any individual who is at least 18 years of age that has items that will fit in any of the supplied category headings. Registration is free.

Business-to-Exchange

Here, you can search for auctions across many different Internet auction sites in order to conduct market studies.

Site Name	Web Address
AuctionWatch	*www.auctionwatch.com*
GoTo Auctions	*www.goto.com*

Reverse Auctions

With reverse auctions, businesses can allow buyers, contractors, and service providers to bid prices down. They are a very valuable time-saver for corporations working under tight deadlines and can't fit the standard request for quote process into their production schedule.

Site Name	Web Address
eBreviate	*www.ebrevia.com*
Respond	*www.respond.com*
imandi	*www.imandi.com*
FreeMarkets	*www.freemarkets.com*
Nextag	*www.nextag.com*

Free—No Listing Fees or Commission

The sites listed in this section were free to use at this writing, but may have decided to start charging fees over time. It's best to check the site for their policies.

Site Name	Web Address
AuctionAddict	*www.auctionaddict.com*
OutBidMe	*www.outbidme.com*

Auction Services

An Internet auction volume seller can take advantage of helpful auction services, including auction managers, news and information updates, bulk uploaders, feedback tools, and Web site building services.

Auction Managers

These sites allow you to view all of your auctions on one page—even if you have auctions listed on more than one site.

Site Name	Web Address
Ándale	*www.andale.com*
Auction Maker	*www.alysta.com/software/auctionmaker.htm*
AuctionInsights	*www.auctioninsights.com*
AuctionShare	*www.auctionshare.com*
BayPal	*www.baypal.com*
Invenna AuctionAmigo Pro	*www.invenna.com*

More About Ándale
Ándale is the premier auction management service, with an array of products and services geared toward all ranges of online sellers.

News and Information

Care to read the latest information concerning the OAI? Check out some of these sites.

Site Name	Web Address
AuctionBytes	*www.auctionbytes.com*
AuctionTribune	*www.auctiontribune.com*
AuctionUser	*www.auctionuser.com*
AuctionWatch	*www.auctionwatch.com*

Uploaders

If you're a regular lister of multiple auctions, these sites provide tools that allow you to schedule and upload numerous auctions with a single effort.

Site Name	Web Address
Ándale	*www.andale.com*

Site Name	Web Address
AuctionWatch	*www.auctionwatch.com*
AuctionWorks	*www.auctionworks.com*
ManageAuctions	*www.manageauctions.com*

Feedback Records

If you're interested in a user feedback reference tool, check out Vrane (see URL below). You can look at only the negative and neutral comments that an eBay user has received, and the ones that he or she has left for other users. You can also enter feedback for many users at once. This site has many different online auction user tools.

Site Name	Web Address
Vrane	*www.vrane.com*

Free Services

Check out these sites for a variety of free auction services. Some of them will help you reach more buyers by giving you access to multiple auction sites and by automating routine tasks.

Site Name	Web Address
Vrane	*www.vrane.com*
AuctionFlow	*www.auctionflow.com*
CollectorOnLine	*www.collectoronline.com/manage*

Free Site for Storefront and Customer List

The sites in the table below allow you to create your own business Web site and product storefront. Most of them offer other Web site creation tools as well.

Site Name	Web Address
BigStep	*www.bigstep.com*
Spree	*www.spree.com*
Merchants Square	*www.merchant-square.com*

Image Hosts

Unless you have your own Web server or you use an Internet auction site that will host your auction images for you, you'll need an image host to handle the job. You can still find free image hosting, but speculation states that it won't last long.

Free

This section shows Web sites that offer free Web space, including image hosting. Check to see if you can use them for auction image hosting, remember that free services often don't stay free forever, despite the service's original intention. By the time this book is on the shelves, these sites may have switched to charging. Check them out.

Site Name	Web Address
AuctionTalk	*www.auctiontalk.com/imagehosting.asp*
BayPal	*www.baypal.com*
FreePicHosting	*www.freepichosting.com*
Portland Communications	*www.portland.co.uk*
ProHosting	*www.prohosting.com*
Tupics	*www.tupics.com*

More About Free Image Hosting

This About.com site has a directory of many free image-hosting sites *(freebies.about.com/shopping/freebies/cs/filestorage)*.

Membership

These image-hosting sites charge a membership fee. You'll usually pay around $12 per year for 5MB to 10MB of image hosting space. Expect the fees to vary from site to site.

Site Name	Web Address
AuctionBuddie	*www.auctionbuddie.com*
AuctionWatch	*www.auctionwatch.com*

Site Name	Web Address
Honesty	*www.honesty.com*
PhotoPoint	*www.photopoint.com*
Yada (Baytown)	*www.baytown.com*

Page Building and HTML

The sites in the table below offer tools or information that will help you create Web pages with the HTML markup code.

Site Name	Web Address
FLFSoft, Inc.	*www.flfsoft.com*
HTML Goodies	*www.htmlgoodies.com*
HTML Made Really Easy	*www.jmarshall.com/easy/html*
Nancy Hix's HTML Guide	*www.nancyandjeff.com/guide.html*
BayPal Tools	*www.baypal.com/tools*
Zelda's Practice Board	*www.zeldas.com*

Trust Building—Settling Disputes

If you find yourself in a dispute with a buyer and you've exhausted all means of resolution that the Internet auction site provides, you might want to consult one of these online agencies to see if there's anything they can do to assist you.

Site Name	Web Address
Square Trade	*www.squaretrade.com*
Federal Trade Commissions' Guide for Internet Auction Buyers and Sellers	*www.ftc.gov/bcp/conline/pubs/online/auctions.htm*

Ads, Banner Ads, and Link Exchanges

The sites listed in this section will help you carry out some of the Internet auction and business Web site promotion ideas that you read about in

Chapter 7. Some of these will help you integrate your advertising strategy to offline as well as online means.

Banner Ads

The sites listed here will create banner ads for you, which you can use in your banner exchanges or on your own business Web site. Some Internet auction sellers also use banner ads in their auction descriptions.

Site Name	Web Address
Animated Communication	*www.animation.com*
Animation Online	*www.animationonline.com*
The Banner Generator	*www.coder.com/creations/banner*
Creative Connectivity	*www.crecon.com*
The Media Builder	*www.mediabuilder.com/abm.html*

Online Advertising Agencies

These sites specialize in advertising on the Internet.

Site Name	Web Address
Lunar Group Interactive	*www.lunargroup.com*
MMG The Online Agency	*www.mmgco.com*
Thielen Online	*www.thielenonline.com*

Ad Networks

These advertising networks offer various means of site promotion in various media, including the Internet.

Site Name	Web Address
24/7 Media	*www.247media.com*
B2B Works	*www.b2bworks.com*
DoubleClick	*www.doubleclick.com*
Flycast Communications	*www.flycast.com*
ValueClick	*www.valueclick.com*

Banner Exchanges

These sites allow you to register and provide a banner ad. In return, you'll agree to host a rotating banner ad on your business Web site.

Site Name	Web Address
The Banner Exchange	*www.bannerexchange.com*
GSAnet	*einets.com/stats/gsa*
LinkExchange	*www.linkexchange.com*
LinkMedia	*www.linkmedia.com/network*
Smart Clicks	*www.smartclicks.com*

Appendix B: HTML for Auction Descriptions and Messages

This short guide is an HTML cheat-sheet—definitely not a comprehensive reference guide for designing sophisticated Web pages. The HTML code included here will assist you in creating great-looking auction descriptions that don't slow the loading time of the Web page when your customer accesses it. You can also use the HTML code here on bulletin boards and message forums (those that have HTML enabled) for creating hyperlinks, adding images, and producing a few other effects.

HTML is a vast and comprehensive coding language. It provides many, many more capabilities than what I describe here. The information in this appendix is enough to help you format eye-catching auction descriptions. If you decide to design Web pages, you may want to invest in an HTML reference book or two. My personal favorite is *HTML: The Definitive Guide*, by Chuck Musciano and Bill Kennedy (O'Reilly & Associates, Inc.).

What Is HTML?

HTML stands for **HyperText Markup Language**, which is the document layout language we use to make pages for the Web. When you combine the HTML tags with your own text, you can control the result of the tags.

Conventions Used

In the HTML-coding examples included in this appendix, the characters that make up the HTML tags, attributes, and values show up in regular typeface. The variable text—which I show here for demonstration purposes—appears in **boldface**. This text is not part of the HTML code. When you do your coding, replace my bold text with your own information. Where you see double quotes, slashes, or arrow brackets, those are important elements of the HTML code. Be sure you include them when you write your code.

Don't add any spaces or unnecessary characters where you don't see them in my examples. Use the code just as shown, except insert your own text between the start tag and the end tag.

HTML Tags

Most HTML tags come in sets—a start tag and an end tag. The start tag indicates that a certain directive occurs after the tag, and the end tag stops the directive. The text you include between the start and end tags is the only text affected by that particular set of tags.

Tags appear inside arrow brackets (< and >). The end tag is the same as the start tag, except the first character after the < is a slash (/) to indicate that the tag's directive stops there.

Example: <CENTER> and </CENTER> are the start and end tags that center text on a Web page.

Formatting Text with HTML Tags

Your HTML tags will appear in your text document as regular text characters. If you know where the < and > keys are, then you're in business. This section will reveal the "secrets" behind making your Web page and auction description text look exactly the way you want it to.

Tags That Affect Text Appearance

You can change the size, typeface, strength, and color of text with certain HTML tags called **physical tags**. Refer to this list when you want to change the appearance of text.

Here's how the text-affecting tags work:

HTML Code	Effect	Result
\<B\>Great Sale!\</B\>	Bold	**Great Sale!**
\<I\>Great Sale!\</I\>	Italics	*Great Sale!*
\<U\>Great Sale!\</U\>	Underline	<u>Great Sale!</u>
\<BLINK\>Great Sale!\</BLINK\>	The text will blink, but this only works when viewing the page with Internet Explorer.	Great Sale! (blinking)
\<SMALL\>Great Sale!\</SMALL\>	Text will be one size smaller than the default.	<small>Great Sale!</small>
\<BIG\>Great Sale!\</BIG\>	Text will be one size larger than the default.	## Great Sale!

One of the most common coding mistakes in HTML is forgetting to close a tag. For instance, the rest of the text on the page will be in boldface if you forget to close your \<B\> tag with \</B\>.

HTML tags are not case sensitive. You can use \<B\>, \<b\>, and any combination for start and end tags. Pick one case and stick with it because it makes it easier to differentiate the code from your text when you edit the HTML file later. You can combine tags for more than one effect. Notice that the tags open and close in mirrored order:

HTML Code	Effect	Result
\<B\>\<I\>Text that is both bold and italic\</I\>\</B\>	The text will be italic boldface.	***Text that is both bold and italic***

An **attribute** gives more direction to the function of the tag. Attributes must be included within the main tag and some have a **value** attached to them with an equal (=) sign.

> \<TAG ATTRIBUTE=VALUE\>text\</TAG\>

Don't put any spaces between the attribute, the equal sign, or the value. Any attribute that is more than one word or that contains spaces or certain characters must be included in quotes. This includes Web site URLs.

> \<TAG ATTRIBUTE="THREE WORD VALUE"\>text\</TAG\>

Assigning Text Color and Font Style

To change the color and font style of the text, you have to use the <FONT> tag with certain attributes. You can use three attributes within the <FONT> tag:

- COLOR—uses any of a hundred or so color names to change the color of the text. You can also use hexadecimal RGB codes if you are familiar with them, but color names are easier. The table that follows lists many color names you can use with the COLOR attribute.

- FACE—indicates what typeface you want the text to be. If the name of the typeface has more than one word, include spaces between the words but enclose the name in double quotes.

- SIZE—changes the size of the text. Your text size can be from 1 to 7 points.

Color
A six-digit hexadecimal code after a pound sign (#) used with the COLOR attribute changes the color of the text. This coding example switches the text color to red, and then changes it back to the default color with the end tag:

```
<FONT COLOR=#CC0000>This will be red text.</FONT>
```

When you look at the HTML code produced by a Web page building program like Microsoft FrontPage or professional designers, you'll usually see hex codes to clearly define hues. For what you're doing, though, you can use colors by their name instead of trying to figure out hexadecimal codes. It works like this:

```
<FONT COLOR=RED>This will also be red text.</FONT>
```

Here's a list of color names recognized by most browsers. Notice there are no spaces in the names:

Color names that can be used with the COLOR attribute

aliceblue	darkviolet	lightskyblue	paleviolet
antiquewhite	deeppink	lightslateblue	palevioletred
aquamarine	deepskyblue	lightslategray	papayawhip
azure	dimgray	lightsteelblue	peachpuff
beige	dodgerblue	lightyellow	pink
bisque	firebrick	limegreen	plum
black	floralwhite	linen	powderblue
blanchedalmond	forestgreen	magenta	purple
blue	gainsboro	maroon	red
blueviolet	ghostwhite	mediumaquamarine	rosybrown
brown	gold	mediumblue	royalblue
burlywood	goldenrod	mediumorchid	saddlebrown
cadetblue	gray	mediumpurple	salmon
chartreus	green	mediumseagreen	sandybrown
chocolate	greenyellow	mediumslateblue	seagreen
coral	honeydew	mediumspringgreen	sienna
cornflowerblue	hotpink	mediumturquoise	skyblue
cornsilk	indianred	mediumvioletred	slateblue
cyan	ivory	midnightblue	slategray
darkblue	khaki	mintcream	snow
darkcyan	lavender	mistyrose	springgreen
darkgoldenrod	lavenderblush	moccasin	steelblue
darkgray	lawngreen	navajowhite	tan
darkgreen	lemonchiffon	navy	thistle
darkkhaki	lightblue	navyblue	tomato
darkolivegreen	lightcoral	oldlace	turquoise
darkorange	lightcyan	olivedrab	violet
darkred	lightgoldenrodyellow	orange	violetred
darksalmon	lightgray	orangered	wheat
darkseagreen	lightgreen	orchid	white
darkslateblue	lightpink	palegoldenrod	whitesmoke
darkslategray	lightsalmon	palegreen	yellow
darkturquoise	lightseagreen	paleturquoise	yellowgreen

If you prefer using hex codes, you'll find numerous charts on the Web that show the color along with the code. Lynda Weinman includes full-color hexadecimal charts in *Designing Web Graphics—How to Prepare Images and Media for the Web* (New Riders Publishing, 1996). Since you'll get a better color match if you see the color right in your

Web browser, check out Weinman's "Non-Dithering Colors by Hue" page (Figure B.1) at *www.lynda.com/hexh.html*.

You'll find another color chart at Gotomy.com, a popular Web services site. Look up *www.gotomy.com/color.html* for colors by hex code and by name.

Face

Within the <FONT> tag, the FACE attribute means "typeface." Here again, if the typeface includes more than one word, like Arial Narrow, you must include the name in double quotes to indicate that it's one value. In this example, note that I used both upper and lower case text for the attribute—either way is fine.

Figure B.1. Lynda Weinman's home page (*www.lynda.com*). Used with permission.

<FONT FACE="Arial Narrow">

Size

The SIZE attribute needs a value from 1 to 7, relative to the default font size. Seventy-two points equal one inch in print matter, but not in a Web browser. Font size is relative to factors like the browser version, video resolution, and the monitor size.

In the following examples, I used the COLOR, FACE, and SIZE attributes and corresponding values to change the color, typeface, and text size:

HTML Code	Result
<FONT FACE="Comic Sans MS"> This text is in Comic Sans MS</FONT>	This text is in Comic Sans MS
<FONT SIZE=3>This text is a size 3. </FONT>	This text is a size 3.
<FONT SIZE=3 FACE=Arial>You can also combine attributes within a tag.</FONT>	**You can also combine attributes within a tag.**

Text Formatting

The format tags allow you to space and center your text, include vertical spacer lines, and add pictures and tables on the page. The first three tags shown in the following table are single tags that don't need an end tag:

HTML Code	Function
<P>	Start a new paragraph. Adds a blank line between the text blocks.
 	Line break with no space between the lines of text.
<HR>	Makes a horizontal line—usually used in an auction description to set off a photograph.
<CENTER> </CENTER>	Anything between the start and end tags appears centered on the page.

Lists

You can create ordered and unordered lists with HTML. Ordered lists contain numbers or letters by each list item. Unordered items have bullets by each item. You can nest any type of list within another list.

Ordered Lists

Use an ordered list when the order of the items listed is important. Ordered lists start with the <OL> tag and end with </OL>. Indicate list items with <LI>, which typically does not require an end tag.

HTML Code	Result
<OL>	
<LI>List item one.	1. List item one.
<LI>List item two.	2. List item two.
<LI>List item three.	3. List item three.
</OL>	

The items in an ordered list automatically start with the Arabic numeral 1. You can begin the list at another number with the START attribute in the <OL> tag.

HTML Code	Result
<OL START=4>	
<LI>List item four.	4. List item four.
<LI>List item five.	5. List item five.
<LI>List item six.	6. List item six.
</OL>	

Use the TYPE attribute within the <OL> tag to change the numbering style. You can use these values with the TYPE attribute:

- **A**—A, B, C, etc.

- **a**—a, b, c, etc.

- **I**—I, II, III, etc.

- **i**—i, ii, iii, etc.

HTML Code	Result
<OL TYPE=I>	
<LI>List item one.	I. List item one.
<LI>List item two.	II. List item two.
<LI>List item three.	III. List item three.
</OL>	

Combine attributes within the <OL> tag. In other words, make your list item start with Roman numeral IV this way:

HTML Code	Result
<OL TYPE=I START=4>	
<LI>List item four.	IV. List item four.
<LI>List item five.	V. List item five.
<LI>List item six.	VI. List item six.
</OL>	

Unordered Lists

Use an unordered list when the order of the items isn't important. Unordered lists start with the <UL> tag and end with </UL>. Indicate list items with <LI>. Items are set off with a bullet.

HTML Code	Result
<UL>	
<LI>Here is an item.	Here is an item.
<LI>Here is another item.	Here is another item.
<LI>Here is a third item.	Here is a third item.
</UL>	

Nested Lists

You can create lists inside of other lists, which is helpful if one of your main list items contains sub-items. You accomplish this by putting the entire sub-list with all associated HTML tags (start tag, list item tags, and end tag) under one main list item. The table below shows an example of how it's done.

HTML Code	Result
<UL>	
<LI>Here is an item.	Here is an item.
<OL>	
<LI>Sub-item one.	1. Sub-item one.
<LI>Sub-item two.	2. Sub-item two.
</OL>	
<LI>Here is another item.	Here is another item.
<LI>Here is a third item.	Here is a third item.
</UL>	

Tables

Tables are a little more complex than lists but you can do a lot more with them:

- Specify the height and width of table cell.

- Include photos.

- Add borders around text and photos.

- Include hyperlinks.

- Use colored backgrounds.

- Use textured backgrounds.

- Span multiple rows or columns.

Define a table with the <TABLE> and </TABLE> tags. You can include almost anything within a table cell—photos, lists, hyperlinks, formatted text, and even another table. You can even give table cells their own background color.

Table Tags

The <TABLE> tag has a few attributes. The one you'll use the most is BORDER. You'll read more about that a little further along. A set of special table tags defines parts of the table.

- The <TR> tag defines a table row. Define the end of the row with </TR>.

- The <TH> tag defines a table header. This may default to bold face type. You don't need to include headers in your tables if you don't want to. End the table header with </TH>.

- The <TD> tag defines a cell of table data. Mark the end of the cell with </TD>

Basic Table Coding

Here is the HTML coding for a basic borderless table:

HTML Code	Result
| ```
<TABLE>
<TR>
<TH>Heading 1</TH>
<TH>Heading 2</TH>
</TR><TR>
<TD>Text 1</TD>
<TD>Text 2</TD>
</TR><TR>
<TD>Text 3</TD>
<TD>Text 4</TD>
</TR></TABLE>
``` | **Heading 1 Heading 2**<br><br>Text 1      Text 2<br><br>Text 3      Text 4 |

Table Borders

As shown in the example above, the border default for <TABLE> is "none," or zero. Use the BORDER attribute within the <TABLE> tag to put a nice chiseled border around your table and between the rows and cells. Use a value from 1 to 5 with the BORDER attribute to alter the thickness.

➠ **Note:** The value numbers represent pixels. A pixel is a picture element or the smallest unit of measure on the computer screen.

HTML Code	Result
| ```
<TABLE BORDER=3>
<TR>
<TH>Heading 1</TH>
<TH>Heading 2</TH>
</TR><TR>
<TD>Text 1</TD>
<TD>Text 2</TD>
</TR><TR>
<TD>Text</TD>
<TD>Text 4</TD>
</TR></TABLE>
``` | **Heading 1 \| Heading 2**<br>Text 1 \| Text 2<br>Text 3 \| Text 4 |

Cell Spacing and Padding

Use the CELLSPACING attribute in the <TABLE> tag to control the thickness of the table grids between the cells and along the outside border of the table. The value for the CELLSPACING attribute is a number in pixels.

HTML Code	Result
<TABLE BORDER=3 CELLSPACING=5> <TR> <TH>Heading 1</TH> <TH>Heading 2</TH> </TR><TR> <TD>Text 1</TD> <TD>Text 2</TD> </TR><TR> <TD>Text 3</TD> <TD>Text 4</TD> </TR></TABLE>	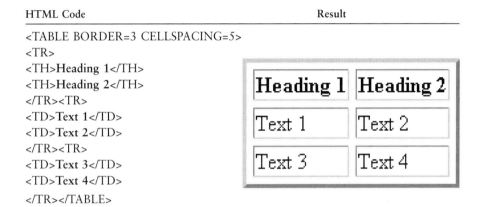

The CELLPADDING attribute in the <TABLE> tag controls the space between the edge of a cell and its contents. The value for the CELLPADDING attribute is a number in pixels.

HTML Code	Result
<TABLE BORDER=3 CELLPADDING=5> <TR> <TH>Heading 1</TH> <TH>Heading 2</TH> </TR><TR> <TD>Text 1</TD> <TD>Text 2</TD> </TR><TR> <TD>Text 3</TD> <TD>Text 4</TD> </TR></TABLE>	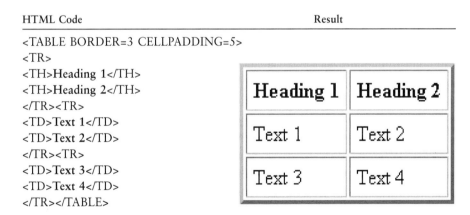

You can use both the CELLPADDING and CELLSPACING attributes within the <TABLE> tag to combine the effect.

Placement Inside of a Cell

The cells used in the examples above are very small because they don't contain a lot of text. As you enter text, images, and links into the table cells, they expand to accommodate the contents. Tables cells will automatically resize to fit the largest amount of data in a row or column. If you have one cell that has a small image or just a few words, you may want that data to appear at the top of the cell. You can control this.

The ALIGN and VALIGN attributes of the <TH> and <TD> tags allow you to control the alignment of the cell contents. The ALIGN attribute controls it horizontally, while VALIGN controls it vertically.

The ALIGN attribute has three values: The VALIGN attribute has three values:

- LEFT
- CENTER
- RIGHT

- TOP
- MIDDLE
- BOTTOM

The following figure shows a table formatted using the ALIGN and VALIGN attributes within <TD> tags.

HTML Code	Result
| ```
<TABLE BORDER=3>
<TR>
<TH>Heading 1</TH>
<tbTH>Heading 2</TH>
<TH>Heading 3</TH>
</TR><TR>
<TD>Paragraph of text for table cell</TD>
<TD ALIGN=RIGHT>Text 2</TD>
<TD VALIGN=TOP>Text 3</TD>
</TR></TABLE>
``` | Heading 1 / Heading 2 / Heading 3; Paragraph of text for table cell / Text 2 / Text 3 |

Spanning Rows and Columns

Let's say you want one cell to span two rows and another to span two columns. Control this with the COLSPAN and ROWSPAN attributes within the <TH> and <TD> tags. The value for each is a number greater than one, not to exceed the number of rows or columns (depending on what you're spanning) in the table.
```

This example illustrates a header spanning two columns in the table:

HTML Code	Result

```
<TABLE BORDER=3>
<TR>
<TH COLSPAN=2>Heading 1</TH>
<TH>Heading 2</TH>
</TR><TR>
<TD>Text 1</TD>
<TD>Text 2</TD>
<TD>Text 3</TD>
</TR></TABLE>
```

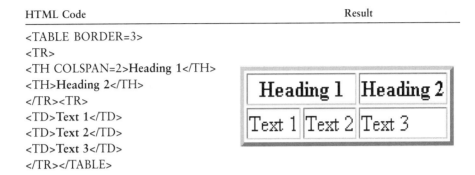

Here's an example of a cell that spans two rows in the table:

HTML Code	Result

```
<TABLE BORDER=3>
<TR>
<TH>Heading 1</TH>
<TH>Heading 2</TH>
<TH>Heading 3</TH>
</TR><TR>
<TD ROWSPAN=2>Text 1</TD>
<TD>Text 2</TD>
<TD>Text 3</TD>
</TR><TR>
<TD>Text 4</TD>
<TD>Text 5</TD>
</TR></TABLE>
```

Notice that the HTML code for the last row only contains information for two columns of data. This is because the first column in that last row is already taken up by "Text 1" as it spans two columns—the second row and the last row. Using ROWSPAN is tricky this way.

Defining the Color of a Cell

If you want to highlight certain cells or just add a little life to your table, try changing the background color of one or more of the cells. Use the BGCOLOR attribute in the <TH> or <TD> tags.

HTML Code	Result

```
<tb><TABLE BORDER=3>
<TR>
<TH>Heading 1</TH>
<TH BGCOLOR=GREEN>Heading 2</TH>
</TR><TR>
<TD>Text 1</TD>
<TD>Text 2</TD>
</TR><TR>
<TD BGCOLOR=GOLD>Text 3</TD>
<TD>Text 4</TD>
</TR></TABLE>
```

Defining the Background Pattern for a Cell

The BACKGROUND attribute of the <TH> or <TD> tag adds a pattern image to a table cell. The value is the URL of an image file that will "tile" to fill the background of the table cell. Here's an example:

HTML Code	Result

```
<TABLE BORDER=3>
<TR>
<TH>Heading 1</TH>
<TH>Heading 2</TH>
</TR><TR>
<TD>Text 1</TD>
<TD BACKGROUND=
"http://www.host.com/back1.jpg">
Text 2 </TD>
</TR><TR>
<TD>Text 3</TD>
<TD>Text 4</TD>
</TR></TABLE>
```

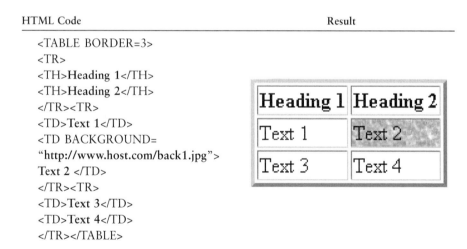

Putting a Picture on your Page

The <IMG> tag lets you include an image on your Web page or within your auction description. Use the SRC attribute with the image URL as the value. Decide where you want your image to appear. At that point, insert the following code just as it appears here:

<IMG SRC="http://www.domain.com/homepage/bird.jpg">

I use *http://www.domain.com/homepage/bird.jpg* as an example. You'll use the image URL you want in your auction description. Note that when you enter the URL, it *must* contain the full path, including the http:// part.

Positioning an Image

Images will automatically align to the left side of the Web page. You can control the position of an image with the ALIGN attribute in the <IMG> tag. Use this only when the image is not inside a table. The values for ALIGN are LEFT, RIGHT, TOP, MIDDLE, and BOTTOM.

The LEFT and RIGHT values flow subsequent text around the image. The others align the image vertically with respect to the surrounding text.

The TOP, MIDDLE, and BOTTOM attribute values only apply to the image relative to any text on the page.

Here's an example of the ALIGN attribute used to position an image to the right of two adjacent paragraphs of text:

HTML Code:
<IMG SRC="http://www.host.com/birdcp.jpg" ALIGN=RIGHT> This little hand-made FIMO bird has a bright yellow belly and rich blue wings. He stands 1½ inch tall.

What a cute little guy! He wears an orange top hat and shiny black shoes. He'll look fabulous perched on your computer monitor, keeping watch over the office. This would make a perfect gift!

Result:

This little hand-made FIMO bird has a bright yellow belly and rich blue wings. He stands 1½" tall.

What a cute little guy! He wears an orange top hat and shiny black shoes. He'll look fabulous perched on your computer monitor, keeping watch over the office. This would make a perfect gift!

The example above is on a small scale, as it would appear in a very small browser or within the defined space of an auction description.

Animation—Image Movers and Shakers

Since animated icons are GIF files, you'll add them to a Web page the same way you do any other image file. You just need to know the URL of the image. Remember that large animated images or those with many frames (the pictures that make up the animation) take a long time to load. Stick with small, simple animation to dress up your auction description, or to populate the image URL field on the auction-entry form. Less is more when it comes to adding extraneous images to your Internet auctions.

Image Banks on the Web

These Web sites have collections with hundreds of images that you can use in your auction descriptions. To maintain control over images you want to use (site owners can and often do move files around), copy the icon to your hard drive and then upload it to your Web directory. You can then code the URL to the image into your auction description.

Remember that linking images back to another host puts a lot of traffic on that server.

Site Name	Web Address
The Icon Factory	*pixelplace.com*
Animation Library	*www.animationlibrary.com*
ScreamDesign	*www.screamdesign.com*
IconBAZAAR	*www.iconbazaar.com*
The Clip Art Connection	*www.clipartconnection.com*
ArtToday	*www.arttoday.com*
Barry's Clip Art Server	*www.barrysclipart.com*
Animation Shack	*www.netmegs.com/~animate*
Buttons, Bullets, and Backgrounds	*www.rewnet.com/bb*

Copying an Icon

The Web gives us a great function for "borrowing" icons from other pages. You can copy and save any icon on any page, unless the image is part of a program. Just place your mouse cursor over the picture, right-click, select "Save Image As" or "Save Picture As" from the menu, and tell your computer where to keep the file.

➤ **Note:** Be sure you don't reuse any copyrighted images on your Web pages. Include credits for any images if the host site specifies that you should.

Finding Your Image's URL

Suppose you're already using the image on a Web page but you don't remember the image's Web address. You need to know the URL of the image to use it in your auction description. Here's how you can find out what it is:

Internet Explorer and AOL users:

- Place your mouse cursor over the image and right-click on it. You'll see a menu.

- Select "Properties" from the menu.

- The Properties box appears. You'll see the Address (URL) of the image.

- Highlight the entire URL (from http).

- Right-click on the highlighted URL, select "Copy," and then paste it into Notepad or another word processing program. Now you have the URL of the image.

Netscape users:

- Place your mouse cursor over the image and right-click. You'll see a menu.

- Select "Copy Image Location" from the menu, then close the menu box.

- Right-click inside Notepad or another word processing program and then select "Paste."

- The URL of your photo writes in the text file.

Now you know the image's unique address on the Web.

Creating Hypertext Links

If the Internet auction site you're using allows external links in your auction description, you can create a link to your business Web page. All you need is the correct URL and some simple HTML code.

Hypertext links start with the <A> (anchor) tag and end with </A>. Use the HREF attribute with the page URL as the value. Whatever you enter between <A> and </A> will appear underlined in the browser. When you pass your mouse cursor over it, the arrow will change into a little hand, indicating that the text is now hypertext. If you click on it, the hyperlinked page loads in your browser.

> **HTML Code:**
> Please visit our <A HREF="http://www.domain.com">Web page</A> for more information about our company.
>
> **Result**
> Please visit our Web page for more information about our company.

The little hand in the result above represents the cursor placed over the words "Web page," which are now hypertext.

Note: Be sure to close the <A> tag because if you don't, the rest of the text (and everything else) on the page will become part of your hyperlink.

Opening External Links in a New Browser

You don't want to draw your bidder's attention away from your Web page. To help keep them there, you can make your hyperlinks open up a new browser. This leaves the host browser with your Web page in it undisturbed. Include the TARGET attribute with _NEW as the value within your <A> tag.

> **HTML Code:**
> <A HREF="http://www.domain.com" TARGET="_NEW">Please visit our Web page!</A>
>
> **Result:**
> When a viewer clicks on the link, a new browser opens for the link, leaving the original browser undisturbed.

Making Your E-mail Address a Hyperlink

If you want your viewers to send you e-mail by clicking on your e-mail address, use the <A> tag with the HREF attribute. The value is MAILTO:**address**, as in this example:

<A HREF="MAILTO:user@email.com">user@email.com<A>

Including your e-mail address between the start and end <A> tags causes it to be a hypertext link. When clicked on, it brings up an e-mail screen addressed to you. This makes it very easy for your customers to contact you.

As you read about in Chapter 8, it's helpful if you use an e-mail link that automatically includes the auction number. You'll achieve that by adding a Subject designation to your <A> tag:

<A HREF="MAILTO:user@email.com?subject=eBay Auction 123456789">user@email.com</A>

When a user clicks on the e-mail address hyperlink created by the HTML code above, the words "eBay Auction 123456789" will automatically appear in the subject line of the e-mail message.

Making an Image a Hyperlink

If you want your reader to be able to click on a picture to access another site, you must code the <IMG> tag information between the starting and ending <A> tags. This causes a two-pixel-wide border to appear around the image by default. If you want a borderless image, use the

BORDER attribute with a value of zero. For a thicker border, increase the value to a number larger than two.

```
HTML Code:
<A HREF="http://www.domain.com">

<IMG SRC="http://www.host.com/bird.jpg" BORDER=0>

</A>
```

Result:

The image is a borderless hyperlink. Here again, the little hand represents the cursor passed over the image.

Creating a Link to Your Auctions

To get the URL for your current auctions, do a seller search on yourself. When the page comes up, copy the URL of the result page into your auction description code file, and make it a hyperlink. Here's an example:

```
<A HREF="http://user.auctions.yahoo.com/user/nancyhix">See my other auctions!</A>
```

The words "See my other auctions" will be hypertext. This gives your customers a quick and easy hyperlink to use to visit your auction listings.

Writing Your Auction Description with HTML

Open Notepad or a word processing program where you can enter and save plain text. Type in your description along with the URL to any additional image files you want to appear with your item description.

Figure B-2 shows raw HTML code viewed in Notepad and Figure B-3 shows the result of the HTML code when viewed in a browser. It might be easier to work with Notepad if you select "Word wrap" from the edit menu. This way you don't have to keep using the scroll bars when you want to view text that extends beyond the screen.

Saving the .html File

All HTML files must end with a file extension of either .html or .htm so your browser software recognizes them. Save your description in a file called practice.html (or any name you choose) and open it in your browser to see how it looks.

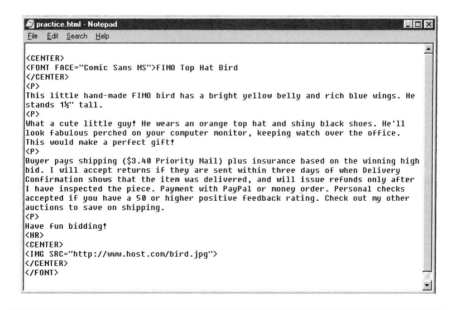

Figure B.2. Microsoft Notepad used to format an auction description.

Figure B.3. HTML file viewed in Internet Explorer.

To save the file, select File from the Notepad menu bar. Then select "Save as" and decide where to save the file on your computer's hard drive. You may want to create a directory in which to store all of your auction description HTML files.

Check Your Results

You can view the results of your auction description in your browser as you create it. Just save the file with an .html or .htm extension. Here's how you open the file in your browser:

With Internet Explorer

1. From the "File" menu on your browser window tool bar, select "Open."

2. Browse to the .html or .htm file you saved on your hard drive.

3. Double click on the filename and it appears in the pop-up window on your browser screen.

4. Click on "OK."

5. The formatted file will appear in your browser.

With Netscape

1. From the "File" menu on your browser window tool bar, select "Open Page."

2. Where you see "Open location or file in:" select Netscape.

3. Click on "Choose File."

4. Browse to the .html or .htm file you saved on your hard drive.

5. Double click on the filename, and it will appear in the pop-up window on your browser screen.

6. Click on "Open."

7. The formatted file will appear in your browser.

If you don't see the formatted file in your browser, check the code. You may have an improperly formed HTML tag somewhere. Also, be sure the file name ends in either .html or .htm.

Keep the file open in Notepad in case you need to make changes or corrections to the description. If you change the file, be sure to save it from the File menu. Hit the "Reload" or "Refresh" button in your browser to view the changes.

Note: When previewing an auction description in your browser, size the browser down to the approximate size of the space in which the description appears on an auction page.

On the Web
You'll find Web sites that allow you to double-check your HTML-coded pages before you actually use them. Dr. Watson (*www.watson.addy.com*) will also analyze your coded page and offer hints for tweaking it (see Figure B-4).

Web Page Indexing

It's important for your business Web page to come up in Web searches. As you read about in Chapter 7, you can add certain HTML code to your Web page that will help the search bots locate and index your page.

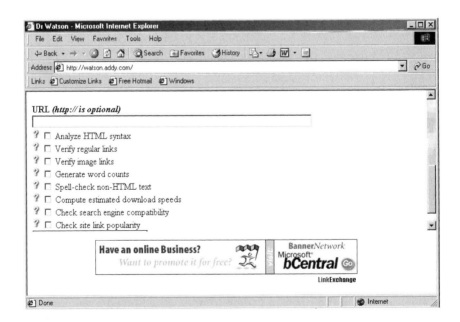

Figure B.4. Dr. Watson by Addy & Associates (*watson.addy.com*).

The <META> Tag

The <META> tag appears between the two <HEAD> tags and acts as a beacon to the search bots. Here's an example of its usage:

```
<HEAD>

<TITLE>GardenGlad</HTML>

<META NAME="description" CONTENT="Your one-stop shop for all your yard and garden needs."

<META NAME="keywords" CONTENT="GardenGlad, garden, garden supplies, flowerpots, peat moss, house plants, yard supplies, insect repellent">

</HEAD>
```

With the <META> tag in place, the search engine will pick up your site when someone searches for one of the keywords you included. If someone conducts a search for "yard supplies," your site will come up. The search result listing will look something like this:

```
GardenGlad
Your one-stop shop for all your yard and garden needs.
```

Sample Auction Description in HTML

I couldn't lead you down the garden path by telling you all the wonderful things HTML can do for you and your auctions, and then not at least give you one complete description to give you an idea of how to format your own. So here it is.

HTML Code for the Sample Description

Copy this code exactly as it appears here into Notepad or another word processing program, and save it as an HTML file.

```
<CENTER>
<TABLE BORDER=2>
<TR>
<TD COLSPAN=2 BGCOLOR=mediumpurple ALIGN=center><FONT
FACE=Verdana COLOR=white SIZE=5><B>FIMO Top Hat Bird</B>
<FONT>
</TR><TR>
<TD ALIGN=CENTER>
<TABLE BORDER=3>
<TR>
<TD><IMG SRC="http://www.host.com/bird.gif">
</TR></TABLE></TD>
<TD><FONT FACE=Verdana SIZE=2><B>What a cute little guy! This
is one fine bird:
<UL>
<LI>He wears an orange hat and shiny black shoes.
<LI>This bird is 100% hand made from FIMO clay.
<LI>His eyes will rock your world.
</UL>
He'll look fabulous perched on your computer monitor, keeping watch
over the office. This bird would also make an excellent gift. You'll want one
for both home and office. Bid early before they're all gone!
<TR>
<TD COLSPAN=2 BGCOLOR=#CCCCFF><FONT FACE=Verdana
SIZE=2><B>Buyer pays shipping ($3.40 Priority Mail) plus insurance based
on the winning high bid. I will accept returns if they are sent within three
days of when Delivery Confirmation shows that the item was delivered,
and will issue refunds only after I have inspected the piece. Payment with
PayPal or money order. Personal checks accepted if you have a 50 or higher
positive feedback rating. Check out my <A HREF="http://
www.auctionsite.com/MyAuctions.html">other auctions</A> to save on
shipping.
<TR>
<TD COLSPAN=2 ALIGN=CENTER BGCOLOR=mediumpurple><FONT
SIZE=5 FACE=Verdana COLOR=white><b>Have fun bidding!</B></
FONT>
</TR>
</TABLE>
</CENTER>
```

Formatted Description

Figure B-5 shows what the above HTML code looks like when it's formatted in your browser:

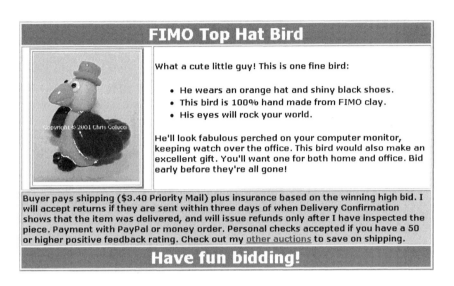

Figure B.5. Formatted sample auction description.

Appendix C: Online Auction Strategy Worksheets

Once your Internet auction business is underway, you can keep much of your Internet auction records online. Many sites offer tools for keeping track of every part of your auction business. These worksheets will help you through the planning phases of your Internet auction listing. The worksheets in Figure C.1 map to the Seven-Step Online Auction Strategy.

When you're first putting together your Internet auction strategy, before you've taken your business online, these worksheets will help you plan your Internet auction product marketing.

Step 1

Target Market Worksheet

This worksheet (Figure C.2 on page 526) will help you determine to whom you'll be selling your products. You'll also be able to determine when your customers are most likely to be online, so you can time your Internet auction closings. Complete one of these worksheets for each type of product you plan to list at an online auction.

Competition Analysis Worksheet

The popularity of Internet auctions draws many sellers to them for the same reason you're going there. This means you'll have competition. Some of your competitors have been there longer than you have, and this worksheet (Figure C.3 on pages 527-528) will help you study how they operate. This will give you an advantage as you launch your Internet auction venture.

Online Auction Strategy Worksheets

Step 1:   Target Market Worksheet

– Competition Analysis Worksheet

– Merchandise Pricing Worksheet

Step 2:   Online Payment Service Worksheet

Step 3:   Auction Site Assessment Worksheet

– Auction Type Assessment Worksheet

– Auction Site Fee Calculation Worksheet

Step 4:   Item Description Worksheet

Step 5:   Promotional Plan Worksheet

Step 6:   Packaging and Shipping Expense Worksheet

Step 7:   Customer Satisfaction Worksheet

– Sales Estimate Worksheet

– Operating Expenses Worksheet

Figure C.1.   List of online auction strategy worksheets.

Merchandise Pricing Worksheet

Use this worksheet (Figure C.4 onpage 529) to determine your price floor, your market variance, and your price ceiling.

Step 2

Auction Site Assessment Worksheet

This worksheet (Figure C.5 on pages 530-531) will help you assess an Internet auction site so you can decide if it meets your business needs. You'll look at some of the essential features of the site. Check if each

Target Market Worksheet	
1. Who are my customers?	
Age group:	
Sex:	
Economic Level:	
Lifestyle:	
Do my customers shop online?	
2. Internet Access	
Where do my customers access the Internet?	
Can they be online at school or work?	
When are they most likely to be online?	
3. Size of Market – How many potential customers do I have for this product?	
More than 100?	
More than 1,000?	
More than 10,000?	
A limitless number?	
4. Demand for Product – What are my customers' needs?	
How can my products meet their needs?	
Can my products be adapted for their needs?	

Figure C.2.   Target market worksheet.

Competition Analysis Worksheet	
1. Who is currently listing the same products that I plan to list?	
Seller #1	
Seller #2	
Seller #3	
Seller #4	
2. What's their market strategy?	
Seller #1	
Seller #2	
Seller #3	
Seller #4	
3. What's their sales record ($ sales from closed auctions over the past 3 months)?	
Seller #1	
Seller #2	
Seller #3	
Seller #4	
4. How many auctions do they have running right now?	
Seller #1	
Seller #2	
Seller #3	
Seller #4	
5. How's their customer feedback – can they handle their auction load?	
Seller #1	Positive: Neutral: Negative:
Seller #2	Positive: Neutral: Negative:
Seller #3	Positive: Neutral: Negative:
Seller #4	Positive: Neutral: Negative:

Figure C.3. Competition analysis worksheet *(continued on next page)*.

Competition Analysis Worksheet
6. What's unique about their Internet auction listings?

Seller #1	
Seller #2	
Seller #3	
Seller #4	

7. What "image" does the seller portray?

Seller #1	
Seller #2	
Seller #3	
Seller #4	

8. What is their pricing structure for the items they're selling that I plan to sell?

Seller #1	
Seller #2	
Seller #3	
Seller #4	

9. What appears to be their marketing strengths?

Seller #1	
Seller #2	
Seller #3	
Seller #4	

10. What appears to be their marketing weaknesses?

Seller #1	
Seller #2	
Seller #3	
Seller #4	

Figure C.3. Competition analysis worksheet *(continued from previous page).*

Merchandise Pricing Worksheet	
A. Product Cost:	
B. Auction Listing Fee and Commission Per Sale:	
C. Price Floor (A + B):	
D. Manufacturer's Suggested Retail Price:	
E. Competitor #1 Price:	
F. Competitor #2 Price:	
G. Competitor #3 Price:	
H. Average Price (D + E + F + G divided by 4):	
I. Price Floor (C):	
J. Variance (H − I):	
K. Price Ceiling: (C + J):	

Figure C.4. Merchandise pricing worksheet.

feature exists at the site, and decide in the "essential" column if the presence or absence of a particular feature would affect your use of the site.

Auction Type Assessment Worksheet

Should you list your auctions at a popular consumer site like eBay, or an Internet auction site that's strictly for business-to-business listings? If you decide to run test auctions at several different sites, this worksheet (Figure C.6 on page 532) will help you keep track of the number of auctions that you listed. Record how many of them resulted in successful transactions and how much you earned by listing at that particular

Auction Site Assessment Worksheet		
Auction Site Name:	URL:	
Type of Auctions	**Offered?** Y/N	**Essential?** Y/N
Consumer-to-Consumer		
Business-to-Consumer		
Business-to-Business		
Business-to-Exchange		
Main Page Features	**Offered?** Y/N	**Essential?** Y/N
Navigation links		
Featured auctions		
Category links		
Site news and information		
Date of last update		
Copyright information		
Link to Terms and Conditions		
Link to site contact		
Types of Auctions	**Offered?** Y/N	**Essential?** Y/N
Standard		
Dutch		
English		
Private		
Restricted		
Reserve		
Sealed bid		
Fixed price		
Open-ended bidding		
Reverse		

Figure C.5.   Auction site assessment worksheet *(continued on next page)*.

Auction Site Assessment Worksheet		
Auction Site Name:	**URL:**	
Search Features	**Offered?** **Y/N**	**Essential?** **Y/N**
Search by keyword		
Search by seller		
Search by bidder		
Search by category		
Search title only		
Search auction descriptions		
Search closed auctions		
Advanced search		
Seller Services	**Offered?** **Y/N**	**Essential?** **Y/N**
Bulk uploading		
Image hosting		
Adjustable auction start and end time		
HTML allowed in description		
Seller Services	**Offered?** **Y/N**	**Essential?** **Y/N**
Site tutorial		
Online payment service		
Escrow		
Site Traffic	**Amount**	**Essential?** **Y/N**
Listing categories		
Registered users		
Active auctions		
Active auctions with at least one bid		

Figure C.5. Auction site assessment worksheet *(continued from previous page)*.

Auction Type Assessment Worksheet				
Auction Site URL	Type of Site (C2C, B2C, etc.)	Number of Auctions Listed	Number of Successful Transac-tions	Total Sales at Site

Figure C.6. Auction type assessment worksheet.

auction site. Under the "type of site" column, indicate whether the site is B2B, C2C, etc.

Auction Site Fee Calculation Worksheet

With this worksheet (Figure C.7) you can calculate how much it will cost you to list an auction, what you'll pay for optional features, and how much you can expect to pay in site commission.

Step 3

Online Payment Service Worksheet

This worksheet (Figure C.8 on page 534) will help you keep track of the fees associated with your Online Payment Service. Keep one of these worksheets for each online payment service you use, including those run by the Internet auction sites you use. Be sure to update this worksheet if the online payment services change their fees.

Auction Site Fee Calculation Worksheet	
Insertion Fee	**Fee**
No insertion fee	
Flat fee for all auctions	
Minimum bid under $10	
Minimum bid $10 to $25	
Minimum bid $25 to $50	
Minimum bid $50 to $100	
Minimum bid $100 to $200	
Minimum bid over $200	
Site Commission	**Percent of sale**
$0–$25	
$25–$100	
$100–$1,000	
Over $1,000	
Other commission fees	
Features	**Fee**
Home page featured	
Bold title	
Reserve auction	
Gallery or thumbnail index fee	
Extended-duration auction	
Other fees	
Auction Services Tools	**Fee**
Bulk-listing tools	
Image hosting	
Auction manager	
Auction tracking	

Figure C.7. Auction site fee calculation worksheet.

Online Payment Service Worksheet	
Site Name	
URL	
Registration Fee	
Transaction Fee	
Business Account Fee	
Referral Bonus	
Comments:	

Figure C.8. Online payment service worksheet.

Step 4

Item Description Worksheet

Not all of these apply to your item, but if you use this worksheet (Figure C.9), you might be able to provide more information about your item than you thought existed. Including it will help your auction come up in more description searches.

Step 5

Promotional Plan Worksheet

How you choose to promote your auctions depends on a few factors. For instance, do you have opportunities to link to your auctions from other sites? In addition, how much do you plan to spend on advertising your auctions? Complete one of these worksheets (Figure C.10 on page 536) for each product you plan to list for auction.

Item Description Worksheet	
Specification:	**Details:**
Item name	
Manufacturer	
Year of manufacture	
Artist	
Model	
Style	
Color	
Dimensions	
Packaging	
Condition	
Damage or defects	
Other:	

Figure C.9. Item description worksheet.

Step 6

Packing Worksheet

Use this worksheet (Figure C.11 on page 537) as a checklist to be sure that you ship items to their new owners along with everything that you need to get them there safely. You can use the buyers' remittance letters, if they enclosed one with their payments, to make out the shipping labels.

Promotional Plan Worksheet

1. How much can you spend promoting your auctions for this campaign?

_____

2. Do you plan to use banner ads? _____

Can you reuse an existing banner? _____

Cost of new banner ad creation: _____

3. Where on the Internet will you place your banner ad?

Site name: _____   Fee: _____

Site name: _____   Fee: _____

Site name: _____   Fee: _____

4. What Web sites will promote your auctions free (not including your own)?

Site name: _____

Site name: _____

Site name: _____

5. What affiliate programs do you have in place?

Site name: _____

Site name: _____

Site name: _____

6. E-mail lists:

Which e-mail list will you use for this campaign?_____

Total costs: _____

Total from Line 1: _____

Are you within your budget? _____

Figure C.10.   Promotional plan worksheet.

Step 7

Customer Satisfaction Worksheet

Your customers' perception of your business practice is the most important measure of your overall effectiveness. This worksheet (C.12 on page 538) will help you keep track of the checkpoints involved in measuring how happy your customers are with you and how likely they are to do repeat business with you.

Monthly Earning Worksheet

Use this worksheet (C.13 on page 539) to track your net earnings on a monthly basis. If you use more than one auction site, you may wish to insert a column to record on which site the auction ran. Only record auctions that successfully close. For those that do, record the auction

Packing Worksheet	
Item	**Check ✓**
Prepared shipping note	
Shipping cartons	
Bubble wrap	
Packing puffies	
Shipping labels	
Enclosures (business card, sample, etc.)	
Packing tape	

Figure C.11. Packing worksheet.

Customer Satisfaction Worksheet		
Value Added	**Yes**	**No**
Potential customers' questions answered before end of auction		
EOA message sent promptly to high bidder(s)		
Customer in agreement with payment terms		
Customer's cleared payment received		
Added appropriate enclosures to shipment		
Item securely packed and promptly shipped		
Customer expressed satisfaction with product received		
Responded to customer complaints promptly		
Customer sent an unsolicited "thank you"		
Customer returned our positive auction site feedback		
Customer agreed to have his or her e-mail added to e-mail list		
Customer agreed to complete and returned e-mail questionnaire evaluating our customer service		
Customer's responses to questionnaire were overall positive		
Customer placed additional orders with us		
Received referrals from satisfied customer		

Figure C.12.　Customer satisfaction worksheet.

numbers, date of closing, and the high bid price on your worksheet. For Dutch or multiple-item listings, use a separate line for every transaction resulting from that auction, and count each sale as one listing.

Monthly Earning Worksheet				
Month and Year:				
Auction Number	Date Closed	High Bid	Site fees (insertion and commission)	Net Earnings

Figure C.13. Monthly earning worksheet.

Operating Expenses Worksheet

Use this worksheet (Figure C.14) to track your Internet auction operating expenses on a monthly basis. This worksheet will not include your cost of goods, since that usually varies. Most of the expenses below will be somewhat constant once you start listing auctions regularly.

Cost of Inventory Worksheet

This worksheet (Figure C.15) will help you manage your inventory in terms of quantity, cost per lot, cost per item, and potential selling price. Use your Merchandise Pricing Worksheet from Step 1 to determine the potential selling price for the items.

Operating Expenses Worksheet	
Expense	**Amount**
Internet Service Provider (ISP) monthly charge	
Auction Service Provider (ASP) monthly charge	
Image host monthly charge	
Auction site monthly membership fees, if applicable	
Monthly listing fees (total)	
Monthly auction site commission (total)	

Figure C.14. Operating expenses worksheet.

Cost of Inventory Worksheet					
Type of merchandise	Type of lot	# of lots in stock	Cost per lot	Cost per item	Price per item

Figure C.15. Cost of inventory worksheet.

Index

Reader Feedback Sheet

Your comments and suggestions are very important in shaping future publications. Please email us at *moreinfo@maxpress.com* or photocopy this page, jot down your thoughts, and fax it to (850) 934-9981 or mail it to:

Maximum Press

Attn: Jim Hoskins

605 Silverthorn Road

Gulf Breeze, FL 32561

_____

_____

_____

_____

_____

_____

_____

_____

_____

_____

_____

_____

_____

_____

_____

_____

101 Internet Businesses You Can Start From Home
by Susan Sweeney, C.A.
520 pages
$29.95
ISBN: 1-885068-59-X

e-Business Formula for Success
by Susan Sweeney, C.A.
360 pages
$34.95
ISBN: 1-885068-60-3

Exploring IBM RS/6000 Computers, Tenth Edition
by Jim Hoskins and Doug Davies
440 pages
$39.95
ISBN: 1-885068-42-5

Exploring IBM @server iSeries and AS/400 Computers, Tenth Edition
by Jim Hoskins and Roger Dimmick
560 pages
$39.95
ISBN: 1-885068-43-3

Exploring IBM @server zSeries and S/390 Servers, Seventh Edition
by Jim Hoskins and Bob Frank
432 pages
$59.95
ISBN: 1-885068-70-0

Exploring IBM e-Business Software
by Casey Young
308 pages
$49.95
ISBN: 1-885068-58-1

Exploring IBM @server xSeries and PCs, Eleventh Edition
by Jim Hoskins and Bill Wilson
432 pages
$39.95
ISBN: 1-885068-39-5

Exploring IBM Technology, Products & Services, Fourth Edition
edited by Jim Hoskins
256 pages
$54.95
ISBN: 1-885068-62-X

To purchase a Maximum Press book, visit your local bookstore
or call 1-800-989-6733 (US/Canada) or 1-850-934-4583 (International)
online ordering available at *www.maxpress.com*